Lecture Notes in Computer Science 14512

Founding Editors

Gerhard Goos
Juris Hartmanis

The series Lecture Notes in Computer Science (LNCS), including its subseries Lecture Notes in Artificial Intelligence (LNAI) and Lecture Notes in Bioinformatics (LNBI), has established itself as a medium for the publication of new developments in computer science and information technology research, teaching, and education.

LNCS enjoys close cooperation with the computer science R & D community, the series counts many renowned academics among its volume editors and paper authors, and collaborates with prestigious societies. Its mission is to serve this international community by providing an invaluable service, mainly focused on the publication of conference and workshop proceedings and postproceedings. LNCS commenced publication in 1973.

Martin Gebser · Ilya Sergey
Editors

Practical Aspects of Declarative Languages

26th International Symposium, PADL 2024
London, UK, January 15–16, 2024
Proceedings

 Springer

Editors
Martin Gebser 🄳
University of Klagenfurt
Klagenfurt, Austria

Ilya Sergey 🄳
National University of Singapore
Singapore, Singapore

ISSN 0302-9743   ISSN 1611-3349 (electronic)
Lecture Notes in Computer Science
ISBN 978-3-031-52037-2   ISBN 978-3-031-52038-9 (eBook)
https://doi.org/10.1007/978-3-031-52038-9

This Springer imprint is published by the registered company Springer Nature Switzerland AG
The registered company address is: Gewerbestrasse 11, 6330 Cham, Switzerland

Paper in this product is recyclable.

Preface

This volume contains the papers presented at the 26th International Symposium on Practical Aspects of Declarative Languages (PADL 2024). The symposium was held on 15–16 January 2024 in London, UK, co-located with the 51st ACM SIGPLAN Symposium on Principles of Programming Languages (POPL 2024).

PADL is a well-established forum for researchers and practitioners to present original work emphasizing novel applications and implementation techniques for all forms of declarative programming, including functional and logic programming, databases and constraint programming, and theorem proving. PADL 2024 especially welcomed new ideas and approaches related to applications, design and implementation of declarative languages going beyond the scope of the past PADL symposia, for example, advanced database languages and contract languages, as well as verification and theorem proving methods that rely on declarative languages.

Originally established as a workshop (PADL 1999 in San Antonio, Texas), the PADL series developed into a regular annual symposium; other previous editions took place in Boston, Massachusetts (2000), Las Vegas, Nevada (2001), Portland, Oregon (2002), New Orleans, Louisiana (2003), Dallas, Texas (2004), Long Beach, California (2005), Charleston, South Carolina (2006), Nice, France (2007), San Francisco, California (2008), Savannah, Georgia (2009), Madrid, Spain (2010), Austin, Texas (2012), Rome, Italy (2013), San Diego, California (2014), Portland, Oregon (2015), St. Petersburg, Florida (2016), Paris, France (2017), Los Angeles, California (2018), Lisbon, Portugal (2019), New Orleans, Louisiana (2020), online (2021), Philadelphia, Pennsylvania (2022), and Boston, Massachusetts (2023).

The 13 papers in this volume, including 12 technical papers and one application paper, were selected by the Programme Committee from 25 submissions. Each of the PADL 2024 submissions received either three or four reviews and was discussed electronically, using the HotCRP conference system, by the Programme Committee and external reviewers before a final decision was made. The reviewing process for PADL 2024 was double-anonymous, and only authors of the eventually accepted papers have been revealed.

The accepted papers span a range of topics related to functional and logic programming, including reactive programming, hardware implementations, implementation of marketplaces, query languages, and applications of declarative programming techniques to artificial intelligence and machine learning. We were also honored to include the two invited talks by Ekaterina Komendantskaya (Southampton University and Heriot-Watt University), "*Whats* and *Whys* of Neural Network Verification (A Declarative Programming Perspective)", and Nicolas Wu (Imperial College London), "Modular Higher-Order Effects", in the PADL 2024 program.

The symposium was supported and sponsored by the Association of Logic Programming (ALP), the Association for Computing Machinery (ACM), and Principles of Knowledge Representation and Reasoning, Incorporated (KR Inc.). We thank all who contributed to the success and the exciting program of PADL 2024. This includes the authors of submissions; the four external reviewers, who provided timely expert reviews; and, of course, the 27 members of the Programme Committee. We are particularly grateful to Esra Erdem, Philippa Gardner, Thomas Eiter, and Marco Gavanelli for their invaluable advice and support.

November 2023   Martin Gebser
                                                                  Ilya Sergey

Organization

Programme Committee Chairs

Marin Gebser   University of Klagenfurt, Austria
Ilya Sergey   National University of Singapore, Singapore

Programme Committee

Alexandra Mendes	University of Porto & HASLab/INESC TEC, Portugal
Anton Trunov	TON Foundation, United Arab Emirates
Arnaud Spiwack	Tweag, France
Daniela Inclezan	Miami University, USA
Emilia Oikarinen	University of Helsinki, Finland
Enrico Pontelli	New Mexico State University, USA
Esra Erdem	Sabanci University, Turkey
Gopal Gupta	University of Texas at Dallas, USA
Jesper Cockx	TU Delft, The Netherlands
Jessica Zangari	University of Calabria, Italy
Johannes P. Wallner	Graz University of Technology, Austria
Leo White	Jane Street, UK
Magnus Myreen	Chalmers University of Technology, Sweden
Manuel Carro	Universidad Politécnica de Madrid and IMDEA Software Institute, Spain
Marcello Balduccini	Saint Joseph's University, USA
Matthew Flatt	University of Utah, USA
Mukund Raghothaman	University of Southern California, USA
Patrick Bahr	IT University of Copenhagen, Denmark
Roland Yap	National University of Singapore, Singapore
Simon Fowler	University of Glasgow, UK
Stefania Costantini	University of L'Aquila, Italy
Tom Schrijvers	KU Leuven, Belgium
Tomi Janhunen	Tampere University, Finland
Weronika T. Adrian	AGH University of Krakow, Poland
Yanhong A. Liu	Stony Brook University, USA
Youyou Cong	Tokyo Institute of Technology, Japan
Zeynep Saribatur	TU Wien, Austria

Additional Reviewers

Aysu Bogatarkan	Sabanci University, Turkey
Francesco Fabiano	New Mexico State University, USA
Muge Fidan	Sabanci University, Turkey
Tuncay Tekle	Stony Brook University, USA

Invited Talks

Whats and *Whys* of Neural Network Verification (A Declarative Programming Perspective)

Ekaterina Komendantskaya

Southampton University and Heriot-Watt University, UK
E.Komendantskaya@soton.ac.uk

Abstract. This talk is an overview of the domain of neural network verification, given from the perspective of the research team implementing the domain-specific language **Vehicle** for specification and verification of properties of neural networks. The talk focuses on *"What?"*s for major successes and *"Why?"*s for major failures in this field so far; and explains the (potential) role of declarative programming in its past and future successes. **Vehicle** uses a range of declarative languages, including the SMT solver Marabou as a backend, Haskell as the main host compiler, and Agda as an additional backend for more complex proofs. It is designed to allow for further declarative backends, such as Coq, Imandra and KeYmaera X. The talk features a quick demo of **Vehicle** in its use, and reflects on its potential applications, including i) natural language processing, ii) security, iii) cyber-physical systems, as well as iv) teaching principles of neural network verification to postgraduate students.

References

1. Casadio, M., et al.: Neural network robustness as a verification property: a principled case study. In: Shoham, S., Vizel, Y. (eds.) CAV 2022. LNCS, vol. 13371, pp. 219–231. Springer, Cham (2022). https://doi.org/10.1007/978-3-031-13185-1_11
2. Daggitt, M.L., Atkey, R., Kokke, W., Komendantskaya, E., Arnaboldi, L.: Compiling higher-order specifications to SMT solvers: how to deal with rejection constructively. In: Proceedings of the 12th ACM SIGPLAN International Conference on Certified Programs and Proofs, CPP 2023, Boston, MA, USA, 16–17 January 2023, pp. 102–120. ACM (2023). https://doi.org/10.1145/3573105.3575674
3. Daggitt, M.L., et al.: The Vehicle tutorial: neural network verification with Vehicle. In: Proceedings of the 6th Workshop on Formal Methods for ML-Enabled Autonomous Systems, FOMLAS 2023, Paris, France, 17–18 July 2023, pp. 1–5. Kalpa Publications in Computing. EasyChair (2023). https://vehicle-lang.github.io/tutorial/
4. Slusarz, N., Komendantskaya, E., Daggitt, M.L., Stewart, R.J., Stark, K.: Logic of differentiable logics: towards a uniform semantics of DL. In: Proceedings of the 24th International Conference on Logic for Programming, Artificial Intelligence and Reasoning, LPAR 2024, Manizales, Colombia, 4–9 June 2023. EPiC Series in Computing, vol. 94, pp. 473–493. Easychair (2023).

Modular Higher-Order Effects

Nicolas Wu

Imperial College London, UK
n.wu@imperial.ac.uk

Abstract. Born out of a vision that human comprehension should be prioritised above mechanical computation, declarative languages prioritise the *purpose* of evaluating programs above of the *process* of evaluating programs. Effect handlers [3] embrace the two perspectives by offering a programming framework where the purpose of a program is given by operations from a given syntax and the process of evaluating such programs is given by handlers that provide a semantics.

The popularity of algebraic effects is partly due to the practical benefits they offer as a tool for describing modular domain-specific languages (DSLs). Algebraic effect handlers enable the creation of specialized, domain-specific languages tailored to address the unique requirements of specific application domains. By encapsulating effectful operations within algebraic theories, these handlers offer a modular and composable framework for defining and interpreting computational effects. This not only enhances the expressiveness of DSLs but also facilitates a more intuitive and maintainable way of reasoning about and orchestrating complex computations within specific problem domains. The adaptability and versatility afforded by algebraic effect handlers empower developers to flexibly extend the domains they are working with and reinterpret those domains differently depending on the context they require.

Unfortunately, the very mechanism that make algebraic effects modular—that is, algebraicity—is also their limitation: not all operations of practical importance are algebraic. In particular, handlers such as `catch` for catching exceptions and `once` for pruning the results of a logic program violate the requirements of algebraic operations.

This shortcoming motivated the exploration of generalisations of algebraic effects into scoped and latent effects [1, 2, 4, 5], whose additional expressivity come at the cost of the inherent modularity offered by algebraic effects. Recent work [6] has shown how to recover modularity by considering *modular models* that can be inherently extended with new operations.

This talk outlines the practical aspects the `effective` library, an implementation of modular higher-order effects in Haskell that is tailored to simplify working with modular models of algebraic and scoped effects. The library enables users to define the syntax and semantics of their own DSLs in a way that is modular and extensible, while integrating well with Haskell's primitive I/O mechanisms and monad transformer infrastructure.

References

1. van den Berg, B., Schrijvers, T., Poulsen, C.B., Wu, N.: Latent effects for reusable language components. In: Oh, H. (ed.) Programming Languages and Systems. APLAS 2021. LNCS, vol. 13008, pp. 182–201. Springer, Cham (2021). https://doi.org/10.1007/978-3-030-89051-3_11
2. Piróg, M., Schrijvers, T., Wu, N., Jaskelioff, M.: Syntax and semantics for operations with scopes. In: Dawar, A., Grädel, E. (eds.) Proceedings of the 33rd Annual ACM/IEEE Symposium on Logic in Computer Science, LICS 2018, Oxford, UK, 9–12 July (2018)
3. Plotkin, G., Pretnar, M.: Handling algebraic effects. Logical Methods Comput. Sci. 9(4) (2013). https://doi.org/10.2168/lmcs-9(4:23)2013
4. Wu, N., Schrijvers, T., Hinze, R.: Effect handlers in scope. In: Proceedings of the 2014 ACM SIGPLAN Symposium on Haskell, pp. 1–12 (2014). http://dl.acm.org/citation.cfm?doid=2633357.2633358
5. Yang, Z., Paviotti, M., Wu, N., van den Berg, B., Schrijvers, T.: Structured handling of scoped effects. In: Sergey, I. (eds) Programming Languages and Systems. ESOP 2022. LNCS, vol 13240. Springer, Cham (2022). https://doi.org/10.1007/978-3-030-99336-8_17
6. Yang, Z., Wu, N.: Modular models of monoids with operations. Proc. ACM Program. Lang. 7(ICFP), 566–603 (2023). https://doi.org/10.1145/3607850

Contents

Forget and Regeneration Techniques for Optimizing ASP-Based Stream Reasoning

Francesco Calimeri⬤, Giovambattista Ianni⬤, Francesco Pacenza⬤, Simona Perri⬤, and Jessica Zangari$^{(\boxtimes)}$⬤

Department of Mathematics and Computer Science, University of Calabria, Rende, Italy
{francesco.calimeri,giovambattista.ianni,francesco.pacenza, simona.perri,jessica.zangari}@unical.it

Abstract. Answer Set Programming (ASP) is a declarative formalism, developed in the field of nonmonotonic reasoning and recognized as a powerful tool for Knowledge Representation and Reasoning. ASP features show potential also in the Stream Reasoning realm. Nevertheless, such a scenario demands for repeated executions and requires reactive reasoning over rapidly changing data streams. Evaluating ASP programs from scratch at each time point represents a bottleneck. To overcome such limits, incremental reasoning techniques have been proposed. Overgrounding is an incremental grounding technique working under the answer set semantics that fully endorses the ASP declarative nature. Given a non-ground program to be repeatedly evaluated in consecutive time points over possibly differing sets of input facts, overgrounding maintains and enriches an overgrounded program, which eventually converges to a propositional theory general enough to be reused together with possible future inputs. In this work, we focus on developments and extensions of overgrounding that could be beneficial in Stream Reasoning applications. In particular, we present forms of forgetting and regeneration strategies purposely intended to mitigate the typical accumulation-oriented behavior of overgrounding by properly dropping accumulated atoms and/or rules.

Keywords: Knowledge Representation and Reasoning · Answer Set Programming · Stream Reasoning · Overgrounding

This work has been supported by the PNRR project FAIR - Future AI Research (PE00000013), Spoke 9 - Green-aware AI, under the NRRP MUR program funded by the NextGenerationEU, and by the project PRIN PE6, Title: "Declarative Reasoning over Streams", funded by the Italian Ministero dell'Università, dell'Istruzione e della Ricerca (MIUR), CUP:H24I17000080001, and by the project "Smart Cities Lab" (CUP J89J21009750007) funded on POR FESR-FSE Calabria 2014–2020.

M. Gebser and I. Sergey (Eds.): PADL 2024, LNCS 14512, pp. 1–17, 2023.
https://doi.org/10.1007/978-3-031-52038-9_1

1   Introduction

A number of applicative contexts, many of which fall within the Stream Reasoning field, require the repeated execution of a reasoning task over a fixed knowledge base, but with changing inputs. They include, e.g., real-time motion tracking [23], robotics [22], artificial players in videogames [7], content distribution [2] and sensor network configuration [12]. Declarative tools based on the answer set semantics are good candidates for reasoning in such domains, as they encompass advanced inference features, declarativity and a potentially good performance [4,5,21].

Recall that the typical workflow of Answer Set Programming (ASP) systems consists in an *instantiation* (or *grounding*) phase and a subsequent *solving* (or *answer sets search*) phase. In the first step, a *grounder* module produces a semantically equivalent propositional program $gr(P \cup F)$ from an input non-ground logic program P and a set of facts F; in the latter step, a *solver* module applies dedicated search techniques on $gr(P \cup F)$ for computing the actual semantics of $P \cup F$ in the form of *answer sets* [18]. Repeated executions, called *shots*, can be conceptually abstracted to the task of finding the set of answer sets $AS(P \cup F_i)$ for a sequence of input fact sets $F_1, \ldots, F_n$. In demanding applications, shots need to be run at very high paces and/or under a high volume of input data.

Many efforts have been done looking both at the grounding and at the solving performance, thus pushing towards the development of efficient incremental reasoning techniques. The overgrounding technique [8,17] focuses on the instantiation stage aiming at incrementally maintaining a so called *overgrounded program* G_P for a non-ground program P. An overgrounded program is monotonically enlarged from a shot to another in order to be made "compatible" with new input facts. Overgrounded programs with tailoring (OPTs) [17] improve over plain overgrounded programs by reducing the size and the number of instantiated rules and thus better controlling the growth of G_P.

Overgrounding is attractive as no operational directives are required to state how to drive the incremental computation; as a distinctive feature, OPTs grow in size from one shot to another while grounding times become fairly low after an initially high grounding cost. The performance of grounding engines with overgrounding is quite interesting, especially over applicative domains in which input data is subject to little or no variation, i.e., when little or no new propositional constants need to be introduced in G_P. For instance, some proposals [12,20] use a form of overgrounding in which G_P is statically predetermined and assumed to be fixed. Given their memory requirements, overgrounded programs are apparently not suitable for applications having some of the following features: *i)* they are subject to an elevated rate of invention of new propositional symbols; *ii)* they are hosted in a device where memory is intrinsically scarce, or *iii)* a given memory limit is needed. The first setting is typical of streams in which one needs to reason on huge sets of timestamped data, whereas the latter two are typical of a reasoner hosted in a mobile or IoT device, or a micro-service-based container [10,14].

To overcome the above limitations, we introduce a form of "forgetting" on top of existing algorithms for overgrounded programs, aimed at reducing the size of overgrounded programs and limiting memory consumption. Intuitively, there are instantiated rules that are less used; these could be dropped (*forgotten*) and possibly regenerated on demand only, in order to contain the size of overgrounded instantiations. However, non-obvious technical obstacles prevent a straightforward extension of overgrounding techniques in the above direction.

This particular context requires (*i*) the development of a suitable *knowledge forgetting and regeneration* method; and, (*ii*) a method for specifying which part of a ground program is "better to be forgotten", considering the impact on performance.

Achieving point (*i*) above shares some similarity with the delete and rederive approach [19]. However, when contextualizing the problem of maintaining ground programs, one has to consider that a ground program does not exactly represent knowledge that can be selectively dropped, like in classic forgetting [13]: in our setting, a ground program can be seen more as a persistent representation of a non-ground program; a ground program contains parts that can be potentially useful or be neglected depending on the evaluation shot at hand. These parts, when "forgotten", might require a future re-materialization, coming at a computational cost, which we call "regeneration".

Point (*ii*) above recalls the possibility of programmatically controlling grounding and solving of ASP modules, available in clingo [15]. Overgrounding follows a different approach, requiring no low-level control to knowledge designers in the spirit of full declarativity. In this paper, we focus our attention on designing forgetting and regeneration techniques for overgrounding-based approaches, and we aim, in future work, to investigate means to automatically trigger and select parts of the ground program at hand to be forgotten.

The paper is structured as follows. We first overview overgrounding techniques (Sect. 2) and show their benefits in a typical Stream Reasoning scenario (Sect. 3). In Sect. 4, we present two forgetting approaches along with a proper regeneration strategy. In Sect. 5, we present our implementation and illustrate its usage; then, in Sect. 6 we report about an experimental evaluation showing how forget and regeneration techniques can significantly impact on memory consumption. Eventually, in Sect. 7, we draw final conclusions.

2   Incremental Instantiation with Overgrounding

Let us briefly recall the overgrounding technique and the context in which it is applied. As mentioned, ASP solvers in general deal with a non-ground ASP program P (made of a set of universally quantified rules) and a set of input facts F. A traditional ASP system performs two separate steps to determine the corresponding models, i.e., the answer sets of P over F, denoted $AS(P \cup F)$. The first step is called *instantiation* (or *grounding*) and consists of the generation of a logic program $gr(P, F)$ by properly replacing variables with constants. Secondly, the solving step is in charge of computing the answer sets $AS(gr(P,F))$. Grounding modules are typically geared towards building $gr(P,F)$ as a "shrunk" version of the theoretical instantiation $grnd(P,F)$ classically defined via the Herbrand base. Still, $gr(P,F)$ preserves semantics, i.e., $AS(gr(P,F)) = AS(grnd(P,F)) = AS(P \cup F)$ (see, e.g., [6] for an overview of grounding optimization techniques).

Performing the grounding and solving steps from scratch when repeating reasoning in multiple shots is rather inefficient and thus incremental evaluation techniques [15,16] are attractive. Overgrounding is an incremental grounding technique, which aims at preserving the declarative nature of ASP, without requiring any operational statements to incrementally drive the computation.

Conceptually, given a non-ground program P and a sequence of input fact sets $F_1, \ldots, F_n$ one per each shot, overgrounding incrementally maintains an *overgrounded program* G_P. G_P is made "compatible" (in the sense of preserving answer sets) with new input facts by monotonically enlarging it from one shot to another. In the standard overgrounding approach [8], G_P is adjusted from one shot to another by adding new rules ΔG and by avoiding input-dependent simplifications; in overgrounding with tailored simplifications [17] ΔG is processed with appropriate simplification filters, which reduce the length of individual rules and the overall size of ΔG. The performance of such incremental techniques is good: in most domains, an overgrounded program, after some update shots, *converges* to a ground theory general enough to be reused together with possible future inputs, without requiring further updates. This virtually eliminates grounding activities in later shots. The first overgrounding-based incremental grounding implementation is $\mathcal{I}^2$-DLV [17][1], the $\mathcal{I}ncremental$ version of $\mathcal{I}$-DLV, a deductive database system and ASP grounder [6]. Lately, *Incremental DLV2* [9][2] has been released as the multi-shot version of the monolithic ASP system $DLV2$ [1], in which incremental grounding is achieved via overgrounding.

In the following, we assume that the reader is familiar with the basic logic programming terminology, including the notions of predicate, atom, literal, rule, and head and body of the latter.

Example 1. We exemplify next the overgrounding approach. Let us consider the program P_0:

$$a : r(X,Y) \coloneq e(X,Y), \; not \; ab(X). \quad b : r(X,Z) \mid s(X,Z) \coloneq e(X,Y), \; r(Y,Z).$$

When taking the set of input facts $F_1 = \{e(3,1), \; e(1,2), \; ab(3)\}$ into account, there are several ways for building a correct instantiation of $P_0 \cup F_1$. For instance, one could simply start from F_1 and then generate new rules in a bottom-up way, by iterating through positive head-body dependencies, obtaining the ground program G_1:

$$a_1 : r(1,2) \coloneq e(1,2), \; not \; ab(1). \quad b_1 : r(3,2) \mid s(3,2) \coloneq e(3,1), \; r(1,2).$$
$$a_2 : r(3,1) \coloneq e(3,1), \; not \; ab(3).$$

Note that G_1 includes only supported rules, i.e., rules having a chance to contribute to the semantics; e.g., substituting $e(1,2)$ to $e(X,Y)$ in rule b would not produce any useful ground instance of b since there is no way for generating an atom compatible with $r(2,Z)$. In addition, one could also cut or simplify rules, e.g. eliminate rules with no chance of firing and remove definitely true atoms, thus obtaining a simplified program G_1':

$$a_1' : r(1,2) :\!-\ \cancel{e(1,2)},\ not\ ab(1). \quad b_1' : r(3,2)\ |\ s(3,2) :\!-\ \cancel{e(3,1)},\ r(1,2).$$
$$a_2' : \cancel{r(3,1) :\!-\ e(3,1),\ not\ ab(3)}.$$

G_1' can be seen as less general and "re-usable" than G_1: adapting G_1' to be "compatible" with different sets of input facts requires the additional effort of retracting no longer valid simplifications as it is done in the overgrounding with tailored simplifications approach. Indeed, enabling simplifications could improve solving performance since smaller overgrounded programs are built.

For the sake of simplicity, let us now focus on the standard overgrounding technique in which no simplification is allowed. Let us assume that, at some point, a subsequent shot requires P_0 to be evaluated over a different set of input facts $F_2 = \{e(3,1),\ e(1,4),\ ab(1)\}$. Note that, with respect to F_1, F_2 features the additions $F^+ = \{e(1,4), ab(1)\}$ and the deletions $F^- = \{e(1,2), ab(3)\}$. G_1 can be easily adapted to the new input F_2 by considering which incremental additions are necessary due to the presence of F^+. More precisely, one can ground P_0 with respect to the new set of possibly true facts $F_1 \cup F_2$; this turns into adding the rules $\Delta G_1 = \{a_3, b_2\}$, must be added, thus obtaining G_2:

$$a_1 : r(1,2) :\!-\ e(1,2),\ not\ ab(1). \quad b_1 : r(3,2)\ |\ s(3,2) :\!-\ e(3,1),\ r(1,2).$$
$$a_2 : r(3,1) :\!-\ e(3,1),\ not\ ab(3). \quad \mathbf{b_2 : r(3,4)\ |\ s(3,4) :\!-\ e(3,1),\ r(1,4).}$$
$$a_3 : \mathbf{r(1,4) :\!-\ e(1,4),\ not\ ab(1).}$$

Interestingly, G_2 is equivalent to P_0, both when evaluated over F_1 and when evaluated over F_2 as input facts, although only different portions of the whole set of rules in G_2 can be considered as relevant when considering either F_1 or F_2 as inputs, respectively. Moreover, if a third shot is done, e.g., over the input facts $F_3 = \{e(1,4),\ e(3,1),\ e(1,2)\}$, we observe that G_2 does not need any further incremental update. This is made possible as G_2 is built on the hypothesis that the possibly true input facts are $F_1 \cup F_2 = F_1 \cup F_2 \cup F_3$, and thus the set ΔG_2 containing new incremental additions to G_2 would be empty.

3 Overgrounding in a Stream Reasoning Scenario

The challenges posed by the unbounded volume and frequent arrival of data become particularly pronounced when addressing advanced stream-based reasoning in the context of AI problem-solving, where tasks such as planning, monitoring, and decision-making [3] need to be seen from a different and more complex perspective. As a testbed scenario, we focus next on a monitoring application, which has been used to assess the capabilities of the Stream Reasoning system *I-DLV-sr* [11]. In this scenario, an Intelligent Monitoring System (IMS) for a simplified photo-voltaic system (PVS) is used to promptly detect major grid malfunctions (*Photo-voltaic System* in the following). The PVS is composed of a grid of interconnected solar panels; each panel is provided with a sensor that tracks the amount of energy produced and continuously sends such data to the IMS. Each panel continuously produces energy to be transferred to a Central Energy Accumulator (CEA), directly or via a path between neighbor panels across the grid. At each second, the working state of panels can be tracked and the following ASP program *PV* is used to identify alerts and possible maintenance interventions.

```
r₁: workingPanel(P) :- energyDelivered_AT_LEAST1_IN_LAST5S(P,W),
                       energyThreshold(Et), W>=Et.
r₂: reachable(cea,P2) :- link(cea,P2), workingPanel(P2).
r₃: reachable(P1,P3) :- reachable(P1,P2), link(P2,P3),
                        workingPanel(P3).
r₄: unlinked :- workingPanel(P), not reachable(cea,P).
r₅: regularFunctioning :- unlinked_AT_MOST2_IN_LAST3S.
r₆: alert :- not regularFunctioning.
r₇: callMaintenance :- alert_ALWAYS_IN_LAST5S.
```

Facts over the `link` predicate describe the connections among solar panels, i.e., an undirected graph representing the PVS grid; a fact over the `energyThreshold` predicate models a threshold defining a lower bound under which a solar panel is considered as no longer working. Both these predicates refer to background information, i.e., static data not changing over time. Dynamic information are given by the `energyDelivered_AT_LEAST1_IN_LAST5S`, `alert_ALWAYS_IN_LAST5S` and `unlinked_AT_MOST2_IN_LAST3S` predicates, requiring a quantification over time. To this end, the Stream Reasoning system carries out a continuous evaluation by looking at specific time windows in the input stream, i.e., a window of 5 s for the former two predicates and a window of 3 s for the latter one.

Rule r_1 is used to model that a panel is working if it is known to have produced an amount of energy greater than a given threshold within the last 5 s; a panel is assumed to be unlinked if it is working but not reachable by the CEA via a path formed of working panels (rule r_4). In this respect, r_2 and r_3 recursively define the set of reachable working panels starting from the CEA. If some working panel has been detected as unlinked more than 2 times in the last 3 s, an alert must be raised since a malfunction has been identified (rule r_6). Furthermore, the IMS must request a maintenance intervention if the failure is continuously observed for 5 s (rule r_7).

In this scenario, the fixed ASP program *PV* has to be repeatedly evaluated at regularly spaced time points over the input stream. In order to assess the effectiveness of overgrounding in such Stream Reasoning context, we assessed performance using either the traditional grounding strategy or overgrounding techniques. We thus considered *DLV2* and its incremental counterpart, *Incremental DLV2*, based on overgrounding. We ran *DLV2* in the one-shot modality, i.e., in a setting in which grounding and solving are performed from scratch every time. *Incremental DLV2* was instead executed in a multi-shot modality, enabling the usage of overgrounding. Table 1 reports total running times (in s) on 60 shots and over different square grid sizes, from 30×30 up to 60×60. In terms of time performance, results show the benefits of overgrounding w.r.t. the traditional one-shot grounding&solving approach, achieving an improvement up to about 37% on the 60×60 grid. As far as memory consumption concerned, as expected, overgrounding tends to be significantly more expensive. Note that the program *PV* is recursive and stratified w.r.t. negation. This program shape and the continuous arrival of new input data, make PVS as a quite grounding-intensive domain, suitable for experimenting with the benefits and limitations of overgrounding. Indeed, as known for this category of logic programs, the main computational effort is in charge of the grounding process.

Table 1. Performance of *DLV2* and *Incremental DLV2* on the *Photo-voltaic System* domain; the total time over all shots is in s, the peak memory in MB.

Size	Total Time (s)		Memory (MB)	
	DLV2	*Incremental DLV2*	*DLV2*	*Incremental DLV2*
30×30	13.2	9.7	17.1	37.7
40×40	49.0	31.4	43.2	100.0
50×50	114.8	81.6	102.3	255.9
60×60	278.7	171.8	202.0	515.6

4 Enriching Overgrounding with Forgetting and Regeneration

Hereafter, we present two *forget and regeneration* techniques and discuss the challenges preventing a direct extension of overgrounding towards this direction.

4.1 Motivations

As discussed in Sect. 2, overgrounded programs grow monotonically among consecutive shots, thus becoming progressively larger but more generally applicable to a wider class of sets of input facts. As a consequence, especially when inputs are similar to each other, grounding times in later shots are significantly reduced as the number of newly added rules tends to decrease.

Nevertheless, the application coverage of overgrounding-based systems can be enlarged in several directions. For instance, there are settings in which either computation times or memory sizes are subject to given cap values.

When evaluation time caps are enforced, stop and restart techniques can be very useful, e.g., one might want to abort a reasoning task yet it might be desirable to reuse part of the effort performed during the allotted time window.

Thanks to the monotonic growth of overgrounding, partially computed instantiations can, in principle, be easily reused in the next shot with almost no rollback burden. On the other hand, when memory caps are enforced, strategies to reduce memory consumption are required. To this end, it is worth exploring strategies aimed to efficiently cache and swap to disk overgrounded programs, as well as *forgetting* strategies aimed to drop and possibly regenerate subsets of ground programs.

In this paper, we focus on memory capped applications. There are non-obvious technical obstacles preventing a straightforward extension in this direction. By its nature, overgrounding tends to accumulate produced (ground) rules and inferred (ground) atoms at each shot. In general, this behavior allows to save grounding time; nevertheless, it can be sometimes counterproductive. Consider, for instance, scenarios where inputs highly vary across different shots: it is very likely that only a small subset of the whole amount of accumulated rules will actually play a role in computing answer sets at the current shot. As a consequence, accumulating rules and atoms may easily lead to a worsening in both time and memory performance as solvers are prompted to process lots of "useless" rules. Moreover, there are several contexts in which memory constraints can be significantly strict. Forget and regeneration is purposely intended to mitigate such issues, and consists in dropping accumulated atoms and/or rules and later regenerating them if needed. One might think of many ways of "cleaning" accumulated ground data, ranging from a total dropping, which basically reduces to switching overgrounding off, to more sophisticated strategies aimed at choosing what to delete and what to spare in the overgrounded program. Furthermore, different forgetting policies can be defined depending on what is actually dropped (e.g., ground rules only, ground atoms and rules, etc.).

We present next two different forgetting policies and discuss the main updates required for extending the original overgrounding technique accordingly. This section is then concluded by illustrating our *regeneration strategy*, which reinstates the correctness of an overgrounded program after a forgetting pass.

4.2   The Forget and Regeneration Techniques

Given a rule r, we define as $B(r)$ (respectively, $H(r)$) the set of all literals in the *body* (respectively, *head*) of r. Moreover, the set of positive body literals in r is referred to as $B^+(r)$. Given a set L of literals, $pred(L)$ denotes the set of predicates appearing in L.

Forget and regeneration works according to the abstract Algorithm 1, which slightly modifies the usual overgrounding approach. At a shot i, the sets G_i of ground rules and A_i of ground atoms possibly true in some answer set are maintained. A ground atom belongs to A_i either because it has been given as an input fact or because it has been inferred *as possibly true* in the current or in some previous shots. When iterating from shot $i-1$ to shot i, A_i is obtained enriching A_{i-1}, while adding new rules ΔG_i to G_{i-1}, so that $G_i = G_{i-1} \cup \Delta G_i$.

The forgetting policies we implemented, namely the *rule-based* and *predicate-based*, work by dropping rules from G_i and/or atoms from A_i after the grounding

Algorithm 1. Overgrounding a program P at a shot i with forgetting

1: $A_i \leftarrow F_i$
2: $\Delta G_i \leftarrow \emptyset$
3: **if** standard overgrounding **then**
4:     $ground(P, \Delta G_i, A_i, A_{i-1})$ ▷ updates ΔG_i and A_i
5: **else if** overgrounding with tailoring **then**
6:     $ground\_and\_desimplify(P, G_{i-1}, \Delta G_i, A_i, A_{i-1})$ ▷ updates ΔG_i and A_i
7: **end if**
8: $G_i \leftarrow G_{i-1} \cup \Delta G_i$
9: $A_i \leftarrow A_i \cup A_{i-1}$
10: $apply\_forgetting(G_i, A_i)$ ▷ apply the chosen forgetting policy, if any

takes place (lines 4 or 6 of Algorithm 1 on the basis of the type of overgrounding applied).

Rule-Based Forgetting. Given a non-ground program P and a non-ground rule r in P, the *rule-based* forgetting of r in a shot i consists in discarding all ground instances of r from the overgrounded program G_i. The non-ground rule r is said to be *forgotten*.

Example 2. Consider again the program P_0 of Example 1. Assume to be at shot 2 when the set of facts $F_2 = \{e(3,1),\ e(1,4),\ ab(1)\}$ is provided as input and to apply a rule-based forgetting over the non-ground rule a. We start updating G_1 by dropping all ground instances of a, marking a as forgotten, thus obtaining a version of G_1 that contains only the rule:

$$b_1 : r(3,2) \mid s(3,2) :- e(3,1),\ r(1,2).$$

Predicate-Based Forgetting. Given a non-ground program P and a predicate p in P, the *predicate-based* forgetting of p in a shot i consists in dropping (1) all ground atoms over p appearing in A_i, and (2) each ground rule r in the overgrounded program G_i containing p in its body or head, i.e., r is such that $p \in pred(H(r)) \cup pred(B(r))$. The predicate p and all corresponding non-ground rules featuring p either in the body or in the head are said to be *forgotten*.

Example 3. Supposing again to be at shot 2 and to consider the program P_0 of Example 1. By applying the predicate-based forgetting over the predicate e, G_1 becomes equal to $\emptyset$, and all atoms over e are dropped. Moreover, both non-ground rules a and b and the predicate e are marked as forgotten.

4.3 The Regeneration Strategy

During the grounding step (lines 4 and 6 of Algorithm 1), each rule $r \in P$ is processed by calling Algorithm 2. This algorithm is in charge of deciding whether the regeneration of forgotten ground rules and atoms is necessary. Note that, by construction, in overgrounding new ground rules are generated only based on new atoms appearing in $A_i \setminus A_{i-1}$, preventing the regeneration of some ground rules that might be necessary to restore correctness.

Example 4. Let us consider again the program P_0 of Example 1. Suppose to be at shot 1 and that $F_1 = \{e(3,1), e(1,2), ab(3)\}$. Let us consider for simplicity standard overgrounding. Then, G_1 consists of the following ground rule:

$a_1 : r(1,2) \text{ :- } e(1,2), \text{ } not \text{ } ab(1). \quad b_1 : r(3,2) \mid s(3,2) \text{ :- } e(3,1), \text{ } r(1,2).$
$a_2 : r(3,1) \text{ :- } e(3,1), \text{ } not \text{ } ab(3).$

In case a naive rule-based forgetting (with no regeneration) is applied on the non-ground rule a of P_0, then $G_1 = \{b_1\}$. If at shot 2, $F_2 = \{e(3,1), e(1,2), ab(3)\}$ since $e(3,1), e(1,2)$, and $ab(3)$ are atoms already seen in the previous shot, no ground rules are generated thus $G_2 = G_1 = \{b_1\}$. This would produce a unique and semantically incorrect answer set comprising only the facts in F_2. Let us now consider predicate-based forgetting on the predicate $r/2$, which causes the forgetting of $r(1,2), r(3,1)$ and $r(3,2)$ as well as all the ground rules containing these atoms in their heads or bodies. Thus, $G_1 = \emptyset$. If, as before, at shot 2 we have $F_2 = \{e(3,1), e(1,2), ab(3)\}$, no new ground rules are generated, thus $G_2 = G_1$ remains empty for the same aforementioned reason, i.e., the lack of unseen atoms. Also in this case, the only answer set computed on the basis of G_2 would be wrong.

We thus introduce a regeneration strategy with two purposes: to avoid as long as possible the (re)-instantiation of forgotten rules, yet to properly regenerate dropped ground rules when necessary, while ensuring that G_i is semantically correct w.r.t. F_i. As observed in the Example 4, regeneration is needed in both the rule-based and the predicate-based policies to ensure that relevant forgotten rules are actually regenerated.

Suppose to be at the shot i, and let r be a non-ground rule that has been forgotten at some shot $j \leq i$. In the following, we first describe the regeneration strategy for the standard overgrounding technique; then, we focus our attention on the overgrounding with tailoring, which requires some different treatment.

Regeneration for Standard Overgrounding. At the current shot i, a forgotten rule r is instantiated again only in case all the predicates in $pred(B^+(r))$ are *updated*. A predicate p is said to be *updated* if at least one of the following conditions holds: (1) a ground atom over p is provided as an input fact; (2) an atom over p is generated via the grounding of some rule r with p appearing in some atom of $H(r)$, in the shot i.

Regeneration for Overgrounding with Tailoring. If overgrounding with tailoring is adopted, simplifications are possibly reverted by applying some desimplification to G_{i-1} during the grounding step (line 6 of Algorithm 1). When simplifications apply, ground rules are moved into a set D if they contain a certainly false literal in the body, i.e., D consists of all *deleted rules*. Note that, differently from rules dropped because of forgetting, deleted rules are kept in memory and possibly restored, whenever necessary by the desimplification step. We modify the notion of *updated* predicate accordingly: in addition to conditions (1) and (2), a predicate p is said to be *updated* if, during the desimplification: (3) there exists a ground rule $g \in D$ such that an atom $a \in H(g)$ has p as predicate, and g is removed from D at the shot i and added to ΔG_i; or (4) there is at least a rule $g \in G_{i-1} \setminus D$ such that an atom $a \in H(g)$ has p as predicate, and all predicates in $pred(B^+(g))$ are tagged as updated. In case (3), all the literals in the body of g can be possibly satisfied at the shot i thus, the head of g can be possibly true. In condition (4), if $B^+(g)$ contains a literal l over a not updated predicate, then l has neither been provided as input nor is inferred through some new or previously deleted and now restored rule in the shot i. Consequently, g does not contribute to the semantics at the shot i.

Algorithm 2. Grounding a rule r at a shot i

1: **if** r is forgotten and all predicates in $pred(B^+(r))$ are updated **then**
2:    $ground\_rule(r, \Delta G_i, A_i \cup A_{i-1})$ $\qquad\qquad\qquad\qquad$ ▷ updates ΔG_i and A_i
3: **else if** r is not forgotten **then**
4:    $incremental\_ground\_rule(r, \Delta G_i, A_i)$ $\qquad\qquad$ ▷ updates ΔG_i and A_i
5: **end if**

Summing things up, the regeneration strategies look for both previously generated and *brand new* atoms, i.e., atoms that are unseen in all the shots preceding i. All of these are, in a sense, atoms that can trigger the instantiation of a forgotten rule r. Algorithm 2 illustrates how each rule is grounded. Once r is identified to be re-grounded, r is "overgrounded" by taking into account all atoms for $pred(B^+(r))$ appearing in A_i, either whether they are brand new or not. Moreover, ΔG_i is enriched with the regenerated instances of r. The grounding of non-forgotten rules is made incrementally on the basis of atoms that are brand new in the current shot i (i.e., $A_i \setminus A_{i-1}$) via an incremental and differential strategy [17]. We show next an example that illustrates the regeneration strategies.

Example 5. Consider again the program P_0 of Example 1. Assume to be at shot 2 when the set of facts $F_2 = \{e(3,1), e(1,4), ab(1)\}$ is provided as input and to apply a rule-based forgetting over the non-ground rule a. We start updating G_1 by dropping all ground instances of a, obtaining $G_1 = \{b_1\}$ and marking a as forgotten; the predicates e and ab are considered to be updated since F_2 contains facts having them as predicates. At this point, rules a and b are instantiated again and G_1 is enriched with the additional set of rules ΔG_2 containing:

$$a_1 : r(1,2) :\!- e(1,2),\ not\ ab(1). \quad b_2 : r(3,4) \mid s(3,4) :\!- e(3,1),\ r(1,4).$$
$$a_2 : r(3,1) :\!- e(3,1),\ not\ ab(3).$$
$$a_3 : r(1,4) :\!- e(1,4),\ not\ ab(1).$$

Note that all previously dropped ground instances of the rule a have been reinstated thanks to the regeneration strategy; indeed, a is forgotten and all its positive body predicates are updated. The rule b instead is not forgotten and it can be incrementally instantiated on the basis of brand new atoms at the shot 2. We thus obtain $G_2 = G_1 \cup \Delta G_2 = \{b_1\} \cup \{a_1, a_2, a_3, b_2\}$ as in Example 1 where no forgetting occurs. Note that, if only brand new atoms were considered for re-instantiating a, we would not generate a_1 and a_2; indeed, since $e(1,2)$ and $e(3,1)$ were provided as input in the shot 1, these atoms are not brand new in the shot 2. However, a_2 is needed to preserve the semantics of G_2 w.r.t. $P_0 \cup F_2$.

Let us now assume to apply, instead, a predicate-based policy that drops the predicate e, then G_1 becomes equal to $\emptyset$ and all atoms over e are dropped. Moreover, all rules and the predicate e are marked as forgotten. The re-instantiation of rules a and b produces:

$$a_2 : r(3,1) :\!\!- e(3,1), \ not \ ab(3). \quad b_1 : r(3,2) \mid s(3,2) :\!\!- e(3,1), \ r(1,2).$$
$$a_3 : r(1,4) :\!\!- e(1,4), \ not \ ab(1). \quad b_2 : r(3,4) \mid s(3,4) :\!\!- e(3,1), \ r(1,4).$$

The rule a_1 is no longer generated as $e(1,2)$ has been dropped and was available only in the shot 1. We would thus have $G_2 = G_1 \cup \Delta G_2 = \emptyset \cup \{a_2, a_3, b_1, b_2\}$, i.e., a cleaner instantiation based on F_2 input only. Indeed, in the predicate-based policy, the forgotten rules necessarily contain in their bodies some forgotten predicate, thus their reinstantiation is automatically driven by brand new atoms available at the shot i.

5 Implementation and Usage

The two forgetting policies along with the rule regeneration strategy have been implemented in *Incremental DLV2*. The system works as a permanent daemon accessible either remotely or locally via TCP connections. Once a client establishes a connection, the system creates a working session and waits for incoming XML commands, which specify tasks to be accomplished. Commands are executed in the order they are provided, and allow e.g., to load a logic program, to perform a reasoning shot, or to stop the system [9]. In the following, we focus on commands and other features related to forgetting policies in *Incremental DLV2*. A user manual illustrating all commands and how the system can be used for multi-shot reasoning, and binaries are available at https://dlv.demacs.unical.it/incremental.

As described in the following, forgetting can be controlled in three ways: via forget commands, via annotations in the logic program, or via command line options. Forget commands allow to enforce forgetting at selected shots, while the other two methods demand forgetting at each shot.

In order to command forgetting after a shot, the user can specify the following XML command:

```
<forget type=''mode''/>
```

where `mode` can be either `r` (rule-based forgetting) or `p` (predicate-based forgetting), which respectively specify one of the two available forgetting policies. Forgetting is applied over the so far accumulated overgrounded program.

In addition, the user can specify within the logic program some *annotations*, consisting in metadata embedded in comments. These allow to specify which predicates or rules have to be forgotten at each shot. Syntactically, all annotations start with the prefix "%@" and end with a dot ("."). The idea is borrowed from Java annotations having no direct effect on the code they annotate but allowing the programmer to inspect the annotated code at runtime, thus changing the code behavior at will. In order to apply the predicate-based forgetting type after each shot over some specific predicates, the user can include in the loaded logic program an annotation [6] of the following form:

```
%@global_forget_predicate(p/n).
```

forcing *Incremental DLV2* to forget all the atoms featuring the predicate p of arity n. To forget more than one predicate, the user can simply specify more than one annotation of this type. Furthermore, an annotation in the form:

```
%@rule_forget().
```

can be used in the logic program before a rule to express that all ground instances of such rule have to be dropped at each shot. The user can annotate more than one rule, each one needs to be preceded by the annotation.

Finally, the command line options -p and -r permit to enable, respectively, the predicate-based and the rule-based forgetting after each shot.

6   Experimental Results

In order to assess the impact of forgetting policies, we conducted an experimental analysis on the *Photo-voltaic System* domain described in Sect. 3. In particular, we considered again 60 shots and different grid sizes varying from 30×30 up to 60×60 and tested *Incremental DLV2* with different forgetting strategies: (*i*) *no forget*, in which the forgetting is disabled; (*ii*) *forget all rules*, in which all ground rules are dropped at each shot; (*iii*) *forget all predicates*, in which all ground rules and atoms are dropped at each shot with the only exception of the predicates link and energyThreshold which represent background facts; (*iv*) *forget energyDelivered*, that coincides with the forgetting of the predicate energyDelivered_AT_LEAST1_IN_LAST5S only; (*v*) *forget energy-Delivered + workingPanel*, that consists of the forgetting of the predicate energy Delivered_AT_LEAST1_IN_LAST5S and workingPanel. The strategies (*iv*) and (*v*), implemented via annotations, have been designed by studying the domain and observing that the predicate energyDelivered_AT_LEAST1_IN_LAST5S shows a high variability from one shot to the other as it represents the amounts of energy delivered by a panel in the window consisting of the last 5 s. Intuitively, such amounts tend to vary quite often depending on possible panel malfunctioning but mostly on the current sunlight, and thus, at each shot it is likely that facts over such a predicate are different in consecutive shots. We also take into account that workingPanel directly depends on energyDelivered_AT_LEAST1_IN_LAST5S and hence, current working panels may easily vary over time.

Results are reported in Table 2. We observe that, as expected, the *no forget* strategy is the one consuming the highest amount of memory. Enabling a form of forgetting generally permits saving memory, and in particular *forget all predicates*

Table 2. Performance of *Incremental DLV2* on the *Photo-voltaic System* domain while varying the forgetting strategy; the total time over all shots is reported in s, the peak memory in MB.

Forgetting Strategy	Total Time (s)	Memory (MB)
30 × 30 nodes - (60654 links)		
None	9.7	37.7
All rules	13.4	9.3
All predicates	12.8	7.3
energyDelivered	7.5	31.1
energyDelivered + workingPanel	12.5	7.5
40 × 40 nodes - (191881 links)		
None	31.4	100.0
All rules	41.0	28.1
All predicates	46.1	24.2
energyDelivered	24.7	98.5
energyDelivered + workingPanel	38.8	24.5
50 × 50 nodes - (468563 links)		
None	81.6	255.9
All rules	96.3	60.4
All predicates	94.8	53.7
energyDelivered	61.6	234.2
energyDelivered + workingPanel	92.4	54.3
60 × 60 nodes - (971731 links)		
None	171.8	515.5
All rules	195.6	120.5
All predicates	228.7	110.1
energyDelivered	138.2	483.3
energyDelivered + workingPanel	194.3	111.0

is the strategy ensuring the best saving since it is the most "aggressive" strategy. The *forget all rules* strategy appears midway between the two just mentioned strategies as it drops only ground rules and saves generated ground atoms.

The impact of forgetting on time performance may significantly vary, depending on the regeneration effort; i.e., dropping atoms/rules which are likely to be regenerated in later shots would increase the instantiation time. Forgetting energyDelivered_AT_LEAST1_IN_LAST5S permits to decrease memory while saving time, confirming the intuition that dropping atoms over highly variable predicates is advantageous. Indeed, the handling of accumulated but "useless" facts is avoided. The strategy (v) that in addition drops the workingPanel predicate appears to be a better alternative w.r.t. to the plain forgetting of all rules

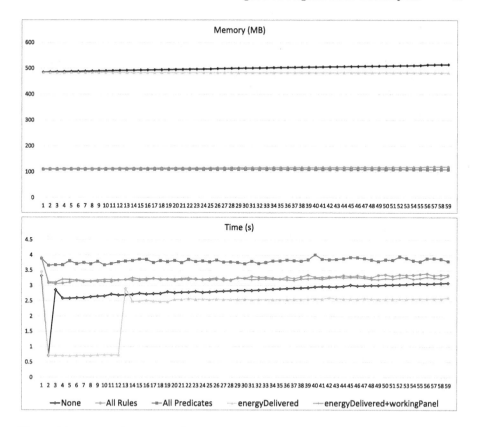

Fig. 1. Memory and time trends over all shots on the *Photo-voltaic System* domain over the 60×60 grid instance.

or predicates; indeed, memory is decreased as in the aggressive forgetting of all predicates, while time is less than the more conservative forgetting of all rules. This suggests that properly choosing a proper subset of rules or predicates to drop out can improve the effectiveness of forgetting. One could build a heuristic selecting particular predicates or rules to be forgotten: for predicates, one could, e.g., look at some metric of variability of the extension of a predicate over the shots, and/or its data distribution; rules can be automatically selected by looking at their dependencies, e.g., one could select highly variable rules forming strongly connected components.

Figure 1 reports a more detailed focus on the executions on the 60x60 grid, plotting memory and time over all 60 shots. Memory consumption is kept steadily low, when forgetting is enabled. Concerning time, the *forget energyDelivered* strategy shows a better scalability.

7   Conclusions

We introduced forgetting as an optimization of the overgrounding technique to make it more efficient in performance demanding applications, such as those emerging in Stream Reasoning scenarios. Indeed, overgrounding was designed by assuming that all ground rules and atoms obtained in previous shots are kept in memory, therefore it does not involve any dropping criterion nor there is any regeneration need. Hence, the herein presented regeneration strategies have been purposely defined to adapt this default behavior in presence of forgetting techniques. As a test bed scenario, we focused on a monitoring application; however, it is worth noting that forgetting tackles an intrinsic aspect related to overgrounding, i.e., memory consumption, which is independent from the benchmark scenario at hand. Experiments demonstrate that overgrounding with forgetting offers significant advantages in terms of both memory saving and time performance, and that a proper choice of the forgetting policy to use can make a difference.

As for future work, several extensions can be identified. Besides rule- and predicate-driven policies, we plan to investigate a more selective "memory cleaning" approach, namely a constant-based forgetting, in which all rules and atoms featuring a specific constant are dropped. Furthermore, for maximizing the gain in terms of memory without affecting time performance, automatically identifying the ideal set of rules and atoms to drop is crucial. For instance, one should avoid dropping rules that depend only on atoms that are consistently "necessary" over all shots. Hence, the definition of heuristics capable of automatically identifying the ideal set of ground rules to be kept in memory is a future direction worth exploring.

References

1. Alviano, M., et al.: The ASP system DLV2. In: Balduccini, M., Janhunen, T. (eds.) LPNMR 2017. LNCS (LNAI), vol. 10377, pp. 215–221. Springer, Cham (2017). https://doi.org/10.1007/978-3-319-61660-5_19
2. Beck, H., Bierbaumer, B., Dao-Tran, M., Eiter, T., Hellwagner, H., Schekotihin, K.: Stream reasoning-based control of caching strategies in CCN routers. In: IEEE International Conference on Communications, ICC 2017, Paris, France, 21–25 May 2017, pp. 1–6. IEEE (2017). https://doi.org/10.1109/ICC.2017.7996762
3. Beck, H., Dao-Tran, M., Eiter, T.: Answer update for rule-based stream reasoning. In: IJCAI, pp. 2741–2747. AAAI Press (2015)
4. Cabalar, P., Fandinno, J., Schaub, T., Wanko, P.: On the semantics of hybrid ASP systems based on clingo. Algorithms 16(4), 185 (2023)
5. Calimeri, F., Fuscà, D., Perri, S., Zangari, J.: External computations and interoperability in the new DLV grounder. In: Esposito, F., Basili, R., Ferilli, S., Lisi, F. (eds.) AI*IA 2017 Advances in Artificial Intelligence. Lecture Notes in Computer Science(), vol. 10640, pp. 172–185. Springer, Cham (2017). https://doi.org/10.1007/978-3-319-70169-1_13
6. Calimeri, F., Fuscà, D., Perri, S., Zangari, J.: I-DLV: the new intelligent grounder of DLV. Intelligenza Artificiale 11(1), 5–20 (2017)

7. Calimeri, F., Germano, S., Ianni, G., Pacenza, F., Perri, S., Zangari, J.: Integrating rule-based AI tools into mainstream game development. In: Benzmüller, C., Ricca, F., Parent, X., Roman, D. (eds.) RuleML+RR 2018. LNCS, vol. 11092, pp. 310–317. Springer, Cham (2018). https://doi.org/10.1007/978-3-319-99906-7_23

8. Calimeri, F., Ianni, G., Pacenza, F., Perri, S., Zangari, J.: Incremental answer set programming with overgrounding. TPLP **19**(5–6), 957–973 (2019)

9. Calimeri, F., Ianni, G., Pacenza, F., Perri, S., Zangari, J.: ASP-based multi-shot reasoning via DLV2 with incremental grounding. In: PPDP, pp. 1–9. ACM (2022)

10. Calimeri, F., et al.: ASP-based declarative reasoning in data-intensive enterprise and IoT applications. Algorithms **16**(3), 159 (2023)

11. Calimeri, F., Manna, M., Mastria, E., Morelli, M.C., Perri, S., Zangari, J.: I-DLV-sr: a stream reasoning system based on I-DLV. Theory Pract. Log. Program. **21**(5), 610–628 (2021)

12. Dodaro, C., Eiter, T., Ogris, P., Schekotihin, K.: Managing caching strategies for stream reasoning with reinforcement learning. Theory Pract. Log. Program. **20**(5), 625–640 (2020). https://doi.org/10.1017/S147106842000037X

13. Eiter, T., Wang, K.: Semantic forgetting in answer set programming. Artif. Intell. **172**(14), 1644–1672 (2008). https://doi.org/10.1016/J.ARTINT.2008.05.002

14. Fuscà, D., Germano, S., Zangari, J., Anastasio, M., Calimeri, F., Perri, S.: A framework for easing the development of applications embedding answer set programming. In: PPDP, pp. 38–49. ACM (2016)

15. Gebser, M., Kaminski, R., Kaufmann, B., Schaub, T.: Multi-shot ASP solving with clingo. TPLP **19**(1), 27–82 (2019)

16. Gebser, M., Leone, N., Maratea, M., Perri, S., Ricca, F., Schaub, T.: Evaluation techniques and systems for answer set programming: a survey. In: IJCAI, pp. 5450–5456. ijcai.org (2018)

17. Ianni, G., Pacenza, F., Zangari, J.: Incremental maintenance of overgrounded logic programs with tailored simplifications. TPLP **20**(5), 719–734 (2020)

18. Kaufmann, B., Leone, N., Perri, S., Schaub, T.: Grounding and solving in answer set programming. AI Mag. **37**(3), 25–32 (2016)

19. Motik, B., Nenov, Y., Piro, R., Horrocks, I.: Maintenance of datalog materialisations revisited. Artif. Intell. **269**, 76–136 (2019). https://doi.org/10.1016/j.artint.2018.12.004

20. Phuoc, D.L., Eiter, T.: An adaptive semantic stream reasoning framework for deep neural networks. In: Conrad, S., Tiddi, I. (eds.) Proceedings of the CIKM 2020 Workshops co-located with 29th ACM International Conference on Information and Knowledge Management (CIKM 2020), Galway, Ireland, 19–23 October 2020. CEUR Workshop Proceedings, vol. 2699. CEUR-WS.org (2020). http://ceur-ws.org/Vol-2699/paper09.pdf

21. Reiter, R.: A logic for default reasoning. Artif. Intell. **13**(1–2), 81–132 (1980)

22. Saribatur, Z.G., Patoglu, V., Erdem, E.: Finding optimal feasible global plans for multiple teams of heterogeneous robots using hybrid reasoning: an application to cognitive factories. Auton. Robots **43**(1), 213–238 (2019). https://doi.org/10.1007/s10514-018-9721-x

23. Suchan, J., Bhatt, M., Walega, P.A., Schultz, C.P.L.: Visual explanation by high-level abduction: On answer-set programming driven reasoning about moving objects. In: AAAI, pp. 1965–1972 (2018). https://www.aaai.org/ocs/index.php/AAAI/AAAI18/paper/view/17303

Asynchronous Reactive Programming with Modal Types in Haskell

Patrick Bahr$^{(\boxtimes)}$, Emil Houlborg, and Gregers Thomas Skat Rørdam

IT University of Copenhagen, Copenhagen, Denmark
{paba,ehou}@itu.dk, gregers@rordam.dk

Abstract. The implementation of asynchronous systems, in particular graphical user interfaces, is traditionally based on an imperative model that uses shared mutable state and callbacks. While efficient, the combination of shared mutable state and callbacks is notoriously difficult to reason about and prone to errors. Functional reactive programming (FRP) provides an elegant alternative and recent theoretical advances in modal FRP suggest that it can be efficient as well.

In this paper, we present Async Rattus, an FRP language embedded in Haskell. The distinguishing feature of Async Rattus is a modal type constructor that enables the composition of asynchronous subsystems by keeping track of each subsystem's clock at compile time which in turn enables dynamically changing clocks at runtime. The central component of our implementation is a Haskell compiler plugin that, among other aspects, checks the stricter typing rules of Async Rattus and infers compile-time clocks. This is the first implementation of an asynchronous modal FRP language. By embedding the language in Haskell we can exploit the existing language and library ecosystem as well as rapidly experiment with new language features and library design. We hope that such experimentation with Async Rattus sparks further research in modal FRP and its applications.

Keywords: Functional reactive programming · Modal types · Space leaks

1 Introduction

Functional reactive programming (FRP) [14] provides an elegant, high-level programming paradigm for reactive systems. This is achieved by making time-varying values (also called *signals* or *behaviours*) first-class objects that are easily composable. For example, assuming a type *Sig a* that classifies signals of type *a*, an FRP library may provide a function $map :: (a \to b) \to Sig\ a \to Sig\ b$ that allows us to manipulate a given signal by applying a function to it.

Haskell has a rich ecosystem of expressive and flexible FRP libraries [1,7, 8,15,19,22,30–32,35]. Devising such FRP libraries is challenging as their APIs must be carefully designed to ensure that reactive programs are *causal* and are

M. Gebser and I. Sergey (Eds.): PADL 2024, LNCS 14512, pp. 18–36, 2023.
https://doi.org/10.1007/978-3-031-52038-9_2

not prone to *space leaks*. A reactive program is causal if the value of any output signal at any time t only depends on the value of input signals at time t or earlier. Due to the high-level nature of FRP programs, they can suffer from *space leaks*, i.e. they keep data in memory for too long. Haskell FRP libraries tackle these issues by providing a set of *abstract* types (i.e. their definitions are not exposed) to represent signals, signal functions, events etc. and only expose a carefully selected set of combinators to manipulate elements of these types.

Over the last decade an alternative to this library-based approach has been developed [3,4,21,24,26,28,29] that uses a modal type operator $\bigcirc$ (pronounced "later") to express the passage of time at the type level. This type modality allows us to distinguish a value of type a, which is available now, from a value of type $\bigcirc a$, which represents data of type a arriving in the next time step. A language with such a modal type operator $\bigcirc$ has been recently implemented as an embedded language in Haskell called Rattus [2].

In Rattus, signals can be implemented as follows:[1]

data $Sig\ a = a ::: (\bigcirc(Sig\ a))$

That is, a signal of type $Sig\ a$ consists of a value of type a now and a signal of type $Sig\ a$ later, thus separating consecutive values of the signal by one time step. Instead of hiding the definition of Sig from the user, Rattus ensures the operational guarantees of causality and absence of space leaks via its type system.

However, the use of the $\bigcirc$ modality limits Rattus to *synchronous* reactive programs where all components of the program progress according to a *global clock*. This is witnessed by the fact that we can implement the following function that takes two delayed integers and produces their delayed sum:

$add :: \bigcirc Int \rightarrow \bigcirc Int \rightarrow \bigcirc Int$
$add\ x\ y = \mathsf{delay}\ (\mathsf{adv}\ x + \mathsf{adv}\ y)$

This only works because the two delayed integers x and y are guaranteed to arrive at the same time, namely at the next tick of the global clock.

Computing according to a *global clock* is a reasonable assumption for many contexts such as simulations and games as well as typical application domains of synchronous (dataflow) languages [6,9,33] such as real-time and embedded systems. However, for many applications, e.g. GUIs and concurrent systems, the notion of a global clock may not be natural and may lead to inefficiencies. A global clock would have to run at least as fast as the updates to the fastest input signal. For example, a GUI may have a component (say a text field) that should react only to keyboard input, while another component (say a button) should only react to mouse clicks. However, in a synchronous implementation of this, both components have to react and perform a computation whenever the user performs a mouse click or uses the keyboard, even though the reaction of one of the components is merely to report that no updates need to be performed on it.

In this paper, we present Async Rattus, an embedded modal FRP language that replaces the *single global clock* of Rattus with *dynamic local clocks* that

---

[1] The data constructor ::: for Sig is written as an infix operator, similarly to : for lists.

enable asynchronous computations. Async Rattus is based on the Async RaTT calculus for asynchronous FRP that has recently been proposed by Bahr and Møgelberg [5] and has been shown to ensure causality and absence of space leaks. Moreover, Async Rattus is implemented as a shallowly embedded language in Haskell, which means that Async Rattus programs can seamlessly interact with regular Haskell code and thus also have access to Haskell's rich library ecosystem.

Similarly to Rattus, the implementation of Async Rattus consists of a library that implements the primitives of the language along with a plugin for the Glasgow Haskell Compiler (GHC). The plugin is needed to check the language's more restrictive variable scope rules and to ensure the eager evaluation strategy that is necessary to obtain the operational properties. However, Async Rattus requires an additional novelty: The underlying core calculus of Async Rattus requires explicit *clocks annotations* in the program. These annotations are necessary to keep track of the dynamic data dependencies in FRP programs at runtime. Instead of relying on the programmer to provide these clock annotations, the Async Rattus plugin infers them and then inserts them into the intermediate code generated by GHC from the Async Rattus code.

The remainder of the paper is structured as follows: Sect. 2 describes the syntax and semantics of Async Rattus with a particular focus on its non-standard typing rules. Section 3 illustrates the expressiveness of Async Rattus and its interaction with Haskell with the help of a selection of example programs. Section 4 describes how Async Rattus is implemented as an embedded language in Haskell. Finally, Sect. 5 and Sect. 6 discuss related and future work, respectively.

Async Rattus is available as a package on Hackage [18]. Apart from the language implementation itself, the package also contains an FRP library implemented in Async Rattus along with example programs using this library. In particular, it contains the full source code of all examples presented in this paper.

2   Introduction to Async Rattus

Async Rattus differs from Haskell in two major ways. Firstly, Async Rattus is eagerly evaluated. This difference in the operational semantics is crucial for the language's ability to avoid space leaks. Secondly, Async Rattus extends Haskell's type system with two type modalities, $\bigcirc$ and $\square$. A value of type $\bigcirc a$ is a delayed computation that waits for an event upon which it will produce a value of type a, whereas a value of type $\square a$ is a thunk that can be forced at any time, now or in the future, to produce a value of type a.

Each value $x :: \bigcirc a$ waits for an event to occur before it can be evaluated to a value of type a. Intuitively, an element of type $\bigcirc a$ is a pair (θ, f) consisting of a (local) *clock* θ and a thunk f, so that f can be forced to compute a value of type a as soon as the clock θ ticks. This intuition is witnessed by the two functions $cl :: \bigcirc a \rightarrow Clock$ and $adv :: \bigcirc a \rightarrow a$ that project out these two components. Conversely, we can construct a value of type $\bigcirc a$ by providing these two components using the function delay $:: Clock \rightarrow a \rightarrow \bigcirc a$. Using these functions, we can implement a function that takes a delayed integer and increments it:

$$\frac{\Gamma, \checkmark_{\mathsf{cl}(t)} \vdash t :: A}{\Gamma \vdash \mathsf{delay}_{\mathsf{cl}(t)} \ t :: \bigcirc A} \quad \frac{\checkmark \notin \Gamma' \text{ or } A \text{ stable}}{\Gamma, x :: A, \Gamma' \vdash x :: A} \quad \frac{\Gamma \vdash t :: \Box A}{\Gamma \vdash \mathsf{unbox} \ t :: A} \quad \frac{\Gamma^{\Box} \vdash t :: A}{\Gamma \vdash \mathsf{box} \ t :: \Box A}$$

$$\frac{\Gamma \vdash s :: \bigcirc A \quad \Gamma \vdash t :: \bigcirc B \quad \checkmark \notin \Gamma'}{\Gamma, \checkmark_{\mathsf{cl}(s) \sqcup \mathsf{cl}(t)}, \Gamma' \vdash \mathsf{select} \ s \ t :: Select \ A \ B} \quad \frac{\Gamma \vdash t :: \bigcirc A \quad \checkmark \notin \Gamma'}{\Gamma, \checkmark_{\mathsf{cl}(t)}, \Gamma' \vdash \mathsf{adv} \ t :: A} \quad \frac{}{\Gamma \vdash \mathsf{never} :: \bigcirc A}$$

$$\text{where} \qquad \cdot^{\Box} = \cdot \qquad (\Gamma, x :: A)^{\Box} = \begin{cases} \Gamma^{\Box}, x :: A & \text{if } A \text{ stable} \\ \Gamma^{\Box} & \text{otherwise} \end{cases}$$
$$(\Gamma, \checkmark_{\theta})^{\Box} = \Gamma^{\Box}$$

Fig. 1. Select typing rules for Async Rattus.

$$incr :: \bigcirc Int \to \bigcirc Int$$
$$incr \ x = \mathsf{delay}_{\mathsf{cl}(x)} \ (\mathsf{adv} \ x + 1)$$

This makes explicit the fact that the integers produced by the delayed computations $x :: \bigcirc Int$ and $incr \ x :: \bigcirc Int$ become available at the same time. We write the first argument of delay as a subscript. As we will see shortly, these clock arguments are annotations that can always be inferred from the context.

Intuitively speaking, a clock θ represents a form of temporal data dependency. In the above example, $incr \ x$ produces an integer as soon as x does. A reactive program processes data received from some input channels (e.g. keyboard, mouse, network connection). A clock θ is simply a set of such input channels, and a tick on θ means that data has been received on some input channel $c \in \theta$. Hence, $\mathsf{delay}_{\theta} \ t$ means that we delay evaluation of t until we have received data on some input channel $c \in \theta$.

2.1 Typing Rules for Delayed Computations

The type signatures that we have given for delay and adv above are a good starting point to understand what delay and adv do, but they are too permissive. If delay were simply a function of type $\mathsf{delay} :: Clock \to a \to \bigcirc a$, we could delay arbitrary computations – and the data they depend on – into the future, which will cause space leaks. Similarly, adv cannot be simply a function of type $\bigcirc a \to a$ as this would allow us to execute future computations now, which would break causality.

Instead, the type system of Async Rattus constrains the use of delay and adv to ensure that programs are causal and do not cause space leaks. Figure 1 shows the most important typing rules of Async Rattus, where we write Γ for typing contexts; s, t for terms; x, y, z for variables; A, B, C for types, and θ for clocks.

Async Rattus uses a *Fitch-style* type system [11], which means that a typing context Γ may contain *tokens* of the form $\checkmark_{\theta}$ (pronounced "tick of clock θ" or just "tick") in addition to the usual typing assumptions of the form $x :: A$. We can think of $\checkmark_{\theta}$ as denoting the passage of one time step on the clock θ, i.e. all variables to the left of $\checkmark_{\theta}$ are one time step older w.r.t. the clock θ compared to those to the right of $\checkmark_{\theta}$. The rule for delay introduces a token $\checkmark_{\mathsf{cl}(t)}$ in the typing context Γ. This means that t sees the variables in Γ as one time step older w.r.t. clock $\mathsf{cl}(t)$, thus matching the intuitive semantics of delay which delays evaluation of t by one time step on the clock $\mathsf{cl}(t)$.

The variable introduction rule explains how ticks influence which variables are in scope: A variable occurring to the left of a tick is no longer in scope unless it is of a type that is time-independent. We call these time-independent types *stable* types, and in particular all base types such as *Int* and *Bool* are stable as are any types of the form $\square a$. For instance, function types are not stable, and thus functions cannot be moved into the future, which means that the type checker must reject the following definition:

$$mapLater :: (a \to b) \to \bigcirc a \to \bigcirc b$$
$$mapLater\ f\ x = \mathsf{delay}_{\mathsf{cl}(x)}\ (f\ (\mathsf{adv}\ x)) \qquad \text{-- f is out of scope}$$

The problem is that functions may store time-dependent data in their closure and thus moving functions into the future could lead to space leaks. We shall return to stable types later when we discuss the $\square$ type modality in Sect. 2.2.

The typing rule for adv only allows us to advance a delayed computation $t :: \bigcirc A$, if we know that the clock of t has already ticked, which is witnessed by the token $\checkmark_{\mathsf{cl}(t)}$ in the context. That is, delay looks ahead one time step on a clock θ and adv then allows us to go back to the present. Variable bindings made in the future, i.e. the context Γ' in the typing rule for adv, are therefore not accessible once we returned to the present.

We can now see why the *add* function from Sect. 1 does not type check:

$$add :: \bigcirc Int \to \bigcirc Int \to \bigcirc Int$$
$$add\ x\ y = \mathsf{delay}_\theta\ (\mathsf{adv}\ x + \mathsf{adv}\ y) \qquad \text{-- no suitable clock } \theta$$

The problem is that there is no clock θ so that both subexpressions adv x and adv y type check. The former only type checks if $\theta = \mathsf{cl}(x)$ and the latter only type checks if $\theta = \mathsf{cl}(y)$. It might very well be that the clocks of x and y are the same at runtime, e.g. if $y = incr\ x$, but that is not guaranteed at compile time.

In order to deal with more than one delayed computation, Async Rattus allows us to form the union $\theta \sqcup \theta'$ of two clocks θ and θ'. The new clock $\theta \sqcup \theta'$ ticks whenever θ or θ' ticks. We interact with such clocks via the select primitive, which takes two delayed computations $s :: \bigcirc A$ and $t :: \bigcirc B$ as arguments, given that a tick on the clock $\mathsf{cl}(s) \sqcup \mathsf{cl}(t)$ is in the context. In return, select produces a value of type *Select A B*, which is defined as follows:[2]

data *Select a b* = *Fst a* $(\bigcirc b)$ | *Snd* $(\bigcirc a)$ *b* | *Both a b*

Given that $\mathsf{cl}(s) \sqcup \mathsf{cl}(t)$ has ticked, select $s\ t$ produces a value with constructor *Fst*, *Snd*, or *Both* if $\mathsf{cl}(s)$ ticked before, after, or at the same time as $\mathsf{cl}(t)$, respectively. For example, the following function waits for two integers and returns the integer that arrives first:

---

[2] Async Rattus is a strict language and all type definitions are strict by default.

$$first :: \bigcirc Int \to \bigcirc Int \to \bigcirc Int$$
$$first\ x\ y = \mathsf{delay}_{\mathsf{cl}(x) \sqcup \mathsf{cl}(y)}\ (\mathbf{case\ select}\ x\ y\ \mathbf{of}\ \ Fst\ \ \ x'\ \_\ \to x'$$
$$Snd\ \ \_\ y' \to y'$$
$$Both\ x'\ \_\ \to x')$$

With the help of select, we can also implement the *add* function from the introduction, but we have to revise the return type:

$$add :: \bigcirc Int \to \bigcirc Int \to \bigcirc(Int \oplus \bigcirc Int)$$
$$add\ x\ y = \mathsf{delay}_{\mathsf{cl}(x) \sqcup \mathsf{cl}(y)}\ (\mathbf{case\ select}\ x\ y\ \mathbf{of}$$
$$Fst\ \ x'\ y' \to Inr\ (\mathsf{delay}_{\mathsf{cl}(y')}\ (x' + \mathsf{adv}\ y'))$$
$$Snd\ \ x'\ y' \to Inr\ (\mathsf{delay}_{\mathsf{cl}(x')}\ (\mathsf{adv}\ x' + y'))$$
$$Both\ x'\ y' \to Inl\ (x' + y'))$$

where $\oplus$ is the (strict) sum type with the two constructors $Inl :: a \to a \oplus b$ and $Inr :: b \to a \oplus b$. The type now reflects the fact that we might have to wait two ticks (of two different clocks) to obtain the result. From now on we will elide the clock annotations for delay as it will always be obvious from the context what the annotation needs to be. Indeed, Async Rattus will infer the correct clock annotation and insert it automatically during compilation.

2.2 Typing Rules for Stable Computations

As we have seen above, only variables of *stable types* can be moved across ticks and thus into the future. A type A is stable if all occurrences of $\bigcirc$ and function types in A are guarded by $\square$. For example $Int \oplus Float$, $\square(Int \to Float)$, and $\square(\bigcirc Int) \oplus Int$ are stable types, but $\square Int \to Float$, $\bigcirc Int$, and $\bigcirc(\square Int)$ are not. That is, the $\square$ modality can be used to turn any type into a stable type, thus making it possible to move functions into the future safely without risking space leaks. Using $\square$, we can implement the *map* function for $\bigcirc$:

$$mapLater :: \square(a \to b) \to \bigcirc a \to \bigcirc b$$
$$mapLater\ f\ x = \mathsf{delay}\ (\mathsf{unbox}\ f\ (\mathsf{adv}\ x))$$

where unbox is simply a function of type $\square a \to a$.

A value of type $\square$ can only be constructed using the introduction form box. The typing rule for box, shown in Fig. 1, restricts the typing context to $\Gamma^{\square}$, which is obtained from Γ by removing all variables of non-stable types and all $\checkmark_\theta$ tokens. Hence, the type system ensures that boxed values may only refer to variables of a stable type.

2.3 Recursive Definitions

Similarly to Rattus and other synchronous FRP languages [3,26], signals can be defined in Async Rattus by the following definition:

data $Sig\ a = a ::: (\bigcirc(Sig\ a))$

That is, a signal of type $Sig\ a$ consists of a current value of type a and a future update to the signal of type $\bigcirc(Sig\ a)$. We can define a map function for signals, but similarly to the $mapLater$ function on the $\bigcirc$ modality, the function argument has to be boxed:

$map :: \square(a \to b) \to Sig\ a \to Sig\ b$
$map\ f\ (x ::: xs) = $ unbox $f\ x :::$ delay $(map\ f\ ($adv $xs))$

In order to ensure productivity of recursive function definitions, Async Rattus requires that recursive function calls, such as $map\ f\ ($adv $xs)$ above, have to be guarded by a delay. More precisely, such a recursive occurrence may only occur in a context Γ that contains a $\checkmark_\theta$.

It may seem that we can get around the need to box the function argument to map by instead using a nested recursive function run:

$map :: (a \to b) \to Sig\ a \to Sig\ b$
$map\ f = run$ **where**
$\quad run :: Sig\ a \to Sig\ b$
$\quad run\ (x ::: xs) = f\ x :::$ delay $(run\ ($adv $xs))$ $\qquad$ -- f is out of scope

However, in this definition, f would no longer be in scope. To type check a recursive definition in a typing context Γ, the body of the recursive definition has to type check in the typing context $\Gamma^\square$. For example, for $run :: Sig\ a \to Sig\ b$ to type check in the context $\Gamma = f :: a \to b$, the body of run has to type check in the context $\Gamma^\square = \cdot$, i.e. f is no longer in scope in the body of run.

While the definition of the signal type looks superficially the same as in synchronous FRP languages, its semantics is quite different because $\bigcirc$ has a different semantics: Updates to a signal do not come at the rate given by a global clock, but rather by some local clock, which may in turn change dynamically. For example, we can implement the constant signal function as follows:

$const :: a \to Sig\ a$
$const\ x = x :::$ never

where never $:: \bigcirc b$ is simply a delayed computation with a clock that will never tick. The $const$ signal function might seem pointless, but we can combine it with a combinator that switches from one signal to another signal:

$switch :: Sig\ a \to \bigcirc(Sig\ a) \to Sig\ a$
$switch\ (x ::: xs)\ d = x :::$ delay (**case** select $xs\ d$ **of**
$\qquad\qquad\qquad\qquad\qquad\qquad\quad Fst\quad xs'\ d' \to switch\ xs'\ d'$
$\qquad\qquad\qquad\qquad\qquad\qquad\quad Snd\ \_\quad d' \to d'$
$\qquad\qquad\qquad\qquad\qquad\qquad\quad Both\ xs'\ d' \to d')$

A signal $switch\ s\ e$ first behaves like s, but as soon as the clock of e ticks the signal behaves like the signal produced by e. For example, given a value $x :: a$

and a delayed value $y :: \bigcirc a$, we can produce a signal that first has the value x and then, as soon as y arrives, has the value that y produces:

$step :: a \rightarrow \bigcirc a \rightarrow Sig\ a$
$step\ x\ y = switch\ (const\ x)\ (\mathsf{delay}\ (const\ (\mathsf{adv}\ y)))$

2.4 Operational Semantics

One of the main features of Async Rattus is that it avoids space leaks. To this end, its type system prevents us from moving arbitrary computations into the future. In addition, the operational semantics is carefully designed so that computations are executed as soon as the data they depend on is available. In short, this means that Async Rattus uses an eager evaluation semantics except for delay and box. That is, arguments are evaluated to values before they are passed on to functions, but special rules apply to delay and box. Furthermore, Async Rattus requires strict data types and any use of lazy data types will produce a warning.

Following the temporal interpretation of the $\bigcirc$ modality, its introduction form delay_θ does not eagerly evaluate its argument since we have to wait until input data arrives, namely when the clock θ ticks. For example, in the expression $\mathsf{delay}\ (\mathsf{adv}\ x + 1)$, we cannot evaluate $\mathsf{adv}\ x + 1$ until the delayed integer value of $x :: \bigcirc Int$ arrives, which is one time step from now on the clock $\mathsf{cl}(x)$. However, evaluation is only delayed until the clock $\mathsf{cl}(x)$ ticks, and this delay is reversed by adv. For example, $\mathsf{adv}\ (\mathsf{delay}\ (1 + 1))$ evaluates immediately to 2.

Several modal FRP calculi [3–5,26] have a similar operational semantics to achieve the same memory property that Async Rattus has. However, similarly to Rattus [2], Async Rattus uses a slightly more eager evaluation strategy for delay: Recall that $\mathsf{delay}_\theta\ t$ delays the computation t by one time step and that adv reverses such a delay. The operational semantics reflects this intuition by first evaluating every term t that occurs as $\mathsf{delay}_{\mathsf{cl}(t)}\ (...\ \mathsf{adv}\ t\ ...)$ before evaluating delay. In other words, $\mathsf{delay}_{\mathsf{cl}(t)}\ (...\ \mathsf{adv}\ t\ ...)$ is equivalent to

$$\mathbf{let}\ x = t\ \mathbf{in}\ \mathsf{delay}_{\mathsf{cl}(x)}\ (...\ \mathsf{adv}\ x\ ...)$$

Similarly, $\mathsf{delay}_{\mathsf{cl}(s) \sqcup \mathsf{cl}(t)}\ (...\ \mathsf{select}\ s\ t\ ...)$ is equivalent to

$$\mathbf{let}\ x = s; y = t\ \mathbf{in}\ \mathsf{delay}_{\mathsf{cl}(x) \sqcup \mathsf{cl}(y)}\ (...\ \mathsf{select}\ x\ y\ ...)$$

This generalisation of the operational semantics of delay allows us to lift some of the restrictions present in the Async RaTT calculus [5] on which Async Rattus is based: Async Rattus allows more than one $\checkmark_\theta$ in the typing context, i.e. delay can be nested; it does not prohibit lambda abstractions in the presence of a $\checkmark_\theta$; and both adv and select can be used with arbitrary terms, not just variables. In Sect. 4, we introduce the technical device that makes it safe to lift these restrictions of Async RaTT, namely the *single tick* program transformation.

3   Reactive Programming in Async Rattus

In this section, we demonstrate the expressiveness of Async Rattus with a number of examples. The full source code of abridged examples along with further example programs can be found in the Async Rattus package [18].

3.1   A Simple FRP Application

To support FRP using the *Sig* type, we implement a library of standard FRP combinators [5] in Async Rattus. Figure 2 lists a small subset of this library.

In addition to the core language constructs of Async Rattus presented in Sect. 2, the language also features primitives for interacting with its environment via *input channels* and *output channels*. The simplest input channel is a timer that ticks at a fixed interval (given in milliseconds):

$$timer :: Int \rightarrow \Box(\bigcirc())$$

Input channels have the type $\Box(\bigcirc a)$, but they can always be turned into signals:

$$mkSig :: \Box(\bigcirc a) \rightarrow \bigcirc(Sig\ a)$$
$$mkSig\ b = \mathsf{delay}\ (\mathsf{adv}\ (\mathsf{unbox}\ b) ::: mkSig\ b)$$
$$timerSig :: Int \rightarrow Sig\ ()$$
$$timerSig\ n = () ::: mkSig\ (timer\ n)$$

That is, the signal *timerSig n* produces a new value every n microseconds. As an example, this timer input channel can be used for implementing the *derivative* and *integral* combinators in Fig. 2 (as in Bahr and Møgelberg [5]).

More general input channels can be constructed using

$$getInput :: IO\ (\Box(\bigcirc a), (a \rightarrow IO\ ()))$$

which produces an input channel of type $\Box(\bigcirc a)$ that we can feed from Haskell by using the callback function of type $a \rightarrow IO\ ()$. Whenever the callback function is called with an argument v, the input channel will produce a new value v. Library authors can use *getInput* to provide an Async Rattus interface to external resources. For example, we can implement an input channel for the console with the following Haskell code:

```
consoleInput :: IO (□(○Text))
consoleInput = do (inp, cb) ← getInput
                  let loop = do line ← getLine; cb line; loop
                  forkIO loop
                  return inp
```

For output channels, Async Rattus provides the function

$$
\begin{array}{ll}
current & :: Sig\ a \rightarrow a \\
future & :: Sig\ a \rightarrow \bigcirc(Sig\ a) \\
map & :: \Box(a \rightarrow b) \rightarrow Sig\ a \rightarrow Sig\ b \\
mapD & :: \Box(a \rightarrow b) \rightarrow \bigcirc(Sig\ a) \rightarrow \bigcirc(Sig\ b) \\
const & :: a \rightarrow Sig\ a \\
scan & :: (Stable\ b) \Rightarrow \Box(b \rightarrow a \rightarrow b) \rightarrow b \rightarrow Sig\ a \rightarrow Sig\ b \\
zipWith & :: (Stable\ a, Stable\ b) \Rightarrow \Box(a \rightarrow b \rightarrow c) \rightarrow Sig\ a \rightarrow Sig\ b \rightarrow Sig\ c \\
interleave & :: \Box(a \rightarrow a \rightarrow a) \rightarrow \bigcirc(Sig\ a) \rightarrow \bigcirc(Sig\ a) \rightarrow \bigcirc(Sig\ a) \\
switch & :: Sig\ a \rightarrow \bigcirc(Sig\ a) \rightarrow Sig\ a \\
switchS & :: Sig\ a \rightarrow \bigcirc(a \rightarrow Sig\ a) \rightarrow Sig\ a \\
\\
derivative & :: Sig\ Float \rightarrow Sig\ Float \\
integral & :: Float \rightarrow Sig\ Float \rightarrow Sig\ Float
\end{array}
$$

Fig. 2. Simple FRP library.

$$setOutput :: Sig\ a \rightarrow (a \rightarrow IO\ ()) \rightarrow IO\ ()$$

which, if given a signal s and a callback function f, calls $f\ v$ whenever s produces a new value v. To support a variety of programming styles beyond the *Sig* type, the type of *setOutput* is in fact more general:

$$setOutput :: Producer\ p\ a \Rightarrow p \rightarrow (a \rightarrow IO\ ()) \rightarrow IO\ ()$$

Instances of *Producer p a* are types p that produce values of type a over time. In particular, we have instances *Producer* $(\bigcirc(Sig\ a))\ a$ and *Producer* $(Sig\ a)\ a$.

Similarly to *getInput*, library authors can use *setOutput* to provide an Async Rattus interface for external resources. For example, we may wish to provide a way to output a signal of integers by printing each new value to the console:

$$
\begin{array}{l}
intOutput :: Producer\ p\ Int \Rightarrow p \rightarrow IO\ () \\
intOutput\ sig = setOutput\ sig\ print
\end{array}
$$

As a simple example, we implement a console application that waits for the user to enter a line, and then outputs the length of the user's input:[3]

$$
\begin{array}{lll}
main = \mathbf{do}\ inp \leftarrow mkSignal\ \langle\$\rangle\ consoleInput & & \text{-- } inp :: \bigcirc(Sig\ Text) \\
\quad\quad\quad\ \mathbf{let}\ outSig = mapD\ (\mathbf{box}\ length)\ inp & & \text{-- } outSig :: \bigcirc(Sig\ Int) \\
\quad\quad\quad\ intOutput\ outSig \\
\quad\quad\quad\ startEventLoop
\end{array}
$$

In the last line we call *startEventLoop* :: *IO* () which starts the event loop that executes output actions registered by *setOutput*. We will look at a more comprehensive example in Sect. 3.3.

---

[3] $\langle\$\rangle$ is the infix notation for the function *fmap* :: *Functor* $f \Rightarrow (a \rightarrow b) \rightarrow f\ a \rightarrow f\ b$.

$$filterMap \quad :: \Box(a \rightarrow Maybe'\ b) \rightarrow Sig\ a \rightarrow IO\ (\Box(\bigcirc(Sig\ b)))$$
$$filterMapD :: \Box(a \rightarrow Maybe'\ b) \rightarrow \bigcirc(Sig\ a) \rightarrow IO\ (\Box(\bigcirc(Sig\ b)))$$
$$filter \quad\quad :: \Box(a \rightarrow Bool) \rightarrow Sig\ a \rightarrow IO\ (\Box(\bigcirc(Sig\ a)))$$
$$filterD \quad\ :: \Box(a \rightarrow Bool) \rightarrow \bigcirc(Sig\ a) \rightarrow IO\ (\Box(\bigcirc(Sig\ a)))$$
$$trigger \quad\ :: (Stable\ a, Stable\ b) \Rightarrow \Box(a \rightarrow b \rightarrow c) \rightarrow Sig\ a \rightarrow Sig\ b \rightarrow IO\ (\Box(Sig\ c))$$
$$triggerD \quad :: Stable\ b \Rightarrow \Box(a \rightarrow b \rightarrow c) \rightarrow \bigcirc(Sig\ a) \rightarrow Sig\ b \rightarrow IO\ (\Box(\bigcirc(Sig\ c)))$$

Fig. 3. Filter functions in Async Rattus.

3.2 Filtering Functions

As Bahr and Møgelberg [5] have observed, the Sig type does not support a filter function $filter :: \Box(a \rightarrow Bool) \rightarrow Sig\ a \rightarrow Sig\ a$. The problem is that a signal of type $Sig\ a$ must produce a value of type a at every tick of its current clock. In order to check the predicate $p :: \Box(a \rightarrow Bool)$ we must wait until the input signal ticks and produces a new value $v :: a$. Hence, we must produce a value for the output signal for that tick as well, regardless of whether $p\ v$ is true or not. Instead, we can implement a variant of $filter$ with the following type:[4]

$$filter' :: \Box(a \rightarrow Bool) \rightarrow Sig\ a \rightarrow Sig\ (Maybe'\ a)$$
$$filter'\ p = map\ (\text{box}\ (\lambda x \rightarrow \textbf{if}\ \text{unbox}\ p\ x\ \textbf{then}\ Just'\ x\ \textbf{else}\ Nothing'))$$

This is somewhat unsatisfactory but workable. We can provide an implementation of standard FRP combinators (like those in Fig. 2) that work with signals of type $Sig\ (Maybe'\ a)$ instead of $Sig\ a$. However, this introduces inefficiencies since programs that work with signals of type $Sig\ (Maybe'\ a)$ have to explicitly check for the $Nothing'$ case for each tick.

A possible solution is to replace the modal operator $\bigcirc$ with the derived operator F that may take several ticks to produce a result:

data $F\ a = Now\ a\ |\ Wait\ (\bigcirc(F\ a))$

data $Sig_F\ a = a ::\!:_F (\bigcirc(F\ (Sig_F\ a)))$

That is, a value of type $F\ a$ is the promise of a value of type a in 0 or more (possibly infinitely many) ticks. Then the definition of Sig_F replaces $\bigcirc$ with the composition of $\bigcirc$ and F. That is, a signal has a current value and the promise that it will update in one or more ticks. With this type, we can implement a function $filter :: \Box(a \rightarrow Bool) \rightarrow Sig_F\ a \rightarrow F\ (Sig_F\ a)$ as well as corresponding versions of the functions in Fig. 2.

Sadly, $Sig_F\ a$ still suffers from the same inefficiency as the $Sig\ (Maybe'\ a)$ type. To implement a more efficient filter function, we instead make use of the $getInput$ and $setOutput$ functions. By composing the two, we can turn a signal of type $Sig\ (Maybe'\ a)$ into a signal of type $Sig\ a$:

$$mkInputSig :: Producer\ p\ a \Rightarrow p \rightarrow IO\ (\Box(\bigcirc(Sig\ a)))$$
$$mkInputSig\ p = \textbf{do}\ (out, cb) \leftarrow getInput$$
$$setOutput\ p\ cb$$
$$return\ \text{box}\ (mkSig\ out)$$

---

[4] $Maybe'$ is a strict variant of the standard $Maybe$ type.

Since we have *Producer* (*Sig* (*Maybe'* *a*)) *a*, we can implement *filter* as follows:

$$filter :: \Box(a \rightarrow Bool) \rightarrow Sig\ a \rightarrow IO\ (\Box(\bigcirc(Sig\ a)))$$
$$filter\ p\ xs = mkInputSig\ (filter'\ p\ xs)$$

Figure 3 lists further filter functions that can be implemented in this fashion: *filterMap* essentially composes the *filter* function with the *map* function. *trigger f xs ys* is a signal that produces a new value unbox *f x y* whenever *xs* produces a new value, where *x* and *y* are the current values of *xs* and *ys* respectively. One can think of *trigger* as a left-biased version of *zipWith*. Finally, we also have versions of these functions that work with delayed signals. We will put this library to use in the next section.

3.3 Extended Example

To demonstrate the use of the FRP library that we have developed above, we implement a simple interactive application. To this end, we extend our simple IO library, which so far consists of *consoleInput* and *intOutput*, with

$$setQuit :: Producer\ p\ a \Rightarrow p \rightarrow IO\ ()$$
$$setQuit\ sig = setOutput\ sig\ (\lambda\_ \rightarrow exitSuccess)$$

which quits the program as soon as the argument *sig* produces its first value.

Figure 4, shows an interactive console application that uses our simple IO API. The application maintains an integer counter *nats* that increments each second. At any time, we can show the current value of the counter by typing "show" in the console: The *showSig* signal triggers output on *showNat*. Moreover, we can manipulate the counter by either writing "negate" or a number "n" to the console, which multiplies the counter with −1 or adds *n* to it, respectively. Finally, we can quit the application by writing "quit".

This example demonstrates the use of the different filter functions to construct new signals (see *quitSig*, *showSig*, *negSig*, *numSig*), the use of *interleave* and *trigger* to combine several signals (see *sig* and *showNat*, respectively), and the use of *switchS* to dynamically change the behaviour of a signal (see *nats'*).

4 Embedding Async Rattus in Haskell

The embedding of Async Rattus in Haskell consists of two main components: (1) the definition of the language's syntax in the form of standard Haskell type and function definitions, and (2) a plugin for GHC which implements the typing rules for the modal type operators and performs the necessary program transformations to obtain the desired operational semantics for Async Rattus. Some

$everySecond :: Sig\ ()$
$everySecond = ()\ :::\ mkSig\ (timer\ 1000000)$

$readInt :: Text \rightarrow Maybe'\ Int$
$readInt\ text = \textbf{case}\ decimal\ text\ \textbf{of}\ Right\ (x, rest)\ |\ null\ rest \rightarrow Just'\ x$
$\phantom{readInt\ text = \textbf{case}\ decimal\ text\ \textbf{of}\ Right\ (x, rest)\ }\ \_ \rightarrow Nothing'$

$nats :: Int \rightarrow Sig\ Int$
$nats\ init = scan\ (\textsf{box}\ (\lambda n\ \_ \rightarrow n + 1))\ init\ everySecond$

$main = \textbf{do}$
  $console\ ::\bigcirc(Sig\ Text)\qquad \leftarrow mkSig\ \langle\$\rangle\ consoleInput$
  $quitSig\ ::\bigcirc(Sig\ Text)\qquad \leftarrow \textsf{unbox}\ \langle\$\rangle\ filterD\ (\textsf{box}\ (\equiv \texttt{"quit"}))\ console$
  $showSig\ ::\bigcirc(Sig\ Text)\qquad \leftarrow \textsf{unbox}\ \langle\$\rangle\ filterD\ (\textsf{box}\ (\equiv \texttt{"show"}))\ console$
  $negSig\ ::\square(\bigcirc(Sig\ Text)) \leftarrow filterD\ (\textsf{box}\ (\equiv \texttt{"negate"}))\ console$
  $numSig\ ::\square(\bigcirc(Sig\ Int))\ \ \leftarrow filterMapD\ (\textsf{box}\ readInt)\ console$

  $\textbf{let}\ sig :: \square(\bigcirc(Sig\ (Int \rightarrow Int)))$
    $sig = \textsf{box}\ (interleave\ (\textsf{box}\ (\circ))$
        $(mapD\ (\textsf{box}\ (\lambda\_\ n \rightarrow -n))\ (\textsf{unbox}\ negSig))$
        $(mapD\ (\textsf{box}\ (\lambda m\ n \rightarrow m + n))\ (\textsf{unbox}\ numSig)))$

  $\textbf{let}\ nats' :: Int \rightarrow Sig\ Int$
    $nats'\ init = switchS\ (nats\ init)$
        $(\textsf{delay}\ (\lambda n \rightarrow nats'\ (current\ (\textsf{adv}\ (\textsf{unbox}\ sig))\ n)))$

  $showNat :: \square(\bigcirc(Sig\ Int)) \leftarrow triggerD\ (\textsf{box}\ (\lambda\_\ n \rightarrow n))\ showSig\ (nats'\ 0)$

  $setQuit\ quitSig$
  $intOutput\ showNat$
  $startEventLoop$

Fig. 4. Example reactive program.

parts of the implementation of Async Rattus are similar to that of Rattus [2], including the $\square$ modality, the *Stable* type constraint, and the check for guarded recursion. We, therefore, focus our attention on the $\bigcirc$ modality as it requires a novel and significantly different approach due to the presence of clocks.

Syntax. Figure 5 shows the implementation of the syntax of $\bigcirc$. A value *Delay* θ f of type $\bigcirc a$ consists of a clock θ and a delayed computation f. In turn, a clock θ is a finite set of input channel identifiers, and we say that θ ticks whenever any of the input channels in θ produces a new value. As soon as θ ticks, by virtue of an input channel $c \in \theta$ producing a new value v of some type b, we can run the delayed computation f by passing both c and v to f as an argument of type *InputValue*. Note that the return type a of f and the type b of v are independent from each other. This is achieved by the fact that the type variable b in the definition of *InputValue* is existentially quantified. Finally, the introduction and elimination forms delay, adv, and select are simply implemented as $\bot$. These dummy implementations are replaced by their correct implementations in a program transformation performed by the compiler plugin. The correct imple-

```
data InputValue where                         -- Not exported
    InputValue :: ChanId → b → InputValue
type Clock = Set ChanId                        -- Not exported
data ○a = Delay Clock (InputValue → a)         -- Constructor not exported
delay :: a → ○a          adv :: ○a → a           select :: ○a → ○b → Select a b
delay _ = ⊥              adv _ = ⊥               select _ _ = ⊥
```

Fig. 5. Implementation of the syntax of ○.

mentations are inserted later since they depend on compile time clocks, which are inferred by the plugin and are thus not part of the surface syntax.

Scope & Clock Check. GHC provides a rich API that allows us to insert custom logic in several phases of its pipeline, which is sketched in Fig. 6. During the type checking phase, GHC will use a constraint solver for the *Stable* type constraint provided by the plugin. Afterwards, the plugin checks the stricter scoping rules of Async Rattus and infers clock annotations. Checking the scoping rules for Async Rattus is similar to Rattus [2]: Variables may no longer be in scope because delay introduced a tick, because adv or select dropped the context to the right of a tick, or because of the restricted context $\Gamma^\square$, e.g. in the rule for box. The clock inference algorithm introduces an existentially quantified clock variable θ for each occurrence of delay, which is then instantiated to $\mathsf{cl}(t)$ or $\mathsf{cl}(s) \sqcup \mathsf{cl}(t)$ as soon as it encounters an occurrence of adv t or select $s\ t$, respectively.

Single Tick, Strictness & Clock Transformation. GHC desugars the typed Haskell AST into the Core intermediate language, on which it then performs various simplification and optimisation steps. The Async Rattus plugin adds three additional transformations. Figure 7 lists the rewrite rules that are applied during these three transformations. In these rewrite rules, we use K to denote a term with a single hole that does not occur in the scope of delay, adv, select, box, or lambda abstraction, and we write $K[t]$ to denote the term obtained from K by replacing its hole with the term t.

The *single tick transformation* rules preserve the typing of the program and once the rules have been exhaustively applied, the resulting program is typable with the more restrictive typing rules of the Async RaTT calculus [5], which only allows at most one tick in the context, requires that adv and select be applied to variables, and disallows lambda abstractions in the scope of a tick. As a consequence, Async Rattus benefits from a less restrictive type system compared to Async RaTT, while still retaining the operational properties that have been proved for the latter. One can prove that the single tick transformation produces a well-typed Async RaTT program using an argument similar to Bahr [2].

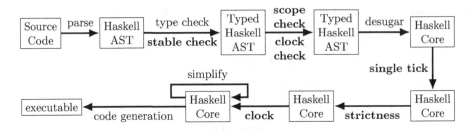

Fig. 6. Simplified pipeline of GHC extended with Async Rattus plugin (in bold).

Single tick transformation:

$$\mathsf{delay}(K[\mathsf{adv}\, t]) \longrightarrow \mathsf{let}\, x = t \,\mathsf{in}\, \mathsf{delay}(K[\mathsf{adv}\, x]) \qquad \text{if } t \text{ is not a variable}$$

$$\mathsf{delay}(K[\mathsf{select}\, s\, t]) \longrightarrow \mathsf{let}\, x = s \,\mathsf{in}\, \mathsf{delay}(K[\mathsf{select}\, x\, t]) \qquad \text{if } s \text{ is not a variable}$$

$$\mathsf{delay}(K[\mathsf{select}\, s\, t]) \longrightarrow \mathsf{let}\, x = t \,\mathsf{in}\, \mathsf{delay}(K[\mathsf{select}\, s\, x]) \qquad \text{if } t \text{ is not a variable}$$

$$\lambda x.K[\mathsf{adv}\, t] \longrightarrow \mathsf{let}\, y = \mathsf{adv}\, t \,\mathsf{in}\, \lambda x.(K[y])$$

$$\lambda x.K[\mathsf{select}\, s\, t] \longrightarrow \mathsf{let}\, y = \mathsf{select}\, s\, t \,\mathsf{in}\, \lambda x.(K[y])$$

Strictness transformation:

$$\lambda x.t \longrightarrow \lambda x.\mathbf{case}\ x\ \mathbf{of}\ \_ \to t$$

$$\mathbf{let}\ x = s\ \mathbf{in}\ t \longrightarrow \mathbf{case}\ s\ \mathbf{of}\ x \to t$$

Clock transformation:

$$\mathsf{delay}(K[\mathsf{adv}\, x]) \longrightarrow Delay\,(\mathsf{cl}(x))(\lambda v \to K[\mathsf{adv}'\, x\, v])$$

$$\mathsf{delay}(K[\mathsf{select}\, x\, y]) \longrightarrow Delay\,(\mathsf{cl}(x) \sqcup \mathsf{cl}(y))(\lambda v \to K[\mathsf{select}'\, x\, y\, v])$$

Fig. 7. Transformation rules.

The *strictness transformation* replaces lambda abstractions and let bindings so that Async Rattus programs have a call-by-value semantics.

The clock inference performed during an earlier compilation phase established that we can find suitable clock annotation for each occurrence of delay. The *clock transformation* inserts these clock annotation and thereby also replaces the dummy functions delay, adv, and select from Fig. 5 with their actual implementations shown in Fig. 8. In addition to inserting the correct clocks, this transformation also propagates the identity of the input channel that caused the tick of the clock as well as the input value that it produced. The identity of the input channel is required for the implementation of select as it needs to check which of the two delayed computations to advance (see select' in Fig. 8), whereas the input value is used to implement the *getInput* function.

$$\text{adv}' :: \bigcirc a \rightarrow InputValue \rightarrow a$$
$$\text{adv}' \ (Delay \ \_ \ f) \ inp = f \ inp$$
$$\text{select}' :: \bigcirc a \rightarrow \bigcirc b \rightarrow InputValue \rightarrow Select \ a \ b$$
$$\text{select}' \ a@(Delay \ \theta_1 \ f) \ b@(Delay \ \theta_2 \ g) \ v@(InputValue \ ch \ \_)$$
$$\quad = \textbf{if} \ ch \in \theta_1 \ \textbf{then if} \ ch \in \theta_2 \ \textbf{then} \ Both \ (f \ v) \ (g \ v)$$
$$\quad \quad \textbf{else} \ Fst \ (f \ v) \ b \quad \quad \quad \textbf{else} \ Snd \ a \ (b \ v)$$

Fig. 8. Implementation of adv and select.

5   Related Work

The use of modal types for FRP has seen much attention in recent years [2–4,10,16,20,23,24,26,28,29]. The first implementation of a modal FRP language we are aware of is AdjS [25], which compiles FRP programs into JavaScript. The language is based on the synchronous modal FRP calculus of Krishnaswami [26] and uses linear types to interact with GUI widgets [27]. To address the discrepancy between the synchronous programming model of AdjS and the inherently asynchronous nature of GUIs, the λ_{Widget} calculus of Graulund et al. [16] combines linear types with an asynchronous modal type constructor $\Diamond$. Similarly to Async Rattus, two values $x : \Diamond A$ and $y : \Diamond B$ arrive at some time in the future, but not necessarily at the same time and thus λ_{Widget} provides a select primitive to observe the relative arrival time. However, we are not aware of an implementation of a language based on λ_{Widget}.

Async Rattus is based on the Async RaTT calculus of Bahr and Mogelberg [5], which proposes the modal operator $\exists$ to model asynchronous signals (in Async Rattus we use the simpler notation $\bigcirc$ instead of $\exists$). Like the synchronous calculus of Krishnaswami [26] (on which AdjS [25] is based), but unlike the asynchronous λ_{Widget} calculus of Graulund et al. [16], Async RaTT comes with a proof of operational guarantees: All Async RaTT programs are causal, productive, and do not have space leaks. Async Rattus generalises the typing rules of Async RaTT in three ways: It allows (1) more than one tick to occur in contexts (thus allowing nested occurrences of delay), (2) function definitions to occur in the scope of ticks in the context, and (3) adv and select to be applied to arbitrary terms instead of just variables. The soundness of this generalisation is based on the single tick program transformation (cf. Sect. 4), introduced by Bahr [2], that is performed by the compiler plugin so that the resulting program will type check using the stricter typing rules of Async RaTT. The implementation of Async Rattus borrows much from the implementation of Rattus [2], which is based on a synchronous modal FRP calculus. However, the asynchronous setting required three key additions: Inference of clocks during type checking, an additional program transformation that inserts inferred clocks into the Haskell code, and finally a new runtime system that allows Async Rattus and Haskell to interact. The latter is enabled by the clock transformation (cf. Sect. 4) and is provided to the user in the form of the *getInput* and *setOutput* functions.

6   Discussion and Future Work

The implementation of Async Rattus as an embedded language further demonstrates the power of GHC's plugin API [12,13,17,34]. In addition to customising the type checker and using program transformations to tweak the operational semantics, we can also use it to implement program elaboration mechanisms like Async Rattus' clock inference.

Our goal is to use Async Rattus to further experiment with asynchronous modal FRP. Interesting topics for further work include: evaluation of asynchronous modal FRP for implementing concurrent programs and GUI applications; library design for asynchronous modal FRP in general as well as specific problem domains; and extending the language with explicit clocks and clock quantification.

References

1. Apfelmus, H.: Reactive banana (2011). URL https://hackage.haskell.org/package/reactive-banana
2. Bahr, P.: Modal FRP for all: Functional reactive programming without space leaks in Haskell. J. Funct. Program. **32**, e15 (2022). ISSN 0956–7968, 1469–7653, publisher: Cambridge University Press
3. Bahr, P., Graulund, C.U., Møgelberg, R.E.: Simply RaTT: a fitch-style modal calculus for reactive programming without space leaks. Proc. ACM Program. Lang. **3**(ICFP), 1–27 (2019)
4. Bahr, P., Graulund, C.U., Møgelberg, R.E.: Diamonds are not forever: liveness in reactive programming with guarded recursion. Proc. ACM Program. Lang. **5**(POPL), 1–28 (2021). 00002
5. Bahr, P., Møgelberg, R.E.: Asynchronous modal FRP. Proc. ACM Program. Lang. **7**(ICFP), 476–510 (2023)
6. Berry, G., Cosserat, L.: The ESTEREL synchronous programming language and its mathematical semantics. In: Brookes, S.D., Roscoe, A.W., Winskel, G. (eds.) CONCURRENCY 1984. LNCS, vol. 197, pp. 389–448. Springer, Heidelberg (1985). https://doi.org/10.1007/3-540-15670-4_19 ISBN 978-3-540-39593-5
7. Blackheath, S.: Sodium (2012). URL https://hackage.haskell.org/package/sodium
8. Bärenz, M., Perez, I.: Rhine: FRP with type-level clocks. In: Proceedings of the 11th ACM SIGPLAN International Symposium on Haskell, Haskell 2018, pp. 145–157. Association for Computing Machinery, New York (2018). ISBN 978-1-4503-5835-4
9. Caspi, P., Pilaud, D., Halbwachs, N., Plaice, J.A.: LUSTRE: a declarative language for real-time programming. In: Proceedings of the 14th ACM SIGACT-SIGPLAN Symposium on Principles of Programming Languages, POPL '87, pp. 178–188. ACM, New York (1987). ISBN 0-89791-215-2
10. Cave, A., Ferreira, F., Panangaden, P., Pientka, B.: Fair Reactive Programming. In: Proceedings of the 41st ACM SIGPLAN-SIGACT Symposium on Principles of Programming Languages, POPL '14, pp. 361–372. ACM, San Diego (2014). ISBN 978-1-4503-2544-8
11. Clouston, R.: Fitch-style modal lambda calculi. In: Baier, C., Dal Lago, U. (eds.) FoSSaCS 2018. LNCS, vol. 10803, pp. 258–275. Springer, Cham (2018). https://doi.org/10.1007/978-3-319-89366-2_14

12. Diatchki, I.S.: Improving Haskell types with SMT. In: Proceedings of the 2015 ACM SIGPLAN Symposium on Haskell, Haskell '15, pp. 1–10. Association for Computing Machinery (2015)
13. Elliott, C.: Compiling to categories. Proc. ACM Program. Lang. **1**(ICFP), 1–27 (2017)
14. Elliott, C., Hudak, P.: Functional reactive animation. In: Proceedings of the Second ACM SIGPLAN International Conference on Functional Programming, ICFP '97, pp. 263–273. ACM, New York (1997). ISBN 0-89791-918-1
15. Elliott, C.M.: Push-pull functional reactive programming. In: Proceedings of the 2Nd ACM SIGPLAN Symposium on Haskell, Haskell '09, pp. 25–36. ACM, New York (2009). ISBN 978-1-60558-508-6, 00145 event-place: Edinburgh, Scotland
16. Graulund, C.U., Szamozvancev, D., Krishnaswami, N.: Adjoint reactive GUI programming. In: FoSSaCS, pp. 289–309 (2021)
17. Gundry, A.: A typechecker plugin for units of measure: domain-specific constraint solving in GHC Haskell. In: Proceedings of the 2015 ACM SIGPLAN Symposium on Haskell, Haskell '15, pp. 11–22. Association for Computing Machinery, New York (2015)
18. Houlborg, E., Rørdam, G., Bahr, P.: Async Rattus (2023). URL https://hackage.haskell.org/package/AsyncRattus
19. Hudak, P., Courtney, A., Nilsson, H., Peterson, J.: Arrows, robots, and functional reactive programming. In: Jeuring, J., Jones, S.L.P. (eds.) AFP 2002. LNCS, vol. 2638, pp. 159–187. Springer, Heidelberg (2003). https://doi.org/10.1007/978-3-540-44833-4_6 ISBN 978-3-540-40132-2
20. Jeffrey, A.: LTL types FRP: linear-time temporal logic propositions as types, proofs as functional reactive programs. In: Claessen, K., Swamy, N. (eds.) Proceedings of the sixth workshop on Programming Languages meets Program Verification, PLPV 2012, Philadelphia, PA, USA, 24 January 2012, pp. 49–60. ACM, Philadelphia (2012). ISBN 978-1-4503-1125-0
21. Jeffrey, A.: Functional reactive types. In: Proceedings of the Joint Meeting of the Twenty-Third EACSL Annual Conference on Computer Science Logic (CSL) and the Twenty-Ninth Annual ACM/IEEE Symposium on Logic in Computer Science (LICS), CSL-LICS '14, pp. 1–9. ACM, New York (2014). ISBN 978-1-4503-2886-9
22. Jeltsch, W.: Grapefruit (2007). URL https://hackage.haskell.org/package/grapefruit
23. Jeltsch, W.: Towards a common categorical semantics for linear-time temporal logic and functional reactive programming. Electr. Notes Theor. Comput. Sci. **286**, 229–242 (2012)
24. Jeltsch, W.: Temporal logic with "until", functional reactive programming with processes, and concrete process categories. In: Proceedings of the 7th Workshop on Programming Languages Meets Program Verification, PLPV '13, pp. 69–78. ACM, New York (2013). ISBN 978-1-4503-1860-0
25. Krishnaswami, N.R.: AdjS compiler (2013). URL https://github.com/neel-krishnaswami/adjs
26. Krishnaswami, N.R.: Higher-order functional reactive programming without space-time leaks. In: Proceedings of the 18th ACM SIGPLAN International Conference on Functional Programming, ICFP '13, pp. 221–232. ACM, Boston (2013). ISBN 978-1-4503-2326-0
27. Krishnaswami, N.R., Benton, N.: A semantic model for graphical user interfaces. In: Proceedings of the 16th ACM SIGPLAN international conference on Functional programming, ICFP '11, pp. 45–57. Association for Computing Machinery, New York (2011). ISBN 978-1-4503-0865-6

28. Krishnaswami, N.R., Benton, N.: Ultrametric semantics of reactive programs. In: 2011 IEEE 26th Annual Symposium on Logic in Computer Science, pp. 257–266. IEEE Computer Society, Washington (2011). ISSN 1043–6871

29. Krishnaswami, N.R., Benton, N., Hoffmann, J.: Higher-order functional reactive programming in bounded space. In: Field, J., Hicks, M. (eds.) Proceedings of the 39th ACM SIGPLAN-SIGACT Symposium on Principles of Programming Languages, POPL 2012, Philadelphia, Pennsylvania, USA, 22–28 January 2012, pp. 45–58. ACM, Philadelphia (2012). ISBN 978-1-4503-1083-3

30. Patai, G.: Efficient and compositional higher-order streams. In: Mariño, J. (ed.) WFLP 2010. LNCS, vol. 6559, pp. 137–154. Springer, Heidelberg (2011). https://doi.org/10.1007/978-3-642-20775-4_8

31. Perez, I., Bärenz, M., Nilsson, H.: Functional reactive programming, refactored. In: Proceedings of the 9th International Symposium on Haskell, Haskell 2016, pp. 33–44. Association for Computing Machinery, New York (2016). ISBN 978-1-4503-4434-0

32. Ploeg, A.v.d., Claessen, K.: Practical principled FRP: forget the past, change the future, FRPNow! In: Proceedings of the 20th ACM SIGPLAN International Conference on Functional Programming, ICFP 2015, pp. 302–314. Association for Computing Machinery, Vancouver (2015). ISBN 978-1-4503-3669-7, 00019

33. Pouzet, M.: Lucid synchrone, version 3. Tutorial and reference manual. Université Paris-Sud, LRI 1, 25 (2006)

34. Prott, K.O., Teegen, F., Christiansen, J.: Embedding functional logic programming in Haskell via a compiler plugin. In: Hanus, M., Inclezan, D. (eds.) Practical Aspects of Declarative Languages, pp. 37–55. Lecture Notes in Computer Science, Springer Nature Switzerland (2023). https://doi.org/10.1007/978-3-031-24841-2_3

35. Trinkle, R.: Reflex (2016). URL https://reflex-frp.org

FOLD-SE: An Efficient Rule-Based Machine Learning Algorithm with Scalable Explainability

Huaduo Wang$^{(\boxtimes)}$ [ID] and Gopal Gupta [ID]

The University of Texas at Dallas, Richardson, USA
{huaduo.wang,gupta}@utdallas.edu

Abstract. We present FOLD-SE, an efficient, explainable machine learning algorithm for classification tasks given tabular data containing numerical and categorical values. The (explainable) model generated by FOLD-SE is represented as a set of *default rules*. FOLD-SE uses a novel heuristic called *Magic Gini Impurity* for *literal selection* that we have devised. FOLD-SE uses a refined data comparison operator and eliminates the long tail effect. Thanks to these innovations, explainability provided by FOLD-SE is scalable, meaning that regardless of the size of the dataset, the number of learned rules and learned literals stay quite small while good accuracy in classification is maintained. Additionally, the rule-set constituting the model that FOLD-SE generates does not change significantly if the training data is slightly varied. FOLD-SE is competitive with state-of-the-art traditional machine learning algorithms such as XGBoost and Multi-Layer Perceptrons (MLP) w.r.t. accuracy of prediction while being an order of magnitude faster. However, unlike XGBoost and MLP, FOLD-SE generates explainable models. The FOLD-SE algorithm outperforms prior rule-learning algorithms such as RIPPER in efficiency, performance, and scalability, especially for large datasets. FOLD-SE generates a far smaller number of rules than earlier algorithms that learn default rules.

Keywords: Inductive Logic Programming · Machine Learning · Explainable AI · Negation as Failure · Answer Set Programming · Data mining

1 Introduction

Dramatic success of machine learning has led to a torrent of Artificial Intelligence (AI) applications. However, the effectiveness of these systems is limited by the machines' current inability to explain their decisions to human users. That is mainly because the statistical machine learning methods produce models that are complex algebraic solutions to optimization problems such as risk minimization or data likelihood maximization. Lack of intuitive descriptions makes it hard for users to understand and verify the underlying rules that govern the model. Also,

© The Author(s), under exclusive license to Springer Nature Switzerland AG 2023
M. Gebser and I. Sergey (Eds.): PADL 2024, LNCS 14512, pp. 37–53, 2023.
https://doi.org/10.1007/978-3-031-52038-9_3

these methods cannot produce a justification for a prediction they compute for a new data sample.

Rule-based machine learning algorithms have been devised that *learn* a set of relational rules that collectively represent the logic of the concept encapsulated in the data. The generated rules are more comprehensible to humans compared to the complicated deep learning models. Examples of such algorithms include FOIL [17] and RIPPER [4]. Some of the rule-based algorithms allow the knowledge learned to be incrementally extended without retraining the entire model. The learned symbolic rules make it easier for users to understand and verify.

Most rule-based algorithms are not efficient for large datasets even those based on a top-down approach. Some of them, e.g., TREPAN [5] extract rules from statistical machine learning models, but their performance and efficiency are limited by the target machine learning model. Yet other algorithms train models with a logic programming based solver, e.g., most Inductive Logic Programming (ILP) based algorithms [6].

An objective of rule-based systems is that they should be scalable, meaning that they should work with large datasets, and learn the rules in a reasonable amount of time. The size of the generated rule-set—represented by the number of rules and the number of conditional predicates (features) involved—has a big impact on human understanding of the rules and in explaining predictions. The more rules and predicates a rule-set contains, the harder it is for humans to understand. For most rule-based systems, as the size of the dataset increases, the number of learned rules and conditional predicates increases. Ideally, we would like for the rule-set size to not increase with dataset size. We call this concept *scalable explainability*, i.e., the size of the rule-set stays small regardless of the dataset size. Thus, even when the input training data is very large, the rule-set representing the model should be small enough for a human to comprehend.

The FOIL algorithm by Quinlan [17] is a popular top-down rule-based machine learning algorithm. The FOLD algorithm by Shakerin [19] is inspired by the FOIL algorithm, it learns a default theory with exceptions represented as a *stratified normal logic program*. The FOLD algorithm uses the *information gain* [16] metric to incrementally generate literals for default rules that cover positive examples while avoiding covering negative examples. It then swaps the positive and negative examples and calls itself recursively to learn exceptions to the default when there are still positive examples uncovered. The FOLD-R++ algorithm, devised by us earlier, has been developed on top of the FOLD algorithm. It utilizes the prefix sum computation technique with special comparison operators to speed up literal selection while avoiding encoding for hybrid-type data [22,23].

FOLD-R++ is able to generate much smaller number of rules than the well-known rule-based algorithm RIPPER while outperforming it in accuracy. Even with this reduction, both the FOLD-R++ and the RIPPER systems often generate too many rules making them incomprehensible to humans. For example, Rain in Australia is a large dataset with over 140K training examples. With the same target class 'No', RIPPER generates 180 rules with over 700 literals that achieve 63% accuracy while FOLD-R++ generates 48 rules with around 120 literals that achieve 79% accuracy. That's too many rules, arguably, for a human to understand. Another explainability-related problem with these rule-based algorithms is that the generated rule-set varies significantly when a small percentage of training data changes. We would like the rule-set to be stable as the training dataset changes.

To deal with the above explainability issues on large datasets, this paper presents a new algorithm that employs a newly created heuristic for literal selection that greatly reduces the number of learned rules and predicates. The learned rules constitute the learned model. In addition, we also improve explainability by introducing a rule-pruning mechanism in the training process. The pruning mechanism ameliorates the long-tail effect, namely, that rules generated later in the learning process cover fewer examples than those generated earlier. The improved learning algorithm, which we call FOLD-SE, provides scalable explainability, i.e., it generates a rule-set that consists of a small number of rules and predicates (features) regardless of the dataset size. Our FOLD-SE algorithm generates just 2 rules and 6 literals with 82% accuracy for the Rain in Australia dataset mentioned earlier. Contrast this with RIPPER which generates 180 rules with 700 literals and FOLD-R++ generates 48 rules with 120 literals. Also, the generated rule-set is stable, i.e., it does not change as the training data is varied. Our experimental results indicate that FOLD-SE is competitive in accuracy and efficiency with well-known machine learning algorithms such as XGBoost classifier and Multi-Layer Perceptron (MLP). The FOLD-SE algorithm *significantly outperforms* FOLD-R++, on which it is based, as well as the RIPPER algorithm w.r.t. the efficiency of the training process.

2 Background

FOLD-SE represents the rule-set that it learns from a dataset as a *default theory* that is expressed as a normal logic program, i.e., logic programming with negation [9]. The logic program is stratified in that there are no recursive calls in the rules. we briefly describe default logic below. We assume that the reader is familiar with logic programming [21] as well as classification problems [1].

Default Logic [18] is a non-monotonic logic to formalize commonsense reasoning. A default D is an expression of the form

$$\frac{A : \mathbf{M} B}{\Gamma}$$

which states that the conclusion Γ can be inferred if pre-requisite A holds and B is justified. $\mathbf{M} B$ stands for "it is consistent to believe B".

Normal logic programs can encode a default theory quite elegantly [9]. A default of the form:

$$\frac{\alpha_1 \wedge \alpha_2 \wedge \cdots \wedge \alpha_n : \mathbf{M} \neg \beta_1, \mathbf{M} \neg \beta_2 \ldots \mathbf{M} \neg \beta_m}{\gamma}$$

can be formalized as the normal logic programming rule:

$$\gamma :\text{-} \alpha_1, \alpha_2, \ldots, \alpha_n, \text{not } \beta_1, \text{not } \beta_2, \ldots, \text{not } \beta_m.$$

where α's and β's are positive predicates and **not** represents negation-as-failure. We call such rules *default rules*. Thus, the default $\frac{bird(X):M\neg penguin(X)}{fly(X)}$ will be represented as the following default rule in normal logic programming:

```
fly(X):- bird(X), not penguin(X).
```

We call **bird(X)**, the condition that allows us to jump to the default conclusion that X can fly, the *default part* of the rule, and **not penguin(X)** the *exception part* of the rule.

3   FOLD-SE Algorithm

3.1   Heuristic for Literal Selection

Most top-down rule-based machine learning algorithms employ heuristics to guide the literal selection process; information gain (IG) and its variations are the most popular ones. The heuristic used in split-based classifiers greatly impacts the accuracy and structure of the learned model, whether it's rule-based or decision tree-based. Specifically, the heuristic used in the literal selection of rule-based algorithms impacts the number of generated rules and literals, therefore it has an impact on explainability.

FOLD-SE employs a heuristic that we have newly created called Magic Gini Impurity (MGI). MGI is inspired by the Gini Impurity heuristic [3] that guides the literal selection process. It helps reduce the number of generated rules and literals while maintaining competitive performance compared to using information gain (IG). Simplified Gini Impurity for binary classification is defined as:

$$GI(tp, fn, tn, fp) = \frac{tp \times fp}{(tp + fp)^2} + \frac{tn \times fn}{(tn + fn)^2} \tag{1}$$

where tp, tn, fp, and fn stand for numbers of true positives, true negatives, false positives, and false negatives, respectively. We replace the IG heuristics used in our FOLD-R++ rule learning algorithm [22] with MGI. Our experiments, discussed later, on this improved rule learning algorithm, show a drastic reduction in the number of rules needed to represent a model.

3.2   Comparison of Feature Values

To evaluate a predicate (literal), FOLD-SE has to compare feature values to the value in the predicate. FOLD-SE employs a carefully designed comparison operator, which is an extension of the comparison operator of our FOLD-R++ algorithm for comparing categorical and numerical values. This gives FOLD-SE the ability to elegantly handle hybrid-type values and, thus, learn from datasets that may have features containing both numerical and categorical values (a missing value is considered a categorical value). The comparison between two numerical values or two categorical values in FOLD-R++ is straightforward, as common-sense would dictate, i.e., two numerical (resp. categorical) values are equal if they are identical, otherwise, they are unequal. The equality between a numerical value and a categorical value is always false, and the inequality between a numerical value and a categorical value is always true. In addition, numerical comparisons ($\leq$ and $>$) between a numerical value and a categorical value are always false. However, the numerical comparisons $\leq$ and $>$ are not complementary to each other with this comparison assumption. For example, $x \leq 4$ means that x is a number and x is less than or equal to 4. The opposite of $x \leq 4$ should be x is a number greater than 4 *or* x is not a number.

Without the opposite of these two numerical comparisons being used, the literal selection process of our FOLD-R++ algorithm would be limited. The FOLD-SE algorithm, thus, extends the comparison operators with $\nleq$ and $\ngtr$ as the opposites of $\leq$ and $>$, respectively. The literals with $\nleq$ and $\ngtr$ will be candidate literals in the literal selection process but converted to their opposites, $\leq$ and $>$, in the final results. An example is shown in Table 1.

Table 1. Comparing numerical and categorical values

comparison	evaluation	comparison	evaluation
$10 =$ 'cat'	False	$10 \neq$ 'cat'	True
$10 \leq$ 'cat'	False	$10 >$ 'cat'	False
$10 \nleq$ 'cat'	True	$10 \ngtr$ 'cat'	True

Given $E^+ = \{3,4,4,5,x,x,y\}$, $E^- = \{1,1,1,2,3,y,y,z\}$, and literal($i, >, 3$) in Table 2, the true positive examples E_{tp}, false negative examples E_{fn}, true negative examples E_{tn}, and false positive examples E_{fp} implied by the literal are $\{4,4,5\}$, $\{3,x,x,y\}$, $\{1,1,1,2,3,y,y,z\}$, $\varnothing$ respectively. Then, the heuristic of literal($i, >, 3$) is calculated as $\mathrm{MGI}_{(i,>,3)}(3,4,8,0) = -0.38$.

Table 2. Evaluation and count for literal($i, >, 3$).

	i^{th} feature values	count
$\mathbf{E^+}$	3 4 4 5 x x y	7
$\mathbf{E^-}$	1 1 1 2 3 y y z	8
$\mathbf{E_{tp(i, >, 3)}}$	4 4 5	3
$\mathbf{E_{fn(i, >, 3)}}$	3 x x y	4
$\mathbf{E_{tn(i, >, 3)}}$	1 1 1 2 3 y y z	8
$\mathbf{E_{fp(i, >, 3)}}$	$\varnothing$	0

3.3   Literal Selection

The FOLD-R++ algorithm starts the learning process with the candidate rule `p(...):- true.`, where `p(...)` is the target predicate to learn. It specializes the rule by adding literals that maximize information gain to its body during the training process. FOLD-SE extends the literal selection process of FOLD-R++ by employing MGI as a heuristic instead of Information Gain. In addition, candidate literals of the form $m \not\leq n$ and $m \not> n$ are also considered.

The literal selection process of FOLD-SE is summarized in Algorithm 2. In line 2, cnt^+ and cnt^- are dictionaries that hold, respectively, the numbers of positive and negative examples of each unique value. In line 3, set_n, set_c are sets that hold, respectively, the unique numerical and categorical values. In line 4, tot_n^+ and tot_n^- are the total number of, respectively, positive and negative examples with numerical values; tot_c^+ and tot_c^- are the total number of, respectively, positive and negative examples with categorical values. In line 6, the prefix sums of numerical values have been computed as preparation for calculating the heuristics of candidate literals. After the prefix sum calculation process, $cnt^+[x]$ and $cnt^-[x]$ represent the number of positive examples and negative examples that have a value less than or equal to x. Preparing parameters correctly is essential to calculating MGI values for candidate literals. In line 11, the MGI value for literal $(i, \leq, x)$ is computed by taking parameters $cnt^+[x]$ as number of true positive examples, $tot_n^+ - cnt^+[x] + tot_c^+$ as the number of false positive examples, $tot_n^- - cnt^-[x] + tot_c^-$ as the number of true negative examples, and $cnt^-[x]$ as the number of false positive examples. The reason for this is as follows: for the literal $(i, \leq, x)$, only numerical values that are less than or equal to x can be evaluated as positive, otherwise negative. $tot_n^+ - cnt^+[x] + tot_c^+$ represents the number of positive examples that have a value greater than x plus the total number of positive examples with categorical values. $tot_n^- - cnt^-[x] + tot_c^-$ represents the number of negative examples that have a value greater than x plus the total number of negative examples with categorical values. $cnt^-[x]$ represents the number of negative examples that have a value less than or equal to x. The heuristic calculation for other candidate literals also follows the same comparison regime mentioned above. Finally, the best_literal_on_attr function returns the best heuristic score and the corresponding literal except the literals that have been used in the current rule-learning process.

Example 1. *Given positive and negative examples in Table 2, E^+, E^-, with mixed type of values on i^{th} feature, the target is to find the literal with the best heuristic score on the given feature. There are 7 positive examples, their values on i^{th} feature are $[3, 4, 4, 5, x, x, y]$, and the values on i^{th} feature of the 8 negative examples are $[1, 1, 1, 2, 3, y, y, z]$.*

With the given examples and specified feature, the number of positive examples and negative examples for each unique value are counted first, which are shown as **count$^+$**, **count$^-$** in Table 3. Then, the prefix sum arrays are calculated for computing heuristic as **sum$_{pfx}^+$**, **sum$_{pfx}^-$**. Table 4 shows the MGI heuristic for each candidate literal and the literal$(i, \not\leq, 2)$ gets selected as it has the highest score.

Algorithm 1: FOLD-SE Algorithm

---

input : E^+: positive examples, E^-: negative examples, *used*: used literals, *ratio*: exception ratio, *tail*: covering limit

output: $R = \{r_1, ..., r_n\}$: a set of default rules with exceptions

1 **Function** learn_rule_set($E^+, E^-, used, tail$)
2      $R \leftarrow \emptyset$
3   **while** $|E^+| > 0$ **do**
4          $r \leftarrow$ learn_rule($E^+, E^-, used, tail$)
5          $E_{fn} \leftarrow$ cover($r, E^+, false$)
6   **if** $|E_{fn}| = |E^+|$ **then**
7   break
8   **end**
9          $E^+ \leftarrow E_{fn}$
10         $R \leftarrow R \cup r$
11   **end**
12   **return** R
13 **end**
14 **Function** learn_rule($E^+, E^-, used, tail$)
15      $L \leftarrow \emptyset$
16      $r \leftarrow rule$
17   **while** *true* **do**
18          $l \leftarrow$ find_best_literl($E^+, E^-, used$)
19          $L \leftarrow L \cup l$
20          $r.default \leftarrow L$
21          $E^+ \leftarrow$ cover($r, E^+, true$)
22          $E^- \leftarrow$ cover($r, E^-, true$)
23   **if** l *is invalid* **or** $|E^-| \leq |E^+| * ratio$ **then**
24   **if** l *is invalid* **then**
25                  $r.default \leftarrow L$
26   **else**
27                  $ab \leftarrow$ learn_rule_set($E^-, E^+, used + L, tail$)
28                  $r.exception \leftarrow ab$
29   **end**
30   break
31   **end**
32   **end**
33   **if** $tail > 0$ **then**
34          $E^+ \leftarrow$ cover($r, E^+, true$)
35   **if** $|E^+| < tail$ **then**
36   **return** invalid
37   **end**
38   **end**
39   **return** r
40 **end**

Algorithm 2: FOLD-SE Find Best Literal function

---

input : E^+: positive examples, E^-: negative examples, *used*: used literals

output: *literal*: the literal that has best heuristic score

1 **Function** best_literal_on_attr($E^+, E^-, i, used$)

2     $cnt^+, cnt^- \leftarrow$ count_class(E^+, E^-, i)

3     $set_n, set_c \leftarrow$ unique_values(E^+, E^-, i)

4     $tot_n^+, tot_n^-, tot_c^+, tot_c^- \leftarrow$ count_total(E^+, E^-, i)

5     $num \leftarrow$ counting_sort(set_n)

6   **for** $i \leftarrow 1$ **to** $|num|$ **do**

7        $cnt^+[num_j] \leftarrow cnt^+[num_j] + cnt^+[num_{j-1}]$

8        $cnt^-[num_j] \leftarrow cnt^-[num_j] + cnt^-[num_{j-1}]$

9   **end**

10   **for** $x \in set_n$ **do**

11        $score[(i, \leq, x)] \leftarrow$
MGI($cnt^+[x], tot_n^+ - cnt^+[x] + tot_c^+, tot_n^- - cnt^-[x] + tot_c^-, cnt^-[x]$)

12        $score[(i, >, x)] \leftarrow$
MGI($tot_n^+ - cnt^+[x], cnt^+[x] + tot_c^+, cnt^-[x] + tot_c^-, tot_n^- - cnt^-[x]$)

13        $score[(i, \nleq, x)] \leftarrow$
MGI($tot_n^+ - cnt^+[x] + tot_c^+, cnt^+[x], cnt^-[x], tot_n^- - cnt^-[x] + tot_c^-$)

14        $score[(i, \ngtr, x)] \leftarrow$
MGI($cnt^+[x] + tot_c^+, tot_n^+ - cnt^+[x], tot_n^- - cnt^-[x], cnt^-[x] + tot_c^-$)

15   **end**

16   **for** $c \in set_s$ **do**

17        $score[(i, =, c)] \leftarrow$
MGI($cnt^+[c], tot_c^+ - cnt^+[c] + tot_n^+, tot_c^- - cnt^-[c] + tot_n^-, cnt^-[c]$)

18        $score[(i, \neq, c)] \leftarrow$
MGI($tot_c^+ - cnt^+[c] + tot_n^+, cnt^+[c], cnt^-[c], tot_c^- - cnt^-[c] + tot_n^-$)

19   **end**

20     $h, literal \leftarrow$ best_pair($score, used$)

21   **return** $h, literal$

22 **end**

23 **Function** find_best_literal($E^+, E^-, used$)

24     $best\_h, literal \leftarrow -\infty, invalid$

25   **for** $i \leftarrow 1$ **to** N **do**

26        $h, lit \leftarrow$ best_literal_on_attr($E^+, E^-, i, used$)

27   **if** $best\_h < h$ **then**

28           $best\_h, literal \leftarrow h, lit$

29   **end**

30   **end**

31   **return** $literal$

32 **end**

3.4   Rule Pruning

The FOLD-R++ algorithm [22] is a recent rule-based machine learning algorithm for classification that generates a normal logic program in which all the default rules have the same rule head (target predicate). An example is covered means that it is predicted as positive. An example covered by any default rule in the set would imply the rule head is true. The FOLD-R++ algorithm generates a model by learning one rule at a time. After learning a rule, the already covered examples would be ruled out for a better literal selection of remaining examples. If the *ratio* of false positive examples to true positive examples drops below the preset threshold, it would next learn exceptions by swapping remaining positive and negative examples then calling itself recursively. The *ratio* stands for the upper bound on the number of false positive examples to the number of true positive examples implied by the default part of a rule. It helps speed up the training process and reduces the number of rules learned. The training process of FOLD-R++ is also a process of ruling out already covered examples. Later-generated rules cover fewer examples than the early-generated ones. In other words, FOLD-R++ suffers from *long-tail effect*. Here is an example:

Table 3. Top: Examples and values on i^{th} feature. Bottom: positive/negative count and prefix sum on each value

	i^{th} feature values							
E^+	3	4	4	5	x	x	y	
E^-	1	1	1	2	3	y	y	z
value	1	2	3	4	5	x	y	z
$count^+$	0	0	1	2	1	2	1	0
sum^+_{pfx}	0	0	1	3	4	NA	NA	NA
$count^-$	3	1	1	0	0	0	2	1
sum^-_{pfx}	3	4	5	5	5	NA	NA	NA

Table 4. The heuristic on i^{th} feature with given examples

	heuristic							
value	1	2	3	4	5	x	y	z
$\leq$ value	$-\infty$	$-\infty$	$-\infty$	$-\infty$	$-\infty$	NA	NA	NA
$>$ value	-0.47	-0.44	-0.38	-0.46	-0.50	NA	NA	NA
$\nleq$ value	-0.39	$\mathbf{-0.35}$	-0.43	-0.49	-0.50	NA	NA	NA
$\ngtr$ value	$-\infty$	$-\infty$	$-\infty$	$-\infty$	$-\infty$	NA	NA	NA
$=$ value	NA	NA	NA	NA	NA	-0.42	$-\infty$	$-\infty$
$\neq$ value	NA	NA	NA	NA	NA	$-\infty$	-0.49	-0.47

Example 2. *The "Adult Census Income" is a classical classification task that contains 32,561 records. We treat 80% of the data as training examples and 20% as testing examples. The task is to learn the income status of individuals (more/less than 50K/year) based on features such as gender, age, education, marital status, etc. FOLD-R++ generates the following model that contains 9 rules:*

```
(1) income(X,'<=50K') :-
  [3428] not marital_status(X,'Married-civ-spouse'),
         not ab3(X,'True').
(2) income(X,'<=50K') :-
  [1999] marital_status(X,'Married-civ-spouse'),
         education_num(X,N1), N1=<12.0, capital_gain(X,N2),
         N2=<5013.0, not ab5(X,'True'), not ab6(X,'True').
(3) income(X,'<=50K') :-  occupation(X,'Farming-fishing'),
  [1]    workclass(X,'Self-emp-not-inc'),
         education_num(X,N1), N1>12.0, capital_gain(X,N2),
         N2>5013.0.
(4) ab1(X,'True') :- not workclass(X,'Local-gov'),
  [2]    capital_gain(X,N2), N2=<7978.0, education_num(X,N1),
         N1=<10.0.
(5) ab2(X,'True') :- capital_gain(X,N2), N2>27828.0,
  [0]    N2=<34095.0.
(6) ab3(X,'True') :- capital_gain(X,N2), N2>6849.0,
  [0]    age(X,N3), N3>20.0, not ab1(X,'True'),
         not ab2(X,'True').
(7) ab4(X,'True') :- workclass(X,'Local-gov'),
  [0]    native_country(X,'United-States').
(8) ab5(X,'True') :- not race(X,'Amer-Indian-Eskimo'),
  [0]    education_num(X,N1), N1=<8.0, capital_loss(X,N4),
         N4>1735.0, N4=<1902.0, not ab4(X,'True').
(9) ab6(X,'True') :- occupation(X,'Tech-support'),
  [0]    not education(X,'11th'), education_num(X,N1),
         N1>5.0, N1=<8.0, age(X,N3), N3=<36.0.
```

The above generated rules achieve 0.85 accuracy and $0.90\,F_1$ score. The first rule covers 3428 test examples and the second rule covers 1999 test examples. Subsequent rules only cover a small number of test examples. This long-tail effect is due to the overfitting on the training data. FOLD-SE introduces a hyperparameter *tail* to limit the minimum number/percentage of training examples that a rule can cover. It helps reduce the number of generated rules and literals by reducing the overfitting of outliers. This rule pruning is not a post-process after training, rather rules are pruned during the training process itself which helps speed-up training. With the *tail* parameter, FOLD-SE can be easily tuned to obtain a trade-off between accuracy and explainability. The FOLD-SE algorithm is summarized in Algorithm 1. Note cover(r, E^+, false) in Algorithm 1 extracts the examples from E^+ that are predicted as false with rule r. The added rule pruning process is carried out in lines 33–38 of Algorithm 1. When a learned rule cannot cover enough training examples, the `learn_rule` function returns.

3.5   Complexity Analysis

If M is the number of training examples and N is the number of features that have been included in the training, the time complexity of finding the best literal of a feature is $O(M)$, assuming that counting sort is used at line 5 in Algorithm 2. Therefore, the complexity of finding the best literal of all features is $O(MN)$. The worst training case is that each generated rule only covers one training example and each literal only helps exclude one example. In this case, $O(M^2)$ literals would be selected in total. Hence, the worst case time complexity of FOLD-SE is $O(M^3N)$. Additionally, it is easy to prove that the FOLD-SE algorithm always terminates (proof is omitted due to lack of space).

4   Experimental Results

We have conducted extensive experiments comparing the performance of various heuristics, as well as comparing our new FOLD-SE rule learning algorithm with state-of-the-art machine learning methods. First, we show the effectiveness of the Magic Gini Impurity (MGI) heuristics in comparison to the Information Gain (IG) heuristics. We supplant the IG heuristics in our FOLD-R++ algorithm with the MGI heuristics and compare the original FOLD-R++ algorithm with the updated one. Note that the FOLD-R++ system is freely available on GitHub [22]. As shown in Table 5, the number of generated rules and generated literals is

Table 5. Comparison of MGI and IG heuristics in FOLD-R++

Data Set			FOLD-R++ with IG						
Name	Rows	Cols	Acc	Prec	Rec	F1	T (ms)	Rules	Predicates
parkinson	765	754	**0.82**	**0.85**	0.93	0.89	10,757	13.7±4.2	21.2±7.5
eeg	14980	15	**0.72**	**0.76**	**0.72**	**0.74**	2,735	69.1±17.3	152.6±35.6
credit card	30000	24	0.82	0.83	0.96	0.89	5,954	19.1±6.4	48.8±14.7
adult	32561	15	0.84	0.86	0.95	0.90	2,508	16.8±2.4	46.7±10.4
rain in aus	145460	24	0.79	**0.87**	0.84	0.86	26,203	48.2±10.6	115.8±39.1
Data Set			FOLD-R++ with MGI						
Name	Rows	Cols	Acc	Prec	Rec	F1	T (ms)	Rules	Predicates
parkinson	765	754	0.81	0.82	**0.96**	0.89	**7,469**	**7.4±1.6**	**13.2±4.2**
eeg	14980	15	0.68	0.75	0.64	0.69	**1,353**	**18.7±7.9**	**40.8±19.5**
credit card	30000	24	0.82	0.83	0.96	0.89	**3,827**	**10.9±3.2**	**25.5±8.7**
adult	32561	15	0.84	0.86	0.95	0.90	**1,414**	**6.8±1.5**	**13.2±3.6**
rain in aus	145460	24	**0.80**	0.86	**0.87**	0.86	**15,003**	**14.6±4.7**	**57.9±31.0**

reduced significantly with MGI compared to IG, while performance remains the same. Table 5 shows the comparison for a few data-sets. Extensive comparison of FOLD-R++ and FOLD-SE (that incorporates MGI and long tail elimination) is shown later in Table 7.

To further verify MGI's effectiveness w.r.t. the FOLD algorithm, a comparison experiment of 4 different heuristics (MGI, information gain, weighted Gini Index [3], Chi-Square [15]) with 2-way split full decision trees on various datasets is also performed. All the heuristics have similar performance in accuracy on decision trees. The number of generated tree nodes and the average depth of leaf nodes are also very close (results are omitted due to lack of space). The interesting point to note is that MGI has a significant impact on FOLD-R++ (where the learned rules are represented as a default theory), but not in learning decision trees.

We next present our experiments with FOLD-SE on UCI [7] and Kaggle datasets (kaggle.com). The XGBoost Classifier is a well-known classification model and is used as a baseline model in our experiments. Multi-Layer Perceptron (MLP) is another widely-used model that is able to deal with generic classification tasks. The settings used for XGBoost and MLP models are kept simple without limiting their performance. However, unlike our FOLD-SE algorithm, both XGBoost and MLP methods cannot directly perform training on hybrid (numerical and categorical values in a row or a column) data. One-hot encoding has been used during data pre-processing for XGBoost and MLP. RIPPER system is another rule-induction algorithm that generates formulas in conjunctive normal form as an explainable model. Both RIPPER and FOLD-R++ are capable of dealing with hybrid data and are used as baselines to compare explainability.

The FOLD-SE algorithm does not need data encoding (such as one-hot encoding) for training, a feature that it inherits from FOLD-R++. After specifying which features are numerical, FOLD-SE can deal with hybrid data directly. Even missing values are handled and do not need to be provided. FOLD-SE has been implemented in Python. The hyper-parameter *ratio* of both FOLD-R++ and FOLD-SE is set to a default value of 0.5 for all experiments. The hyper-parameter *tail* of the FOLD-SE algorithms is set to the default percentage 0.5% of training data size. All the training processes have been performed on a small form factor desktop with Intel i7-8705G and 16 GB RAM. To have good performance tests, we performed 10-fold cross-validation tests on each dataset. The experimental results comparing FOLD-SE with XGBoost and MLP are listed in Table 6. FOLD-SE *always* takes an order of magnitude less time to train compared to XGBoost and MLP, especially for large datasets with many unique values. FOLD-SE can achieve equivalent scores w.r.t. accuracy and F_1 score. For the "credit card" dataset, XGBoost, and MLP failed training because of the 16 GB memory limitation of the testing machine, the one-hot encoding process needs around 39 GB memory consumption. However, FOLD-SE only consumes 53 MB (Megabytes) of memory at peak for training on the same dataset. Compared to XGBoost and MLP, the FOLD-SE algorithm is more efficient and lightweight.

Table 6. Comparison of XGBoost, MLP, and FOLD-SE on various Datasets credit card dataset is excluded in computing average*

Data Set			XGBoost			MLP			FOLD-SE		
Name	Rows	Cols	Acc	F1	T (ms)	Acc	F1	T (ms)	Acc	F1	T (ms)
acute	120	7	**1.0**	**1.0**	122	0.99	0.99	22	**1.0**	**1.0**	1
heart	270	14	**0.82**	**0.83**	247	0.76	0.78	95	0.74	0.77	13
ionosphere	351	35	0.88	0.91	2,206	0.79	0.81	1,771	**0.91**	**0.93**	119
kidney	400	25	0.99	0.99	273	0.99	0.99	218	1.0	1.0	16
voting	435	17	0.95	0.93	149	0.95	0.93	43	0.95	**0.94**	11
credit-a	690	16	**0.85**	**0.86**	720	0.82	0.84	356	**0.85**	0.85	36
breast-w	699	10	0.95	0.96	186	**0.97**	**0.98**	48	0.94	0.92	9
autism	704	18	**0.97**	**0.98**	236	0.96	0.97	56	0.91	0.94	29
parkinson	765	754	0.76	0.85	270,336	0.60	0.71	152,056	**0.82**	**0.89**	9,691
diabetes	768	9	0.66	0.76	839	0.66	0.73	368	**0.75**	**0.81**	38
cars	1728	7	**1.0**	**1.0**	210	0.99	1.0	83	0.96	0.97	20
kr vs. kp	3196	37	**0.99**	**0.99**	403	**0.99**	**0.99**	273	0.97	0.97	152
mushroom	8124	23	1.0	1.0	697	1.0	1.0	394	1.0	1.0	254
churn-model	10000	11	**0.85**	**0.91**	97,727	0.81	0.88	18,084	**0.85**	**0.91**	600
intention	12330	18	**0.90**	**0.94**	171,480	0.81	0.89	41,992	**0.90**	**0.94**	661
eeg	14980	15	0.64	**0.71**	46,472	**0.69**	**0.71**	9,001	0.67	0.68	1,227
credit card	30000	24	NA	NA	NA	NA	NA	NA	0.82	0.89	3,513
adult	32561	15	**0.87**	**0.92**	424,686	0.81	0.87	300,380	0.84	0.90	1,746
rain in aus	145460	24	**0.84**	**0.90**	385,456	0.81	0.88	243,990	0.82	0.89	10,243
average*	13872	57	0.83	0.87	73,812	0.81	0.84	40,485	**0.88**	**0.91**	1,493

The experimental results shown in Table 7 indicate that FOLD-SE outperforms the RIPPER algorithm in accuracy and explainability (the numbers of generated rules and literals/predicates). The FOLD-SE algorithm outperforms FOLD-R++ in explainability while maintaining comparable performance in accuracy, especially for large datasets. With enough data, the FOLD-SE algorithm can generate really concise rules that can capture patterns in datasets. The most dramatic result is that for the Rain in Australia dataset, FOLD-SE generates a model with 2.5 rules on average with 6.1 literals in these rules on average with an average accuracy of 0.82, while RIPPER and FOLD-R++ report much higher values for the number of rules and literals (180.1 rules and 776.4 literals for RIPPER and 48.2 rules and 115.8 predicates for FOLD-R++) and lower value for accuracy (0.63 for RIPPER and 0.79 for FOLD-R++). *FOLD-SE, thus, not only generates far fewer rules, the generated rules provide higher accuracy of prediction.*

Table 8 shows the results of the comparison between a full binary decision tree and FOLD-SE. Nodes of a binary decision tree are equivalent to predicates

Table 7. Comparison of RIPPER, FOLD-R++, and FOLD-SE on various Datasets

Data Set	RIPPER					FOLD-R++					FOLD-SE				
Name	Acc	F1	T (ms)	Rules	Preds	Acc	F1	T (ms)	Rules	Preds	Acc	F1	T (ms)	Rules	Preds
acute	0.93	0.92	95	**2.0**	4.0	0.99	0.99	2	2.7	**3.0**	1.0	1.0	1	**2.0**	**3.0**
heart	0.76	0.77	317	5.4	12.9	**0.77**	**0.79**	38	15.9	32.2	0.74	0.77	13	4.0	9.1
ionosphere	0.72	0.73	1,161	8.5	13.9	0.90	0.92	275	12.4	19.7	0.91	0.93	119	3.6	7.1
kidney	0.98	0.98	750	7.1	8.5	0.99	0.99	16	4.9	5.9	1.0	1.0	16	4.9	6.1
voting	0.95	0.92	172	4.1	8.9	0.94	0.92	23	10.0	27.2	0.95	0.94	11	7.3	20.2
credit-a	0.89	0.89	944	10.1	21.4	0.83	0.83	84	10.3	23.3	0.85	0.85	36	2.4	5.8
breast-w	0.93	0.90	319	14.4	19.9	**0.95**	**0.96**	34	10.5	18.6	0.94	0.92	9	3.5	6.3
autism	0.93	0.95	359	10.3	25.2	0.93	0.95	62	25.4	54.8	0.91	0.94	29	9.9	23.
parkinson	0.70	0.78	159,556	8.9	13.4	0.82	0.89	10,757	13.7	21.2	0.82	0.89	9,691	5.7	12.5
diabetes	0.58	0.56	511	8.7	14.8	0.74	0.80	66	8.3	19.4	0.75	0.81	38	2.7	5.9
cars	0.99	0.99	385	14.2	39.8	0.96	0.97	31	12.3	29.8	0.96	0.97	20	7.2	14.0
kr vs. kp	0.99	0.99	609	8.1	16.2	0.99	0.99	226	19.3	46.7	0.97	0.97	152	5.0	10.4
mushroom	1.0	1.0	923	8.3	12.7	1.0	1.0	281	7.9	11.9	1.0	1.0	254	5.7	10.6
churn-model	0.54	0.60	9,941	11.6	39.2	0.85	0.91	987	28.1	66.9	0.85	0.91	600	2.9	9.1
intention	0.88	0.93	8,542	25.2	91.6	0.90	0.94	1,085	8.4	23.0	0.90	0.94	661	2.0	5.1
eeg	0.55	0.36	12,996	43.4	134.7	**0.72**	**0.74**	2,735	69.1	152.6	0.67	0.68	1,227	5.1	12.1
credit card	0.76	0.84	49,940	36.5	150.7	0.82	0.89	5,954	19.1	48.8	0.82	0.89	3,513	2.0	3.0
adult	0.71	0.77	63,480	41.4	168.4	0.84	0.90	2,508	16.8	46.7	0.84	0.90	1,746	2.0	5.0
rain in aus	0.63	0.70	3118,025	180.1	776.4	0.79	0.86	26,203	48.2	115.8	0.82	0.89	10,243	2.5	6.1
average	0.81	0.82	180,475	23.6	82.8	**0.88**	**0.91**	2,704	18.1	40.4	**0.88**	**0.91**	1,493	4.2	9.2

of FOLD-SE, because both compare a feature value with a trained value to designate it as positive or negative outcome. Therefore, the number of decision-tree nodes and the number of literals (predicates) in FOLD-SE rule-set, intuitively, are comparable. The rule-sets generated by FOLD-SE are much easier to comprehend than the generated binary decision trees because there are far fewer predicates in the generated rule-sets. For example, the generated binary decision tree for UCI Adult Dataset consists of over 8,000 nodes while the logic program generated by FOLD-SE only contains 5 predicates. As Table 8 shows, FOLD-SE is also considerably faster in terms of execution time.

FOLD-SE has also been extended for multi-class classification. The performance of the extended system w.r.t. XGBoost and MLPs on multi-class tasks is similar to FOLD-SE.

5   Explainability

With the new heuristic and rule pruning, the FOLD-SE algorithm pushes interpretability and explainability to a significantly higher level. For Example 2 (UCI Adult Dataset), FOLD-SE generates the following logic program with *only two rules*:

```
(1) income(X,'<=50K') :-
 [3457] not marital_status(X,'Married-civ-spouse'),
        capital_gain(X,N1), N1=<6849.0.
(2) income(X,'<=50K') :-
```

Table 8. Comparison of Decision Tree, and FOLD-SE

| Data Set | | | Decision Tree | | | FOLD-SE | | |
Name	Rows	Cols	Acc	Nodes	T (ms)	Acc	Preds	T (ms)
acute	120	7	1.0	7.4±0.8	3	1.0	**3.0±0.0**	**1**
heart	270	14	**0.75**	79.6±6.1	38	0.74	**9.1±8.5**	**13**
ionosphere	351	35	0.88	42.0±3.8	377	**0.91**	**7.1±0.7**	**119**
kidney	400	25	0.98	19.6±2.4	53	**1.0**	**6.1±0.3**	**16**
voting	435	17	0.95	48.8±6.3	27	0.95	**20.2±6.7**	**11**
credit-a	690	16	0.80	158.8±3.3	137	**0.85**	**5.8±5.5**	**36**
breast-w	699	10	0.92	70.4±4.0	48	**0.94**	**6.3±1.4**	**9**
autism	704	18	**0.92**	95.0±4.4	48	0.91	**23.6±4.3**	**29**
parkinson	756	764	0.81	79.6±2.8	18,253	**0.82**	**12.5±3.9**	**9,691**
diabetes	768	9	0.68	233.8±10.9	166	**0.75**	**5.9±3.7**	**38**
cars	1728	7	**1.0**	94.8±2.4	53	0.96	**14.0±3.2**	**20**
kr vs. kp	3196	37	**1.0**	73.4±4.3	422	0.97	**10.4±2.5**	**152**
mushroom	8124	23	1.0	21.4±2.3	1,463	1.0	**10.6±1.3**	**254**
churn-model	10000	11	0.80	2450.2±38.3	5,610	**0.85**	**9.1±1.6**	**600**
intention	12330	18	0.86	1686.0±25.6	6,886	**0.90**	**5.1±0.3**	**661**
eeg	14980	15	**0.85**	2282.8±32.8	11,820	0.67	**12.1±4.5**	**1,227**
credit card	30000	24	0.73	7790.0±68.3	62,112	**0.82**	**3.0±0.0**	**3,513**
adult	32561	16	0.82	8125.8±71.6	40,943	**0.84**	**5.0±0.0**	**1,746**
average	6562	59	0.88	1297.7±16.1	8,248	0.88	**9.4±2.7**	**1,007**

```
[1998] marital_status(X,'Married-civ-spouse'),
       capital_gain(X,N1), N1=<5013.0,
       education_num(X,N2), N2=<12.0.
```

The above rules achieve 0.85 accuracy, 0.86 precision, 0.96 recall, and 0.91 F_1 score, the first rule covers 3457 test examples and the second rule covers 1998 test examples. The generated rule-set can be understood easily due to the symbolic representation: Who makes less than 50K dollars a year: (1) unmarried people with capital gain less than \$6,849; (2) married people with capital gain less than \$5,013 and education level not over 12. The generated rule-set for this dataset in the 10-fold cross-validation test are almost all identical, only the values in the literals change slightly.

Example 3. *The "Rain in Australia" is another classification task that contains 145,460 records with 24 features. We treat 80% of the data as training examples and 20% as testing examples. The task is to find out if it is not rainy tomorrow, the FOLD-SE generates the following rules:*

```
(1) raintomorrow(X,'No') :- humidity3pm(X,N1), N1=<64.0,
       rainfall(X,N2), N2=<182.6.
```

```
(2) raintomorrow(X,'No') :- rainfall(X,N2), N2=<2.2,
        humidity3pm(X,N1), not(N1=<64.0), not(N1>81.0).
```

The generated rules achieve 0.83 accuracy, 0.85 precision, 0.94 recall, and $0.89\,F_1$ score.

6   Related Work and Conclusions

Rule-base Machine Learning is a long-standing interest of the research community. Some rule-based algorithms perform training directly on the input data: ALEPH [20] is a well-known Inductive Logic Programming algorithm that induces rules by using bottom-up approach, it cannot handle numerical features; those have to be handled manually. ILASP [12] system is another ILP algorithm that is able to generate normal logic program, it needs to work with a solver and requires a rule-set to describe the hypothesis space. Some other rule-based algorithms rely on statistical machine learning models: SVM+ProtoTypes [14] extracts rule from Support Vector Machine (SVM) models by using K-Means clustering algorithm. RuleFit [8] algorithm learns weighted rules from ensemble models of shallow decision trees. TREPAN [5] produces a decision tree from trained Neural Networks by querying. Support Vector ILP [13] uses ILP-learned clauses as the kernel in dual form of SVM. nFOIL [10] system employs the naive Bayes criterion to guide its rule induction. The kFOIL [11] algorithm integrates the FOIL system with kernel methods. The TILDE [2] algorithm generate propositional rules for paths from the root to every leaf node of a trained C4.5 decision tree. TILDE produces too many rules for large datasets when the generated decision tree has many leaf nodes. Compared to the above systems, our approach is more efficient and scalable due to being top-down and using prefix-sum technique for literal selection. Thus, the rule-set learned in our approach is much more concise because of the use of default rules with exceptions and use of the Magic Genie Impurity heuristics. Finally, our approach is able to provide scalable explainability which, to the best of our knowledge, no other rule-based algorithm achieves.

Acknowledgement. Authors acknowledge support from NSF grant IIS 1910131, US DoD, and Atos Corp.

References

1. Bishop, C.M.: Pattern Recognition and Machine Learning. Information Science and Statistics, Springer, Heidelberg (2006)
2. Blockeel, H., De Raedt, L.: Top-down induction of first-order logical decision trees. Artif. Intell. **101**(1), 285–297 (1998). https://doi.org/10.1016/S0004-3702(98)00034-4. https://www.sciencedirect.com/science/article/pii/S0004370298000344
3. Breiman, L.: Classification and Regression Trees. Wadsworth International Group, Draper (1984). https://doi.org/10.5555/55768

4. Cohen, W.W.: Fast effective rule induction. In: Proceedings of the Twelfth International Conference on International Conference on Machine Learning, pp. 115–123. ICML'95, Morgan Kaufmann Publishers Inc., San Francisco, CA, USA (1995)

5. Craven, M.W., Shavlik, J.W.: Extracting tree-structured representations of trained networks. In: Proceedings of the 8th International Conference on Neural Information Processing Systems, pp. 24–30. NIPS'95, MIT Press, Cambridge, MA, USA (1995)

6. Cropper, A., Dumancic, S.: Inductive logic programming at 30: a new introduction (2020). https://arxiv.org/abs/2008.07912

7. Dua, D., Graff, C.: UCI machine learning repository (2017). http://archive.ics.uci.edu/ml

8. Friedman, J.H., Popescu, B.E., et al.: Predictive learning via rule ensembles. Ann. Appl. Stat. **2**(3), 916–954 (2008)

9. Gelfond, M., Kahl, Y.: Knowledge representation, reasoning, and the design of intelligent agents: the answer-set programming approach. Cambridge University Press (2014)

10. Landwehr, N., Kersting, K., Raedt, L.D.: nFOIL: integrating naïve bayes and FOIL. In: Proceedings of the AAAI, pp. 795–800 (2005)

11. Landwehr, N., Passerini, A., Raedt, L.D., Frasconi, P.: kFOIL: learning simple relational kernels. In: Proceedings of the AAAI, pp. 389–394 (2006)

12. Law, M.: Inductive learning of answer set programs. Ph.D. thesis, Imperial College London, UK (2018)

13. Muggleton, S., Lodhi, H., Amini, A., Sternberg, M.J.E.: Support vector inductive logic programming. In: Hoffmann, A., Motoda, H., Scheffer, T. (eds.) DS 2005. LNCS (LNAI), vol. 3735, pp. 163–175. Springer, Heidelberg (2005). https://doi.org/10.1007/11563983_15

14. Núñez, H., Angulo, C., Català, A.: Rule extraction from support vector machines. In: Proceedings of European Symposium on Artificial Neural Networks, pp. 107–112 (2002)

15. Pearson, K.: On the criterion that a given system of deviations from the probable in the case of a correlated system of variables is such that it can be reasonably supposed to have arisen from random sampling. Philos. Mag. Ser. **50**(302), 157 175 (1900). https://doi.org/10.1080/14786440009463897

16. Quinlan, J.R.: Induction of decision trees. Mach. Learn. **1**(1), 81–106 (1986). https://doi.org/10.1023/A:1022643204877

17. Quinlan, J.R.: Learning logical definitions from relations. Mach. Learn. **5**, 239–266 (1990)

18. Reiter, R.: A logic for default reasoning. Artif. Intell. **13**(1–2), 81–132 (1980)

19. Shakerin, F., Salazar, E., Gupta, G.: A new algorithm to automate inductive learning of default theories. TPLP **17**(5–6), 1010–1026 (2017)

20. Srinivasan, A.: The aleph manual (2001). http://web.comlab.ox.ac.uk/oucl/research/areas/machlearn/Aleph/

21. Sterling, L., Shapiro, E.: The Art of Prolog. MIT Press, Cambridge (1994)

22. Wang, H., Gupta, G.: FOLD-R++: a scalable toolset for automated inductive learning of default theories from mixed data. In: Hanus, M., Igarashi, A. (eds.) FLOPS 2022. LNCS, vol. 13215, pp. 224–242. Springer, Heidelberg (2022). https://doi.org/10.1007/978-3-030-99461-7_13

23. Wang, H., Shakerin, F., Gupta, G.: FOLD-RM: a scalable, efficient, and explainable inductive learning algorithm for multi-category classification of mixed data. Theory Pract. Logic Program. **22**, 658–677 (2022). https://doi.org/10.1017/S1471068422000205

Marketplace Logistics via Answer Set Programming

Mario Alviano[1]([✉]) [iD], Danilo Amendola[2,3] [iD],
and Luis Angel Rodriguez Reiners[1] [iD]

[1] DEMACS, University of Calabria, Via Bucci 30/B, 87036 Rende, CS, Italy
{mario.alviano,luis.reiners}@unical.it
[2] Oliveru – Smartly Engineering, Rome, Italy
danilo.amendola@oliveru.com
[3] Joint Research Centre – European Commission,
Retieseweg 111, 2440 Geel, Belgium
Danilo.Amendola@ec.europa.eu

Abstract. Marketplaces aggregate products from several providers and handle orders involving several suppliers automatically. We report on an application of Answer Set Programming for automatically selecting products from different warehouses within the network of a marketplace to fulfill a given order. The presented solution easily accommodates different objective functions that are employed at different stages of managing an order, enabling economic savings for the customer as well as simplification of logistics for both the marketplace and its suppliers.

Keywords: Answer Set Programming · combinatorial search and optimization · logistics marketplace

1 Introduction

E-commerce changed the world of retail by making the Internet the preferred place to buy commodities of any kind [1], and several recent works deal with computational problems related to e-commerce logistic [2–7]. Early e-commerce websites were focused on business-to-consumer (B2C) transactions, and essentially consisted in online stores advertising and selling their own products. Nowadays, marketplaces of different sizes and targeting several commercial fields are emerging, bringing e-commerce to a more profitable level [8]. In fact, a marketplace provides a uniform view over products sold by different suppliers and stored in different warehouses, hence giving the possibility to their end-users to complete orders that would not be manageable by any single supplier. It is the marketplace that takes care of coordinating the associated suppliers in order to provide the products that are requested by a customer order. Moreover, the marketplace platform handles the B2C transaction associated with an order, and the subsequent business-to-business (B2B) transactions to the suppliers, hence simplifying an important financial aspect of online sales.

The development of a profitable marketplace platform presents a number of challenges, in particular due to the increasing complexity of the supply chain.

M. Gebser and I. Sergey (Eds.): PADL 2024, LNCS 14512, pp. 54–63, 2023. .
https://doi.org/10.1007/978-3-031-52038-9_4

Despite the challenges, marketplaces are becoming increasingly popular, and in 2022 they accounted for over half of the global e-commerce sales, estimated in more than 5 trillions USD[1]. Given the substantial amount of money involved, optimization of the chain of distribution can lead to significant savings. First of all, a marketplace needs to track the inventory of several suppliers in order to let end-users compose eligible orders. Given the fact that the same product is possibly available by different suppliers, an eligible order can be managed by shipping products from different suppliers. A reasonable criteria to decide which suppliers have to be involved in managing an eligible order is therefore required. Should the goal be to minimize the end-user expenses? Or is it better to simplify the marketplace logistic? What about the logistic of suppliers?

In this article we consider a marketplace in which suppliers expose products whose prices are agreed with the platform. Each supplier synchronizes the supplies in its warehouse with the marketplace platform, so that end-users can compose eligible orders. Moreover, each supplier offers the possibility to waive shipping fees when the total cost of the products to ship reaches a threshold, where the threshold is decided by the supplier. In order to maximize the attractiveness of the marketplace for end-users, the total cost of the composed order is minimized by distributing the order among suppliers with cheaper shipping fees, possibly trying to capture as many free-shipping opportunities. The total cost is updated within each product addition and removal to achieve a pleasant user experience, and therefore the optimization task must be completed with negligible computational effort. Before completing the order, the platform confirms the estimated cost and informs the end-user on the number of shipments the requested products will be distributed. This information is obtained by addressing a slightly more complex combinatorial problem that selects among the solutions with the same minimum cost those that simplify the marketplace logistic as much as possible, that is, those that involve a minimum number of suppliers. Finally, after the order is paid by the end-user, the platform employs a broader combinatorial problem to simplify also the logistic of the involved suppliers, essentially by minimizing the number of pairs warehouse–product involved in the process. This way, the marketplace platform offers advantages to its end-users and suppliers, as well as to its own business.

The combinatorial problems addressed by the analyzed marketplace are formalized and addressed by means of Answer Set Programming (ASP, [9,10]) specifications (see Sect. 3). Actually, a small fragment of ASP is sufficient to empower the proposed specifications (see Sect. 2). An experiment aiming at assessing the quality of the developed specifications is also reported (see Sect. 4), comparing solutions obtained within ASP with those obtained by a greedy algorithm. ASP provides much better results as well as the flexibility to uniformly address all three combinatorial tasks of interest.

---

[1] https://on.emarketer.com/Report-20220308ChannelAdvisor_BusRegpageProgPro.

2 Background

We consider a restricted syntax in which aggregates only occur in (weak) constraints, and all other rules are choice rules to select exactly one atom. Such a restricted syntax is sufficient for our encodings, and simplifies the definition of the semantics of the language. We refer the ASP-Core-2 format for a description of a broader fragment of ASP [11].

A *constant* is any natural number in $\mathbb{N}$. Strings starting by an uppercase letter denote (object) *variables*. *Interpreted functions* are prefixed by @: an interpreted function maps a sequence of constants to a single constant. *Terms* are inductively defined as follows: constants and object variables are terms; if $@f$ is an interpreted function and $\bar{t}$ is a sequence of terms, then $@f(\bar{t})$ is a term. For a sequence $\bar{t}$, let $|\bar{t}|$ denote its length and $\bar{t}_i$ denote its i-th element. An *atom* is of the form $p(\bar{t})$, where p is a predicate name and $\bar{t}$ is a sequence of $n \geq 0$ terms. An *interval* has the form $t = l..u$ where t, l, u are terms; t is referred to as the left-hand-side of the interval. A (sum) *aggregate* has the form

$$\#\mathrm{sum}\{\bar{t} : conj\} \odot b \tag{1}$$

where $\bar{t}$ is a sequence of terms, $conj$ is a sequence of atoms and intervals (a conjunction), $\odot \in \{<, \leq, \geq, >, =, \neq\}$, and b is a term (the bound).

A (rule) *body* is a conjunction of atoms, intervals and aggregates. An (exactly-one) *choice* rule has the form

$$\{\alpha : conj\} = 1 \ \text{:-} \ body. \tag{2}$$

where α is an atom, $conj$ is a (possibly empty) sequence of atoms and intervals, and $body$ is an aggregate-free body. The left-hand-side of a choice rule is called the head of the rule. A *fact* is a choice rule of the form $\{p(\bar{t})\} = 1 \ \text{:-}$, and usually simply denoted as $p(\bar{t})$. A *constraint* has the form

$$\text{:-} \ body. \tag{3}$$

where $body$ is a body. A *weak constraint* has the form

$$\text{:}\sim \ body. \ [w@l, \bar{t}] \tag{4}$$

where $body$ is a body, w and l are terms, and $\bar{t}$ is a sequence of terms. Choice rules, constraints and weak constraints are jointly called rules. A *program* Π is a set of rules.

Variables of different rules are distinct (even if they share the same string representation). *Global variables* of a rule are those occurring in at least one atom of its body and those on the left-hand-side of an interval of its body. Global variables are (virtually) expanded by substituting them with constants, in all possible ways. Any remaining *(local) variable* inside an aggregate of the form (1) or in a head of a choice rule of the form (2) is *safe* if it occurs in at least one atom or left-hand-side of an interval in $conj$. Any remaining variable in weak constraints (in squared brackets) is unsafe. Only programs with safe variables are considered here.

An expression (term, atom, interval, and so on) is *ground* if all its terms are constants. Let $expand(E)$ be the set obtained by expanding an expression E. An *interpretation* I is a set of ground atoms. Variable-free terms are interpreted independently by the chosen interpretation as follows: $I(c) = c$ if $c \in \mathbb{N}$; $I(@f(\bar{t})) = f(I(t_1), \ldots, I(t_{|\bar{t}|}))$, where f is the mapping associated with $@f$. An interpretation I is a *model* of a program Π if $I \models \Pi$, where relation $\models$ is defined as follows: $I \models p(\bar{t})$ if $p(I(\bar{t})) \in I$; $I \models t = l..u$ if $I(l) \leq I(t) \leq I(u)$; $I \models A$, where A is an aggregate of the form (1), if

$$\left(\sum_{\{\overline{t'} \mid (\overline{t'} : conj') \in expand(\overline{t} : conj)\}} \overline{t'}_1 \right) \odot I(b); \tag{5}$$

$I \models body$ if $I \models body_i$ for all $i = 1..|body|$; $I \models r$, where r is a choice rule of the form (2), if $I \not\models body$ or

$$|\{\alpha' \mid (\alpha' : conj') \in expand(\alpha : conj),\ I \models conj'\}| = 1; \tag{6}$$

$I \models r$, where r is a constraint of the form (3), if $I \not\models body$; $I \models r$, where r is a weak constraint of the form (4), if $I \not\models body$; $I \models \Pi$ if $I \models r$ for all choice rules and constraints $r \in expand(\Pi)$. Weak constraints of Π associate a cost function $cost_\Pi : I \times \mathbb{N} \to \mathbb{N}$ to I as follows:

$$cost_\Pi(I, l) = \sum_{(w,\bar{t}):(:\sim x body.\ [w@l,\bar{t}]) \in expand(\Pi),\ I \not\models body} w. \tag{7}$$

The *answer sets* of Π are its subset-minimal models. An answer I of Π is *optimal* if there is no answer set J of Π such that there exists $l \in \mathbb{N}$ with $cost_\Pi(J, l') = cost_\Pi(I, l')$ for all $l' > l$, and $cost_\Pi(J, l) < cost_\Pi(I, l)$.

3 Problem Statement and Solution

Let us first formalize the problem introduced in Sect. 1 (Sect. 3.1). After that, we report a greedy algorithm not guaranteeing the computation of optimal solutions (Sect. 3.2). Finally, we present a declarative ASP encoding which guarantees the computation of optimal solutions (Sect. 3.3).

3.1 Problem Formalization

The input includes the following elements: a set P of products, i.e., the integer interval $[1..|P|]$; a set W of warehouses, i.e., the integer interval $[1..|W|]$; a function $product\_price : P \to \mathbb{N}^+$ assigning a price to each product; a function $product\_request : P \to \mathbb{N}^+$ representing the requested amount of each product; a function $shipping\_fee : W \to \mathbb{N}^+$ assigning a shipping fee to each warehouse; a function $shipping\_free\_threshold : W \rightarrow \mathbb{N}^+$ representing the minimum expense to waive the shipping fee of each warehouse; a function $products\_in\_warehouse : P \times W \rightarrow \mathbb{N}$ providing the available amount of each product in each warehouse. The goal is to select the requested amount of products from warehouses (i.e., computing a function $select : P \times W \rightarrow \mathbb{N}$) minimizing shipping costs, possibly breaking ties by minimizing the number of warehouses involved, and possibly breaking further ties by minimizing the number of pairs warehouse–product involved.

Example 1. Let us consider an instance with $P = [1..2]$, $W = [1..3]$, $product\_request = \{1 \mapsto 7, 2 \mapsto 8\}$, $product\_price = \{1 \mapsto 4, 2 \mapsto 2\}$, $products\_in\_warehouse = \{(1,1) \mapsto 6, (1,2) \mapsto 1, (1,3) \mapsto 9, (2,1) \mapsto 4, (2,2) \mapsto 8, (2,3) \mapsto 0\}$, $shipping\_fee = \{1 \mapsto 1, 2 \mapsto 1, 3 \mapsto 2\}$, $shipping\_free\_threshold = \{1 \mapsto 8, 2 \mapsto 5, 3 \mapsto 20\}$. Below are three admissible solutions:

$$\{(1,1) \mapsto 6, (1,2) \mapsto 0, (1,3) \mapsto 1, (2,1) \mapsto 4, (2,2) \mapsto 4, (2,3) \mapsto 0\} \tag{8}$$

$$\{(1,1) \mapsto 1, (1,2) \mapsto 0, (1,3) \mapsto 6, (2,1) \mapsto 4, (2,2) \mapsto 4, (2,3) \mapsto 0\} \tag{9}$$

$$\{(1,1) \mapsto 6, (1,2) \mapsto 1, (1,3) \mapsto 0, (2,1) \mapsto 1, (2,2) \mapsto 7, (2,3) \mapsto 0\} \tag{10}$$

$$\{(1,1) \mapsto 0, (1,2) \mapsto 0, (1,3) \mapsto 7, (2,1) \mapsto 0, (2,2) \mapsto 8, (2,3) \mapsto 0\} \tag{11}$$

Note that (8) involves warehouse 3 without reaching the threshold for waiving its shipping fee, while (9)–(11) benefit from completely free shipping. Additionally, (10)–(11) also minimize the number of warehouses involved. Finally, (11) also minimizes the number of warehouse–product pairs involved.   ∎

3.2   Greedy Algorithm

A first solution to the problem formalized in Sect. 3.1 is reported as Algorithm 1. It is a greedy algorithm iteratively selecting a warehouse that maximizes the number of requested products available within its supplies, until all requested products are covered by the selection process. In more details, the algorithm builds a *select* function with signature $select : W \times P \rightarrow \mathbb{N}$ representing how many products are taken from each warehouse in order to fulfil the requested amount of products. To this aim, the algorithm repeats the following greedy choices until there are products to cover (line 1): Each warehouse is assigned a *utility* value being the number of requested products available within its supplies (lines 2–3). A warehouse w with maximal utility is selected (line 4), and the maximum amount of requested products is selected from w (lines 6–10). Actually, in case no new products are covered by w, the algorithm terminates reporting the inconsistency of the instance in input (line 5). Note that each warehouse is selected at most once due to the fact that its product supply is updated by line 9, making its utility value 0 for the next iteration.

Algorithm 1 finds an admissible solution if one exists, but cannot guarantee its optimality or an estimate on the distance to the optimum possible value for the shipment cost. In fact, Algorithm 1 returns (8) when run on the instance from Example 1. Moreover, it cannot guarantee to include in the computed solution

---

Algorithm 1: GreedySelect

Input   : sets P and W; functions *product_request* and *products_in_warehouse*
(of type $\mathbf{int}[|P|]$ and $\mathbf{int}[|P|][|W|]$, 1–based arrays)
Output: function *select* (of type $\mathbf{int}[|P|][|W|]$, initially all zeros), or **fail**

1 **while** $\exists\, p \in P$ *such that* $product\_request[p] > 0$ **do**
2   **for** $w \in W$ **do**
3      $utility_w := \sum_{p \in P} \min(product\_in\_warehouse(p, w), product\_request(p))$;
4    $w := \arg\max_{w \in W} utility_w$;
5   **if** $utility_w = 0$ **then return fail**;
6   **for** $p \in P$ **do**
7      $select\_qty := \min(product\_in\_warehouse(p, w), product\_request(p))$;
8      $select[p][w] := select[p][w] + select\_qty$;
9      $product\_in\_warehouse[p][w] := product\_in\_warehouse[p][w] - select\_qty$;
10      $product\_request[p] := product\_request[p] - select\_qty$;

11 **return** *select*;

---

a minimal number of warehouses or pairs of warehouse–product. Therefore, the more sophisticated objective functions defined in Sect. 3.1 are not within its reach. Nonetheless, it can represent a baseline for more thoughtful algorithms.

3.3   ASP Encoding

Given the formalization of the problem reported in Sect. 3.1, developing an ASP encoding for computing optimal solutions of problem instances is quite natural. Products in P and warehouses in W are identified by constants. The input is encoded by the following facts: `product`(p), for each $p \in P$; `warehouse`(w), for each $w \in W$; `product_price`(p,p), for each $p \in P$, where $product\_price(p) = p'$; `product_request`(p,r), for each $p \in P$, where $product\_request(p) = r$; `shipping_fee`(w,f), for each $w \in W$, where $shipping\_fee(w) = f$; `shipping_free_threshold`(w,t), for each $w \in W$, where $shipping\_free\_threshold(w) = t$; `product_in_warehouse`$(p,w,q)$, for each $p \in P$ and each $w \in W$, where $product\_in\_warehouse(p, w) = q$. The output is encoded by facts `select`(p,w,q), for each $p \in P$ and $w \in W$, where q is the quantity of product p selected from warehouse w.

The listing reported in Fig. 1 encodes required conditions. Specifically, it relies on the @-term `@min` implemented in Python (lines 1–3) to limit how many products to select from each warehouse (lines 4–5) so to cover all requested products (line 6). The objective functions are encoded by the weak constraints in lines 7–11. In particular, to minimize the shipment cost is sufficient to include the weak constraint in lines 7–9 alone (the resulting encoding is referred to as $\Pi_{\$}$); if ties have to be broken by minimizing the number of warehouses involved, then also the weak constraint in line 10 is included (the resulting encoding is referred to as $\Pi_{\$W}$); if ties have to be further broken by minimizing the number of warehouse–product pairs involved in the solution, then all weak constraints

```
1 #script(python)
2 def min(a, b): return a if a < b else b
3 #end.
4 {select(P,W,Q') : Q' = 0..@min(Q,R)} = 1 :-
5   product_request(P,R), products_in_warehouse(P,W,Q).
6 :- product_request(P,R), #sum{Q,W : select(P,W,Q)} != R.
7 :~ warehouse_shipping_cost(W,C), warehouse_free_shipping(W,T),
8   #sum{Q' * Price,P : select(P,W,Q'), product_price(P,Price)} < T,
9   select(_,W,Q), Q > 0.  [C@3, W]
10 :~ warehouse(W), select(P,W,Q), Q > 0.  [1@2, W]
11 :~ select(P,W,Q), Q > 0.  [1@1, P,W]
```

Fig. 1. ASP encoding to select products from warehouses

are included in the encoding (the resulting encoding is referred to as $\Pi_{\$WP}$). For the instance from Example 1, solutions (9)–(11) are all accepted by $\Pi_\$$, (10)–(11) are accepted by $\Pi_{\$W}$, while $\Pi_{\$WP}$ only accepts (11).

4 Experiment

The ASP encodings presented in Sect. 3.3 were fast prototyped with ASP CHEF[2] [12], consolidated using the CLINGO PYTHON API [13], and assessed empirically over synthetic instances whose size is uniformly selected among sizes typically handled by the analyzed marketplace. Specifically, the most frequent case for the https://oliveru.com marketplace is an end-user buying no more than 10 different products, usually with a single unit per product. Currently, the number of warehouses registered to the marketplace is 10. Therefore, we generated instances with a random number of products in the range [1..20], each one with random multiplicity in the range [1..20]. The number of warehouses was randomly chosen between 1 and 20, and the available products within each warehouse was randomly chosen in the range [1..20]. A total of 1,000 instances were generated. Generated instances were processed using CLINGO (version 5.6.2) by activating the *unsatisfiable core analysis algorithm* K [14] with *reiterated geometric search unsatisfiable core shrinking* [15] (command line --opt-strategy=usc,k,0,5 --opt-usc-shrink=rgs). Tests were run on an Intel(R) Core(TM) i7-8565U CPU @ 1.80GHz with 12GB of RAM. The measured values are the execution time, the cost of the computed solution, the number of warehouses involved, and the number of warehouse–product pairs involved.

Experimental result are reported in Fig. 2. First of all, we observe that the greedy algorithm terminates in less than 0.01 s on all tested instances, while running the ASP encodings $\Pi_\$$, $\Pi_{\$W}$, $\Pi_{\$WP}$ requires around 0.05 s, 0.05 s, 0.08 s

---

[2] Example 1 available on https://asp-chef.alviano.net/s/marketplace@padl2024; accessed on 23 November 2023.

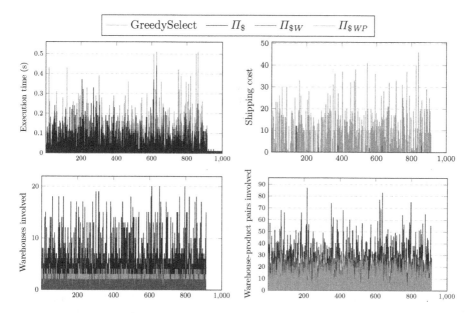

Fig. 2. Experimental results (bar plots with instance number of the x-axis)

on average. For completeness we report that running CLINGO with its default configuration takes several seconds to process $\Pi_{\$WP}$, which is not compatible with the requirements of the marketplace. Moreover, 86 of the 1,000 generated instances do not have feasible solutions, and their statistics are shown on the rightmost positions in the plots. It can be noted that CLINGO detects the inconsistency with negligible effort. The other plots in Fig. 2 measure the quality of the computed solution. Regarding the shipping cost, all ASP encodings obtain the same result, and therefore we focus on $\Pi_{\$}$. Interestingly, the shipping cost is often 0, meaning that shipping fees are correctly waived when possible. As for the number of warehouses involved, the same result is obtained by $\Pi_{\$W}$ and $\Pi_{\$WP}$, and therefore we consider only $\Pi_{\$}$ and $\Pi_{\$W}$, as well as the greedy algorithm. It can be observed that the greedy algorithm is more targeted on minimizing the number of warehouses involved rather than the resulting shipping cost. Nonetheless, the activation of the weak constraint of level 2 significantly reduces the number of warehouses involved, aligning them to the small number obtained by the greedy algorithm but keeping the minimum shipping cost. A similar observation applies to the number of warehouse-product pairs involved in the process, with the greedy algorithm performing well, and ASP slightly improving such a baseline thanks to the activation of the weak constraint of level (i.e., program $\Pi_{\$WP}$).

5   Conclusion

ASP proved to be effective in addressing the combinatorial problems of the analyzed platform, for instances of expected size for the volume of the business managed handled by the marketplace. Apart from computational efficiency, the ASP specification given in Sect. 3.3 provides a uniform solution to the three combinatorial problems of interest, depending on the weak constraints that are kept active. The generated assignment of products to deliver from each warehouse can be the subject of subsequent optimization in-warehouse logistics. For example, an automated warehouse would need to compute a collision-free schedule of robot movements and actions to deliver all required products [16].

Acknowledgment. This work was partially supported by Italian Ministry of Research (MUR) under PRIN project PRODE "Probabilistic declarative process mining", CUP H53D23003420006 under PNRR project FAIR "Future AI Research", CUP H23C22000860006, under PNRR project Tech4You "Technologies for climate change adaptation and quality of life improvement", CUP H23C22000370006, and under PNRR project SERICS "SEcurity and RIghts in the CyberSpace", CUP H73C22000880001; by Italian Ministry of Health (MSAL) under POS projects CAL.HUB.RIA (CUP H53C22000800006) and RADIOAMICA (CUP H53C22000650006); by the LAIA lab (part of the SILA labs) and by GNCS-INdAM.

References

1. Radhakrishnan, V.: E-commerce industry and its effect on the world today. Int. Res. J. Adv. Sci. Hub **3**, 23–29 (2021)
2. Catalán, A., Fisher, M.: Assortment allocation to distribution centers to minimize split customer orders. SSRN Electr. J. (2012)
3. Dutta, P., Mishra, A., Khandelwal, S., Katthawala, I.: A multiobjective optimization model for sustainable reverse logistics in Indian e-commerce market. J. Clean. Prod. **249**, 3 (2020)
4. Zhang, C., Ma, H.M.: Introduction of the marketplace channel under logistics service sharing in an e-commerce platform. Comput. Industr. Eng. **163**, 107724 (2022)
5. Qin, X., Liu, Z., Tian, L.: The strategic analysis of logistics service sharing in an e-commerce platform. Omega (United Kingdom) **92**, 102153 (2020)
6. Sunil Kumar and Rajendra Prasad Mahapatra: Design of multi-warehouse inventory model for an optimal replenishment policy using a rain optimization algorithm. Knowl.-Based Syst. **231**, 11 (2021)
7. Ali Reza Moazzeni and Ehsan Khamehchi: Rain optimization algorithm (ROA): a new metaheuristic method for drilling optimization solutions. J. Petrol. Sci. Eng. **195**, 12 (2020)

8. OECD. Unpacking E-commerce: Business Models, Trend and Policies. OECD Publishing, Paris (2019)
9. Marek, V., Truszczyński, M.: Stable models and an alternative logic programming paradigm. In: Apt, K.R., Marek, V.W., Truszczynski, M., Warren, D.S. (eds.) The Logic Programming Paradigm. Artificial Intelligence, pp. 375–398. Springer, Berlin (1999). https://doi.org/10.1007/978-3-642-60085-2_17
10. Niemelä, I.: Logic programming with stable model semantics as a constraint programming paradigm. Ann. Math. Artif. Intell. **25**(3,4), 241–273 (1999)
11. Calimeri, F., et al.: ASP-Core-2 input language format. Theory Pract. Log. Program. **20**(2), 294–309 (2020)
12. Alviano, M., Cirimele, D., Reiners, L.A.R.: Introducing ASP recipes and ASP chef. In: Arias, J., et al. (eds.) Proceedings of the International Conference on Logic Programming 2023, Workshops co-located with the 39th International Conference on Logic Programming (ICLP 2023), London, United Kingdom, July 9th and 10th, 2023, volume 3437 of CEUR Workshop Proceedings. CEUR-WS.org (2023)
13. Gebser, M., Kaufmann, B., Schaub, T.: Conflict-driven answer set solving: from theory to practice. Artif. Intell. **187**, 52–89 (2012)
14. Alviano, M., Dodaro, C., Ricca, F.: A MaxSAT algorithm using cardinality constraints of bounded size. In: Yang, Q., Wooldridge, M.J. (eds.) Proceedings of the Twenty-Fourth International Joint Conference on Artificial Intelligence, IJCAI 2015, Buenos Aires, Argentina, 25–31 July 2015, pp. 2677–2683. AAAI Press (2015)
15. Alviano, M., Dodaro, C.: Anytime answer set optimization via unsatisfiable core shrinking. Theory Pract. Log. Program. **16**(5–6), 533–551 (2016)
16. Rajaratnam, D., Schaub, T., Wanko, P., Chen, K., Liu, S., Son, T.C.: Solving an industrial-scale warehouse delivery problem with answer set programming modulo difference constraints. Algorithms **16**(4), 216 (2023)

Rhyme: A Data-Centric Expressive Query Language for Nested Data Structures

Supun Abeysinghe$^{(\boxtimes)}$ and Tiark Rompf

Purdue University, West Lafayette, IN 47906, USA
{tabeysin,tiark}@purdue.com

Abstract. We present Rhyme, an expressive language designed for high-level data manipulation, with a primary focus on querying and transforming nested structures such as JSON and tensors, while yielding nested structures as output. Rhyme draws inspiration from a diverse range of declarative languages, including Datalog, JQ, JSONiq, Einstein summation (Einsum), GraphQL, and more recent functional logic programming languages like Verse. It has a syntax that closely resembles existing object notation, is compositional, and has the ability to perform query optimization and code generation through the construction of an intermediate representation (IR). Our IR comprises loop-free and branch-free code with program structure implicitly captured via dependencies. To demonstrate Rhyme's versatility, we implement Rhyme in JavaScript (as an embedded DSL) and illustrate its application across various domains, showcasing its ability to express common data manipulation queries, tensor expressions (à la Einsum), and more.

Keywords: Declarative query languages · Logic programming · Tensor expressions · Multi-paradigm languages · Rhyme

1 Introduction

Declarative programming represents a paradigm in which users articulate *what* computation needs to be performed, without the explicit specification of the procedural steps required for its execution. Declarative programming languages find application across a diverse array of domains. Notable examples include SQL, employed for data querying and manipulation, Datalog [14], used for data querying as well as in domains like declarative program analysis [21,28,34] and binary decompilation [16], Einstein notation (or similar domain specific languages [35]) for expressing tensor computations mathematically, and GraphQL [19] for data querying within the context of web application front-ends, and so on.

In practical scenarios where diverse paradigms of workloads are combined (e.g., data frames + tensors), the necessity arises to employ multiple query languages or systems in tandem. Each of these languages interfaces with the respective engines tasked with handling individual workloads. However, this approach is inherently inefficient, both from a performance perspective, due to the reliance

M. Gebser and I. Sergey (Eds.): PADL 2024, LNCS 14512, pp. 64–81, 2023.
https://doi.org/10.1007/978-3-031-52038-9_5

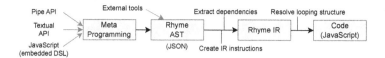

Fig. 1. End-to-end workflow of Rhyme, with green markers indicating various entry points leading to the common entry point, Rhyme AST. The Rhyme AST can be constructed directly from external tools or via metaprogramming using different APIs. This AST serves as the basis for generating an IR (with dependencies), driving subsequent code generation.

on multiple isolated backends, and from a programmer productivity standpoint, as it necessitates learning and maintaining code written in multiple query languages.

A promising approach to address the performance challenge is to construct common intermediate layers across multiple domain-specific systems [8,27,32]. In such cases, the respective query languages or system interfaces for different domains act as frontends that emit fragments of intermediate representation (IR) logic corresponding to their portion of the computation. These IR fragments are then assembled to create a unified IR for the combined workload, allowing for global optimizations and the generation of a unified executable. However, a common limitation in these systems is the requirement for individual system developers to implement *all* their operators using a limited set of generic IR operators, which becomes a bottleneck in practice [8].

In this work, we address this challenge by introducing a unified query language, named Rhyme[1], that comprises a general substrate capable of accommodating a wide array of different use cases. While our approach shares some similarities with the idea of constructing common IRs, it distinguishes itself by focusing on a higher-level, more expressive common substrate. This distinction allows for the intuitive expression of various workload paradigms, as elaborated throughout the paper. Rhyme takes inspiration from many existing declarative languages including GraphQL, JQ [3], XQuery [4], JSONPath [18], Einstein notation, Datalog, recent functional logic programming languages like Verse [10], etc. Rhyme is designed to serve as an expressive language for high-level data manipulation, enabling the querying and transformation of nested data structures (e.g., JSON, tensors) and producing nested structures as output.

There are several key defining characteristics of Rhyme. First, Rhyme adopts a query syntax that closely mirrors existing object notation, meaning that queries are essentially expressed as JSON objects. Second, Rhyme is designed in a way that permits query optimization and code generation via the construction of an intermediate representation (IR). This IR contains loop-free and branch-free code with dependencies that implicitly capture the program structure. Third, Rhyme is compositional and easy to meta-program, recognizing that data transformation queries are typically used as part of larger programs and are often generated programmatically.

---

[1] https://rhyme-lang.github.io.

```
// input dataset
let data = [
  {key: "A", val: 10},
  {key: "B", val: 15},
  {key: "A", val: 25}
]
// query
sum('data.*.val')
// AST constructed from the query:
{agg: 'sum', param: 'data.*.val'}
// result: 50
```

```
1 let tmp = {}
2 // ??= is assign if null operator
3 tmp[0] ??= 0
4 for (let star in data) {
5   tmp[0] += data[star]['val']
6 }
7 return tmp[0]
```

(a) A query computing the sum of all values

```
// query
{
  total: sum('data.*.val'),
  'data.*.key': sum('data.*.val')
}
// AST constructed from the query:
{
  total:
    {agg: 'sum', param: 'data.*.val'},
  'data.*.key':
    {agg: 'sum', param: 'data.*.val'}
}
// result:
// { total: 50,
//   'A': 35,
//   'B': 15 }
```

```
1 let tmp = {}
2 tmp[0] ??= {}
3 tmp[0]['total'] ??= 0
4
5 for (let star in data) {
6   tmp[0]['total'] += data[star]['val']
7   tmp[0][data[star]['key']] ??= 0
8   tmp[0][data[star]['key']] += data[star]['val']
9 }
10 return tmp[0]
```

(b) A query computing sum of all values (**total**) and sum per each key

```
// query
{
  'data.*A.key': div(sum('data.*A.val'),
                     sum('data.*B.val'))
}
// AST constructed from the query:
{
  'data.*.key': {
    path: 'div',
    param: [
      {agg: 'sum', param: 'data.*A.val'},
      {agg: 'sum', param: 'data.*B.val'}
    ]
  }
}
// result:
// {'A': 0.7, 'B': 0.3}
```

```
1 let tmp = {}
2 tmp[1] ??= {}
3 tmp[2] ??= 0
4
5 for (let starB in data) { // loop hoisted!
6   tmp[2] += data[starB]['val']
7 }
8
9 tmp[0] ??= {}
10 for (let starA in data) {
11   tmp[1][data[starA]['key']] ??= 0;
12   tmp[1][data[starA]['key']] +=
                     data[starA]['val']
13   tmp[0][data[starA]['key']] =
                     tmp[1][data[starA]['key']] / tmp[2]
14 }
15 return tmp[0]
```

(c) A query computing key-specific relative aggregate proportions

Fig. 2. The end-to-end workflow of Rhyme for three queries, starting with the query and the corresponding AST (left; Sect. 2.5), followed by the construction of the IR (center; Sect. 4.1), and the final generated code (right).

Figure 1 provides an overview of the end-to-end workflow of Rhyme. The central point of entry into this workflow is the Rhyme AST (Sect. 2.5). Notably, this AST is represented in JSON format and is hence serializable, enabling the ability to be exported/imported from various other environments. We implement Rhyme as an embedded DSL in JavaScript (JS), which constructs the Rhyme AST from Rhyme queries. Additionally, alternative interfaces can be used, such as pipes (Sect. 3.1), or entirely textual inputs that can be processed by a parser to construct the same AST. Once the AST is constructed, it gets transformed into Rhyme IR. During this transformation, declarative query operators are mapped to IR instructions along with their dependencies. Subsequently, this IR is used to analyze the looping structure and generate the final code.

Consider the query in Fig. 2a. In Rhyme, `data.*.val` is called a *path* expression, a notation inspired by JSONPath [18]. The ∗ symbol serves as an iterator, facilitating iteration through the `val` values, while the aggregator `sum` calculates the sum of these iterated values. Rhyme's IR (shown in the center) consists of two main types of operators. First, it has *generators* (represented as *rounded rectangles*), which represents iterators that enumerate a list of items (ultimately translated into loops in the generated code). In our example, `data.*` is a generator, iterating values from the data object. Second, the IR has *assignments* (represented as rectangles), comprising the computations required for executing the query. In the case of our first query, the initialization logic `tmp[0] ??= 0` and the subsequent sum computation `tmp[0] += ...` are assignments.

Notably, the IR operates without the need for explicit control flow constructs. Instead, the program's structure is implicitly inferred through dependencies. For our example query, the assignment `tmp[0] += ...` has dependencies to both the initializer (because initialization must come first) and the generator (because its operand is the iterated value). Additionally, it is worth noting that computations are performed on temporary state variables (`tmp[0]` in the first example). This approach, utilizing intermediate temporaries, draws inspiration from works such as RPAI [7] and DBToaster [22]. These systems utilize such state variables to maintain values for various sub-queries of the main query, which are then used to compute the final result. Finally, the IR is translated into JS code (and eventually run using `eval()`), taking dependencies into account to extract the program structure and performing optimizations as part of this transformation process.

Figure 2b and Fig. 2c illustrate two additional queries executed on the same dataset. Specifically, in Fig. 2b, we compute both the total sum of all values (similar to the query in Fig. 2a) and the sum of values per key, effectively a group-by sum operation. A key characteristic of Rhyme lies in the contextual interpretation of expressions such as `sum(data.*.val)`. That is, the semantics of this expression differs depending on its context. This is similar to local unification semantics in Verse [10]. For instance, when it is nested within {`data.*.key:` ...}, the expression signifies a group-by sum operation. Conversely, if it is not nested within an iterator (i.e., ∗), it calculates the aggregate over the entire set of values. This distinction is exemplified in the query presented in Fig. 2c. Here, `sum(data.*A.val)` is nested within {`data.*A.key:` ...}, signifying a group-by aggregate operation. Conversely, `sum(data.*B.val)` computes a total aggregate, as it is not nested within a ∗B iterator.

Additionally, Fig. 2c also demonstrates an optimization that occurs at the IR level. Specifically, even though the `sum(data.*B.val)` appears as a nested sub-query in the original query, the Rhyme backend can determine that the generated ∗B can be hoisted out as a separate loop by analyzing the IR dependencies. This is essentially similar to sub-query hoisting that happens at the logical plan level in other traditional query optimizers.

These examples provide a broad overview of Rhyme's functionalities and its syntactic structure. In the subsequent sections of this paper, we will delve deeper into the syntax and capabilities of Rhyme and discuss the process of IR construction and code generation. Moreover, the previous example queries focused on Rhyme's capability to express analytical queries on JSON objects. However, Rhyme covers an even broader spectrum of use cases, including the ability to express tensor computations and declaratively specify visual components (e.g., tables, charts) of web applications.

Our specific contributions are as follows.

- We introduce the syntax of Rhyme, showcasing the ability to express common data manipulation operators such as selections, group-bys, joins, user-defined functions (UDFs), and others (Sect. 2).
- We highlight the versatility of Rhyme across various use cases, including the expression of visual elements in web applications (e.g., tables, charts using SVG), declarative tensor computations (akin to Einsum), and alternative 'pipe' APIs via metaprogramming (Sect. 3).
- We elucidate the process of lowering queries into an IR that features loop-free and branch-free code, with dependencies implicitly representing the program structure. Then, we illustrate how this IR facilitates code generation by constructing the optimal program structure from dependencies (Sect. 4).
- We evaluate the performance of Rhyme on several JSON analytics workloads to demonstrate the effectiveness of our code generation approach (Sect. 5).

We discuss related work in Sect. 6, followed by conclusions and potential future research directions in Sect. 7.

2   The Rhyme Query Language

In the previous section, we saw Rhyme in action for a set of relatively simple queries. In this section, we will introduce the syntax of Rhyme, illustrating how it facilitates the expression of common data manipulation operations like selections, aggregates, group-bys, and so on. The formal grammar is shown in Fig. 3. The rest of this section illustrates how each of these components are used to express different kinds of queries. To improve understanding, we will employ a running illustrative example dataset, as depicted below. The dataset contains populations of several major cities, along with the respective country. Our chosen dataset is deliberately kept simple, devoid of intricate nested structures. However, Rhyme has the capacity to seamlessly query nested JSON data in the same way. We will see such examples later in Sect. 3.

```
let data = [
  {country: "Japan",   city: "Tokyo",      population: 14},
  {country: "China",   city: "Beijing",    population: 22},
  {country: "France",  city: "Paris",      population: 3},
  {country: "UK",      city: "London",     population: 9},
  {country: "Japan",   city: "Osaka",      population: 3},
  {country: "UK",      city: "Birmingham", population: 2}
]
```

$$\begin{aligned}
\text{Ident} &::= \texttt{[a-zA-Z\_][a-zA-Z0-9\_]}^* \\
\text{Num} &::= \texttt{[0-9]+} \\
\text{Var} &::= *\ \text{Ident} \\
\text{ScalarOp} &::= \texttt{get} \mid \texttt{apply} \mid \texttt{plus} \mid \texttt{minus} \\
&\quad\mid \texttt{div} \mid \texttt{fdiv} \mid \texttt{times} \mid \texttt{mod} \\
\text{ReductionOp} &::= \texttt{sum} \mid \texttt{count} \mid \texttt{max} \mid \texttt{min} \\
&\quad\mid \texttt{first} \mid \texttt{last} \mid \texttt{array}
\end{aligned}$$

$$\begin{aligned}
\text{Atom} &::= \text{Ident} \mid \text{Num} \mid \text{Var} \\
\text{Path} &::= \text{Atom} \ (\ .\ \text{Atom}\ )^* \\
\text{Expr} &::= \ \text{Path} \\
&\quad\mid \text{Expr ScalarOp Expr} \\
&\quad\mid \text{ReductionOp (Expr)} \\
&\quad\mid [\ \text{Expr}\ ] \\
&\quad\mid \{\ (\ \text{Path} : \text{Expr}\ )^*\ \} \\
\text{Query} &::= \text{Expr}
\end{aligned}$$

Fig. 3. Syntax for expressing Rhyme queries.

2.1 Basics

First we will look at how to perform several basic query operations on the afore-mentioned dataset. For instance, if we want to select a particular key of the dataset at a given index, we can use the following syntax.

```
'data.2.country'        // result: France
{first : 'data.0.country'}  // result: {first: Japan}
```

Here, the reference `data` refers to the dataset object, and can be simply indexed through integer indices. Furthermore, specific keys can be selected by specifying the desired key names (e.g., `.country`). Notably, Rhyme offers the convenience of the familiar JS-like syntax for constructing structured output from extracted values, as exemplified in the second instance.

While this form of explicit indexing into the array can be useful for several use cases, generally, queries involve some form of iterating over the dataset. Rhyme offers this capability through the * operator, serving as an implicit iteration operator. Moreover, as we saw in Fig. 2c, we can perform controlled iteration with multiple generator symbols (e.g., *A, *B, etc.). In fact, these generator symbols behave like logic variables in Datalog, Prolog, and other logic programming languages as we see in Sect. 3.2. Below, we present three example queries that leverage iterators and compute aggregates over the iterated values.

```
['data.*.city']         // result: [Tokyo, Beijing, ..., Birmingham]
sum('data.*.population') // result: 53
max('data.*.population') // result: 22
```

These queries are self-explanatory in nature. In the first example, we illustrate a scenario where an array can be constructed from the values obtained through iteration, employing the [...] syntax. Moreover, users can compute aggregates over the iterated values using the relevant aggregate functions, such as `sum`, `max`, and so forth. As discussed previously, these queries can be used as parts of object construction logic and combined flexibly, as shown below.

```
{ total: sum('data.*.population'),    // result:
  highest: max('data.*.population') }  // {total: 53, highest: 22}
```

2.2 Group By

Another vital query operator, especially relevant to JSON-style objects, is the group-by query. Rhyme offers an intuitive means of implicitly expressing group-bys. The following query exemplifies this, grouping records based on the `country` attribute and subsequently calculating the total population for each group:

```
{ 'data.*.country': sum('data.*.population') }
// result: {Japan: 17, China: 22, France: 3, UK: 11}
```

Here, specifying `{data.*.country: ...}` as the key implies that any iteration carried out within this key utilizing the same iterator (∗) is performed for records with each unique value of `country` separately. The next example shows how to use this form of grouping to compute aggregates at different levels. It computes the total population of all records, breaks it down by country, and subsequently computes the population proportion of each city with respect to total population:

```
let query = {
  total: sum('data.*.population'),           // total population
  'data.*.country': {
    total: sum('data.*.population'),          // population per country
    'data.*.city': div(sum('data.*.population'),   // population proportion
                       sum('data.*A.population'))}  // (per each city)
}
// result: {total: 53, Japan: {total: 17, Tokyo: 0.26, Osaka: 0.06}, ...}
```

In the given query, the `sum('data.*.population')` at each query level computes distinct results: total population, total population per country, and population per city, respectively. If we had multiple population values for a given city (e.g., county data), then the last aggregation would compute the per city sum. As previously discussed, since `sum('data.*A.population')` is not nested within a ∗A key, it performs a total aggregation, which sums all the population values. It is worth noting that our implementation employs calls like `div` for some operators since it functions as an embedded DSL in JS. In a textual frontend, the query could appear even more concise, using standard operators like `/` for division.

2.3   Join

Joins are another fundamental operator in data querying. To illustrate how joins work in Rhyme, consider the following new dataset named `other`, which includes information about the `region` to which each country belongs:

```
let other = [
  {country: "Japan",  region: "Asia"},
  {country: "China",  region: "Asia"},
  {country: "France", region: "Europe"},
  {country: "UK",     region: "Europe"},
]
```

Now, consider a scenario where we aim to compute aggregate population values based on regions. For this, we must perform a join between our original `data` and this new `other` object to acquire the corresponding region for each country. The following Rhyme query illustrates how this is expressed.

```
let countryToRegion = {             // create a mapping of
  'other.*0.country': 'other.*0.region'   // country -> region
}
let query = {
  '-': keyval(get(countryToRegion, 'data.*.country'), { // Use of "-" and keyval is because
```

```
total: sum('data.*.population')                    // JS enforces JSON keys to be
  'data.*.country' : sum('data.*.population')       // strings and our key is a var
})
}
// result: {Asia: {total:39, Japan:17, China:22}, Europe: {total:14, France:3, UK:11}}
```

Here, we use a distinct query (`countryToRegion`) to retrieve the corresponding region for a given country. The main query conducts a group-by based
on the `region` (retrieved using `get`) first, followed by another group-by based
on `country`, ultimately computing the desired aggregates. We use `'-'` in our
implementation due to JS's requirement that JSON keys be represented as
strings. Consequently, specifying `get(countryToRegion, 'data.*.country')` as
the key directly is not possible. Hence, we introduce `keyval(<key>, <value>)` as
a workaround that allows arbitrary arguments to be used as a key. It is worth
noting that in a textual frontend, such workarounds would not be necessary.

2.4   User-Defined Functions

Rhyme allows using user-defined functions (UDFs) written in JS seamlessly with
the queries. Consider a simple query where we want to obtain the percentage
population per each country from our dataset.

```
let udf = {
  formatPercent: v => (v*100).toFixed(2) + "%
}
let query = {
  'data.*.country':
    apply(udf.formatPercent, div(sum('data.*.population'), sum('data.*A.population')))
}
// result: {Japan: 32.05%
```

We have defined the UDF `formatPercent` that, given a proportion value,
computes the percentage and adds a % sign at the end. We can then use `apply`
in the query to call this UDF to convert the proportions to percentages.

2.5   Rhyme AST

As we saw in Figs. 1 and 2, all the queries above construct a Rhyme AST representation which serves as the basis for the dependency analysis and IR construction. This AST representation is in JSON format, and closely mirrors the query
JSON structure. The difference is, all the calls to reducers like `sum`, `count`, etc.
and other operations like `plus`, `minus`, etc. will be translated to explicit object
components with `agg` (or `path`) and the corresponding arguments. Here, `agg` is
for reducers (which are stateful), and `path` is for operations simply performs
a lookup and some computation. For instance, Fig. 2c (left) shows how `sum` is
translated to `agg` and `param`, and `div` is translated to `path` and `param`.

This AST representation serves as the entry point for our compiler backend,
and gets translated into an IR, as elucidated in Sect. 4. Moreover, as depicted in
Fig. 1, the creation of this AST is not limited to the aforementioned JS embedding. Instead, it can be constructed using different APIs, (e.g., Fluent API introduced in Sect. 3.1), or a textual frontend with a parser, and so on.

3   Case Studies

3.1   Fluent API

Rhyme's query frontend (JSON) we saw in Sect. 2 describes the query using the structure of the computed *result*. However, sometimes, it is more natural to start from the structure of the *input*, and specify a sequence of transformation steps. Given that our frontend is embedded in JS, we can use metaprogramming to layer a LINQ-style [24] pipeline API on top.

To illustrate the advantages of such an interface, consider a simple task borrowed from Advent of Code 2022 [1]. The task involves processing a sequence of values partitioned into chunks, each containing multiple values. The objective is to calculate the sum of values for each chunk and subsequently identify the maximum sum among those computed. To begin, let us examine how the Rhyme query appears when utilizing the familiar JSON-style API for data parsing and computation. First, we define several user-defined functions (UDFs) to assist with data parsing. The role of each UDF is simple and self-explanatory.

```
let input = '100,200,300|400|500,600|700,800,900|1000' // sample input
// some UDFs for parsing the data
let udf = {
  'splitPipe'  : x => x.split('|'),
  'splitComma' : x => x.split(','),
  'toNum'      : x => Number(x)
}
```

Shown below is the Rhyme query responsible for executing the required computation, with comments provided alongside to elucidate each section of the query (numbered for clarity):

```
1 let query = max(get({         // 5. find maximum among group sums
2   '*chunk': sum(              // 4. group-by chunk and compute sum
3     apply('udf.toNum',        // 3. convert each string number to a number object
4     get(apply('udf.splitComma', // 2. split by comma to get numbers of each chunk
5       get(apply('udf.splitPipe', '.input'), '*chunk')), // 1. split into chunks
6       '*line')))
7 },'*'))
```

Function `apply()` is used to apply UDFs to arguments; `get()`, when used with an unbounded generator symbol (e.g., *chunk), binds the iterator to the object in the first argument. For example, in Line 5, `get(..., '*chunk')` binds the iterator *chunk to the result of splitting the output by the pipe symbol (|). While this approach works as intended and yields the correct results, for these kinds of workloads, it is more natural to think starting from the input instead of the output structure. In such cases, Rhyme's 'fluent' interface offers an alternative way to express this query concisely as shown below. Here, we specify the query as a sequence of transformation steps on the input. This high-level fluent API essentially functions as a metaprogramming layer that generates an equivalent Rhyme AST as before.

```
let query =
  pipe('.input')
    .map('udf.splitPipe').get('*chunk') // 1. split into chunks (and bind to *chunk)
    .map('udf.splitComma').get('*line') // 2. split by comma to get numbers of each chunk
    .map('udf.toNum')                   // 3. convert each string number to a number object
```

```
.sum().group('*chunk').get('*')      // 4. group-by chunk and compute sum
.max()                               // 5. find maximum among group sums
```

The `pipe()` function creates a `Pipe` object equipped with methods `sum`, `max`, and so on, all of which return a `Pipe`. The `map()` function, similar to `apply()` mentioned earlier, is employed to apply a UDF, and `group()` is used to perform a group-by (i.e., `e.group(x)` is `{x : e}`).

3.2   Tensor Expressions

Rhyme provides an elegant framework for expressing tensor computations, drawing inspiration from the Einstein summation (Einsum) notation frequently employed in tensor frameworks and Einops [29]. The Einsum notation offers a concise means of articulating tensor computations. For instance, $ik, kj \rightarrow ij$ specifies a standard matrix product that takes two two-dimensional tensors (i.e., matrices A and B), and yields a third tensor (say C), as the result, computed as $C_{ij} = \sum_k A_{ik} \times B_{kj}$. Likewise, complex tensor computations involving multiple n-dimensional tensors can be specified using such declarative expressions.

Rhyme provides a similar way to express tensor computations in a declarative fashion. To perform tensor computations, we rely on using the notion of unbounded iterators in Rhyme. Specifically, in prior cases, we explicitly specified the data source from which we iterate, as seen in constructs like `data.*A`. However, if instead we only specify the iterator as the key, Rhyme's backend automatically determines the appropriate data source by examining the query body. For instance, when we have a query like `{*i: sum(times(A.*i, B.*i))}`, the backend selects either `A` or `B` as the data source for iteration. Subsequently, the generated code ensures that the iterated values exist in both `A` and `B`. This concept essentially parallels the notion of unification in logic programming, and more specifically narrowing in functional logic programming [10, 20].

To demonstrate how tensor computations are expressed in Rhyme, let's consider some examples. While Rhyme accommodates tensors in various nested formats, for the sake of simplicity, we will consider a scenario where we represent tensors using JS Arrays, as illustrated below:

```
let A = [[1, 2], [3, 4]]; let B = [[1, 2, 3], [4, 5, 6]]
```

Shown below are a set of example tensor computations expressed in Rhyme. Einsum notation counterparts (which closely mirror Rhyme query structure) are shown in parentheses for each example.

```
// tensor transpose (ij->ji)              // matrix multiplication (ik,kj->ij)
{'*j': {'*i': 'B.*i.*j'}}                 {'*i': {'*j': sum(
// sum of all elements (ij->)               times('A.*i.*k', 'B.*k.*j')) }}
sum('B.*i.*j')                            // Hadamard product (ij,ij->ij)
// column sum (ij->j)                     {'*i': {'*j': times('A.*i.*j', 'B.*i.*j') }}
{'*j': sum('B.*i.*j')}                    // general tensor contraction (n-d Tensors)
// row sum (ij->i)                        // e.g., pqrs,tuqvr->pstuv
{'*i': sum('B.*i.*j')}                    {'*p':{'*s':{'*t':{'*u':{'*v':sum(
// dot product (vector-vector) (i,i->)      times('T1.*p.*q.*r.*s',
sum(times('vecA.*i', 'vecB.*i'))              'T2.*t.*u.*q.*v.*r')) }}}}}
```

One benefit of having a unified query language for both data manipulation and tensor computations is the ability to handle combined workloads efficiently.

To illustrate this, consider a simplified version of computing a city's 'crime index' (taken from [27]). We first select a set of features of cities (e.g., population, adult population and number of robberies), followed by a dot product with a predefined weight vector.

```
let cityVec = { 'data.*.city': ['data.*.pop', 'data.*.adultPop', 'data.*.numRobs'] }
let weightVec = [1.0, 1.0, -2000.0] // weight of each feature
let crimeIndex = { // dot product
  'data.*.city': sum(times('weightVec.*i', get(get(cityVec, 'data.*.city'), '*i')))
} // computes the crime index for each city
```

We can specify both the data manipulation component (i.e., the projection) and the tensor computation (i.e., dot product) within the same query language, and we generate a unified code for the combined task. While we kept the example simple for brevity, this has the potential to optimize practical intricate workloads that combine data processing with tensor computations.

3.3   Declarative Visualizations

Since Rhyme is embedded within JS, we can extend its capabilities by introducing a means to *declaratively* specify the visual components of websites using a similar structural approach. This allows the seamless integration of data querying logic with the corresponding data visualization logic, such as creating tables. This is enabled by a special key called '$display'. To illustrate this, consider the following example query, alongside its corresponding output:

```
{
  '$display': 'table'    // display data in a table
  rows: [0], cols: [1], // row:data index, col:keys
  data: [
    {region:"Asia",city:"Beijing",
      "population":{'$display':'bar',value:40}},
    {region:"Asia",city:"Tokyo",
      "population":{'$display':'bar',value:70}}
  ]
}
```

	region	city	population
0	Asia	Beijing	▭
1	Asia	Tokyo	▭

The query above produces the visualization shown on the right. Specifically, it declaratively specifies to display a table that has data as the underlying data. This data can be some raw JSON or another Rhyme query. Notice that we can mix, and manipulate these components as valid values inside Rhyme queries, and compose them as necessary. For instance, the progress bars are manipulated as values in the query. These visualizations can take various forms, including standard DOM elements like h1, p, or high-level components like table, bar, select, and more, as well as SVG objects.

To exemplify the practical utility of this approach, consider a scenario involving the visualization of data related to mobile phone supplier warehouses. Imagine the raw data is represented as an array of JSON objects, each featuring attributes such as warehouse, product, model, and quantity. Before delving into the main query, shown below is a helper query. This auxiliary query calculates the sum of quantities, generates a formatted percentage total, and presents this information as a progress bar displaying the corresponding percentage.

```
let computeEntry = {
  'Quantity': sum('data.*.quantity'),
  'Percent': apply('udf.formatPercent',
      div(sum('data.*.quantity'),sum('data.*B.quantity'))),
  'Bar Chart': {
    '$display': 'bar',
    value: apply('udf.percent', div(sum('data.*.quantity'), sum('data.*B.quantity')))
  }
}
```

As previously discussed, the semantics of these aggregations varies depending on the calling context. For instance, when invoked within the context of {'data.*.warehouse': ...}, the aggregates computed on * iterators are grouped based on the warehouse attribute. Below, we present a query that leverages the above sub query and visualizes our data in a pivot table. This query performs aggregations at multiple levels and displays each level of aggregate in a single table as shown on the right. Naturally, this repeated structure could be abstracted further into a single operation such as rollup('data.*', [model, product, warehouse], computeEntry).

```
let query = {
  '$display': 'table',
  ...
  data: { Total: {
    props: computeEntry, // total aggregate
    children: {'data.*.warehouse': {
    props: computeEntry, // warehouse-level aggr
    children: 'data.*.product': {
    props: computeEntry, // product-level aggr
    children: {
      'data.*.model': // model-level aggr
        computeEntry
    }
  }
  ...
}
```

	Quantity	Bar Chart	Percent Total
Total	1210		100 %
San Jose	650		53 %
iPhone	300		24 %
7	50		4 %
6s	100		8 %
X	150		12 %
Samsung	350		28 %
Galaxy S	200		16 %
Note 8	150		12 %
San Francisco	560		46 %
iPhone	260		21 %
7	10		0 %
6s	50		4 %

We can similarly use Rhyme to visualize data in different types of charts using SVG graphics (such examples are omitted due to space concerns). Regarding how this visualizations are handled in the backend, we start by building the necessary helper functions to create these components (tables, bars, etc.) programmatically. Then, the backend is augmented to use these functions whenever a '$display' is encountered. Our ultimate goal of these kinds of integrations is to enable users to use Rhyme to build interactive dashboards and CRUD applications directly from a single query.

4 IR and Code Generation

Up to this point, we have provided an introduction to the syntax of Rhyme and explored its versatility across various domains. In Fig. 1 and Fig. 2, we gained a preliminary understanding of how Rhyme queries are transformed into an IR, which subsequently serves as the basis for generating optimized code. In this section, we will delve into a detailed discussion of the IR structure and the code generation process.

4.1   IR Structure

As discussed in Sect. 1 (Fig. 2), the IR structure of Rhyme consists of two primary types of instructions: *generators* and *assignments*. Generators correspond to iterators responsible for enumerating input or intermediate nested objects, and these generators are transformed into loops in the generated code. Assignments, on the other hand, encompass any form of computation that updates or initializes an intermediate or output state.

Rhyme queries inherently exhibit nested iterating structures that could be simply translated into a series of nested loop structures in the generated code. However, performing this transformation naively and enforcing the 'program structure' implied by the user query would lead to missed optimization opportunities like hoisting computations and loops that are independent of outer loops, common sub-query/expression elimination, and more. Therefore, rather than naively transforming queries and directly imposing the program structure, we extract a set of generators, iterators, and their dependencies during IR construction. While the IR does not explicitly capture the program structure, the optimal program structure can be derived from an analysis of these dependencies.

4.2   Constructing the IR

The dependency structure is relatively straightforward. As demonstrated in the generated code snippet in Fig. 2, we utilize objects such as `tmp[0]`, `tmp[1]`, and so on, to maintain intermediate results required for computing the final query result. Assignment operators have these temporaries as operands, creating data dependencies in the process. Generators can also iterate values from these temporaries, and in such cases, we introduce similar dependencies for the generators. Similarly, when a generator symbol is used in an assignment or another generator, a dependency is added. To illustrate how dependencies are created, consider the following assignment instruction extracted from Line 13 in Fig. 2c:

```
13 tmp[0][data[starA]['key']] = tmp[1][data[starA]['key']] / tmp[2]
```

This instruction relies on `tmp[0]`, `tmp[1]`, and `tmp[2]` as operands. As a result, this instruction is associated with the last (write) operations of all three temporaries as dependencies, as depicted in the IR visualization presented in Fig. 2c. Furthermore, since it employs the *A iterator, it also exhibits a dependency on the corresponding generator.

The final missing piece in our lowering process is determining the appropriate IR instruction from our query AST. This is done distinctly for reduction operators (those with a key in the AST) and other operators (those with a path in the AST). For reduction operators, which require the management of state, we introduce stateful temporary variables indexed by the current grouping path. In this context, 'path' refers to the pertinent 'parent' grouping keys within the query nest. In contrast, other types of operators are simpler to handle. We retrieve the operands and subsequently create an instruction that performs the desired computation. For example, for plus, we retrieve the left and right operands and create a binary operation utilizing the + operator.

4.3   Code Generation

Once the IR is constructed for a query, the next step is to generate the final code taking into account the instruction dependencies. Specifically, it entails determining where to insert loops, how to nest loops within one another, where to place assignment instructions, and so on. We will use the query from Fig. 2c as a running example for this section.

The first step is computing two auxiliary relations: `tmpInsideLoop` and `tmpAft- erTmp`. These relations track which temporaries should be scheduled inside particular loops and which temporaries should be scheduled after certain other temporaries. This can be done by analyzing assignment to assignment dependencies and generator to assignment dependencies.

The next step involves computing the relation `tmpAfterLoop` based on the two relations computed above. Specifically, if we determined that a temp variable `t2` should be scheduled after another temp variable `t1` (i.e., `tmpAfterTmp[t2][t1]`), which resides inside a loop `l` (with the condition that `t2` itself is not within loop `l`), then this implies that `t2` should be scheduled after the loop `l`. For instance, in our sample query, `tmp[0]` should be scheduled after `*A`.

Subsequently, as the final analysis step before code generation, we determine `loopAfterLoop` and `loopInsideLoop`. These essentially help identify how the loops should be scheduled. In particular, if we ascertain that a given temp `t` should be scheduled inside both loops `l1` and `l2`, it implies that `l1` and `l2` should belong to the same loop nest. Conversely, if we determined that for a particular temp `t`, it resides within loop `l2`, and we also know that `t` should be scheduled after another loop `l1`, then this indicates that the loop `l2` should be scheduled after `l1` (provided they are not part of the same loop nest).

Once the analysis steps are completed, we proceed with the code generation process. Our approach to code generation draws inspiration from the IR scheduling algorithm utilized in Lightweight Modular Staging (LMS) [11,12,31]. In particular, we schedule generators and assignments in an 'outside-in' fashion, commencing with the outer loops before progressing to the inner ones.

Since we did not have program control structures enforced from the front end, this code scheduling mechanism freely schedules assignments and generators in an optimal manner. For instance, any generator that does not have dependencies to the 'outer query' would be hoisted and scheduled as a separate query instead of repeating the computation multiple times inside a nested loop.

5   Experiments

In this section, we conduct a performance evaluation of our current Rhyme implementation, comparing it against two established JSON processing systems: JQ [3] and Rumble [25], the latter of which utilizes Spark for distributed processing. We acknowledge that systems like Rumble are primarily designed for large-scale, cluster execution and may not exhibit optimal performance in a single-node, single-threaded context. Nevertheless, we consider it a valuable baseline for comparison. Moreover, we report the end-to-end execution time, including time for loading data.

5.1 Experimental Setup

We run three queries on a simple synthetic dataset comprising 1 million records of JSON objects. Each object in the dataset contains two string keys, key1 and key2, as well as an integer value. The first query calculates the sum of all values, the second query performs an aggregate sum after grouping by the key1, and the third query computes a two-level aggregate using key1, then key2.

We run all the experiments using a single thread, on a NUMA machine with 4 sockets, 24 Intel(R) Xeon(R) Platinum 8168 cores per socket, and 750GB RAM per socket (3 TB total) running Ubuntu 18.04.4 LTS. We have used JQ v1.6, Rumble v1.21.0, and Node v18.18.0 (for running our JS code). All experiments are run five times, reporting the mean execution time.

5.2 Results

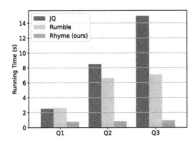

Fig. 4. Running time (left) for JQ, Rumble, and Rhyme for three different queries

Across the three queries, Rhyme demonstrates the best performance. This can be attributed to its ability to generate optimized JS code tailored to a specific query, which significantly reduces overhead compared to the general execution engines employed by systems like Rumble. JQ performs the worst, as it lacks any form of 'query planning' and executes queries naively without optimizations such as loop fusion (Fig. 4).

While these results highlight the potential performance gains achievable through Rhyme's code generation capabilities, it is important to note that this benchmark does not provide a comprehensive analysis that contains the full spectrum of representative cases in JSON analytics. Such a comprehensive evaluation is deferred to future research.

6   Related Work

There are several query languages designed for working with semi-structured data like JSON, each with its own focus and strengths. JSONiq [5,17] is a notable query language explicitly tailored for JSON data, borrowing most of its syntax from XQuery [4] (e.g., FLWOR expressions). Zorba [6] and RumbleDB [25] are examples of engines that support JSONiq, with RumbleDB using Spark [37] as a backend, leveraging the scalability of Spark for execution. AsterixDB, designed for semi-structured data, employs AQL [2] and SQL++ [26] as its query languages. GraphQL [19], on the other hand, is widely used in web application development for querying data from backend services. Most of these languages are specifically targeted towards large-scale JSON analytics workloads and are not expressive enough to support cases like the ones in Sects. 3.1 to 3.3. While we take inspiration from these languages for the design of the language, Rhyme is designed to handle various forms of nested data (e.g., tensors), and it offers support for efficient code generation and optimizations through its IR.

Rhyme's path expressions are inspired by JSONPath [18] (a descendent of XPath). Although not discussed extensively in this paper, it is possible to extend Rhyme to support the full set of JSONPath operators, which include conditions, recursion, etc. Rhyme also borrows many ideas from functional logic programming languages like Verse [10], Curry [20], miniKanren [13] and Scalogno [9], and adapts them into a new data-centric declarative language.

7   Conclusions and Future Work

In this paper, we introduced Rhyme, a new query language tailored for high-level data manipulation. We illustrated how Rhyme's design facilitates query optimization and code generation through the construction of an IR. This IR comprises loop-free branch-free code, with program structure implicitly captured by dependencies. Throughout the paper, we demonstrated the versatility of Rhyme by showcasing its applicability in expressive data manipulations, tensor computations, manipulation of visual aspects, and so on in a declarative manner. It is worth noting that Rhyme is still in its early developmental stages, and we are excited about exploring various avenues of interesting future work.

Incrementality. While not extensively covered in this paper, the concept of utilizing intermediate temporaries within the generated code is inspired by prior works in incremental execution, such as DBToaster [22] and RPAI [7]. An immediate focus of our future work involves introducing support for incremental execution. Notably, our generated code is inherently designed to be 'incremental-friendly'. This implies that we have the capability to generate code akin to update triggers, which are invoked whenever a modification is made to the dataset. Specifically, instead of dense loops used in the current version, update triggers generate 'sparse' loops in the sense that they iterate only over the deltas.

Another dimension of incrementality involves managing query changes. This entails finding ways to accommodate changes in queries while maximizing the utilization of previously computed temporaries and sharing state across multiple queries. Such an approach will be useful in interactive applications, where users can dynamically modify their queries.

Performance. While the ability to generate JS for browser-based execution is undeniably valuable, there are specific scenarios where optimizing performance becomes paramount. In such cases, the generation of low-level, specialized C code becomes imperative to eliminate any potential overhead associated with managed runtimes. A substantial body of prior research has already demonstrated the efficacy of such compilation mechanisms [15,30,33,36]. Furthermore, it is feasible to leverage existing compiler infrastructures such as LMS [31] or MLIR [23] for streamlined handling of tasks like IR construction, dependency analysis, and the eventual generation of highly specialized low-level code.

Acknowledgements. We would like to thank our anonymous reviewers for their valuable feedback that helped improve the paper significantly. This work was supported in part by NSF awards 1553471, 1564207, 1918483, 1910216, DOE award DE-SC0018050, as well as gifts from Meta, Google, Microsoft, and VMware.

References

1. Advent of code 2022. https://adventofcode.com/2022/day/1. Accessed 27 Sept 2023
2. The asterix query language (aql). https://asterixdb.apache.org/docs/0.9.8/aql/manual.html. Accessed 27 Sept 2023
3. jq manual. https://jqlang.github.io/jq/manual/. Accessed 27 Sept 2023
4. Xquery 3.1: an xml query language (2017). https://www.w3.org/TR/xquery-31/. Accessed 27 Sept 2023
5. Jsoniq (2018). https://www.jsoniq.org/. Accessed 27 Sept 2023
6. Zorba (2018). https://www.zorba.io/. Accessed 27 Sept 2023
7. Abeysinghe, S., He, Q., Rompf, T.: Efficient incrementialization of correlated nested aggregate queries using relative partial aggregate indexes (RPAI). In: SIGMOD Conference, pp. 136–149. ACM (2022)
8. Abeysinghe, S., Wang, F., Essertel, G.M., Rompf, T.: Architecting intermediate layers for efficient composition of data management and machine learning systems. CoRR abs/2311.02781 (2023)
9. Amin, N., Byrd, W.E., Rompf, T.: Lightweight functional logic meta-programming. In: Lin, A.W. (ed.) APLAS 2019. LNCS, vol. 11893, pp. 225–243. Springer, Cham (2019). https://doi.org/10.1007/978-3-030-34175-6_12
10. Augustsson, L., et al.: The verse calculus: a core calculus for deterministic functional logic programming. Proc. ACM Program. Lang. **7**(ICFP), 417–447 (2023)
11. Bracevac, O., et al.: Graph IRS for impure higher-order languages (technical report). CoRR abs/2309.08118 (2023)
12. Bračevac, O., et al.: Graph IRS for impure higher-order languages: making aggressive optimizations affordable with precise effect dependencies. Proc. ACM Program. Lang. **7**(OOPSLA2), 236:1–236:31 (2023)
13. Byrd, W.E.: Relational programming in miniKanren: techniques, applications, and implementations. Ph.D. thesis, Indiana University (2009)
14. Ceri, S., Gottlob, G., Tanca, L.: What you always wanted to know about Datalog (and never dared to ask). IEEE Trans. Knowl. Data Eng. **1**(1), 146–166 (1989)
15. Essertel, G.M., Tahboub, R.Y., Decker, J.M., Brown, K.J., Olukotun, K., Rompf, T.: Flare: optimizing apache spark with native compilation for scale-up architectures and medium-size data. In: OSDI, pp. 799–815. USENIX Association (2018)
16. Flores-Montoya, A., Schulte, E.M.: Datalog disassembly. In: USENIX Security Symposium, pp. 1075–1092. USENIX Association (2020)
17. Florescu, D., Fourny, G.: JSONiq: the history of a query language. IEEE Internet Comput. **17**(5), 86–90 (2013)

18. Goessner, S.: Jsonpath - xpath for json (2007). https://goessner.net/articles/JsonPath/. Accessed 27 Sept 2023
19. GraphQL: A query language for your api. https://graphql.org/. Accessed 27 Sept 2023
20. Hanus, M.: Functional logic programming: from theory to curry. In: Voronkov, A., Weidenbach, C. (eds.) Programming Logics. LNCS, vol. 7797, pp. 123–168. Springer, Heidelberg (2013). https://doi.org/10.1007/978-3-642-37651-1_6
21. Jordan, H., Scholz, B., Subotić, P.: Souffle: on synthesis of program analyzers. In: Chaudhuri, S., Farzan, A. (eds.) CAV 2016. LNCS, vol. 9780, pp. 422–430. Springer, Cham (2016). https://doi.org/10.1007/978-3-319-41540-6_23
22. Koch, C., et al.: DBToaster: higher-order delta processing for dynamic, frequently fresh views. VLDB J. **23**(2), 253–278 (2014)
23. Lattner, C., et al.: MLIR: a compiler infrastructure for the end of Moore's law. CoRR abs/2002.11054 (2020)
24. Meijer, E., Beckman, B., Bierman, G.M.: LINQ: reconciling object, relations and XML in the.net framework. In: SIGMOD Conference, p. 706. ACM (2006)
25. Müller, I., Fourny, G., Irimescu, S., Cikis, C.B., Alonso, G.: Rumble: data independence for large messy data sets. Proc. VLDB Endow. **14**(4), 498–506 (2020)
26. Ong, K.W., Papakonstantinou, Y., Vernoux, R.: The SQL++ semi-structured data model and query language: a capabilities survey of SQL-on-Hadoop, NoSQL and NewSQL databases. CoRR abs/1405.3631 (2014)
27. Palkar, S., et al.: A common runtime for high performance data analysis. In: CIDR. www.cidrdb.org (2017)
28. Reps, T.: Solving demand versions of interprocedural analysis problems. In: Fritzson, P.A. (ed.) CC 1994. LNCS, vol. 786, pp. 389–403. Springer, Heidelberg (1994). https://doi.org/10.1007/3-540-57877-3_26
29. Rogozhnikov, A.: EINOPS: clear and reliable tensor manipulations with Einstein-like notation. In: ICLR. OpenReview.net (2022)
30. Rompf, T., Amin, N.: A SQL to C compiler in 500 lines of code. J. Funct. Program. **29**, e9 (2019)
31. Rompf, T., Odersky, M.: Lightweight modular staging: a pragmatic approach to runtime code generation and compiled DSLs. Commun. ACM **55**(6), 121–130 (2012)
32. Sujeeth, A.K., et al.: Delite: A compiler architecture for performance-oriented embedded domain-specific languages. ACM Trans. Embed. Comput. Syst. **13**(4s), 134:1–134:25 (2014)
33. Tahboub, R.Y., Essertel, G.M., Rompf, T.: How to architect a query compiler, revisited. In: SIGMOD Conference, pp. 307–322. ACM (2018)
34. Ullman, J.D.: Principles of Database and Knowledge-Base Systems, vol. II. Computer Science Press, Kuala Lumpur (1989)
35. Vasilache, N., et al.: Tensor comprehensions: framework-agnostic high-performance machine learning abstractions. CoRR abs/1802.04730 (2018)
36. Wei, G., Chen, Y., Rompf, T.: Staged abstract interpreters: fast and modular whole-program analysis via meta-programming. Proc. ACM Program. Lang. **3**(OOPSLA), 126:1–126:32 (2019)
37. Zaharia, M., et al.: Apache spark: a unified engine for big data processing. Commun. ACM **59**(11), 56–65 (2016)

Rethinking Answer Set Programming Templates

Mario Alviano[✉][iD], Giovambattista Ianni[iD], Francesco Pacenza[iD],
and Jessica Zangari[iD]

DEMACS, University of Calabria, Via Bucci 30/B, 87036 Rende, CS, Italy
{mario.alviano,giovambattista.ianni,francesco.pacenza,
jessica.zangari}@unical.it

Abstract. In imperative programming, the Domain-Driven Design methodology helps in coping with the complexity of software development by materializing in code the invariants of a domain of interest. Code is cleaner and more secure because any implicit assumption is removed in favor of invariants, thus enabling a fail fast mindset and the immediate reporting of unexpected conditions. This article introduces a notion of template for Answer Set Programming that, in addition to the *don't repeat yourself* principle, enforces locality of some predicates by means of a simple naming convention. Local predicates are mapped to the usual global namespace adopted by mainstream engines, using universally unique identifiers to avoid name clashes. This way, local predicates can be used to enforce invariants on the expected outcome of a template in a possibly empty context of application, independently by other rules that can be added to such a context. Template applications transpiled this way can be processed by mainstream engines and safely shared with other knowledge designers, even when they have zero knowledge of templates.

Keywords: Answer Set Programming · secure coding · clean code · Domain-Driven Design · Test-Driven Development

1 Introduction

Answer Set Programming (ASP) is a declarative specification language suited to address combinatorial search and optimization [12,26]. In ASP, problem requirements are represented in terms of a program made of logic rules, and solutions are obtained by computing stable models of the program, that is, classical models satisfying an additional stability condition. Fast prototyping is very likely the most appreciated strength of ASP, as it provides several linguistic constructs to ease the representation of complex knowledge and allows for quickly testing alternative solutions to the same problem of interest [2]. The linguistic capabilities of ASP are accompanied by several efficient algorithms addressing a broad variety of computational problems, therefore different solving strategies can be attempted with minimal design effort [31]. Nonetheless, ASP has a few shortcomings when used in broad development environments. In this paper we are

M. Gebser and I. Sergey (Eds.): PADL 2024, LNCS 14512, pp. 82–99, 2023.
https://doi.org/10.1007/978-3-031-52038-9_6

particularly interested in *1)* the issue of knowledge reuse, and *2)* in the difficulty of enforcing *invariants* [13,27] (literally *something that does not change or vary*) over logic programs written under ASP semantics.

Concerning knowledge reuse, a programming language should ideally have linguistic constructs to ease the reuse of code [1]. Macros, subroutines and templates are often used to address such a concern, and some constructs in this direction were defined and implemented also for ASP [3,7,9]. Much work suggests that some predicates should be considered *hidden*, that is, they should be essentially *auxiliary* to the definition of other *visible* predicates that actually define the semantics of programs or modules of a program [4,5]. As such, auxiliary predicates should not be taken into account when checking equivalence of programs, and should not be shared between different contexts. The formalization of such an intuition is not necessarily trivial, nor it is trivial to enforce the uniqueness of auxiliary names in practical systems combining multiple modules possibly coming from different authors; moreover, one has to take into account that the successful adoption of an implementation by practitioners strongly depends on how easy is to specify that a predicate is auxiliary, how easily modules can be exchanged and combined, and how many features and constructs of mainstream systems are compatible with the implemented linguistic extension.

To understand the importance of enforcing invariants, we observe that in a typical development environment multiple programmers with several roles contribute to writing code. Likewise, a large ASP-based project involves multiple programmers writing knowledge, and in particular we distinguish two roles. *End-user knowledge designers* are simply interested in writing declarative code, possibly with the aid of existing code. On the other hand, *library knowledge designers* contribute with reusable code and often have a deeper understanding of technical aspects of ASP; their interest is on developing sound and thoroughly tested code that can be combined with code written by other programmers. Without invariants, any property of the tested code is possibly lost when the code is extended and combined with other programs. However, note that ASP programs are often seen as a whole, with rules interacting in any possible way. This is in part due to the stable model semantics adopted by ASP, which is nonmonotonic and therefore not friendly to the definition of invariants. An invariant is essentially an assumption taken within a block of code to guarantee correctness of computation. For example, consider a function written in C to implement the factorial of a number n by multiplying all positive integers less than or equal to n. If numbers are stored as `uint32_t`, *the function is correct under the assumption that $n \leq 12$*, as 13! exceeds the limit of `uint32_t` (and an integer overflow would occur). If the function starts by raising an error when $n > 12$, integer overflows are impossible and the computation of the factorial is guaranteed to be correct (if no errors are raised). In ASP, guaranteeing that some properties of the stable models of a program are preserved when the program is extended with other rules is nontrivial [4,16,29].

This work contributes to the reuse of ASP code by introducing and implementing a simple notion of *template*. The notion of template is here intended in the broad sense of a set of rules, not explicitly identifying input and output predicates, with the capability of being applied multiple times by specifying possibly different renaming mappings for *visible* predicates. Auxiliary predicates are kept *local* to their template applications by an automatic renaming policy that appends a *universally unique identifier* (UUID [24]), generated at application time, to predicate names. This way, visible and auxiliary predicates of different template applications can coexist in the usual *global* namespace adopted by ASP engines. To ease the implementation of this idea and its adoption by practitioners, local predicates are automatically identified by introducing a naming convention commonly used in Python objects to declare *private* methods, that is, names starting by *double underscore* are associated with local predicates.

The main advantage that off-the-shelf templates can provide to end-user knowledge designers is isolation from tedious technical aspects of the ASP semantics: understanding the interface of a template is sufficient for its usage, while a full understanding of its internal properties is not required. On the other hand, library knowledge designers can additionally benefit from the invariant on local predicates to test for other invariants and expected properties of the developed templates: since local predicates cannot be accessed from outside the template they are declared, any property enforced by local predicates is preserved when the template is used in broader code bases. Moreover, templates constitute a natural *unit to be tested*. In order to enable the verification of some invariants that a template imposes on any program it is applied to, we focus on *here-and-there* models, that is, models of the monotonic, modal logic of here-and-there. (In this work here-and-there logic is used to establish correctness of some tests. Users are not expected to interface with the logic of here-and-there, and the framework is open to the definition of other automatic tests.) Intuitively, here-and-there models of a program Π are pairs of the form $\langle H, T \rangle$ such that T is a stable model candidate, and H is a model of the program reduct Π^T, so that stable models are characterized as here-and-there models of the form $\langle T, T \rangle$ such that there is no here-and-there model $\langle H, T \rangle$ with $H \subset T$ [14,30]. Being a monotonic logic, here-and-there models of a set of rules are necessarily an overestimate of the here-and-there models of any broader set of rules. This is an invariant that can power the definition of tests providing guarantees on the behavior of a template; for example, it is possible to define tests to guarantee that some atoms have a specific assignment in all stable models of any program extending a template application; to guarantee that some interpretations cannot be stable models even if consistent with all rules of a broader program; or also to guarantee coherence of some atoms w.r.t. some interpretations (intended as derivation in the associated program reducts).

In summary, the contributions of this work are the following:

– We propose a notion of template made of rules with global and local predicates. Templates can be applied and mixed with other programs by means of a versatile form of predicate renaming that overcomes the inflexible practice of fixing input and output predicates, and therefore broadens the reusability of code snippets. Global predicates are mapped according to the preferences of knowledge designers, while the renaming of local predicates is automatic and clash-free without the need for synchronizing template applications.

- We define a transpiler that expands programs with templates to ordinary ASP programs. Note that only library knowledge designers need to use the transpiler, while end-user knowledge designers can use transpiled modules in their standard solver of choice. Indeed, transpiled programs can be evaluated by mainstream ASP engines, and combined with other programs with a practical guarantee that local predicate names do not clash. Our transpiler and its testing constructs are powered by the CLINGO PYTHON API.
- For library knowledge designers, we enable the possibility to enforce some invariants of templates, some of which are verified by our implementation by analyzing here-and-there models with the help of mainstream ASP engines; note that knowledge designers are not required to reason in terms of here-and-there models. A context of application for the template is possibly given by specifying other rules, and invariants are obtained thanks to the impossibility to refer local predicates outside the template.

2 Background

A *universally unique identifier* (UUID) is a 128-bit label generated according to standard methods that guarantee uniqueness for practical purposes [24] (i.e., even if the probability of generating duplicated UUIDs is not zero, it is generally considered close enough to zero to be negligible).

A *normal program* is a set of rules of the form

$$p_0(\overline{t_0}) \leftarrow p_1(\overline{t_1}), \ \ldots, \ p_m(\overline{t_m}), \ not \ p_{m+1}(\overline{t_{m+1}}), \ \ldots, \ not \ p_n(\overline{t_n}) \qquad (1)$$

where $n \geq m \geq 0$, and each $p_i(\overline{t_i})$ is an atom made of a predicate p_i from a fixed set $\mathbf{P}$ and a sequence $\overline{t_i}$ of terms; terms are either variables (uppercase strings) from a fixed set $\mathbf{V}$ or constants (integers and lowercase strings) from a fixed set $\mathbf{C}$. Sets $\mathbf{P}$, $\mathbf{V}$ and $\mathbf{C}$ are countably infinite and pairwise disjoint. For a rule r of the form (1), let $H(r)$ denote the *head* atom $p_0(\overline{t_0})$, and $B^+(r), B^-(r)$ denote the sets $\{p_i(\overline{t_i}) \mid i = 1..m\}$ and $\{p_i(\overline{t_i}) \mid i = m+1..n\}$ of atoms occurring in *positive* and *negative literals* of r. A rule of the form (1) is a *fact* if $n = 0$. We adopt the usual shortcut p/n for referring to predicate p of arity n. Let $pred(\Pi)$ be the set of predicate names occurring in program Π.

The *grounding* $grd(\Pi)$ of Π is $\bigcup_{r \in \Pi} grd(r)$, where $grd(r)$ is obtained from r by replacing variables from $\mathbf{V}$ with constants from $\mathbf{C}$, in all possible ways. An *interpretation* I is a set of ground atoms (i.e., atoms without variables): atoms in I are true, other atoms are false. The relation $\models$ (is model of) is defined inductively: for a ground atom $p(\overline{c})$, $I \models p(\overline{c})$ if $p(\overline{c}) \in I$, and $I \models not \ p(\overline{c})$ if $p(\overline{c}) \notin I$; for a ground rule r, $I \models B(r)$ if I is a model of all literals in $B(r)$, and $I \models r$ if $I \models H(r)$ whenever $I \models B(r)$; for a program Π, $I \models \Pi$ if $I \models r$ for all $r \in grd(\Pi)$. The *reduct* Π^I of Π w.r.t. I is $\{H(r) \leftarrow B^+(r) \mid r \in grd(\Pi),$ $I \models B(r)\}$. I is a *stable model* of Π if $I \models \Pi$ and there is no $J \subset I$ such that $J \models \Pi^I$. Let $SM(\Pi)$ be the set of stable models of Π.

Example 1. Consider the following example in ASP-Core-2 syntax [6]:

```
a(X) :- e(X), not b(X).      e(1).  e(2).
b(X) :- e(X), not a(X).      fail :- a(1), b(2), not fail.
```

The above program has three stable models, namely $X = \{e(1), e(2)\}$, $X \cup \{a(1), a(2)\}$, $X \cup \{b(1), a(2)\}$, and $X \cup \{b(1), b(2)\}$. It is using the fact that `fail` only occurs in the head of rules of the form *fail ← body, not fail*, a well-known pattern to simulate constraints in ASP.   ■

In the following, $\perp \leftarrow body$ is used as syntactic sugar for *fail ← body, not fail*, where *fail* is not used elsewhere (note that this assumption will be turned into an invariant by Example 7).

A program can be mapped to a theory of the logic of here-and-there (HT for short; [19]) by replacing each rule of the form (1) with a formula

$$p_1(\overline{t_1}) \wedge \cdots \wedge p_m(\overline{t_m}) \wedge (p_{m+1}(\overline{t_{m+1}}) \rightarrow \perp) \cdots \wedge (p_n(\overline{t_n}) \rightarrow \perp) \rightarrow p_0(\overline{t_0}) \quad (2)$$

and by expanding variables with constants from $\mathbf{C}$ (as done for the grounding). Let Γ_Π denote the theory associated with program Π. A HT-interpretation is a pair $\langle I_H, I_T \rangle$ of interpretations such that $I_H \subseteq I_T$; intuitively, $\langle I_H, I_T \rangle$ represents two worlds, namely H and T, with $H \leq T$. Relation $\models$ is extended to $\langle I_H, I_T \rangle$ and world $w \in \{H, T\}$ as follows: $\langle I_H, I_T, w \rangle \not\models \perp$; for a ground atom $p(\overline{c})$, $\langle I_H, I_T, w \rangle \models p(\overline{c})$ if $p(\overline{c}) \in I_w$; for formulas F, G, $\langle I_H, I_T, w \rangle \models F \wedge G$ if $\langle I_H, I_T, w \rangle \models F$ and $\langle I_H, I_T, w \rangle \models G$; for formulas F, G, $\langle I_H, I_T, w \rangle \models F \rightarrow G$ if $I_{w'} \models F \rightarrow G$ for all $w \leq w'$; for a formula F, $\langle I_H, I_T \rangle \models F$ if $\langle I_H, I_T, H \rangle \models F$; for a set of formulas Γ, $\langle I_H, I_T \rangle \models \Gamma$ if $\langle I_H, I_T \rangle \models F$ for all $F \in \Gamma$. A HT-interpretation $\langle I_H, I_T \rangle$ is a HT-model of a program Π if $\langle I_H, I_T \rangle \models \Gamma_\Pi$. Let $HT(\Pi)$ be the set of HT-models of Π. A HT-interpretation $\langle T, T \rangle$ is an equilibrium model of Π if $\langle T, T \rangle \in HT(\Pi)$ and there is no $\langle H, T \rangle \in HT(\Pi)$ with $H \subset T$ [30]. Let $EQ(\Pi)$ be the set of equilibrium models of Π.

Example 2. For Π being the program in Example 1, the theory Γ_Π includes $e(1) \wedge (b(1) \rightarrow \perp) \rightarrow a(1)$ and other formulas. For $X = \{e(1), e(2), a(1), b(2)\}$, $HT(\Gamma_\Pi)$ includes $\langle X, X \cup \{fail\} \rangle$, and no pair of the form $\langle I_H, X \rangle$.   ■

Proposition 1. $I \in SM(\Pi)$ *if and only if* $\langle I, I \rangle \in EQ(\Pi)$.

3   Templates

A *template* π is a set of rules (like a program). Let $\mathbf{P_L} \subseteq \mathbf{P}$ be the set of *local predicates*, i.e., predicates whose name starts by double underscore. Predicates in $\mathbf{P} \setminus \mathbf{P_L}$ are *global* and play the role of (renamable) *parameters* in templates. A *renaming* ρ is a function with signature $\rho : \mathbf{P} \longrightarrow \mathbf{P}$. A *local renaming* ρ is a renaming being the identity on predicates from $\mathbf{P} \setminus \mathbf{P_L}$. In contrast, a *global renaming* ρ is a renaming being the identity on predicates from $\mathbf{P_L}$. In the following, the term *universally unique predicate* refers to a predicate name that is guaranteed to be unique, and the notation $\rho(\pi)$ is abused to refer to the set of rules in π with all predicates renamed according to ρ; similarly, $\rho(I)$ is the interpretation obtained from I by renaming predicates according to ρ.

Example 3. The renaming $[fail \mapsto \_\_fail]$ is global; it maps *fail* to $\_\_fail$, and is the identity for other predicates. The renaming $[\_\_fail \mapsto \_\_fail\_7b905af5\_de82\_49b3\_9db7\_415d4d048c76]$ is local; with a very good probabilistic confidence the predicate $\_\_fail\_7b905af5\_de82\_49b3\_9db7\_415d4d048c76$ is unique if obtained appending a newly generated UUID to $\_\_fail$.   ∎

The *application* $\pi\rho$ of a template π w.r.t. a global renaming ρ is the set of rules $\rho(\rho_L(\pi))$, where ρ_L is a local renaming mapping each local predicate in $pred(\pi)$ to a universally unique predicate in $\mathbf{P_L}$. Note that, by the way they are defined, a template π (being a set of rules) can include the application of another template $\pi'\rho$ (i.e., a set of rules): in this case, $\pi \supseteq \pi'\rho$, and the sets of local predicates occurring in $\pi'\rho$ and $\pi \setminus \pi'\rho$ are disjoint because those in $\pi'\rho$ are universally unique by construction; moreover, any application $\pi\rho'$ of π, by construction, is guaranteed to map local predicates of $\pi'\rho$ to new universally unique predicates, hence preserving the invariant that different applications of π are associated with different local predicates.

Example 4. Let π_{tc} (for transitive closure) be the template comprising of

$$closure(X,Y) \leftarrow relation(X,Y) \tag{3}$$
$$closure(X,Z) \leftarrow closure(X,Y), \ relation(Y,Z) \tag{4}$$

that is, π_{tc} is expected to define the transitive closure of *relation/2*. The application $\pi_{tc}[relation \mapsto link, closure \mapsto reach]$ is expected to produce (at least) the transitive closure of *link/2* in predicate *reach/2* (an invariant). Similarly, the application $\pi_{tc}[relation \mapsto link, closure \mapsto link]$ is expected to enforce that relation *link/2* is closed under transitivity (an invariant).

Let $\pi_{acyclic}$ comprise of the following rules:

$$\_\_closure(X,Y) \leftarrow relation(X,Y) \tag{5}$$
$$\_\_closure(X,Z) \leftarrow \_\_closure(X,Y), \ relation(Y,Z) \tag{6}$$
$$\bot \leftarrow \_\_closure(X,X) \tag{7}$$

Intuitively, the template $\pi_{acyclic}$ is expected to discard interpretations in which the relation encoded by predicate *relation/2* has cycles (an invariant). Note that rules (5)–(6) can be obtained as the template application $\pi_{tc}[closure \mapsto \_\_closure]$; predicate *closure* of template π_{tc} is mapped to a local predicate of $\pi_{acyclic}$ so to inhibit external reference (an invariant). The template application $\pi_{acyclic}[relation \mapsto link]$ could map $\_\_closure$ to $\_\_closure\_6bd3728a\_36b4\_4fb9\_8019\_61af6363420b$.

Let π_{tcg} (for transitive closure guaranteed) comprise rules (3)–(6) and

$$\bot \leftarrow closure(X,Y), \ not \ \_\_closure(X,Y) \tag{8}$$

to compute the transitive closure of *relation/2* in *closure/2*, and enforce failure if *closure* is extended externally by other rules mentioning *closure* (an invariant). Note that (3)–(6) are obtained as $\pi_{tc}[] \cup \pi_{tc}[closure \mapsto \_\_closure]$.   ∎

Algorithm 1: Expand($[\pi_1, \ldots, \pi_n]$: a program with templates; *templates*: a map from names to templates): a program Π

---

1 $\Pi := \emptyset$;
2 **foreach** $i \in 1..n$ **do**
3   **if** π_i *is* `__template__("name")`. *content* `__end__`. **then**
4 | $templates[name] :=$ Expand(*content, templates*);
5   **else if** π_i *is* `__apply_template__("name",`ρ`)`. **then**
6 | $\pi := templates[name]$; $\Pi := \Pi \cup \pi\rho$;
7   **else**
8 | $\Pi := \Pi \cup \{\pi_i\}$;

9 **return** Π;

---

4 Implementation

Templates are implemented in DUMBO ASP, a prototype PYTHON library powered by the CLINGO PYTHON API [23]. The implementation is available at: https://github.com/alviano/dumbo-asp. Templates can be declared and applied via a serialization format based on ASP rules, as explained next. Predicates `__apply_template__`, `__template__` and `__end__` are reserved. A *program with templates* is a sequence $[\pi_1, \ldots, \pi_n]$ $(n \geq 0)$, where each π_i is one of the followings: (i) a rule of the form (1); (ii) a template application

    `__apply_template__("`*name*`",` *mapping*`).`

where *name* identifies a template occurring at some previous index $j < i$, and *mapping* is a comma-separated list of pairs of the form (*old_predicate, new_predicate*); (iii) a template declaration, that is, a block

    `__template__("`*name*`").`
      content
    `__end__.`

where *name* identifies the template, and *content* is a sequence of rules and applications of previous templates. Note that recursive template applications are disallowed by design, but arbitrary dependencies among predicates defined by different template applications are permitted, including recursion.

A program with templates can be expanded by Algorithm 1. Elements of the program are processed in order (line 2). Ordinary rules are added to the output program (line 8), which is initially empty (line 1). If a template declaration is found (lines 3–4), the *templates* map (initially containing built-in templates from our core library) is extended with a template comprising rules obtained by calling Algorithm 1; note that the nested call to the algorithm is not reiterated thanks to the serialization format given above (templates' content cannot declare other templates). Whenever the application of a template is found, the content of the template is retrieved from the *templates* map, and the global renaming ρ is used to produce rules $\rho(\rho_L(\pi))$ for the output program (lines 3–4); in our implementation, $\rho_L(\_p) = \_p\_u$, where u is a UUID generated when π is applied.

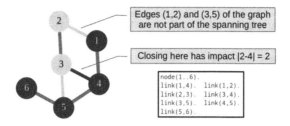

Fig. 1. Example of input and output for the running problem of Sect. 5

Example 5 (Continuing Example 4). Let us consider the following program:

```
1 __template__("@dumbo/transitive closure").
2     closure(X,Y) :- relation(X,Y).
3     closure(X,Z) :- closure(X,Y), relation(Y,Z).
4 __end__.
5 __template__("@dumbo/transitive closure guaranteed").
6     __apply_template__("@dumbo/transitive closure", (closure,__closure
      )).
7     closure(X,Y) :- __closure(X,Y).
8     :- closure(X,Y), not __closure(X,Y).
9 __end__.
10 link(a,b).  link(a,c).
11 __apply_template__("@dumbo/transitive closure guaranteed",
12     (relation, link), (closure, reach)).
13 reach(foo,bar).  % this is going to cause an inconsistency
```

Template `@dumbo/transitive closure guaranteed` materializes the transitive closure in the local predicate `__closure` by applying `@dumbo/transitive closure` (line 6); `__closure` is then "copied" to the global predicate `closure`, subject to a constraint guaranteeing that it cannot be further extended elsewhere (lines 7–8). In fact, line 13 causes an inconsistency with such an invariant of the program. Also note that these templates are part of the core templates of DUMBO ASP. ∎

5   Application Scenario

Let us consider a hypothetical (partial) problem specification to be addressed by two teams of developers, say *Alpha* and *Bravo*. Given a graph representing road segments, we are interested in finding a spanning tree to build a highway network. For each such network proposal, we want to understand the impact of closing every single road segment in terms of the resulting tree-size-difference between connected points. An example input graph, one of its spanning trees and the impact of closing one of its segments are shown in Fig. 1.

Team Alpha develops a declarative model for spanning trees, and Team Bravo develops the impact measurement. The two teams agree on using predicates

```
1 link(X,Y) :- link(Y,X).              1 {out(X,Y) : tree(X,Y)} = 1.
2 {tree(X,Y) : link(X,Y), X < Y} = C-1  2 in(X,Y) :- tree(X,Y), not out(X,Y).
             :- C = #count {X : node(X)}. 3 in(X,Y) :- in(Y,X).
3 tree(X,Y) :- tree(Y,X).              4 reach(X) :- X = #min {Y : node(Y)}.
4 reach(X) :- X = #min {Y : node(Y)}.  5 reach(Y) :- reach(X), in(X,Y).
5 reach(Y) :- reach(X), tree(X,Y).     6 impact(X,Y,|C|) :- out(X,Y), C = #sum{1,Z :
6 :- node(X), not reach(X).                   reach(Z); -1,Z : node(Z), not reach(Z)}.
```

Fig. 2. Programs written by Team Alpha (left) and Team Bravo (right)

```
1  __template__("@dumbo/symmetric closure").
2      closure(X,Y) :- relation(Y,X).
3      closure(X,Y) :- relation(Y,X).
4  __end__.
5  __template__("@dumbo/reachable nodes").
6      reach(X) :- start(X).
7      reach(Y) :- reach(X), link(X,Y).
8  __end__.
9  __template__("@dumbo/connected graph").
10     __start(X) :- X = #min{Y : node(Y)}.
11     __apply_template__("@dumbo/reachable nodes", (start, __start), (reach, __reach)).
12     :- node(X), not __reach(X).
13 __end__.
14 __apply_template__("@dumbo/symmetric closure", (relation, link), (closure, link)).
15 __template__("spanning tree").
16     {tree(X,Y) : link(X,Y), X < Y} = C-1 :- C = #count{X : node(X)}.
17     __apply_template__("@dumbo/symmetric closure", (relation, tree), (closure, __tree)).
18     __apply_template__("connected graph", (node, node), (link, __tree)).
19 __end__.
20 __apply_template__("spanning tree").
```

Fig. 3. Program written by Team Alpha (lines 13–19) using core templates (lines 1–12)

node/1 and link/2 for the input graph, tree/2 for the spanning tree, and impact /3 for measuring the impact of closing one segment. The two teams produce respectively the ASP-Core-2 programs in Fig. 2. Taken individually, the two programs are correct, which is not the case for their union because reach/1 is used with different meanings; after some synchronization between the two teams, the bug is fixed by changing reach/1 to reach'/1 in one of the two programs. Besides this, there is another bug due to the fact that Alpha enforces the symmetric closure of tree/2, while Bravo works under the assumption that tree/2 is anti-symmetric; the bug can be fixed by adding X < Y in lines 1–2 of Bravo. Moving the code to a new project may lead to similar issues, especially for very common predicate names like in/2 and out/2. In addition, observe that some rules are essentially repeating (e.g., lines 4–5 of Alpha and lines 4–5 of Bravo).

Let us consider a different development timeline. The Alpha team wears the role of a library knowledge designer: it is thus aware of templates and the program in Fig. 3 is produced, where relevant core templates from our library are also shown for convenience. The Bravo team wears the role of an end-user knowledge designer: it is not aware of templates and follows the traditional ASP development lifecycle, using a plain solver of choice. Alpha is ready to share

```
1 __apply_template__("@dumbo/symmetric closure", (relation, tree), (closure, tree)).
2 {__out(X,Y) : tree(X,Y)} = 1.
3 __in(X,Y) :- tree(X,Y), not __out(X,Y).
4 __apply_template__("@dumbo/symmetric closure", (relation, __in), (closure, __in)).
5 __start(X) :- X = #min{Y : node(Y)}.
6 __apply_template__("@dumbo/reachable nodes", (start,__start), (link, __in), (reach,__reach)).
7 impact(X,Y,|C|) :- __out(X,Y), C = #sum{1,Z : __reach(Z); -1,Z : node(Z), not __reach(Z)}.
```

Fig. 4. Program written by Team Bravo using core templates

```
1 {select(T)} :- town(T).  :~ select(T). [1@1, T]
2 __apply_template__("@dumbo/symmetric closure", (relation, connected), (closure, connected)).
3 length(L-1) :- townsintravel(L).
4 __apply_template__("@dumbo/all simple directed paths of given length",
5    (node, town), (link, connected), (path, path'), (in_path, in_path)).
6 __apply_template__("@dumbo/discard duplicate sets",
7    (set, path'), (in_set, in_path), (unique, path)).
8 :- path(P), #count{T : in_path(T,P), select(T)} = 0.
```

Fig. 5. A program addressing the *Fighting with the gang of Billy the Kid* problem. Towns are guessed and minimized (line 1). The graph is symmetrically closed (line 2) and the requested length is adjusted (line 3) to apply the @dumbo/all simple directed paths of given length template, hence obtaining all paths in path'/1 and in_path (lines 4–5). Duplicates are then discarded (lines 6–7) so that the remaining paths can be checked for including at least one selected town (line 8).

their code with Bravo, actually in the form of an expanded, transpiled program obtained by Algorithm 1, so that a clash of names is essentially impossible. In this timeline Bravo can use the transpiled code of Alpha without installing any additional software. This timeline may evolve with Bravo liking the idea of templates, and reusing some of the templates written by Alpha. The result is shown in Fig. 4. The two teams may also add closure constraints to guarantee that the extension of tree/2 and impact/3 is not accidentally extended by other external rules; for this purpose, we provide templates @dumbo/exact copy (arity n) for $n \geq 0$, which have the following form:

```
__template__("@dumbo/exact copy (arity n)").
   output(X1,...,Xn) :- input(X1,...,Xn).
   :- output(X1,...,Xn), not input(X1,...,Xn).
__end__.
```

Even better, as reachable nodes, connected graph and spanning tree are very likely reusable in other programs, Alpha may propose their addition to the core library, or publish them elsewhere.

For another example, more focused on end-user knowledge designers, let us consider the *Fighting with the gang of Billy the Kid* problem: Given a graph encoded by predicates town/1 and connected/2, and a length encoded by predicate townsintravel/1, select a minimum number of towns so that each simple path of the given length includes at least one selected town. Let us consider the following templates from our core library: (1) @dumbo/all simple directed paths of given length materializes in path/1 and in_path/2 all simple paths of

```
 1 {select(T)} :- town(T).  :~ select(T). [1@1, T]
 2 connected(X,Y) :- connected(X,Y).  connected(X,Y) :- connected(Y,X).
 3 length(L-1) :- townsintravel(L).
 4 __path_length_1((N,nil),0) :- town(N).
 5 __path_length_1((N',(N,P)),(L+1)) :- __path_length_1((N,P),L); length(M); L < M;
 6     connected(N,N'); not __in_path_1(N',P).
 7 __in_path_1(N,(N,P)) :- __path_length_1((N,P),_).
 8 __in_path_1(N',(N,P)) :- __path_length_1((N,P),_); __in_path_1(N',P).
 9 __path_1(P) :- __in_path_1(_,P).
10 path'(P) :- __path_1(P); __path_length_1(P,L); length(L).
11 in_path(N,P) :- path'(P); __in_path_1(N,P).
12 __equals_2(S,S') :- path'(S); path'(S'); S < S';
13     in_path(X,S): in_path(X,S'); in_path(X,S'): in_path(X,S).
14 path(S) :- path'(S); not __equals_2(S,_).
15 :- path(P), #count{T : in_path(T,P), select(T)} = 0.
```

Fig. 6. The transpiled program obtained by the program in Fig. 5 (UUIDs replaced by progressive integers). All predicates starting with double underscore are used by templates, of no interest for the end-user knowledge designer, and actually dealing with non-trivial modeling involving uninterpreted function symbols (lines 4–8).

length `length/1` in graph (`node/1`, `link/2`); the length of a path is the number of edges in the path. (2) `@dumbo/discard duplicate sets` selects in `unique/1` all sets from `set/1` and `in_set/2` that are not duplicate of another selected set; in case of duplicates, the set with the smallest ID, according to their natural order, is selected. Figure 5 reports a program using such templates: it is simple and isolated by the complexity of inner details of the applied templates (shown by the expanded program in Fig. 6).

6   Template Testing

Some properties of templates based on their HT-models can be used to establish invariants on the stable models of broader programs, in addition and thanks to the invariant that local predicate names are isolated in their template applications. This can be helpful for library knowledge designers interested in having some form of testing before deploying a template. We first consider a pair Π, Π' of programs, their HT-models, and possibly the fact that some predicates occur only in Π. Later on, we recast the results for templates. Let us start with simple conditions guaranteeing that some atoms have fixed truth values in all stable models of programs extending Π. Intuitively, as the possible interpretations of world T provide an overestimate on stable models, their intersection and union can be analyzed to identify atoms that are necessarily true or false in all (stable) models; see (9)–(10) below. On the other hand, for a fixed interpretation of world T, the possible interpretations of world H provide an overestimate on the models of a program reduct, and therefore their intersection can be analyzed to identify atoms that are necessarily true in the reduct; see (11) below.

Proposition 2. *Let Π, Π' be programs. It holds that*

$$\bigcap_{\langle I_H, I_T \rangle \in HT(\Gamma_\Pi)} I_T \subseteq \bigcap_{\langle I_H, I_T \rangle \in HT(\Gamma_\Pi \cup \Gamma_{\Pi'})} I_T \tag{9}$$

$$\bigcup_{\langle I_H, I_T \rangle \in HT(\Gamma_\Pi)} I_T \supseteq \bigcup_{\langle I_H, I_T \rangle \in HT(\Gamma_\Pi \cup \Gamma_{\Pi'})} I_T. \tag{10}$$

Moreover, for any interpretation I_T, it holds that

$$\bigcap_{\langle I_H, I_T \rangle \in HT(\Gamma_\Pi)} I_H \subseteq \bigcap_{\langle I_H, I_T \rangle \in HT(\Gamma_\Pi \cup \Gamma_{\Pi'})} I_H. \tag{11}$$

Proof. $HT(\Gamma_\Pi) \supseteq HT(\Gamma_\Pi \cup \Gamma_{\Pi'})$ follows from the monotonicity of here-and-there, and in turn implies (9)–(11). □

From (9)–(10) we obtain (12) below, and from (11) we obtain (13) below.

Corollary 1. *Let Π, Π' be programs, and I, J be interpretations with $J \subseteq I$.*

$$I \models \Pi \cup \Pi' \implies \bigcap_{\langle I_H, I_T \rangle \in HT(\Gamma_\Pi)} I_T \subseteq I \subseteq \bigcup_{\langle I_H, I_T \rangle \in HT(\Gamma_\Pi)} I_T. \tag{12}$$

$$I \models \Pi \cup \Pi' \wedge J \models (\Pi \cup \Pi')^I \implies \bigcap_{\langle I_H, I_T \rangle \in HT(\Gamma_\Pi)} I_H \subseteq J. \tag{13}$$

Example 6. Let Π be the following set of rules:

`:- a(X).   b(1).   g :- b(X), not a(X).   :- not d.   e :- not f.   f :- not e.`

For any Π', atom $a(c)$ is false in all models of $\Pi \cup \Pi'$, for all $c \in \mathbf{C}$; indeed, one can see that $a(c)$ is false in all I_T such that $\langle I_H, I_T \rangle \in HT(\Gamma_\Pi)$, and therefore (12) applies. Similarly, $b(1)$ is true in all models of $\Pi \cup \Pi'$ and their reducts; indeed, $b(1)$ is true in all I_H and I_T such that $\langle I_H, I_T \rangle \in HT(\Gamma_\Pi)$, and therefore (12)–(13) apply. We can go on and conclude that g is true in all models of $\Pi \cup \Pi'$ and their reducts, and that d is true in all models of $\Pi \cup \Pi'$ (but not necessarily in their reducts). Finally, it can be checked that e is true in all models of $(\Pi \cup \Pi')^I$ such that $I \models \Pi \cup \Pi'$ and e belongs to I (similar for f); (13) applies. ∎

As shown in the next proposition, further interpretations can be guaranteed to not be stable models of $\Pi \cup \Pi'$: the truth value of atoms whose predicates are guaranteed to occur in Π only, cannot compromise the satisfiability of Π'. Hence, if the instability of a model of Π only depends on such predicates, the instability extends to $\Pi \cup \Pi'$.

Proposition 3. *Let Π, Π' be programs, and X be a nonempty set of atoms of the form $p(\bar{c})$, with $p \in pred(\Pi) \setminus pred(\Pi')$. If $\langle I, I \cup X \rangle \in HT(\Gamma_\Pi)$, then $I \cup X \notin SM(\Pi \cup \Pi')$.*

Proof. The only interesting case is $I \cup X \models \Pi \cup \Pi'$, for which we shall show that $I \models (\Pi \cup \Pi')^{I \cup X}$. Since $\langle I, I \cup X \rangle \in HT(\Gamma_\Pi)$ by assumption, we thus have $I \models \Pi^{I \cup X}$, and therefore it remains to show $I \models (\Pi')^{I \cup X}$. From the assumption $I \cup X \models \Pi \cup \Pi'$, we have $I \cup X \models \Pi'$; combining with the assumption that atoms in X have predicates in $pred(\Pi) \setminus pred(\Pi')$, we can conclude that $I \models \Pi'$ and $(\Pi')^{I \cup X} = (\Pi')^I$. Hence, $I \models (\Pi')^{I \cup X}$, i.e. $I \cup X$ is not an equilibrium model of $\pi \cup \pi'$, and we are done. □

Example 7. Let Π be `__fail:- foo, not __fail`. Note that $HT(\Pi)$ includes $\langle \{\texttt{foo}\} \cup X, \{\texttt{foo}, \texttt{\_\_fail}\} \cup X \rangle$ and $\langle X, \{\texttt{\_\_fail} \cup X\} \rangle$, for every set X of atoms not including `foo` or `__fail`. For every Π' not mentioning `__fail`, $SM(\Pi \cup \Pi')$ cannot contain $\{\texttt{\_\_fail}\} \cup X$ and $\{\texttt{foo}, \texttt{\_\_fail}\} \cup X$; Proposition 3 applies. ∎

Elaborating on the above claim, it is possible to conclude that a specific set I of atoms cannot be extended to a stable model without including at least one atom in another given set I'. As a special case, when $I = \{\alpha\}$ and $I' = \emptyset$, falsity of α is guaranteed in all stable models; this is the case for `__fail` in Example 7.

Corollary 2. *Let Π, Π' be programs, and be I, I' disjoint sets of atoms. If every I_T with $I \subseteq I_T$ and $I' \cap I_T = \emptyset$ is such that there is $\langle I_H, I_T \rangle \in HT(\Gamma_\Pi)$ with $I_H \subset I_T$ and $p \in pred(\Pi) \setminus pred(\Pi')$ for all $p(\bar{c}) \in I_T \setminus I_H$, then there is no $I_T \in SM(\Pi \cup \Pi')$ with $I \subseteq I_T$ and $I' \cap I_T = \emptyset$.*

All in all, given a program Π whose local predicate names are guaranteed to be universally unique, we are interested in the following test types on Π:

T1. Given sets I, J of atoms, apply Corollary 1 to verify that atoms in I are true in all (classical) models of $\Pi \cup \Pi'$, and atoms in J are false in all models of $\Pi \cup \Pi'$, where Π' is any program.
T2. Given a model I of Π, and a set $J \subseteq I$, apply Corollary 1 to verify that atoms in J are true in all models of $(\Pi \cup \Pi')^I$, where Π' is any program.
T3. Given disjoint sets I, I' of atoms, apply Corollary 2 to verify that there is no $I \cup X \in SM(\Pi \cup \Pi')$ such that $X \cap I' \neq \emptyset$, for any set X of atoms and program Π' (i.e., some atom in I' must be true when atoms in I are true).

Note that the above tests are sound, and not intended to be complete. For instance, it is possible that there is no $I \cup X \in SM(\Pi \cup \Pi')$ such that $X \cap I' \neq \emptyset$, for any set X of atoms and program Π', but this is not captured by Corollary 2. Finally, template instantiation guarantees that local predicate names are universally unique.

Theorem 1. *Let π be a template, ρ be a global renaming ρ, and $\Pi = \pi\rho$. The requirement $p \in pred(\Pi) \setminus pred(\Pi')$ in Proposition 3 and Corollary 2 is guaranteed for predicates in $pred(\pi\rho) \cap \mathbf{P_L}$, under the assumption that generated UUIDs are unique and Π' has zero knowledge of the local renaming used by $\pi\rho$.*

Proof. By construction, $pred(\pi\rho) \cap \mathbf{P_L}$ are universally unique, and therefore they cannot occur in Π'. □

Regarding test support in DUMBO ASP, we expect Π to be the application of a template possibly extended with other rules providing a context for specific behaviors of the template. Our implementation is powered by meta encodings coupled with the *reification* of Π [23], as well as other rules to check for specific conditions. Tests of type **T1** are implemented by respectively computing the intersection and union of all models of Π. This can be respectively done by means of cautious reasoning tasks, i.e. finding whether an atom a belongs to all stable models, and brave reasoning task, i.e. finding whether an atom a belongs to some stable model. Type **T2** is implemented by computing the intersection of all models of Π^I by means of cautious reasoning. **T3** tests are implemented by enumerating the models of Π including I and disjoint from I', and for each of them checking that there is a model for their reduct satisfying the requirements of Corollary 2; both computational tasks are addressed by stable model search. We provide functions raising exceptions if some of **T1**–**T3** fail:

```
validate_in_all_models(program, true_atoms, false_atoms)
validate_in_all_models_of_the_reduct(program, model, true_atoms)
validate_cannot_be_extended_to_stable_model(program, true_at, false_at)
```

Example 8. Let Π be the following program obtained by applying the symmetric closure template from Sect. 5:

```
__apply_template__("@dumbo/symmetric closure",
        (relation, __relation), (closure, __closure)).
__relation(1,2).
```

The following tests are satisfied:

```
validate_in_all_models(Π, [__closure(1,2), __closure(2,1)], [])
validate_cannot_be_extended_to_stable_model(Π, [__closure(1,1)], [])
```

The first test above verifies that the expected atoms are true in all models of all extensions of Π. Note that the falsity of other instances of `__closure` cannot be guaranteed by analyzing classical models alone. To circumvent such a limitation, the second test above is used to effectively guarantee the falsity of atom `__closure(1,1)`, which is impossible to achieve without the notion of local predicate: if the addition of `__closure(1,1)` or `__relation(1,1)` to Π were not inhibited, there would be extension of Π having `__closure(1,1)` occurring in their stable models. For example, consider Π to be

```
__apply_template__("@dumbo/symmetric closure").
relation(1,2).
```

and the failing test

```
validate_cannot_be_extended_to_stable_model(Π, [closure(1,1)], [])
```

Knowledge designers can understand from the above failing test that the truth of atom `closure(1,1)` cannot be excluded by expansions of the above fragment of code. Consequently, they can opt for the version relying on local predicate names, which instead guarantees the desired property. ∎

7 Related Work

Our work has clear points of connection with three, not necessarily disjoint, lines of research: *a)* studies on modular ASP, *b)* practical approaches at verifying, debugging and unit testing ASP programs, and *c)* studies on relativized equivalence of logic programs under stable models semantics.

Regarding *a)*, *modular extensions to ASP* are historically classified in *programming-in-the-large* approaches, where the focus is on the composition of arbitrary sets of rules [22], with no explicit notion of scope, and *programming-in-the-small* approaches, where some form of scoping and notions of input/output predicates are proposed. The proposal of generalized quantifiers in [10], macros in [3], templates in [7] and module atoms in [8] fall in this latter category, while multi-context systems [9] feature aspects of both approaches. It must be noted that we propose a mixed approach which is mainly based on macro expansion, yet bringing aspects of programming-in-the-large. In particular, within a template we do not require an explicit distinction between input and output predicates, and definitions of predicates are not confined to the template. This is in contrast with macros and the previous proposal of templates, where input and output relations need to be specified ahead; moreover, in previous works name clashes were not explicitly addressed, although it was hinted at weaker handling of this issue without providing an actual invariant in this respect, especially in case transpiled code is moved in other projects. Note also that we aim to reuse templates in combination with future, unknown, logic specifications: in a way, we aim to compose programs from smaller building blocks, in a bottom-up fashion. Among the modular approaches, a somewhat orthogonal, top-down methodology proposed by Cabalar et al. [5] suggests that single logic programs, built by individual knowledge designers, can be devised in a modular structure. The correctness of such program parts, expressed in terms of a form of strong equivalence, helps in verifying the entire module structure (i.e. the original program).

Concerning *b)*, practical approaches to debugging and testing in the context of ASP, such as unit tests and TDD, have been considered mainly at the level of easing the embedding of test cases within a program. In this respect, linguistic extensions have been proposed to specify that some rules extended with a provided set of facts are expected to produce a stable model, or on the contrary that some stable models are not expected [2,15,18,20,21,28,32]. While it is clear that such linguistic extensions provide valuable tools for developers, they are not meant to guarantee that a set of rules can be used in another program still behaving in a controlled way. In part, this is due to the nonmonotonicity of stable model semantics, but there are also assumptions that cannot be enforced, among them the fact that a predicate is not used elsewhere. Another way of checking properties of a program is by defining *achievements* [25], that is, statements on the behavior of the first n rules of a program (said *prefixes*), for some $n \geq 1$. While achievements can be given in terms of first-order logic assertions, and can be automatically verified for linguistic fragments of ASP, by design they cannot be used to check properties of any portion of a program not being a prefix. Actually, the properties of a prefix of the program may be lost when other rules of the program are added, possibly due to the very last considered rules. Active research in this context led to ANTHEM [13], enabling the possibility of verifying that *io-programs* conform to first-order specifications, where an io-program is essentially a program with distinguished input and output predicates; input predicates only occur in rule bodies, and predicates not being input or output are called private. Since our templates provide a simple mechanism to guarantee that local predicates are essentially private, ANTHEM can be employed to verify some of their properties. The idea is to not use input predicates in rule heads, define all relations using local predicates, and finally define output predicates by applying the @dumbo/exact copy (arity$n$) templates.

Example 9. Recall the spanning tree template shown in Fig. 3. Let Π be

```
__apply_template__("spanning tree", (tree, __t)).
__apply_template__("@dumbo/exact copy (arity 2)",
    (input, __t), (output, tree)).
```

The application of Π w.r.t. the identity renaming, $\Pi[\,]$, is

```
{__t(X,Y) : link(X,Y), X < Y} = C-1 :- C = #count{X : node(X)}.

__t_1(X,Y) :- __t(X,Y).  % symmetric closure
__t_1(X,Y) :- __t(Y,X).  % symmetric closure

% connectedness
__start_2_1(X) :- X = #min{Y : node(Y)}.
__reach_2_1(X) :- __start_2_1(X).
__reach_2_1(Y) :- __reach_2_1(X), __t_1(X,Y).
:- node(X), not __reach_3_1(X).

tree(X0,X1) :- __t(X0,X1).    :- tree(X0,X1); not __t(X0,X1).  % output
```

(UUIDs replaced by progressive integers.) $\Pi[\,]$ is essentially an io-program with input predicates node/1 and link/2, and output predicate tree/2.   ∎

Finally, regarding *c)*, the notions of *relativised strong equivalence with projection* [11,17] and *visible strong equivalence* [4] address the issue of excluding hidden predicates when verifying the invariant properties of (parts of) logic programs. These notions might provide material for extending the testing functionalities of our library beyond invariants based on plain here-and-there models.

8   Conclusion

Templates introduce a naming convention to separate local and global names, and transpilation to ordinary ASP so to map local names to universally unique predicates. This way transpiled programs can be simply combined by concatenation with the invariant that local names of different template applications do not clash. Such an invariant can enforce other invariants, as for example ensuring that a global predicate is not further extended by other rules, including those that have not been written yet. Some testing functionalities in this direction are given in Sect. 6, and more are expected in our future work. Finally, we expect to enrich the core template library with other common patterns of ASP.

Acknowledgment. This work was partially supported by Italian Ministry of Research (MUR) under PRIN project PRODE "Probabilistic declarative process mining", CUP H53D23003420006 under PNRR project FAIR "Future AI Research", CUP H23C22000860006, under PNRR project Tech4You "Technologies for climate change adaptation and quality of life improvement", CUP H23C22000370006, and under PNRR project SERICS "SEcurity and RIghts in the CyberSpace", CUP H73C22000880001; by Italian Ministry of Health (MSAL) under POS projects CAL.HUB.RIA (CUP H53C22000800006) and RADIOAMICA (CUP H53C22000650006); by the LAIA lab (part of the SILA labs) and by GNCS-INdAM.

References

1. AlOmar, E.A., Wang, T., Raut, V., Mkaouer, M.W., Newman, C.D., Ouni, A.: Refactoring for reuse: an empirical study. Innov. Syst. Softw. Eng. **18**(1), 105–135 (2022)
2. Amendola, G., Berei, T., Ricca, F.: Testing in ASP: revisited language and programming environment. In: Faber, W., Friedrich, G., Gebser, M., Morak, M. (eds.) JELIA 2021. LNCS (LNAI), vol. 12678, pp. 362–376. Springer, Cham (2021). https://doi.org/10.1007/978-3-030-75775-5_24
3. Baral, C., Dzifcak, J., Takahashi, H.: Macros, macro calls and use of ensembles in modular answer set programming. In: Etalle, S., Truszczyński, M. (eds.) ICLP 2006. LNCS, vol. 4079, pp. 376–390. Springer, Heidelberg (2006). https://doi.org/10.1007/11799573_28
4. Bomanson, J., Janhunen, T., Niemelä, I.: Applying visible strong equivalence in answer-set program transformations. ACM Trans. Comput. Log. **21**(4), 33:1–33:41 (2020)
5. Cabalar, P., Fandinno, J., Lierler, Y.: Modular answer set programming as a formal specification language. Theory Pract. Log. Program. **20**(5), 767–782 (2020)
6. Calimeri, F., et al.: Asp-core-2 input language format. Theory Pract. Log. Program. **20**(2), 294–309 (2020)
7. Calimeri, F., Ianni, G.: Template programs for disjunctive logic programming: an operational semantics. AI Commun. **19**(3), 193–206 (2006)
8. Dao-Tran, M., Eiter, T., Fink, M., Krennwallner, T.: Modular nonmonotonic logic programming revisited. In: Hill, P.M., Warren, D.S. (eds.) ICLP 2009. LNCS, vol. 5649, pp. 145–159. Springer, Heidelberg (2009). https://doi.org/10.1007/978-3-642-02846-5_16
9. Dao-Tran, M., Eiter, T., Fink, M., Krennwallner, T.: Distributed nonmonotonic multi-context systems. In: KR. AAAI Press (2010)
10. Eiter, T., Gottlob, G., Veith, H.: Modular logic programming and generalized quantifiers. In: Dix, J., Furbach, U., Nerode, A. (eds.) LPNMR 1997. LNCS, vol. 1265, pp. 289–308. Springer, Heidelberg (1997). https://doi.org/10.1007/3-540-63255-7_22
11. Eiter, T., Tompits, H., Woltran, S.: On solution correspondences in answer-set programming. In: IJCAI, pp. 97–102. Professional Book Center (2005)
12. Erdem, E., Gelfond, M., Leone, N.: Applications of answer set programming. AI Mag. **37**(3), 53–68 (2016)
13. Fandinno, J., Lifschitz, V., Lühne, P., Schaub, T.: Verifying tight logic programs with anthem and vampire. Theory Pract. Log. Program. **20**(5), 735–750 (2020)

14. Fandinno, J., Pearce, D., Vidal, C., Woltran, S.: Comparing the reasoning capabilities of equilibrium theories and answer set programs. Algorithms **15**(6), 201 (2022)

15. Febbraro, O., Reale, K., Ricca, F.: Testing ASP programs in ASPIDE. In: CILC. CEUR Workshop Proceedings, vol. 810, pp. 115–129. CEUR-WS.org (2011)

16. Fink, M.: A general framework for equivalences in answer-set programming by countermodels in the logic of here-and-there. Theory Pract. Log. Program. **11**(2–3), 171–202 (2011)

17. Geibinger, T., Tompits, H.: Characterising relativised strong equivalence with projection for non-ground answer-set programs. In: Calimeri, F., Leone, N., Manna, M. (eds.) JELIA 2019. LNCS (LNAI), vol. 11468, pp. 542–558. Springer, Cham (2019). https://doi.org/10.1007/978-3-030-19570-0_36

18. Greßler, A., Oetsch, J., Tompits, H.: Harvey: a system for random testing in ASP. In: Balduccini, M., Janhunen, T. (eds.) LPNMR 2017. LNCS (LNAI), vol. 10377, pp. 229–235. Springer, Cham (2017). https://doi.org/10.1007/978-3-319-61660-5_21

19. Heyting, A.: Die formalen regeln der intuitionistischen logik, pp. 42–56. Deütsche Akademie der Wissenschaften zu Berlin, Mathematisch-Naturwissenschaftliche Klasse (1930)

20. Janhunen, T., Niemelä, I., Oetsch, J., Pührer, J., Tompits, H.: On testing answer-set programs. In: ECAI. Frontiers in Artificial Intelligence and Applications, vol. 215, pp. 951–956. IOS Press (2010)

21. Janhunen, T., Niemelä, I., Oetsch, J., Pührer, J., Tompits, H.: Random vs. structure-based testing of answer-set programs: an experimental comparison. In: Delgrande, J.P., Faber, W. (eds.) LPNMR 2011. LNCS (LNAI), vol. 6645, pp. 242–247. Springer, Heidelberg (2011). https://doi.org/10.1007/978-3-642-20895-9_26

22. Janhunen, T., Oikarinen, E., Tompits, H., Woltran, S.: Modularity aspects of disjunctive stable models. J. Artif. Intell. Res. **35**, 813–857 (2009)

23. Kaminski, R., Romero, J., Schaub, T., Wanko, P.: How to build your own asp-based system?! Theory Pract. Log. Program. **23**(1), 299–361 (2023)

24. Leach, P., Mealling, M., Salz, R.: A universally unique identifier (UUID) urn namespace. Internet Requests for Comments, July 2005. https://tools.ietf.org/html/rfc4122

25. Lifschitz, V.: Achievements in answer set programming. Theory Pract. Log. Program. **17**(5–6), 961–973 (2017)

26. Lifschitz, V.: Answer Set Programming. Springer, Cham (2019). https://doi.org/10.1007/978-3-030-24658-7

27. Lühne, P.: Discovering and proving invariants in answer set programming and planning. CoRR abs/1905.03196 (2019)

28. Oetsch, J., Prischink, M., Pührer, J., Schwengerer, M., Tompits, H.: On the small-scope hypothesis for testing answer-set programs. In: KR. AAAI Press (2012)

29. Oetsch, J., Seidl, M., Tompits, H., Woltran, S.: Beyond uniform equivalence between answer-set programs. ACM Trans. Comput. Log. **22**(1), 2:1–2:46 (2021)

30. Pearce, D.: Equilibrium logic. Ann. Math. Artif. Intell. **47**(1–2), 3–41 (2006)

31. Son, T.C., Pontelli, E., Balduccini, M., Schaub, T.: Answer set planning: a survey. Theory Pract. Log. Program. **23**(1), 226–298 (2023)

32. Vos, M.D., Kisa, D.G., Oetsch, J., Pührer, J., Tompits, H.: Annotating answer-set programs in LANA. Theory Pract. Log. Program. **12**(4–5), 619–637 (2012)

Cutting the Cake into Crumbs: Verifying Envy-Free Cake-Cutting Protocols Using Bounded Integer Arithmetic

Martin Mariusz Lester[(✉)] [ID]

University of Reading, Reading, UK
m.lester@reading.ac.uk

Abstract. Fair division protocols specify how to split a continuous resource (conventionally represented by a cake) between multiple agents with different preferences. Envy-free protocols ensure no agent prefers any other agent's allocation to his own. These protocols are complex and manual proofs of their correctness may contain errors. Recently, Bertram and others [5] developed the DSL *Slice* for describing these protocols and showed how verification of envy-freeness can be reduced to SMT instances in the theory of quantified non-linear real arithmetic. This theory is decidable, but the decision procedure is slow, both in theory and in practice.

We prove that, under reasonable assumptions about the primitive operations used in the protocol, counterexamples to envy-freeness can always be found with bounded integer arithmetic. Building on this result, we construct an embedded DSL for describing cake-cutting protocols in declarative-style C. Using the bounded model-checker CBMC, we reduce verifying envy-freeness of a protocol to checking unsatisfiability of pure SAT instances. This leads to a substantial reduction in verification time when the protocol is unfair.

Keywords: fair division · constraint programming · declarative C

1   Introduction

Alice and Bob wish to divide a cake fairly. Alice cuts the cake into two slices, which she believes to be of equal size. Bob chooses the slice he believes to be bigger. Alice takes the remaining slice. Neither Alice nor Bob *envies* the other. This is true regardless of the actual relative sizes of the slices. Maybe the cake is slightly taller at one end and Alice's cut failed to take this into account, but she did not realise. Or maybe the slices have equal weight, but one slice has a strawberry on top and Bob really likes strawberries, so he chose that slice. In any case, Alice believes that both slices are equal, so is happy with whichever slice was left; Bob believes that he chose a slice better than or as good as Alice's.

This story illustrates how competing agents may amicably agree to divide a continuous resource. Problems of this kind are widely studied in economics.

© The Author(s), under exclusive license to Springer Nature Switzerland AG 2023
M. Gebser and I. Sergey (Eds.): PADL 2024, LNCS 14512, pp. 100–115, 2023.
https://doi.org/10.1007/978-3-031-52038-9_7

```
#define SLICES 2
#define AGENTS 2

#include "crumbs.h"

int main() {
    slice whole, left, right;
    // Create the cake.
    whole = cake();
    // Agent 1 halves the cake.
    halve(1, left, right, whole);
    // Agent 2 picks the bigger slice.
    if (smaller(2, left, right)) {
        // Agent 2 picks the right slice.
        alloc(1, left);
        alloc(2, right);
    }
    else {
        // Agent 2 picks the left slice.
        alloc(1, right);
        alloc(2, left);
    }
    // Check that the focused agent doesn't feel envious.
    check();
}
```

Fig. 1. The well-known cut-and-choose protocol expressed in our cake-cutting protocol DSL *Crumbs*, which is embedded in C. Envy-freeness is verified using the bounded model-checker CBMC.

We represent the resource as a cake, but it could equally be land, advertising space or many other things. Similarly, the agents could (for example) be friends, companies or governments. But in general, we refer to such protocols for resource allocation, where the divisions are proposed and evaluated by the competing agents, as *cake-cutting protocols*. A protocol is *envy-free* if, on termination, no agent would prefer any other agent's allocation.

The *cut and choose* protocol we described is alluded to in Genesis [10], the first book of the Bible, but only works for two agents. Selfridge and Conway independently developed a protocol for three agents in the 1960s [16]. In this protocol, slices cut by one agent are further cut into smaller slices by another agent, with each agent ultimately receiving multiple discontinuous slices. The question of whether bounded protocols for larger numbers of agents existed remained unanswered for many years. It was resolved in 2016 by Aziz and Mackenzie [3,4], who developed a protocol for any number of agents. The bound on the number of queries (markings of the cake by an agent or evaluations of the value of a slice) required by the protocol depends only on the number of agents, but is a tower of exponentials.

But with protocols being so complex, how can we specify them unambiguously and ensure they are correct? Recently, Bertram and others [5] addressed this problem through a Domain-Specific Language (DSL) called *Slice* for specifying cake-cutting protocols. Furthermore, they showed how to verify envy-freeness of a protocol using a translation from a *Slice* program into an SMT instance, which can be solved using Z3 [15].

While this approach performs acceptably in verifying correctness of the protocols they examine, it fails to find counterexamples even on trivially unfair protocols. The root cause seems to be that they encode axioms about properties of agents' valuations. This in turn requires that they target the theory of quantified real arithmetic, which is decidable, but has doubly exponential time complexity, which often manifests in practice.

We propose an alternative approach in our DSL *Crumbs* in Sect. 3. We observe that, if we restrict our DSL to higher-level primitives, such as dividing a cake into equally sized pieces, or comparing two pieces to see which is bigger, we need only rely on properties of valuations that follow from the standard axioms of arithmetic. Furthermore, in Sect. 4.2, we show that to find counterexamples to envy-freeness for a bounded number of slices, we need only consider valuations consisting of bounded integers.

Our DSL is embedded in C. Following the approach demonstrated by Manthey [14] and by Lester [12], we write *declarative C* specifications for our cake-cutting operations in Sect. 4.3, then use bounded model-checker *CBMC* [8,11] to compile the program into a SAT instance that encodes the constraint satisfaction problem of finding an envy-inducing allocation; CBMC solves the SAT instance using a SAT solver (in our experiments, we use *Kissat* [6]). If it is unsatisfiable, the protocol is envy-free. If it is satisfiable, CBMC extracts an envy-inducing run of the protocol.

We evaluate *Crumbs* empirically and compare it with *Slice* in Sect. 5. We find that it is comparable in speed on correct protocols and significantly faster on incorrect protocols, where *Slice* does not terminate in a reasonable amount of time.

Our contributions are:

- the design (Sect. 3) and implementation (Sect. 4.3) of the embedded DSL *Crumbs* in declarative C;
- the novel reduction of verification of envy-freeness to bounded integer arithmetic in Sect. 4.1 and Sect. 4.2;
- the experimental evaluation in Sect. 5, which shows that *Crumbs* is competitive on correct protocols and faster on erroneous protocols.

The artifact supporting this paper [13] includes the implementation of *Crumbs* and scripts necessary to reproduce our experiments.

2   Preliminaries

Let us first formalise what we mean by a cake-cutting protocol.

A whole cake is represented by the real interval $[0, 1]$. A cake-cutting protocol is an algorithm that involves a fixed set of agents, A. Each agent a has a valuation function $V_a : \mathcal{P}([0, 1]) \to \mathbb{R}$, which specifies how much the agent desires different allocations of cake. The input to the protocol is the set of agents' valuation functions and the output is an allocation of a portion of the cake to each agent, $P : A \to \mathcal{P}([0, 1])$. A slice $s \subseteq [0, 1]$ is a connected subinterval of the cake. We require that allocations consist of a finite number of slices.

A feasible allocation is one where all $P(a)$ are disjoint: $\forall a_1, a_2.P(a_1) \cap P(a_2) = \emptyset$. A complete allocation is one where the whole cake is allocated: $\bigcup P(A) = [0, 1]$. An envy-free allocation is one where no agent would prefer any other agent's allocation: $\forall a_1, a_2.V_{a_1}(P(a_1)) \geq V_{a_1}(P(a_2))$.

In practice, we need to introduce some restrictions on the permitted valuation functions and allocations to develop interesting, realisable protocols. In their DSL *Slice*, Bertram and others adopt a reasonable set of assumptions on valuations, which we follow. Valuations must be normalised, non-negative, additive and continuous. In effect, this means that each agent's valuation function is fully described by a continuous, non-negative, everywhere-integrable density function v_a, such that $V_a([l, r]) = \int_l^r v_a(x)\, dx$ with $V_a([0, 1]) = 1$ and $V_a([l_1, r_1] \cup [l_2, r_2]) = V_a([l_1, r_1]) + V_a([l_2, r_2])$, assuming $[l_1, r_1]$ and $[l_2, r_2]$ are disjoint.

Returning to our initial example of Alice and Bob cutting a cake, these restrictions allow Alice to express that the value of a slice is proportional to its weight, and allow Bob to express that the value of a slice increases linearly with the weight of strawberries in the slice. However, they do not allow Alice to express that she is not very hungry and has no interest in having more than $\frac{1}{3}$ of the cake, or allow Bob to express that he would rather have a whole strawberry than two half strawberries.

We also do not allow the algorithm within the protocol to access the valuation functions directly. (They might in any case not be finitely representable.) Instead, the protocol is restricted to making a finite number of queries of the agents. Agents are assumed to respond truthfully and accurately at all times.

A common query model, adopted by *Slice*, is the Robertson-Webb model. In this model, agents may be asked to *evaluate* or *mark* a slice:

evaluate Given $[l, r]$, the agent returns the value of $V_a([l, r])$.
mark Given l and v, the agent picks r such that $V_a([l, r]) = v$.

Here we diverge from *Slice*, instead choosing the higher-level primitives *split*, *trim* and *compare*:

split The agent splits a slice into a number of smaller slices that he believes have equal value.
trim Given a reference slice and a bigger slice, the agent trims the bigger slice down to the size of the reference slice.
compare The agent says which of two slices he prefers.

This selection allows us to express well-known protocols without resorting to real arithmetic, which will be important for our approach to developing an efficient verification procedure.

3   The Crumbs DSL

We now give an overview of the *Crumbs* DSL, which is embedded in C. Figure 2 shows the first part of the Selfridge-Conway procedure, which illustrates most of the language's features.

Crumbs uses two datatypes to describe cake-cutting protocols: *agents* are represented by integer IDs, starting from 1; *slices* are contiguous intervals of cake.

Crumbs provides the following operations for cutting and allocating slices of cake:

cake() Returns a single slice, consisting of a whole cake.

halve(a, l, r, w) Agent *a* splits the slice *w* into 2 equal slices, which are assigned to *l* and *r*.

third(a, l, m, r, w) Agent *a* splits the slice *w* into 3 equal slices, which are assigned to *l*, *m* and *r*. (Variants for splits into equal numbers of smaller pieces can be supported analogously.)

trim(a, l, r, w, s) Agent *a* trims the slice *w* into 2 slices, assigned to *l* and *r*, such that he believes *l* is equal to slice *s*. (It is an error to trim *w* if *a* believes it is smaller than *s*.)

alloc(a, s) Allocates slice *s* to agent *a*.

check() Checks that the allocation is envy-free.

Note that the operations that cut the cake require empty slice variables to be passed in, which are used to store the resulting slices.

Slices can be compared with the following operations:

smaller(a, l, r) Returns true if agent *a* believes slice *l* is strictly smaller (lower value) than slice *r*.

lteq(a, l, r) Returns true if agent *a* believes slice *l* is less than or equal to slice *r*.

equal(a, l, r) Returns true if agent *a* believes slice *l* is less than or equal to slice *r*.

remember(s) Returns a copy of *s*, which can be compared, but should not be allocated.

same(s1, s2) Returns true if *s1* and *s2* are the same slices of cake. (That is, they represent the same interval of the cake, not two distinct intervals with the same perceived value.)

These operations are side-effect free functions.

For convenience, the following operations for sorting and swapping slices are also defined:

sort2(a, s1, s2) Agent *a* rearranges slices *s1* and *s2*, so that he believes they are sorted in increasing order.

sort3(a, s1, s2, s3) Agent *a* rearranges slices *s1*, *s2* and *s3*, so that he believes they are sorted in increasing order. (Variants for sorting larger numbers of slices can be supported analogously.)

```
#define SLICES 4
#define AGENTS 3

#include "crumbs.h"

int main() {
    slice whole, a, b, c;
    whole = cake();
    third(1, a, b, c, whole); // P1 divides cake into 3.

    sort3(2, c, b, a); // P2 thinks largest piece is A.

    if(equal(2, a, b)) {
        sort3(3, c, b, a);
        alloc(3, a);     // If P2 thinks 2 biggest parts equal,
        sort2(2, c, b); // P3, P2 and P1 choose a piece in order.
        alloc(2, b);
        alloc(1, c);
    }
    else {
        slice a1, a2;           // P2 trims A to match B.
        trim(2, a1, a2, a, b); // Call trimmed piece A1.

        slice trimmed = remember(a1); // Remember A1 for later.

        sort3(3, c, b, a1); // P3 chooses a piece.
        alloc(3, a1);

        // P2 chooses a piece, then P1.
        // If P3 didn't choose trimmed piece, P2 must.
        if (same(trimmed, a1)) {
            sort2(2, c, b);
            alloc(2, b);
            alloc(1, c);
        }
        else if (same(trimmed, b)) {
            alloc(2, b);
            alloc(1, c);
        }
        else { // Trimmed piece is c.
            alloc(2, c);
            alloc(1, b);
        }
    }
    check();
}
```

Fig. 2. The first part of the Selfridge-Conway protocol in *Crumbs*. The allocation generated is envy-free, but not complete.

swap(s1, s2) Swaps slices $s1$ and $s2$.

rol(s1, s2, s3) Rotates the slices $s1, s2, s3$ left, so that $s1 \leftarrow s2$, $s2 \leftarrow s3$ and $s3 \leftarrow s1$.

ror(s1, s2, s3) Rotates the slices $s1, s2, s3$ right; inverse of rol().

These operations move slice objects between variables. They are specified solely in terms of the preceding slice manipulation and comparison operations.

As our higher-level primitives are all expressible in the Robertson-Webb model, any *Crumbs* protocol will be expressible in *Slice*. Conversely, there may be *Slice* protocols that, because of the arithmetic they perform on slice sizes and valuations, are not expressible in *Crumbs*. However, we have not encountered any reasonable protocols like this.

Crumbs is embedded in C, so the usual C control flow features, such as loops and functions, are available. Here, *Crumbs* is more expressive than *Slice* from the user's perspective, as the latter does not support loops or recursive functions. However, this does not really affect the range of protocols that can be expressed, as the underlying verification procedure requires that control flow be bounded. For example, loops must have a statically computable bound on the number of iterations possible.

4   Verifying Protocols in Crumbs

4.1   Practical Verification of Envy-Freeness

A path of execution through a cake-cutting protocol consists of a sequence of operations: agents can cut slices of cake; agents can compare slices of cake; and slices of cake can be allocated to agents.

When execution terminates, the cake has been cut into a number of slices. Each slice has a size and, for each agent, a perceived value; these must all be non-negative. Operations on the path induce further constraints on the sizes and values of the slices. When an agent cuts a slice into two smaller slices, this induces a constraint that the sizes and values of the resulting slices are non-negative and sum to the size and values of the parent slice. Furthermore, if the agent cuts a slice into child sizes that he believes to be of equal value, this induces the constraint that the agent's values of the child slices are equal. If an agent compares two slices and declares that one is smaller than another, this induces the constraint that the agent's value of one slice is smaller than the other.

A protocol is envy-free if all paths that terminate have the property that, for all agents, the sum of an agent's perceived total value of allocated slices is not less than the agent's perceived total value of any other agent's allocated slices. That is, a protocol is not envy-free only if there is a path where an agent perceives his sum of slices to be smaller than another's. We can verify that a protocol is envy-free by verifying that no such path exists.

To get to a practical verification procedure from here, we need two further observations. Firstly, we can verify envy-freeness for each agent separately, *focusing* on one agent at a time. When we focus on one agent, it is sound to ignore the actual sizes of any slices and the valuations of other agents. We may lose completeness if there is an envy-inducing but infeasible path, whose infeasibility depends on these ignored details, for example, if a non-focused agent compares the same pair of slices twice. However, such situations are unlikely to occur in practice, other than as a result of an implementation error. This observation means that we can safely model a slice as a pair of numbers representing an interval over the focused agent's value, rather than a pair for each agent, plus a pair to represent the actual size.

Secondly, if agents are restricted to cutting and comparing slices, but cannot declare their perceived value numerically, all constraints on a path are equalities or inequalities of sums of the focused agent's value for a subset of slices; there are no constants, other than 0 and 1 (which represent the left and right ends of the whole cake). This observation will ultimately allow us to model slice values using bounded integers, rather than as real or rational numbers.

4.2 Bounded Integer Arithmetic

So that we can avoid having to invoke an SMT solver for real arithmetic, we would like to encode our constraint problem for finding envious runs using bounded integer arithmetic. Then it can be translated into a pure SAT instance, which may be faster to solve.

For a fixed number of slices n, even with real values, there are only finitely many different possible conjunctions of inequalities between sums of values of subsets of slices. Furthermore, we can clearly model all such relationships using integers, as we can approximate reals to arbitrary precision with rationals and, as we consider only sums with a bounded number of terms, we will not encounter any behaviour that is specific to irrational numbers, such as convergence of infinite sums. Multiplying by the denominator(s) of the rational numbers will then give integers. So a bound on the size of integers we need to consider to model the same relationships as with reals clearly exists, but in order to use this fact to construct a SAT instance for verification, we need to compute it explicitly. The following theorem gives an explicit bound.

Theorem 1. *Consider a finite set $X \subseteq \mathbb{R}$ of n non-negative real numbers. There is mapping $f : X \to \mathbb{N}$ of elements of X to non-negative integers that, extended point-wise to sets, preserves the sign (positive, negative or zero) of linear combinations of elements of X with coefficients -1, 0 or 1. Furthermore, $\sum f(X) \leq \frac{1}{6}(4^n + 2)$.*

Proof. We begin by proving the existence of f, leaving the bound on $\sum f(X)$ until later. Sort the elements of X in non-decreasing order, so that $X = \{x_1, \ldots, x_n\}$ with $x_1 \leq \ldots \leq x_n$. Argue by induction over n.

Base case: $n = 0$, so $X = \emptyset$ with f being the empty mapping and $\sum f(X) = 0$.

Inductive step: Suppose we have built a suitable mapping f_k for $X_k = \{x_1, \ldots, x_k\}$. We aim to build a mapping f_{k+1} for $X_{k+1} = \{x_1, \ldots, x_k, x_{k+1}\}$.

We need an f_{k+1} that preserves sign of linear combinations of interest. We attempt to construct f_{k+1} by extending f_k. This will preserve the sign of any linear combination over X_k.

For the new linear combinations over X_{k+1}, we need to choose a value for $f_{k+1}(x_{k+1})$ somewhere between $f_k(x_k)$ (in the case that $x_k = x_{k+1}$) and $\sum f(X_k) + 1$ (in the case that $\sum X_k - f(x_{k+1})$ is positive) that gives them the correct sign. If there is such an integer value available, we pick it and we are done. If not, the value we would like to assign lies between two integers, say i and $i + 1$. In this case, we pick $f_{k+1}(x_{k+1}) = i + \frac{1}{2}$, then double all values assigned by f_{k+1} to restore integrality.

We now turn our attention to the bound $\sum f(X) \leq \frac{1}{6}(4^n + 2)$. The construction above gives the recurrence relation $\sum f(X_0) = 0$ and $\sum f(X_{k+1}) \leq max(\sum f(X_k) + 1, 4 \sum f(X_k) - 1)$, which solves to the required bound.

Note that, for any $Y, Z \subseteq X$, if $\sum Y \leq \sum Z$, the theorem gives us $\sum f(Y) \leq \sum f(Z)$. Thus, as a corollary, if there is an envious run of a protocol that creates at most n slices with real values, then there is an envious run with n slices with non-negative integer values with total sum at most $\frac{1}{6}(4^n + 2)$. Conversely, if there is an envious run with integer values, it is trivially an envious run with real values; if we wish, we can divide by the sum of all slices to normalise the values to the range $[0, 1]$.

When we use integers to measure the value of a slice, according to a focused agent, we call them *focused agent crumbs* or simply *crumbs*.

4.3   Embedding Crumbs in Declarative C

Crumbs is implemented as a C header file, to be included at the top of a C program that describes a cake-cutting protocol using the supplied datatypes and operations. Although protocols in *Crumbs* are written in an imperative style as C programs, they are not intended to be compiled and executed. Rather, through the use of verifier-level nondeterminism, assumptions and assertions, the program specifies a constraint satisfaction problem, which can be solved using the program model-checker CBMC. We refer to this style of C program, which repurposes C as a constraint programming language, as *declarative C*.

Figure 3 shows the definition of some of the primitive operations and datatypes used in *Crumbs*. Internally, the *slice* datatype is a C `struct` storing two points `l` and `r`, representing the left-hand and right-hand ends of a slice of cake, as distances from the left-hand end of the cake, measured in *focused agent crumbs*. The datatype `P` is an unsigned integer used to represent a distance, weight or value in crumbs.

The constant `MAX_RIGHT` is the bound on the number of crumbs needed for sound verification. The function `cake()` creates a new slice representing the whole cake. As the value of the right end of the slice is uninitialised, CBMC will treat it as a nondeterministic integer that can take any value within the range of its datatype. The assumption (introduced by `__CPROVER_assume`) tells CBMC that it need only consider values up to the bound.

```
// Maximum crumbs needed for this number of slices.
#define MAX_RIGHT (((1 << ((SLICES) * 2)) + 2) / 6)

// Type of a slice of cake.
struct slice {
    P l; // Left end of slice.
    P r; // Right end of slice.
};

typedef struct slice slice;

// Create a whole cake.
inline slice cake() {
    slice s;
    s.l = 0;
    __CPROVER_assume(s.r <= MAX_RIGHT);
    return s;
}

// In: left/right are new slice objects; whole is a slice
// Out: left and right are a division of whole
#define cut(left, right, whole)
    // Pick a mid-point between the ends of the slice.
    P mid;
    __CPROVER_assume(whole.l <= mid && mid <= whole.r);
    left.l = whole.l;
    left.r = mid;
    right.l = mid;
    right.r = whole.r;

// Return value of a slice according to the focused agent.
P inline value(slice s) {
    return s.r - s.l;
}

// Totals for each focused agent.
P totals[AGENTS] = {0};

// Return the total of agent X (lvalue).
#define total(X) totals[(X)-1]
```

Fig. 3. Definitions of low-level primitives in *Crumbs*. Some details have been elided for readability.

```
// According to agent a, is slice l smaller than r?
#define smaller(a, l, r) \
    ((a) == AGENT ? value(l) < value(r) : nondet_char())

// Cut a slice of cake in half.
// w is whole slice; l and r are new slice objects; a is agent cutting.
// Afterwards, l and r are slices.
#define halve(a, l, r, w) \
    cut(l, r, w);
    // If focused agent is cutting, he must think slices are same size.
    __CPROVER_assume(((a) != AGENT) || (value(l) == value(r)));

// Trim slice s1 so it is same size as slice s2, according to agent a.
// Slice s1a is the same size as s2; s1b is the trimmings.
// Requires that agent a believes s1 is at least as big as s2.
#define trim(a, s1a, s1b, s1, s2)
    assert(((a) != AGENT) || (value(s1) >= value(s2)));
    cut(s1a, s1b, s1);
    __CPROVER_assume(((a) != AGENT) || (value(s1a) == value(s2)));

// Allocate slice s to agent a.
#define alloc(a, s)
    totals[a-1] += value(s);

// Check that the focused agent doesn't feel envious of anyone else.
void inline check() {
    for (int n = 1; n <= AGENTS; n++) {
        assert(total(n) <= total(AGENT));
    }
}
```

Fig. 4. Definitions of higher-level operations in *Crumbs*. Some details have been elided for readability.

The operations described in the Sect. 3 are implemented using the following lower-level operations:

cut(l, r, w) Cuts the slice *w* into 2 slices, which are assigned to *l* and *r*.
value(s) Returns the value of slice *s* for the currently focused agent.
total(a) The total value of all slices allocated to agent *a*, according to the currently focused agent.

cut() merits some further explanation. Here we use verifier nondeterminism to allow a slice to be cut anywhere. The assumption ensures that the cut must be between the left and right ends of the slice.

Figure 4 shows the implementation of a representative sample of higher-level operations. As explained earlier, we need only consider the valuation of a single agent at any particular time. We call this agent the *focused agent*, represented by the constant `AGENT`. A common pattern is that we implement operations performed by other agents using nondeterminism. We can see this most simply in `smaller()`: the focused agent does not know or care whether other agents consider one slice to be smaller than another; his envy or lack thereof depends only on his own valuations.

To have an agent `halve()` a slice, we cut it nondeterministically, then, if the agent doing the cutting is focused, use an assumption to restrict the verifier to considering only paths of execution in which the agent believes the two slices are equal. The implementation of `trim()` is similar, but also uses an `assert()` to check that the agent does believe that the slice to be trimmed is bigger than the reference slice.

When slices are allocated to an agent, `alloc()` adds their value to a running total. At the end of a protocol, `check()` asserts that the focused agent does not believe any other agent has a bigger portion. If there is a path of execution that violates this assertion, CBMC will flag it as a verification failure.

4.4   Verifying Other Safety Properties

There are some other safety properties that our implementation does not verify. We do not verify whether all slices are allocated, or whether all slices are allocated at most once. (The former intentionally does not hold in some protocols.) Nor do we verify that the number of slices generated is at most `SLICES`. However, these properties can also be verified relatively cheaply using CBMC, at least at the level of accuracy comparable to a standard static analysis, by adjusting the header file to provide different definitions of the cake-cutting operations, which ignore the size of slices and instead track the number of slices.

Firstly, we need to check that slices cannot be copied, other than using `remember()`. We can do this by turning `slice` into a C++ object with private copy constructor and copy assignment operator, then type-checking the protocol as a C++ program.

Next, to check that `SLICES` is big enough, we need to add a global variable to track the number of slices created, which we increment on calls to `cut()` and compare with `SLICES` in `check()`.

To check that no slice is allocated twice, we can augment `slice()` with a flag indicating that a slice is "live", set on creation by `cake()`, preserved on child slices and cleared on parent slices slices by `cut()`, and cleared by calls to `alloc()` and `remember()`. Then we can add an assertion to forbid `alloc()` on a slice without the flag.

Finally, to check that all slices are allocated (if this is intended by the protocol), we can add a global variable to track the number of slices allocated, which we increment on calls to `alloc()`, then modify `check()` to compare this with the number actually created.

We do not explicitly verify that protocols necessarily terminate, and our definition of envy-freeness permits non-terminating protocols. However, CBMC's translation to SAT will not terminate if it cannot statically bound the number of iterations of a loop or the depth of recursive function calls, so implicitly it does verify that protocols terminate.

5   Evaluation

We evaluated our implementation of *Crumbs* experimentally by benchmarking verification of envy-freeness for the same protocols used by Bertram and others in their presentation of *Slice*. As *Crumbs* does not support some of the low-level primitives used in *Slice*, the *Crumbs* programs are necessarily different from their *Slice* counterparts, but the high-level structure and sequence of operations is similar.

All benchmarks were run on a machine running Debian GNU/Linux 12 with an Intel i5-7500 CPU at 3.40 GHz and 64 GB RAM. As our backend verifier for *Crumbs*, we used *CBMC 5.83.0* with external SAT solver *Kissat sc2022-bulky*. Code and scripts to reproduce our results are in the artifact [13] accompanying this paper.

The results of our benchmarks are shown in Table 1. For most of the protocols, verification takes around a second for both *Crumbs* and *Slice*. The full Selfridge-Conway protocol is somewhat more complicated than the others, and here we see a meaningful difference. *Crumbs* is slower than *Slice*, but still roughly comparable.

Table 1. Time taken to verify envy-freeness for cake-cutting protocols for 2–3 agents, in both *Crumbs* and *Slice*. *Crumbs* verification times combine CBMC compilation and Kissat solving; CBMC time was negligible.

	Crumbs verification time (s)				Slice verification time (s)		
Protocol	*Agent 1*	*Agent 2*	*Agent 3*	*Total*	*Compile*	*Z3*	*Total*
Cut-Choose	0.02	0.02	-	0.04	0.11	0.04	0.15
Surplus	0.03	0.06	-	0.09	1.14	0.04	1.18
Selfridge-Conway-Surplus	0.34	1.52	1.74	3.60	1.22	0.93	2.15
Selfridge-Conway-Full	9.84	20.38	22.83	53.05	1.20	21.71	22.91

To demonstrate our claim that our approach is good for finding counterexamples to incorrect protocols, we deliberately introduced errors to each protocol. Table 2 shows the time taken to find counterexamples to envy-freeness for the dissatisfied agent with *Crumbs*. With *Slice*, Z3 did not terminate in less than 30 min on any of the examples we tried. Thus it is clear that our approach performs better for disproving envy-freeness.

Verifying envy-freeness corresponds to showing that a SAT instance is unsatisfiable, which is a co-NP problem. Conversely, finding a counterexample corresponds to showing that it is satisfiable, which is an NP problem. SAT solvers are typically faster on satisfiable instances than on unsatisfiable instances of comparable problems, which explains why our approach is fast for disproving envy-freeness.

Table 2. Time taken to find counterexamples to envy-freeness for erroneous cake-cutting protocols for 2–3 agents in *Crumbs*.

Protocol	Agent	Time (s)	Description of error introduced
Cut-Allocate	2	0.02	Agent 1 cuts and chooses.
Cut-Choose	2	0.02	Slices allocated wrong way round in one branch.
Surplus	2	0.05	Unsafe trim of slice smaller than reference.
S-C-S (1)	2	0.13	Allocates trimmings of slice instead of trimmed slice.
S-C-S (2)	1	0.05	Agent 2 not forced to take trimmed slice if available.
S-C-F	1	0.07	Trimmings cut by agent who took trimmed slice.

6   Related Work

The literature on fair division is broad. We surveyed some of the main results in cake cutting in Sect. 1. For an overview, see Procaccia's article [16]. For a sample of the breadth of the field, see the two Dagstuhl seminars on the topic [2,7].

Slice [5] verifies envy-freeness using an encoding in quantified non-linear real arithmetic, which it solves using the SMT solver Z3 [15]. Decidability of this theory was proved by Tarski using quantifier elimination. Most modern implementations use a variant of the algorithm Cylindrical Algebraic Decomposition (CAD), but its time complexity is doubly exponential. The SMT solver SMT-RAT [9] is specialised for solving problems involving real arithmetic and manages to avoid the worst-case time complexity in many cases.

Although we reduced verification of envy-freeness to integer arithmetic, the model of cake-cutting we adopted would also permit a reduction to Mixed Integer Linear Programming (MILP), which may be faster in practice. Linear inequalities over the reals can be solved using Fourier-Motzkin elimination. Although we derived our bound on the size of integers required directly, it may also be possible to find a bound through an analysis of Fourier-Motzkin elimination.

CBMC [8,11] is a bounded model-checker for C programs. It uses a variety of program transformations, such as loop unrolling and function inlining, to bound behaviour in programs and reduce program verification to SAT. Manthey [14] illustrated how to use declarative C and CBMC to generate SAT instances corresponding to a puzzle game for the SAT Competition. Meanwhile, Lester used this approach to build the constraint programming system CoPTIC [12] and the XCSP3 constraint solver Exchequer [1]. Kissat is a leading SAT solver [6]; variants of Kissat dominated the SAT Competition 2022.

7   Conclusion

We have developed and presented the embedded DSL *Crumbs* for describing cake-cutting protocols and verifying envy-freeness. Our verification procedure uses a novel encoding of envy-freeness as a constraint satisfaction problem in declarative C that requires only integer arithmetic. This enables us to implement it efficiently using the bounded model-checker for C programs CBMC, which in turn translates the verification problem into a pure SAT instance. We have evaluated *Crumbs* experimentally on a number of well-known protocols and some erroneous versions of those protocols. Verification of correct protocols was comparable in speed to the existing cake-cutting DSL *Slice*. For erroneous protocols, the verification procedure employed in *Slice* was too slow to be practical, whereas our approach was very fast.

There are further safety properties that we could verify by extending our implementation, but we leave that for future work. By combining our encoding with ideas from syntax-guided synthesis, it would be possible to encode the problem of constructing an envy-free cake-cutting protocol with a bounded number of slices as a QBF instance, although we do not expect this approach to be fast enough to be practical. It may also be worthwhile to attempt an encoding of envy-freeness as a MILP instance; we suspect this may be faster than both the integer arithmetic used in *Crumbs* and the quantified real arithmetic used in *Slice*.

References

1. Audemard, G., Lecoutre, C., Lonca, E.: Proceedings of the 2022 XCSP3 competition. CoRR abs/2209.00917 (2022). https://doi.org/10.48550/arXiv.2209.00917
2. Aumann, Y., Lang, J., Procaccia, A.D.: Fair division (dagstuhl seminar 16232). Dagstuhl Rep. **6**(6), 10–25 (2016). https://doi.org/10.4230/DagRep.6.6.10
3. Aziz, H., Mackenzie, S.: A discrete and bounded envy-free cake cutting protocol for any number of agents. In: Dinur, I. (ed.) IEEE 57th Annual Symposium on Foundations of Computer Science, FOCS 2016, 9–11 October 2016, Hyatt Regency, New Brunswick, New Jersey, USA, pp. 416–427. IEEE Computer Society (2016). https://doi.org/10.1109/FOCS.2016.52
4. Aziz, H., Mackenzie, S.: A bounded and envy-free cake cutting algorithm. Commun. ACM **63**(4), 119–126 (2020). https://doi.org/10.1145/3382129
5. Bertram, N., Levinson, A., Hsu, J.: Cutting the cake: a language for fair division. CoRR abs/2304.04642 (2023). https://doi.org/10.48550/arXiv.2304.04642
6. Biere, A., Fleury, M.: Gimsatul, IsaSAT and Kissat entering the SAT competition 2022. In: Balyo, T., Heule, M., Iser, M., Järvisalo, M., Suda, M. (eds.) Proceedings of the SAT Competition 2022 - Solver and Benchmark Descriptions. Department of Computer Science Series of Publications B, vol. B-2022-1, pp. 10–11. University of Helsinki (2022). http://hdl.handle.net/10138/359079
7. Brams, S.J., Pruhs, K., Woeginger, G.J. (eds.): Fair Division, 24.06.–29.06.2007, Dagstuhl Seminar Proceedings, vol. 07261. Internationales Begegnungs- und Forschungszentrum fuer Informatik (IBFI), Schloss Dagstuhl, Germany (2007). http://drops.dagstuhl.de/portals/07261/
8. Clarke, E., Kroening, D., Lerda, F.: A tool for checking ANSI-C programs. In: Jensen, K., Podelski, A. (eds.) TACAS 2004. LNCS, vol. 2988, pp. 168–176. Springer, Heidelberg (2004). https://doi.org/10.1007/978-3-540-24730-2_15
9. Corzilius, F., Kremer, G., Junges, S., Schupp, S., Ábrahám, E.: SMT-RAT: an open source C++ toolbox for strategic and parallel SMT solving. In: Heule, M., Weaver, S. (eds.) SAT 2015. LNCS, vol. 9340, pp. 360–368. Springer, Cham (2015). https://doi.org/10.1007/978-3-319-24318-4_26

10. Klarreich, E.: How to cut cake fairly and finally eat it too. Quanta Magazine, October 2016. https://www.quantamagazine.org/new-algorithm-solves-cake-cutting-problem-20161006/

11. Kroening, D., Tautschnig, M.: CBMC – C bounded model checker. In: Ábrahám, E., Havelund, K. (eds.) TACAS 2014. LNCS, vol. 8413, pp. 389–391. Springer, Heidelberg (2014). https://doi.org/10.1007/978-3-642-54862-8_26

12. Lester, M.M.: CoPTIC: constraint programming translated into C. In: Sankaranarayanan, S., Sharygina, N. (eds.) Tools and Algorithms for the Construction and Analysis of Systems. TACAS 2023. LNCS, vol. 13994, pp. 173–191. Springer, Cham (2023). https://doi.org/10.1007/978-3-031-30820-8_13

13. Lester, M.M.: Crumbs: A DSL for Verifying Envy-Free Cake-Cutting Protocols using Bounded Integer Arithmetic, January 2024. https://doi.org/10.5281/zenodo.10205142

14. Manthey, N.: Solving summle.net with SAT. In: Balyo, T., Heule, M., Iser, M., Järvisalo, M., Suda, M. (eds.) Proceedings of the SAT Competition 2022 - Solver and Benchmark Descriptions. Department of Computer Science Report Series B, vol. B-2022-1, pp. 70–71. University of Helsinki (2022). http://hdl.handle.net/10138/359079

15. de Moura, L., Bjørner, N.: Z3: an efficient SMT solver. In: Ramakrishnan, C.R., Rehof, J. (eds.) TACAS 2008. LNCS, vol. 4963, pp. 337–340. Springer, Heidelberg (2008). https://doi.org/10.1007/978-3-540-78800-3_24

16. Procaccia, A.D.: Cake cutting: not just child's play. Commun. ACM **56**(7), 78–87 (2013). https://doi.org/10.1145/2483852.2483870

A Direct ASP Encoding for Declare

Francesco Chiariello[1], Valeria Fionda[2], Antonio Ielo[2(✉)],
and Francesco Ricca[2]

[1] University of Naples Federico II, Naples, Italy
`francesco.chiariello@unina.it`
[2] University of Calabria, Rende, Italy
{`valeria.fionda,antonio.ielo,francesco.ricca`}`@unical.it`

Abstract. Answer Set Programming (ASP), a well-known declarative programming paradigm, has recently found practical application in Process Mining, particularly in tasks involving declarative specifications of business processes. Declare is the most popular declarative process modeling language. It provides a way to model processes by sets of constraints, expressed in Linear Temporal Logic over Finite Traces (LTL$_f$), that valid traces must satisfy. Existing ASP-based solutions encode a Declare constraint by the corresponding LTL$_f$ formula or its equivalent automaton, derived using well-established techniques. In this paper, we propose a novel encoding for Declare constraints, which models their semantics *directly* as ASP rules, without resorting to intermediate representations. We evaluate the effectiveness of the novel approach on two Process Mining tasks by comparing it to alternative ASP encodings and a Python library for Declare.

Keywords: Answer Set Programming · Process Mining · Declare

1 Introduction

A process, as defined in the Project Management Body of Knowledge [1], is (sic) *"a set of interrelated actions and activities performed to achieve a specified set of products, results, or services"*, typically performed in a periodic, recurrent or continuous fashion. Process Mining [2] is an interdisciplinary field that analyzes processes, using a blend of formal methods, data science, computer science, and business process management tools. One of the main tasks of Process Mining is *conformance checking*, which evaluates the validity of a particular process execution, referred to as a *trace*, with respect to a *process model*. This process model is a formal mathematical representation that allows

This work was partially supported by the Italian Ministry of Research (MUR) under PRIN project PINPOINT - CUP H23C22000280006, PRIN project HypeKG - CUP H53D23003710006, PRIN PNRR project DISTORT - CUP H53D23008170001, PNRR projects FAIR "Future AI Research" - Spoke 9 - WP9.1 and WP9.2- CUP H23C22000860006 and by the project "Borgo 4.0", POR Campania FESR 2014–2020.

M. Gebser and I. Sergey (Eds.): PADL 2024, LNCS 14512, pp. 116–133, 2023.
https://doi.org/10.1007/978-3-031-52038-9_8

for various forms of reasoning related to the underlying process. Process models can be expressed using either *imperative* or *declarative* languages. Imperative process models explicitly describe all possible execution traces and are effective in representing well-structured routine processes. However, their use is impractical when the process involves a large number of activities characterized by intricate coordination patterns. In such cases, declarative process models may be more convenient. Declarative process modeling uses logic-based languages to provide a set of constraints on the possible executions, where every execution is allowed unless a constraint explicitly prohibits it. Linear temporal logic over finite traces (LTL$_f$) emerged as a natural formalism for declarative process modeling [24]. However, in Process Mining applications, *"free-form"* LTL$_f$ formulae are rarely used for specification purposes. Instead, a limited set of predefined patterns, derived from the realm of systems' verification literature [14], is exploited. Restricting modeling languages to a set of predefined patterns accomplishes two important objectives: *(i)* it simplifies the tasks of modelers [25], and *(ii)* it paves the way for ad-hoc implementations that may outperform generic LTL$_f$ techniques in terms of efficiency. In particular, the most widely used declarative process modeling language in Process Mining applications is Declare [4], which consists of a set of patterns ("templates") whose semantics can be formalized in LTL$_f$. Although, historically, the initial semantics of Declare was not provided in terms of LTL$_f$, its LTL$_f$ formalization became the cornerstone of many reasoning tasks within Declare [12]. Answer Set Programming (ASP; [6,21,32]) has been used in planning applications to inject domain-dependent knowledge rules, similar to a predefined set of patterns, obtained by encoding an action theory language into ASP [35]. Recently, ASP has been proposed to tackle various computational tasks in Declare-based Process Mining [10,26]. The work of [11] proposes a solution based on the well-known LTL$_f$-to-automata translation [22]. This transformation maps a LTL$_f$ formula φ into a symbolic automaton $\mathcal{M}_\varphi$ such that, given a trace π, $\pi \models \varphi$ if and only if $\mathcal{M}_\varphi$ recognizes π. In a different study [28], authors suggested a method for encoding the semantics of temporal operators into a logic program, enabling the encoding of arbitrary LTL$_f$ formulae, by a reification of their syntax tree. Nevertheless, as far as we know, there has been no prior attempt to *directly* encode the Declare LTL$_f$ patterns library using ASP – "directly" refers to an encoding that represents the semantics of Declare constraints without relying on any intermediary translation. In this paper, we fill this gap by proposing a direct encoding of the most common Declare constraints and comparing it to existing ASP-based encodings on several logs commonly used in Process Mining literature [31]. The experimental evaluation aims to achieve two primary objectives: *(i)* compare the ASP-based methods on the conformance and query checking tasks; and, *(ii)* evaluate the performance of our direct encoding approach. Code and data to reproduce our experiments are publicly available at https://github.com/ainnoot/padl-2024.

2   Preliminaries

In this section fundamental concepts related to Process Mining, linear temporal logic over finite traces, the Declare process modeling language, and Answer Set Programming are discussed.

2.1   Process Mining

Process Mining [2] is a research area at the intersection of Process Science and Data Science. It leverages data-driven techniques to extract valuable insights from operational processes by analyzing event data (i.e., event logs) collected during their execution. A process can be seen as a sequence of activities that collectively allow to achieve a specific goal. A trace represents a concrete execution of a process recording the exact sequence of events and decisions taken in a specific instance. Process Mining plays a significant role in Business Process Management [36], by providing data-driven approaches for the analysis of events logs directly extracted from enterprise information systems. Typical Process Mining tasks include: *Conformance checking* that aims at verifying if a trace is conformant to a specified model and, for logic-based techniques, *Query Checking* that evaluates *queries* (i.e., formulae incorporating variables) against the event log. Several formalisms can be used in process modelling, with Petri nets [3] and BPMN [37] being among the most widely used, both following an imperative paradigm. Imperative process models explicitly describe all the valid process executions and can be impractical when the process under consideration is excessively intricate. In such cases, declarative process modelling [1] is a more appropriate choice. Declarative process models specify the desired properties (in terms of constraints) that each valid process execution must satisfy, rather than prescribing a step-by-step procedural flow. Using declarative modeling approaches allows to easily specify the desired behaviors: everything that does not violate the rules is allowed. Declarative specifications are typically expressed in Declare [4], Linear Temporal Logic over Finite Traces (LTL$_f$) [16], or Linear Temporal Logic over Process Traces (LTL$_p$) [17].

2.2   Linear Temporal Logic over Finite Traces

This section recaps minimal notions of Linear Temporal Logic over Finite Traces (LTL$_f$) [24]. We start by introducing its syntax and semantics, and then we informally describe its temporal operators, and some Process Mining application-specific notation.

Syntax. Let $\mathcal{A}$ be a finite set of propositional symbols. A *finite trace* is a sequence $\pi = \pi_0 \cdots \pi_{n-1}$, with $n \in \mathbb{N}$. For each i, $\pi_i \subseteq \mathcal{A}$ is its i-th *state*, and $|\pi| = n$ denotes the trace *length*. LTL$_f$ is an extension of propositional logic that can be used to reason about temporal properties of traces. It shares the same syntax as Linear Temporal Logic (LTL) [33], but it is interpreted over

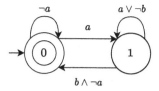
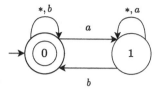

Fig. 1. Left: Minimal automaton for the LTL$_f$ formula $\varphi = $ G $(a \rightarrow$ X F $b)$. Models of propositional formulae (labeling the transitions) compactly represent sets of symbols; Right: Minimal automaton for φ interpreted as a LTL$_p$ formula, where $*$ denotes any $x \in \mathcal{A} \setminus \{a, b\}$. A comma on edges denotes multiple transitions.

finite traces rather than *infinite* ones. An LTL$_f$ formula φ over $\mathcal{A}$ is defined according to the following grammar:

$$\varphi ::= \top \mid a \mid \neg\varphi \mid \varphi \wedge \varphi \mid \mathsf{X}\, \varphi \mid \varphi_1 \ \mathsf{U} \ \varphi_2,$$

where $a \in \mathcal{A}$. We assume common propositional ($\vee$, $\rightarrow$, $\longleftrightarrow$, etc.) and temporal logic shorthands. In particular, for temporal operators, we define *eventually* operator F $\varphi \equiv \top$ U φ, the *always* operator G $\varphi \equiv \neg$F $\neg\phi$, the *weak until* operator φ W $\varphi' \equiv$ G $\varphi \vee \varphi$ U φ' and *weak next* operator X$_w$ $\varphi \equiv \neg$X $\neg\varphi \equiv$ X $\varphi \vee \neg$X $\top$.

Semantics. Let φ be an LTL$_f$ formula, π a finite trace, $0 \leq i < |\pi|$ an integer. The *satisfaction relation*, denoted by $\pi, i \models \varphi$, is defined recursively as follows:

- $\pi, i \models \top$;
- $\pi, i \models p$ iff $p \in \pi_i$;
- $\pi, i \models \neg\varphi$ iff $\pi, i \models \varphi$ does not hold;
- $\pi, i \models \varphi_1 \wedge \varphi_2$ iff $\pi, i \models \varphi_1$ and $\pi, i \models \varphi_2$;
- $\pi, i \models$ X φ iff $i < |\pi| - 1$ and $\pi, i + 1 \models \varphi$;
- $\pi, i \models \varphi_1$ U φ_2 iff $\exists j$ with $i \leq j \leq |\pi|$ s.t. $\pi, j \models \varphi_2$ and $\forall k$ with $i \leq k < j$, $\pi, k \models \varphi_1$.

We say that π is a *model* for φ if $\pi, 0 \models \varphi$, denoted as $\pi \models \varphi$. Each LTL$_f$ formula φ can be associated to a minimal automaton $\mathcal{M}(\varphi)$ over $2^{\mathcal{A}}$ such that for whatever trace π it holds that $\pi \models \varphi$ if and only if π, interpreted as a string over $2^{\mathcal{A}}$, is accepted by $\mathcal{M}(\varphi)$ [22,24]. A common assumption in LTL$_f$ applications to Process Mining, referred to as *Declare assumption* [23] or *simplicity assumption* [11], is that exactly one activity occurs in each state. LTL$_f$ with this additional restriction is known as LTL$_p$ [17], and traces therein, known as *process traces*, can be seen as strings over the alphabet $\mathcal{A}$. This has the following practical implication: given a LTL$_p$ formula φ, the minimal automaton $\mathcal{M}(\varphi)$ of φ can be simplified into a deterministic automaton [11], as shown in Fig. 1.

Table 1. Some Declare templates as LTL_p formulae along with their informal description, as reported in [23]. We slightly edit the definitions for ChainPrecedence(a,b) and AlternatePrecedence(a,b), to align their semantics to the informal description commonly assumed in Process Mining applications. Changes w.r.t the original source [23] are highlighted in red. The Succession (resp. AlternateSuccession, ChainSuccession) template is defined as the conjunction of (Alternate, Chain) Response and Precedence templates.

Template	LTL_p	Description
Choice(a,b)	$F\ (a \vee b)$	a or b must be executed
ExclusiveChoice(a,b)	$\text{Choice(a,b)} \wedge \neg(F\ a \cdot \wedge F\ b)$	Either a or b must be executed, but not both
RespEx(a,b)	$F\ a \rightarrow F\ b$	If a is executed, then b must be executed as well
CoExistence(a,b)	$\text{RespEx(a,b)} \wedge \text{RespEx(b,a)}$	Either a and b are both executed, or none of them is executed
Response(a,b)	$G\ (a \rightarrow F\ b)$	Every time a is executed, b must be executed afterwards
Precedence(a,b)	$\neg b\ W\ a$	b can be executed only if a has been executed before
Alt.Response(a,b)	$G\ (a \rightarrow X\ (\neg a\ U\ b))$	Every a must be followed by b, without any other a in between
Alt.Precedence(a,b)	$\text{Precedence(a,b)}\quad \wedge G\ (b \rightarrow X_w\ \text{Precedence(a,b)})$	Every b must be preceded by a, without any other b inbetween
ChainResponse(a,b)	$G\ (a \rightarrow X\ b)$	If a is executed then b must be executed next
ChainPrecedence(a,b)	$G\ (X\ b \rightarrow a) \wedge \neg b$	Task b can be executed only immediately after a

2.3   Declare Modeling Language

Declare [4] is a declarative process modeling language that consists of a set of *templates* that express temporal properties of process execution traces. The semantics of each Declare template is defined in terms of an underlying LTL_p formula. Table 1 provides the LTL_p definition of some Declare templates, as reported in [23]. Declare templates can be classified into four distinct categories, each addressing different aspects of process behavior: *existence* templates, specifying the necessity or prohibition of executing a particular activity, potentially with constraints on the number of occurrences; *choice* templates, centered around the concept of execution choices as they model scenarios where there is an option regarding which activities may be executed; *relation* templates, establishing a dependency between activities as they dictate that the execution of one activity necessitates the execution of another, often under specific conditions or requirements; *negation* templates, modelling mutual exclusivity or prohibitive conditions in activity execution. In Table 1, Choice(a,b) and ExclusiveChoice(a,b) are examples of *choice* templates; while the others fall under the *relation* category. A Declare model is a set of *constraints*, where a constraint is a particular instantiation of a template, over specific activities, called respectively *activation* and *target* for binary constraints. Informally, the activation of a Declare constraint is the activity whose occurrence imposes a constraint over the occurrence of the target on the rest of the trace. A more formal account of activation-target semantics of Declare constraints can be found in [8]. The following example showcases the informal semantics of the Response template, which will serve as a running example in the rest of the paper.

Example 1 (Semantics of the Response template). The informal semantics for Response(a,b) is that *whenever a occurs in the trace, b will appear in the future.* Formally, the template is defined as G $(a \rightarrow F\ b)$. Thus, if a occurs at time t in a trace π, in order for the constraint to be satisfied, b must appear in the trace suffix $\pi_{t+1}, \ldots, \pi_n$. In the context of a customer service process, let's consider the response template instantiated with a = customer_complains and b = address_complain, corresponding to the template instantiation, i.e., the constraint, Response(customer_complains,address_complain). Such constraint imposes that when a customer complaint is received (activation activity), a follow-up action, such as addressing the complaint (target activity), must be executed. The trace π = customer_complains, logging_complain, address_complain, feedback_collection satisfies the above constraint while the trace π' = customer_complains, logging_complain, address_complain, customer_complains, feedback_collection does not, indeed the second occurrence of customer_complains is not followed by any address_complain event.

This paper focuses on the Declare *conformance checking* and Declare *(template) query checking* tasks, as defined below:

Conformance Checking. Let $\mathcal{L}$ be an event log (a multiset of traces) and $\mathcal{M}$ a Declare model. The conformance checking task $(\mathcal{L}, \mathcal{M})$ consists in computing the subset of traces $\mathcal{L}' \subseteq \mathcal{L}$ such that for each $\pi \in \mathcal{L}'$, $\pi \models c$ for all $c \in \mathcal{M}$.

Query Checking. Let $\mathcal{L}$ be an event log, and c a constraint. The support of c on $\mathcal{L}$, denoted by $\sigma(c, \mathcal{L})$, is defined as the fraction of traces $\pi \in \mathcal{L}$ such that $\pi \models c$. High support for a constraint is usually interpreted as a measure of relevance for the given constraint on the log $\mathcal{L}$. Given a Declare template t and a *support threshold* $s \in (0, 1]$, the query checking task $(t, \mathcal{L}, s)$ consists in computing variable-activity bindings such that the constraint c we obtain by instantiating t with such bindings has a support greater than s on $\mathcal{L}$.

Interested readers can refer to [12,14] as a starting point for Declare.

2.4   Answer Set Programming

Answer set programming (ASP) [6,21] is a declarative programming paradigm based on the stable models semantics, which has been used to solve many complex AI problems [15]. We now provide a brief introduction describing the basic language of ASP. We refer the interested reader to [6,19,21] for a more comprehensive description of ASP. The syntax of ASP follows Prolog's conventions: variable terms are strings starting with an uppercase letters; constant terms are either strings starting by lowercase letter or are enclosed in quotation marks, or are integers. An *atom* of arity n is an expression of the form $p(t_1, \ldots, t_n)$ where

p is a predicate and $t_1, \ldots, t_n$ are terms. A (positive) *literal* is an atom a or its negation (negative literal) *not* a where *not* denotes negation as failure. A *rule* is an expression of the form $h \leftarrow b_1, \ldots, b_n$ where $b_1, \ldots, b_n$ is a conjunction of literals, called the *body*, $n \geq 0$, and h is an atom called the *head*. All variables in a rule must occur in some positive literal of the body. A *fact* is a rule with an empty body (i.e., $n = 0$). A *program* is a finite set of rules. Atoms, rules and programs that do not contain variables are said to be ground. The Herbrand Universe U_P is the collection of constants in the program P. The Herbrand Base B_P is the set of ground atoms that can be generated by combining predicates from P with the constants in U_P. The ground instantiation of P, denoted by $ground(P)$, is the union of ground instantiations of rules in P that are obtained by replacing variables with constants in U_P. An *interpretation* I is a subset of B_P. A positive (resp. negative) literal ℓ is true w.r.t. I, if $\ell \in I$ (resp. $\bar{\ell} \notin I$); it is false w.r.t. I if $\ell \notin I$ (resp. $\bar{\ell} \in I$). An interpretation I is a *model* of P if for each $r \in ground(P)$, the head of r is true whenever the body of r is true. Given a program P and an interpretation I, the (Gelfond-Lifschitz) reduct [21] P^I is the program obtained from $ground(P)$ by (i) removing all those rules having in the body a false negative literal w.r.t. I, and (ii) removing negative literals from the body of remaining rules. Given a program P, the model I of P is a *stable model* or *answer set* if there is no $I' \subset I$ such that I' is a model of P^I.

In the paper, also use more advanced ASP constructs such as *choice rules* and *function symbols*. We refer the reader to [7] for a description of more advanced ASP constructs. In the rest of the paper, ASP code examples will use CLINGO [20] input language.

3   Translation-Based ASP Encodings for Declare

This section introduces ASP encodings for conformance checking of Declare models and query checking of Declare constraints with respect to an input event log, based on the translation to automata and syntax trees. Both encodings share the same input fact schema to specify which Declare constraints belong to the model, or which constraint we are performing query checking against. These encodings are *indirect*, since they rely on a translation, but also *general* in the sense that they can be applied to the evaluation of arbitrary LTL$_p$ formulae. This is achieved, in the case of the syntax tree encoding, by reifying the syntax tree of a formula and by explicitly modeling the semantics of each LTL$_p$ temporal operator through a logic program, and in the case of the automaton encoding, by exploiting the well-known LTL$_p$-to-automaton translation [11,24]. Thus, one can use these two encodings to represent Declare constraints by their LTL$_p$ definitions. The automaton-based encoding is adapted from [10], the syntax tree-based encoding is adapted from [28] - integrating changes to allow for the above-mentioned shared fact schema and evaluation over multiple traces. A similar encoding has also been used in [27] to learn LTL$_f$ formulae from sets of example traces, using the ASP-based inductive logic programming system ILASP [29]. We start by defining how event logs and Declare constraints are encoded into facts, then introduce conformance checking and query checking encodings with the two approaches.

Encoding Process Traces. For our purposes, an event log $\mathcal{L}$ is a multiset of process traces, thus a multiset of strings over an alphabet of propositional symbols $\mathcal{A}$ (representing activities). We assume that each trace $\pi \in \mathcal{L}$ is uniquely indexed by an integer, and we denote that the trace π has index i by $id(\pi) = i$. This is a common assumption in Process Mining, where i is referred to as the *trace identifier*. Traces are modeled through the predicate `trace/3`, where the atom $trace(i, t, a)$ encodes that $\pi_t = a, id(\pi) = i$ — that is, the t-th activity in the i-th trace π is a. Given a process trace π, we denote by $E(\pi)$ the set of facts that encodes it. Thus, an event log $\mathcal{L}$ is encoded as $E(\mathcal{L}) = \bigcup_{\pi \in \mathcal{L}} E(\pi)$.

Example 2 (Encoding a process trace). Consider an event log composed of the two process traces $\pi^0 = abc$ and $\pi^1 = xyz$, respectively with identifiers 0 and 1, over the propositional alphabet $\mathcal{A} = \{a, b, c, x, y, z\}$. This is encoded by the following set of facts:

```
trace(0,0,a). trace(0,1,b). trace(0,2,c).
trace(1,0,x). trace(1,1,y). trace(1,2,z).
```

Each Declare template, informally, can be understood as a "LTL$_p$ formula with variables". Substituting these variables with activities yields a Declare constraint. How templates are instantiated into constraints, and how constraints are evaluated over traces, depends on the ASP encoding we use. However, all encodings share a common fact schema where constraints are expressed as templates with bound variable substitutions.

Encoding Declare Constraints. A Declare constraint is modeled by predicates `constraint/2` and `bind/3`. The former model which Declare template a given constraint is instantiated from and the latter which activity-variable bindings instantiate the constraint. An atom $constraint(cid, template)$ encodes that the constraint uniquely identified by cid is an instance of the template $template$. The atom $bind(cid, arg, value)$ encodes that the constraint uniquely identified by cid is obtained by binding the argument arg to the activity $value$. Given a Declare model $\mathcal{M} = \{c_1, \ldots, c_n\}$, where the subscript i uniquely indexes the constraint c_i, we denote by $E(\mathcal{M})$ the set of facts that encodes $\mathcal{M}$, that is $E(\mathcal{M}) = \bigcup_{c \in \mathcal{M}} E(c)$. Recall that in Declare $\pi \models \mathcal{M}$ if and only if $\pi \models c$ for all $c \in \mathcal{M}$, thus there is no notion of "order" among the constraints within $\mathcal{M}$ and it does not matter how indexes are assigned to constraints as long as they are unique.

Example 3 (Encoding a Declare model). Consider the model $\mathcal{M}$ composed of the two constraints Response(a_1, a_2) and Precedence(a_2, a_3). $\mathcal{M}$ is encoded by the following facts:

```
constraint(0,"Response").         constraint(1,"Precedence").
bind(0,arg_0,a_1).                bind(1,arg_0,a_2).
bind(0,arg_1,a_2).                bind(1,arg_1,a_3).
```

3.1   Encoding Conformance Checking

All the Declare conformance checking encodings we propose consist of a stratified normal logic program P_{CF}. Given a log $\mathcal{L}$ and a Declare model $\mathcal{M}$, it holds that for every trace $\pi_i \in \mathcal{L}$, $\pi_i \models c_j \in \mathcal{M}$ if and only if the unique model of $P_{CF} \cup E(\mathcal{M}) \cup E(\mathcal{L})$ contains the atom $sat(i, j)$. Complete encodings for all the templates in Table 1 are available online.

Automaton Encoding. The automaton encoding, reported in Fig. 2, models Declare templates through their corresponding automaton obtained by translating the template's LTL_p definition [22]. The automaton's complete transition function is reified into a set of facts that defines the template in ASP. The predicates `initial/2`, `accepting/2` model the initial and accepting states of the automaton, while `template/4` stores the transition function of the template-specific automaton. In particular, `arg_0` refers to the template *activation*, and `arg_1` refers to the template *target*. A constraint c instantiated from a template binds its `arg_0`, `arg_1` to specific activities. The constant "$\star$" is used as a place-holder for any activity in $\mathcal{A} \setminus \{x, y\}$ – where x and y are the bindings of `arg_0` and `arg_1`. Activities not explicitly mentioned as within the atomic propositions in an LTL_p formula φ have the same influence to $\pi \models \varphi$. Consequently, all unbound activities can be denoted by the symbol "$\star$" in the automaton transition table. As an example, consider the constraint $c = $ Response(a,b), shown in Fig. 4. Evaluating the trace abwqw is equivalent to evaluating the trace abtts, which would be equivalent to evaluating the trace ab$\star\star\star$, since a and b are the only propositional formulae that appear in the definition of Response(a,b).

Syntax Tree-Based Encoding. The syntax tree encoding, shown in Fig. 3, reifies the syntax tree of a LTL_p formula into a set of facts, where each node represents a sub-formula. The semantics of temporal operators and propositional operators is defined in terms of ASP rules. Analogously to the automaton encoding, templates are defined in terms of reified syntax trees, which are used to evaluate each constraint according to the template they are instantiated from. The following normal rules define the semantics of each temporal and propositional operator. We report the rules for operators $\{ \cup, X, \neg, \wedge \}$ which are the basic operators of LTL_p. The full encoding, that also includes definitions of derived operators, is available online. In particular, the `true/4` predicate tracks which sub-formula of a constraints' definition is true at any given time. As an example, the atom $true(c, f, t, i)$ encodes that *at time t the constraint sub-formula f of constraint c is satisfied on the i-th trace*. The predicates `conjunction/3`, `negate/2`, `next/2`, `until/3` model the topology of the syntax tree of the corresponding formula. The first term refers to a node identifier, while the other terms (one for unary operators, two for the binary operators are the node identifiers of its child nodes. The `atom/2` predicate models that a given node (first term) is an atom, bound to a particular argument (second term) by the `bind/3` predicate which is used in encoding of Declare constraints. Figure 5 shows an example.

```
% Automaton initial state
cur_state(C,TID,S,0) :-
   trace(TID,_,_),
   initial(Template,S),
   constraint(C,Template).

% Last point of each trace
last(TID,T) :-
   trace(TID,T,_),
   not trace(TID,T+1,_).

% A trace is accepted
sat(TID,C) :-
   cur_state(C,TID,S,T+1),
   last(TID,T),
   template(Template,C),
   constraint(C, Template),
   accepting(Template,S).
```

```
% Reads activation/target
cur_state(C,TID,S2,T+1) :-
   cur_state(C,TID,S1,T),
   constraint(C,Template),
   template(Template,S1,Arg,S2),
   trace(TID,T,A),
   bind(C,Arg,A).


% Reads "*"
cur_state(C,TID,S2,T+1) :-
   cur_state(C,TID,S1,T),
   constraint(C,Template),
   template(Template,S1,"*",S2),
   trace(TID,T,A),
   not bind(C,_,A).
```

Fig. 2. ASP program to execute a finite state machine corresponding to a constraint, encoded as template/4 facts, on input strings encoded by trace/3 facts.

3.2 Encoding Query Checking

The query checking problem takes as input a Declare template $\mathcal{T}$, an event log $\mathcal{L}$ and consists in deciding which constraints c can be instantiated from $\mathcal{T}$ such that $\sigma(c, \mathcal{L}) \geq k$, where $\sigma(c, \mathcal{L})$ is the support and denotes the fraction of traces in $\mathcal{L}$ that are models of c. The problem has been formally introduced in [9] for temporal logic formulae, and in [34] it has been framed into a Process Mining setting, in the context of LTL$_f$. An ASP-based solution to the problem has been provided in [10], through the same automaton encoding we have been referring to throughout the paper, and instead an exhaustive search-based, Declare-specific implementation is provided in the Declare4Py [13] library. From the ASP perspective, a conformance checking encoding can be easily adapted to perform query checking, by searching over possible variable-activities bindings that yield a constraint above the chosen support threshold. In particular, we adapt the query checking encoding presented in [18] to the LTL$_f$ setting. In order to encode the query checking problem, we slightly change our input model representation, as reported in the following example.

Example 4. Consider the query checking problem instance over the template *Response*, with both its activation and target ranging over $\mathcal{A}$. The var_bind/3 predicate, analogously to bind_3, models that in a given template a parameter is bound to a variable. Notice that the ASP formulation can be easily generalized to query check sets of Declare constraints, while available tools address only a single constraint at a time. For the query checking problem, we are interested in tuples of activities that, when substituted to the constraints' variables, yield a

```
last(TID,T) :-                        sat(C,TID) :-
  trace(TID,T,_),                       true(C,0,0,TID).
  not trace(TID,T+1,_).
                                      true(C,F,Ti,TID) :-
true(C,F,T,TID) :-                      constraint(C,Template),
  constraint(C,Template),               template(Template,next(F,G)),
  template(Template,                    trace(TID,Ti,_),
    atom(F,Arg)                         Tj=Ti+1,
  ),                                    Ti<M,
  bind(C,Arg,A),                        last(TID,M),
  trace(TID,T,A).                       true(C,G,Tj,TID).

true(C,F,T,TID) :-                    true(C,F,Ti,TID) :-
  constraint(C,Template),               constraint(C,Template),
  template(Template,                    template(Template,
    conjunction(F,G,H)                      until(F,G,H)),
  ),                                    trace(TID,Ti,_),
  trace(TID,T,_),                       trace(TID,Tj,_),
  true(C,G,T,TID),                      Tj>=Ti,
  true(C,H,T,TID).                      Tj<=M,
                                        last(TID,M),
true(C,F,T,TID) :-                      X {true(C,G,T,TID):
  constraint(C,Template),                   trace(TID,T,_), T >=Ti,
  template(Template,negate(F,G)),           T<Tj} X,
  not true(C,G,T,TID),                  X = Tj-Ti,
  trace(TID,T,_).                       true(C,H,Tj,TID).
```

Fig. 3. ASP program to evaluate each sub-formula of the LTL_p definition of a given template, encoded as template/2 facts, on input strings encoded by a syntax tree representation through the conjunction/3, negate/2, until/3, next/2 and atom/2.

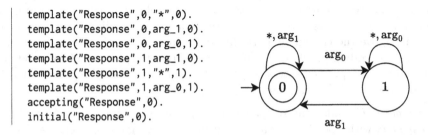

```
template("Response",0,"*",0).
template("Response",0,arg_1,0).
template("Response",0,arg_0,1).
template("Response",1,arg_1,0).
template("Response",1,"*",1).
template("Response",1,arg_0,1).
accepting("Response",0).
initial("Response",0).
```

Fig. 4. Left: Facts that encode the Response template; Right: A minimal finite state machine whose recognized language is equal to the set of models of Response, under LTL_p semantics.

```
template("Response",always(0,1)).
template("Response",implies(1,2,3)).
template("Response",atom(2,arg_0)).
template("Response",eventually(3,4)).
template("Response",atom(4,arg_1)).
```

$$G^0$$
$$|$$
$$\overset{1}{\rightarrow}$$
$$arg_0^2 \overset{}{\swarrow} \qquad \overset{}{\searrow} F^3$$
$$|$$
$$arg_1^4$$

Fig. 5. Left: Facts that encode the Response template; Right: Syntax tree of the Response template LTL_p definition.

constraint whose support is above the threshold over the input log. The domain/2 predicate can be used to give each variable its own subset of possible values, but in this case, for both variables, the domain of admissible substitutions spans over $\mathcal{A}$. The choice rule generates candidate substitutions that are pruned by the constraints if they are above the maximum number of violations. Given an input support threshold $s \in (0, 1]$, the constant max_violations is set to the nearest integer above $(1 - s) \cdot |\mathcal{L}|$.

```
constraint(c,"Response").
var_bind(c,arg_0,var(a)).
var_bind(c,arg_1,var(b)).
domain(var(a),A) :- trace(_,_,A).
domain(var(b),A) :- trace(_,_,A).
{ bind(C,Arg,Value): domain(Var,Value) } = 1 :- var_bind(C,Arg,Var).
:- #count{X: not sat(C, X), trace(X, _, _)} > max_violations.
```

4   Direct ASP Encoding for **Declare**

The previous encodings are general techniques that enable reasoning over arbitrary LTL_p formulae. The encoding discussed in this section instead is an ad-hoc, direct translation of the semantics of Declare constraints into ASP rules. The general approach we followed in defining the templates, is to model *constraint failures* through a fail/2 predicate. Due to the activation-target semantics of Declare templates, sometimes it is required to assert that an activation condition is matched in the suffix of the trace by a correlation condition. In the encoding, this is modeled by the witness/3 predicate. This mirrors the *activation* and *target* concepts in the definition of Declare constraints. However, the encodings are not based on a systematic, algorithmic rewriting. We show an example using the Response and Precedence templates, typical patterns in the verification literature [14].

Example 5 (Modeling the Response template directly in ASP). Recall from Table 1 that the template Response(a, b) is defined as the LTL_p formula $G \ (a \rightarrow F \ b)$, whose informal meaning is that *whenever a happens, b must happen somewhere in the future.* Thus, every time we observe an a at time t, in order for

Response(a, b) to be true, we have to observe b at a time instant $t' \geq t$. The first rule below encodes this situation. If we observe at least one a that is not matched by any b in the future, the constraint fails, which is encoded in the second rule.

```
witness(C,T,TID) :-
    constraint(C, "Response"),
    bind(C,arg_0,X),
    bind(C,arg_1,Y),
    trace(TID,T,X),
    trace(TID,T',Y), T'>=T.
```

```
fail(C,TID) :-
    constraint(C,"Response"),
    bind(C,arg_0,X),
    bind(C,arg_1,Y),
    trace(TID,T,X),
    not witness(C,T,TID).
```

Example 6 (Modeling the Precedence template directly in ASP). Recall from Table 1 that the constraint Precedence(x, y) is defined as the LTL_p formula $\neg x \ W \ y = G \ (\neg x) \ \lor \ \neg x \ U \ y$, whose informal meaning is that *if* y *happens,* x *must have happened before.* Notice that in order to witness the failure of this constraint, it is enough to reason about the trace prefix up to the first occurrence of y.

```
fail(C,TID) :-
    constraint(C,"Precedence"),
    bind(C,arg_0,X),
    bind(C,arg_1,Y),
    trace(TID,T',Y),
    T = #min{Q: trace(TID,Q,X)},
    trace(TID,T,X), T'<=T.
```

```
fail(C,TID) :-
    constraint(C,"Precedence"),
    bind(C,arg_0,X),
    bind(C,arg_1,Y),
    trace(TID,_,Y),
    not trace(TID,_,X).
```

Let P_{CF} denote the logic program that encodes LTL_p semantics or Declare semantics. The logic program $P \cup E(\mathcal{M}) \cup E(\mathcal{L})$ has a unique model, and contains the atom $sat(c, i)$ if and only if $\pi_i \models c$. We validate our direct encoding definitions of Declare semantics by a bounded model checking approach, searching for a counterexample trace π that is accepted (rejected) by the direct encoding but rejected (accepted) by the automaton of the corresponding constraint, over the propositional alphabet $\{a, b, *\}$ which represents respectively the first two parameters of the Declare constraint under test, and a placeholder "everything else" character, as discussed in the automata encoding subsection.

5   Experiments

In this section, we report the results of our experiments comparing different methods to perform conformance checking and query checking of Declare models, using the ASP-based representations outlined in the previous sections and Declare4Py, a Python library for Declare tasks. Methods will be referred as $\text{ASP}_\mathcal{D}$, $\text{ASP}_\mathcal{A}$, $\text{ASP}_\mathcal{S}$ and D4Py - denoting respectively our direct encoding, the automata and syntax tree-based translation methods and Declare4Py. We start by describing datasets (logs and Declare models), and execution environment to conclude by discussing experimental results.

Table 2. Statistics for the logs used in the experiments: $|\mathcal{A}|$ denotes the number of activities for the log; Average $|\pi|$ is the average trace length for the log; $|\mathcal{L}|$ is the number of traces in the log; $|\mathcal{C}^{IV}|$ is the total number of Declare constraints above 50% support in the log, by Declare4Py miner.

Log name	$|\mathcal{A}|$	Average $|\pi|$	$|\mathcal{L}|$	$|\mathcal{C}^{IV}|$
Sepsis Cases (SC)	16	14.5	1050	76
Permit Log (PL)	51	12.3	7065	26
BPI Challenge 2012 (BC)	23	12.6	13087	10
Prepaid Travel Cost (PC)	29	8.7	2099	52
Request For Payment (RP)	19	5.4	6886	52
International Declarations (ID)	34	11.2	6449	152
Domestic Declarations (DD)	17	5.4	10500	52

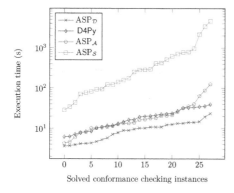

Fig. 6. Conformance checking cactus.

Table 3. Run time in seconds to perform conformance checking on $\mathcal{C}^{IV}$, the model that contains the most constraints, on each log.

Log	$\text{ASP}_\mathcal{D}$	D4Py	$\text{ASP}_\mathcal{A}$	$\text{ASP}_\mathcal{S}$
ID	**23.3**	39.5	124.9	4621.7
RP	**10.8**	16.3	25.8	409.8
PT	**5.2**	8.5	12.6	121.6
SC	**4.3**	11.6	13.4	141.2
PL	**10.8**	35.6	20.7	624.1
DD	**14.2**	22.4	40.1	963.2
BC	**14.1**	23.7	20.5	796.6

Data. We validate our approach on real-life event logs from past BPI Challenges [31]. These event logs are well-known and actively used in Process Mining literature. For each event log $\mathcal{L}_i$, we use Declare4Py to mine the set of Declare constraints $\mathcal{C}_i$ whose support on $\mathcal{L}_i$ is above 50%. Then, we define four models, $\mathcal{C}_i^{I}, \mathcal{C}_i^{II}, \mathcal{C}_i^{III}, \mathcal{C}_i^{IV}$, containing respectively the first 25%, 50%, 75% and 100% of the constraints in a random shuffling of $\mathcal{C}_i$, such that $\mathcal{C}_i^{I} \subset \mathcal{C}_i^{II} \subset \mathcal{C}_i^{III} \subset \mathcal{C}_i^{IV}$. Table 2 summarizes some statistics about the logs and the Declare models we mined over the logs. All resource measurements take into account the fact that ASP encodings require an additional translation step from the XML-based format of event logs to a set of facts. The translation time is included in the measurement times and is comparable with the time taken by Declare4Py.

Execution Environment. The experiments in this section were executed on an Intel(R) Xeon(R) Gold 5118 CPU @ 2.30 GHz, 512 GB RAM machine, using CLINGO version 5.4.0, Python 3.10, Declare4Py 1.0 and pyrunlim [5] to mea-

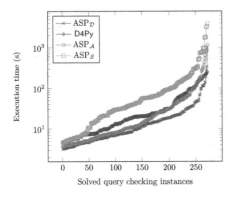

Fig. 7. Query checking cactus plot.

Table 4. Cumulative run time in seconds to perform all query checking tasks on a given log.

Log	$ASP_{\mathcal{D}}$	D4Py	$ASP_{\mathcal{A}}$	$ASP_{\mathcal{S}}$
ID	**817.2**	1624.5	1654.0	3522.4
RP	884.2	565.8	**318.2**	1179.4
PT	**223.6**	451.1	236.1	427.9
SC	**163.8**	267.0	173.1	665.1
PL	**1614.0**	4227.7	3926.8	5397.5
DD	**407.7**	698.2	479.2	2436.2
BC	**2304.8**	2467.7	6636.0	27445.3

sure resources usage. Experiments were run sequentially. All data and scripts to reproduce our experiments are available at this repository.

Conformance Checking. We consider the conformance checking tasks $(\mathcal{L}_i, \mathcal{M})$, with $\mathcal{M} \in \{\mathcal{C}_i^{I}, \mathcal{C}_i^{II}, \mathcal{C}_i^{III}, \mathcal{C}_i^{IV}\}$, over the considered logs and its Declare models. Figure 6 reports the solving times for each method in a cactus plot. Recall that a point (x, y) in a cactus plot represents the fact that a given method solves the x-th instance, ordered by increasing execution times, in y seconds. Table 3 reports the same data aggregated by the event log dimension, best run-time in bold. Overall, our direct encoding approach is faster than the other ASP-based encodings as well as Declare4Py on considered tasks. $ASP_{\mathcal{A}}$ and Declare4Py perform similarly, whereas $ASP_{\mathcal{S}}$ is less efficient.

Query Checking. We consider the query checking instances $(t, \mathcal{L}_i, s)$ where t is a Declare template, from the ones defined in Table 1, $s \in \{0.50, 0.75, 1.00\}$ is a support threshold, and $\mathcal{L}_i$ is a log. Figure 7 summarizes the results in a cactus plot, and Table 4 aggregates the same data on the log dimension, best runtime in bold. $ASP_{\mathcal{D}}$ is again the best method overall, outperforming other ASP-based methods with the exception of $ASP_{\mathcal{A}}$ on the RP log tasks. Again, $ASP_{\mathcal{A}}$ and D4Py perform similarly and $ASP_{\mathcal{S}}$ is the worst.

Discussion. We conjecture that the significant increase in maximum memory usage, as indicated in Table 5, is the primary factor contributing to the performance gap observed for $ASP_{\mathcal{S}}$ in both tasks. In fact, we observe that in conformance checking $ASP_{\mathcal{D}}$ is more efficient w.r.t. memory consumption when compared to D4Py, and, when combined, these two methods collectively show better memory efficiency when compared to other ASP-based methods. As for the query checking tasks, D4Py is the most efficient method memory-wise. This is expected, since the imperative nature of its implementation allows to *"iterate and discard"* candidate assignments, rather than requiring their explicit grounding, as in the ASP-based techniques. In conclusion, it is worth noticing that for

Table 5. Max memory usage (MB) over all the conformance checking and query checking tasks, aggregated by log, for all the considered methods. Lowest value in boldface.

Log	Conformance Checking				Query Checking			
	$ASP_\mathcal{D}$	D4Py	$ASP_\mathcal{A}$	$ASP_\mathcal{S}$	$ASP_\mathcal{D}$	D4Py	$ASP_\mathcal{A}$	$ASP_\mathcal{S}$
BC	**323.6**	566.3	546.0	8757.9	3157.0	**580.7**	1450.8	18866.5
DD	536.6	**386.0**	927.2	14473.8	728.1	**336.4**	513.0	2706.0
ID	837.1	**578.4**	2338.9	55435.2	1498.5	**583.5**	763.6	5029.8
PL	**312.8**	2062.2	579.5	11388.3	2434.2	2071.0	**1023.3**	7006.2
PC	**222.2**	281.9	341.2	5211.2	435.3	283.4	**282.8**	1209.3
RP	372.3	**347.6**	610.8	9706.0	574.8	**312.3**	396.9	1843.3
SC	**195.0**	245.6	336.4	5786.5	480.4	**244.6**	247.2	2146.7

both tasks, $ASP_\mathcal{S}$ is the least efficient memory-wise implementation, and it also tends to exhibit lower efficiency in terms of running times across nearly all logs.

6   Conclusion

Declare is a declarative process modeling language, which describes processes by sets of temporal constraints. Declare specifications can be expressed as LTL_p formulae, and traditionally have been evaluated by executing the equivalent automata [12]. Translation-based approaches (on automata, or syntax trees) are at the foundation of existing ASP-based solutions [10,28]. This paper proposes a novel direct encoding of Declare in ASP that is not based on translations. Moreover, for the first time, we put on common ground (regarding input fact schema) and compare available ASP solutions for conformance checking and query checking. Our experimental evaluation over well-known event logs provides the first aggregate picture of the performance of the methods considered. The results show that our direct encoding outperforms other methods in terms of execution time, and thus that ASP provides a compact, declarative and efficient way to implement Declare constraints in the considered tasks. As far as future work is concerned, we plan to extend our approach to the *data perspective* [30], i.e., attaching data payloads to each activity in a trace, as well as considering other Process Mining tasks such as log generation tasks, along the lines of [10].

References

1. A Guide To The Project Management Body Of Knowledge (PMBOK Guides). Project Management Institute, 2004. ISBN: 193069945X

2. van der Aalst, W.M.P.: Process mining: a 360 degree overview. In: van der Aalst, W.M.P., Carmona, J. (eds.) Process Mining Handbook. LNBIP, vol. 448, pp. 3–34. Springer, Cham (2022). https://doi.org/10.1007/978-3-031-08848-3_1

3. van der Aalst, W.M.P.: The application of petri nets to workflow management. J. Circuits Syst. Comput. **8**(1), 21–66 (1998)

4. van der Aalst, W.M., Pesic, M., Schonenberg, H.: Declarative workflows: balancing between flexibility and support. Comput. Sci. Res. Dev. **23**(2), 99–113 (2009)

5. Alviano, M.: The pyrunlim tool (2014). https://github.com/alviano/python/tree/master/pyrunlim

6. Brewka, G., Eiter, T., Truszczynski, M.: Answer set programming at a glance. Commun. ACM **54**(12), 92–103 (2011)

7. Calimeri, F., et al.: ASP-Core-2 input language format. Theory Pract. Log. Program. **20**(2), 294–309 (2020)

8. Cecconi, A., et al.: Measuring the interestingness of temporal logic behavioral specifications in process mining. Inf. Syst. **107**, 101920 (2022). https://doi.org/10.1016/j.is.2021.101920

9. Chan, W.: Temporal-logic queries. In: Emerson, E.A., Sistla, A.P. (eds.) Computer Aided Verification. CAV 2000. LNCS, vol. 1855, pp. 450–463. Springer, Berlin, Heidelberg (2000). ISBN: 978-3-540-45047-4, https://doi.org/10.1007/10722167_34

10. Chiariello, F., Maggi, F.M., Patrizi, F.: ASP-based declarative process mining. In: AAAI, pp. 5539–5547. AAAI Press (2022)

11. Chiariello, F., Maggi, F.M., Patrizi, F.: From LTL on process traces to finite-state automata. In: BPM, vol. 3469, pp. 127–131. CEUR WP. CEUR-WS.org (2023)

12. Di Ciccio, C., Montali, M.: Declarative process specifications: reasoning, discovery, monitoring. In: van der Aalst, W.M.P., Carmona, J. (eds.) Process Mining Handbook. LNBIP, vol. 448, pp. 108–152. Springer, Cham (2022). https://doi.org/10.1007/978-3-031-08848-3_4

13. Donadello, I., et al.: Declare4Py: a python library for declarative process mining. In: BPM (PhD/Demos), vol. 3216, pp. 117–121. CEUR WP. CEURWS.org (2022)

14. Dwyer, M.B., Avrunin, G.S., Corbett, J.C.: Patterns in property specifications for finite-state verification. In: ICSE. ACM, pp. 411–420 (1999)

15. Erdem, E., Gelfond, M., Leone, N.: Applications of answer set programming. AI Mag. **37**(3), 53–68 (2016)

16. Finkbeiner, B., Sipma, H.: Checking finite traces using alternating automata. Form. Meth. Syst. Des. **24**(2), 101–127 (2004)

17. Fionda, V., Greco, G.: LTL on finite and process traces: complexity results and a practical reasoner. J. Artif. Intell. Res. **63**, 557–623 (2018)

18. Fionda, V., Ielo, A., Ricca, F.: Logic-based composition of business process models. In: Marquis, P., Son, T.C., Kern-Isberner, G. (eds.) Proceedings of the 20th International Conference on Principles of Knowledge Representation and Reasoning, KR 2023, Rhodes, Greece, 2–8 September 2023, pp. 272–281 (2023). https://doi.org/10.24963/KR.2023/27

19. Gebser, M., et al.: Answer Set Solving in Practice. Synthesis Lectures on Artificial Intelligence and Machine Learning. Morgan & Claypool Publishers, San Rafael (2012)

20. Gebser, M., et al.: Multi-shot ASP solving with clingo. Theory Pract. Log. Program. **19**(1), 27–82 (2019)

21. Gelfond, M., Lifschitz, V.: Classical negation in logic programs and disjunctive databases. New Gener. Comput. **9.3/4**, 365–386 (1991)

22. De Giacomo, G., Favorito, M.: Compositional approach to translate LTLf/LDLf into deterministic finite automata. In: ICAPS, pp. 122–130. AAAI Press (2021)

23. De Giacomo, G., De Masellis, R., Montali, M.: Reasoning on LTL on finite traces: insensitivity to infiniteness. In: AAAI, pp. 1027–1033. AAAI Press (2014)

24. De Giacomo, G., Vardi, M.Y.: Linear temporal logic and linear dynamic logic on finite traces. In: IJCAI. IJCAI/AAAI, pp. 854–860 (2013)

25. Greenman, B., et al.: Little tricky logic: misconceptions in the understanding of LTL. Art Sci. Eng. Program. **7**(2) (2023)

26. Ielo, A., Pontieri, L., Ricca, F.: Declarative mining of business processes via ASP. In: PMAI@IJCAI, vol. 3310, pp. 105–108. CEUR WP. CEUR-WS.org (2022)

27. Ielo, A., et al.: Towards ILP-based LTLf passive learning. In: ILP 2023, (To Appear)

28. Kuhlmann, I., Corea, C., Grant, J.: An ASP-based framework for solving problems related to declarative process specifications. In: NMR, vol. 3464, pp. 129–132. CEUR WP. CEUR-WS.org (2023)

29. Law, M.: Conflict-driven inductive logic programming. Theory Pract. Log. Program. **23**(2), 387–414 (2023). https://doi.org/10.1017/S1471068422000011

30. De Leoni, M., Van Der Aalst, W.M.: Data-aware process mining: discovering decisions in processes using alignments. In: SAC. ACM, pp. 1454–1461 (2013)

31. Lopes, I.F., Ferreira, D.R.: A survey of process mining competitions: the BPI challenges 2011–2018. In: Di Francescomarino, C., Dijkman, R., Zdun, U. (eds.) BPM 2019. LNBIP, vol. 362, pp. 263–274. Springer, Cham (2019). https://doi.org/10.1007/978-3-030-37453-2_22

32. Niemelä, I.: Logic programs with stable model semantics as a constraint programming paradigm. Ann. Math. Artif. Intell. **25**(3–4), 241–273 (1999)

33. Pnueli, A.: The temporal logic of programs. In: FOCS, pp. 46–57. IEEE Computer Society (1977)

34. Räim, M., Di Ciccio, C., Maggi, F.M., Mecella, M., Mendling, J.: Log-based understanding of business processes through temporal logic query checking. In: Meersman, R., et al. (eds.) OTM 2014. LNCS, vol. 8841, pp. 75–92. Springer, Heidelberg (2014). https://doi.org/10.1007/978-3-662-45563-0_5

35. Son, T.C., et al.: Domain-dependent knowledge in answer set planning. ACM Trans. Comput. Log. **7**(4), 613–657 (2006). https://doi.org/10.1145/1183278.1183279

36. Weske, M.: Business Process Management - Concepts, Languages, Architectures, Third Edition. Springer, Berlin, Heidelberg (2019). https://doi.org/10.1007/978-3-540-73522-9

37. White, S.A.: Introduction to BPMN. In: IBM 2.0 (2004)

Using Logic Programming and Kernel-Grouping for Improving Interpretability of Convolutional Neural Networks

Parth Padalkar[(✉)][iD], Huaduo Wang[iD], and Gopal Gupta[iD]

The University of Texas at Dallas, Richardson, USA
{parth.padalkar,huaduo.wang,gupta}@utdallas.edu

Abstract. Within the realm of deep learning, the interpretability of Convolutional Neural Networks (CNNs), particularly in the context of image classification tasks, remains a formidable challenge. To this end, we present a neurosymbolic framework, NeSyFOLD-G that generates a symbolic rule-set using the last layer kernels of the CNN to make its underlying knowledge interpretable. We find groups of similar kernels in the CNN (kernel-grouping) using the cosine-similarity score between the feature maps generated by various kernels. Once such kernel groups are found, we binarize each kernel group's output and use it to generate a rule-set using a Rule Based Machine Learning (RBML) algorithm called FOLD-SE-M. We present a novel kernel grouping algorithm and show that grouping similar kernels leads to a significant reduction in the size of the rule-set generated by FOLD-SE-M, consequently, improving the interpretability. The rule-set can be viewed as a stratified Answer Set Program wherein each predicate's truth value depends on a kernel group in the CNN. Each predicate in the rule-set is mapped to a semantic concept using a novel semantic labeling algorithm that utilizes a few semantic segmentation masks of the images used for training. The last layers of the CNN can then be replaced by this rule-set to obtain the NeSy-G model which can then be used for the image classification task. The goal-directed ASP system s(CASP) can be used to obtain the justification of any prediction made using the NeSy-G model.

Keywords: CNN · Neurosymbolic AI · Answer Set Programming · Rule-Based Machine Learning · Interpretable Image Classification

1 Introduction

Interpretability of deep learning models is an important issue that has resurfaced in recent years as these models have become larger and are being applied to an increasing number of tasks. Some applications such as autonomous vehicles [9], disease diagnosis [27], and natural disaster prevention [12] are very sensitive areas where a wrong prediction could be the difference between life and death. The above tasks rely heavily on good image classification models such as Convolutional Neural Networks (CNNs). A CNN is a deep learning model used for a wide

© The Author(s), under exclusive license to Springer Nature Switzerland AG 2023
M. Gebser and I. Sergey (Eds.): PADL 2024, LNCS 14512, pp. 134–150, 2023.
https://doi.org/10.1007/978-3-031-52038-9_9

range of image classification and object detection tasks, first introduced by Y. Lecun et al. [15]. Current CNNs are extremely powerful and capable of outperforming humans in image classification tasks. A CNN is inherently a blackbox model, though attempts have been made to make it more interpretable [36,37]. There is no way to tell whether the predictions made by the model are based on concepts meaningful to humans, or are simply the outcome of coincidental correlations. If the knowledge of the trained CNN becomes interpretable then domain experts can scrutinize this knowledge and point out any biases or spurious correlations that the CNN might have learnt which could lead to wrong predictions. Thus retraining with better and more targeted data can be suggested by the experts.

We propose a framework for interpretable image classification using CNNs called NeSyFOLD-G. A CNN, like any deep neural network is composed of multiple layers. We focus on the convolution layer, more specifically the last convolution layer of a CNN in this work. The convolution layer is composed of kernels.

A kernel, also known as a filter, is a 2D matrix. It acts like a small, specialized magnifying glass that slides over an image to help recognize specific features or patterns in the image, like edges, curves, or textures. It does this by multiplying its values with the pixel values of the image in a small region, and then it adds up those products. This process helps highlight important parts of the image. As the kernel slides over the entire image, it creates a new, simplified version of the image that emphasizes the patterns it's looking for. This simplified version is called a feature map. The CNN then uses these feature maps to understand the image and make predictions.

The NeSyFOLD-G framework can be used to create a *NeSy-G* model which is a composition of the CNN and a rule-set generated from kernels in its last convolution layer. A Rule Based Machine Learning (RBML) algorithm called FOLD-SE-M [30] is used for generating the rule-set by using binarized outputs of the groups of similar kernels in a trained CNN. The rule-set is a default theory represented as a stratified answer set program. The binarized output (0/1) of the kernel groups influences the truth value of the predicates appearing in the rule body. The s(CASP) [1] ASP system can be used to obtain justifications of the predictions made by the NeSy-G model. The rule-set also serves as a global explanation for the predictions made by the CNN.

Our first novel contribution is the *kernel grouping algorithm* that finds groups of similar kernels in the CNN based on the cosine similarity score of their corresponding generated feature maps.

Secondly, we introduce a semantic labelling algorithm that can be used to label the predicates in the rule-set with the semantic concept(s) that their corresponding kernel groups represent in the images. For example, the predicate 52(X) corresponding to kernel group 52 in the last convolution layer of the CNN will be replaced by bathtub(X) in the rule-set, if kernel group 52 has learnt to look for "bathtubs" in the image. Figure 1 illustrates the NeSyFOLD-G framework.

Padalkar et al. proposed the NeSyFOLD framework [18] which shares similarities with the NeSyFOLD-G framework. The major difference that separates NeSyFOLD-G from NeSyFOLD is that the truth values of predicates in the generated rule-set is influenced by the binarized output of *groups* of similar kernels. In NeSyFOLD each predicate's truth value is influenced by single kernels in the CNN. However, it is known that groups of kernels in the last layer are responsible for representing a single concept. Yang et al. [33] proposed an attention-based masking mechanism for finding the concept learnt by a single kernel by accounting for the other kernels with similar attention weights. Their approach serves as motivation behind our kernel grouping algorithm that uses the cosine similarity score between feature maps of various kernels to find the groups of similar kernels.

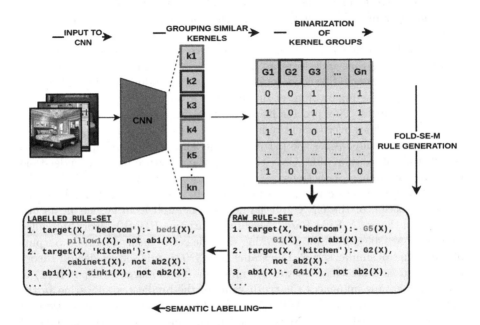

Fig. 1. The NeSyFOLD-G framework. Each kernel group is depicted with a unique color in the rule-set. (Color figure online)

The size of the rule-set generated can be used as a metric for interpretability. Lage et al. [13] comprehensively showed through human evaluations that as the size of the rule-set increases the difficulty in interpreting the rule-set also increases. Padalkar et al. show that NeSyFOLD framework generates a smaller rule-set than the ERIC system [28] which was the previous SOTA. We show that NeSyFOLD-G, achieves a significant reduction in the size of the rule-set generated while maintaining or improving on the accuracy and fidelity in comparison to the NeSyFOLD framework.

To summarize, our contributions are as follows:

1. We present a novel kernel grouping algorithm that constitutes the heart of the NeSyFOLD-G framework for improving interpretability of the generated rule-set.
2. We also introduce a semantic labeling algorithm for labeling the predicates of the rule-set generated by the NeSyFOLD-G framework.

2   Background

FOLD-SE-M: The FOLD-SE-M algorithm [30] that we employ in our framework, learns a rule-set from data as a *default theory*. Default logic [21] is a non-monotonic logic used to formalize commonsense reasoning. A default D is expressed as:

$$D = A : \mathbf{M}B \over \Gamma \tag{1}$$

Equation 1 states that the conclusion Γ can be inferred if pre-requisite A holds and B is justified. $\mathbf{M}B$ stands for "it is consistent to believe B". Normal logic programs can encode a default theory quite elegantly [8]. A default of the form:

$$\alpha_1 \wedge \alpha_2 \wedge \cdots \wedge \alpha_n : \mathbf{M}\neg\beta_1, \mathbf{M}\neg\beta_2 \ldots \mathbf{M}\neg\beta_m \over \gamma$$

can be formalized as the normal logic programming rule:

$$\gamma :\!- \alpha_1, \alpha_2, \ldots, \alpha_n, \texttt{not } \beta_1, \texttt{not } \beta_2, \ldots, \texttt{not } \beta_m.$$

where α's and β's are positive predicates and **not** represents negation-as-failure. We call such rules *default rules*. Thus, the default

$$bird(X) : M\neg penguin(X) \over flies(X)$$

will be represented as the following default rule in normal logic programming:

```
flies(X) :- bird(X), not penguin(X).
```

We call `bird(X)`, the condition that allows us to jump to the default conclusion that X flies, the *default part* of the rule, and **not** `penguin(X)` the *exception part* of the rule.

FOLD-SE-M [30] is a Rule Based Machine Learning (RBML) algorithm. It generates a rule-set from tabular data, comprising rules in the form described above. The complete rule-set can be viewed as a stratified answer set program. It uses special `abx` predicates to represent the exception part of a rule where x is unique numerical identifier. FOLD-SE-M incrementally generates literals for *default rules* that cover positive examples while avoiding covering negative examples. It then swaps the positive and negative examples and calls itself recursively to learn exceptions to the default when there are still negative examples falsely covered.

There are 2 tunable hyperparameters, *ratio*, and *tail*. The *ratio* controls the upper bound on the number of false positives to the number of true positives implied by the default part of a rule. The *tail* controls the limit of the minimum number of training examples a rule can cover. FOLD-SE-M generates a much smaller number of rules than a decision-tree classifier and gives higher accuracy in general.

3   Learning

In this section we describe the process of generating a rule-set from the CNN and obtaining the NeSy-G model. We start by training the CNN on the input images for the given image classification dataset. Any optimization technique can be used for updating the weights. Figure 1 illustrates the learning pipeline.

Binarization: Once the CNN has been fully trained to convergence, we pass the full training set consisting of n images to the CNN. For each image i in the training set, let $A_{i,k}$ denote the feature map generated by kernel k in the last convolutional layer. The feature map $A_{i,k}$ is a $2D$ matrix of dimension determined by the CNN architecture. For each image i there are K feature maps generated where K is the total number of kernels in the last convolutional layer of the CNN. To convert each of the feature maps to a single value we take the norm of the feature maps as demonstrated by Eq. (2) to obtain $a_{i,k}$.

Kernel Grouping Algorithm: We then find the groups of similar kernels in the CNN. Consider a kernel $\hat{k}$ for which we need to identify the most similar kernels. We do this by first finding the *top-10* images $\hat{i}_1, \hat{i}_2, ..., \hat{i}_{10}$ that activate $\hat{k}$ the most, according to the norm values of the feature maps generated by $\hat{k}$ for these images. Now, we compute the cosine similarity score between $A_{\hat{i}_g, \hat{k}}$ and $A_{\hat{i}_g, k'}$, where g $\in [1, 10]$ and k' is some kernel in the last layer the last layer of the CNN. The similarity score of kernel k' w.r.t. $\hat{k}$ is calculated by taking the mean of the cosine similarity scores for all the *top-10* images $\hat{i}_1, \hat{i}_2, ..., \hat{i}_{10}$ as $sim_{\hat{k}, k'}$. The similarity score is a value between 0 and 1. Thus, we calculate the similarity score of all kernels in the last layer of the CNN w.r.t. to $\hat{k}$. The group of kernel $\hat{k}$ would then constitute of all kernels that have a similarity score w.r.t. $\hat{k}$ greater than a user-defined similarity threshold θ_s.

Hence, we find a group of similar kernels G_k for all the kernels k in the last layer of the CNN. Note that the total number of kernel groups G_k is the same as the total number of kernels in the last layer of the CNN.

Next, for each kernel group G_k we obtain the group norm a_{i,G_k} for each image i in the training set. This is achieved by taking the mean of the norms corresponding to each kernel in G_k for each image i. This leads to the creation of a table T_G with each row representing an image and each column representing the group norm for each of the kernel groups G_k.

Finally, for each kernel group we convert the group norm values to either 0 or 1 which symbolizes the kernel group "activating" or "deactivating" for each image. This is called *binarization* of the kernel groups. This is done by determining an appropriate threshold θ_{G_k} for each kernel group G_k to binarize its output. The threshold θ_{G_k} is calculated as a weighted sum of the mean and the standard deviation of the group norms a_{i,G_k} for all images i in the training set, denoted by Eq. (3) where α and γ are user-defined hyperparameters.

Thus a binarization table B_G is created. Each row in the table represents an image and each column is the binarized kernel group value represented by either a 0 if $a_{i,G_k} \leq \theta_{G_k}$ or 1 if $a_{i,G_k} > \theta_{G_k}$ (*cf.* Fig. 1 (right)).

$$a_{i,k} = ||A_{i,k}||_2 \tag{2}$$

$$\theta_{G_k} = \alpha \cdot \overline{a_{G_k}} + \gamma \sqrt{\frac{1}{n} \sum (a_{i,G_k} - \overline{a_{G_k}})^2} \tag{3}$$

Rule-Set Generation: The binarization table B_G is given as an input to the FOLD-SE-M algorithm to obtain a rule-set in the form of a stratified answer set program. The FOLD-SE-M algorithm finds the most influential features in the B_G and generates a rule-set that has these features as predicates. Since B_G has features as kernel group ids, the raw rule-set has predicates with names in the form of their corresponding kernel group's id. An example rule could be:

```
target(X,'2')  :- not 3(X), 54(X), not ab1(X).
```

This rule can be interpreted as "Image X belongs to class '2' if kernel group 3 is not activated and kernel group 54 is activated and the abnormal condition (exception) ab1 does not apply". There will be another rule with the head as ab1(X) in the rule-set. The binarized output of a kernel group would determine the truth value of its predicate in the rule-set. The rule-set generated is in the form of a decision list, i.e., the next rule is checked only if the current rule and all the rules above it were not satisfied.

Semantic Labeling: Groups of kernels activate in synergy to identify concepts in the CNN. Since we capture the outputs of the kernel groups as truth values of predicates in the rule-set, we can label the predicates with the semantic concept(s) that the corresponding kernel group has learnt. Thus, the same example rule from above may now look like:

```
target(X,'bathroom')  :- not bed(X), bathtub(X), not ab1(X).
```

We introduce a novel semantic labelling algorithm to automate the semantic labelling of the predicates in the rule-set generated. The details of the algorithm are discussed later.

The NeSy-G model is conceptualized as the model obtained after replacing all the layers following the last convolutional layer with the rule-set generated by applying the FOLD-SE-M algorithm on the binarization table B_G.

4   Inference

For using the NeSy-G model to obtain predictions on the test set, we first obtain the kernel feature maps for each kernel in the last convolutional layer. Then, we compute the group norms for all kernel groups that were found in the learning process to obtain the table $T_{G_k}^{test}$. From $T_{G_k}^{test}$ we obtain the binarization table B_G^{test} by binarizing the output of each kernel group in $T_{G_k}^{test}$ by using the threshold θ_{G_k} calculated in the learning phase. Next, for each binarized vector b in B_G^{test}, we use the labeled/unlabelled rule-set obtained in the learning phase to make predictions. The truth value of the predicates in the rule-set is determined by the corresponding binarized kernel group values in b. FOLD-SE-M toolkit's built-in rule-interpreter can be used to obtain the predicted class of b given the rule-set. The binarized kernel group values in b can also be listed as facts and the rule-set which is a stratified answer set program, can be queried with the s(CASP) interpreter [1] to obtain the justification as well as the target class. Note that s(CASP) searches for the answer set in a goal directed manner, which implies that the rules are checked from the top to the bottom one by one. Hence, the first answer set that is found to satisfy the rule-set with the given facts entails the intended prediction made by the NeSy-G model.

5   Semantic Labelling of Predicates

The raw rule-set generated by FOLD-SE-M initially has kernel group ids as predicate names. Also, since the FOLD-SE-M algorithm finds only the most influential kernel groups, the number of kernel groups that actually appear in the rule-set is usually very low in comparison to the total number of kernel groups. We present a novel algorithm for automatically labelling the corresponding predicates of the kernel groups with the semantic concept(s) that the kernel groups represent.

Xie et al. [32] showed that each kernel in the CNN may learn to represent multiple concepts in the images. Hence each kernel group may also represent multiple concepts. As a result, we assign semantic labels to each predicate, denoting the names of the semantic concepts learnt by the corresponding kernel group. To regulate the extent of approximation, i.e., to dictate the number of concept names to be included in the predicate label, we introduce a hyperparameter *margin*. This hyperparameter exercises control over the precision of the approximation achieved. Figure 2 illustrates the semantic labelling of a given predicate. The algorithm requires a dataset that has semantic segmentation masks of the training images. This essentially means that for every image i in the dataset I, there is an image i_M where every pixel is annotated with the label of the object (concept) that it belongs to (Fig. 2 middle). We denote these by I_M.

The CNN that is trained on the training set is used to obtain the norms $a_{i,k}$ of the feature maps $A_{i,k}$ generated by each kernel k in the last convolution layer. Next, as the respective kernel groups for each kernel are known, the table $T_{G_k}^{I_m}$ is created where each row represents the images whose corresponding semantic segmentation masks are available and the columns are the kernel group norms.

Now, consider some kernel group $G_{\hat{k}}$ that has l kernels in the group namely, $\hat{k}_1, \hat{k}_2, ..., \hat{k}_l$. The *top-m* images $i'_1, i'_2, ..., i'_m \in I'_m$, according to the group norm values are selected. We need to calculate the group's *Intersection over Union* (*IoU$_c$*) score for each concept c visible in the *top-m* images that most activate the group. Then according to this score for each concept c, the label of the kernel group's predicate should comprise of the top concepts that the kernel group is detecting.

$$IoU_c(i^{Mask}, i) = \frac{\text{no. of non-zero pixels in } c \cap i}{\text{no. of non-zero pixels in } i} \qquad (4)$$

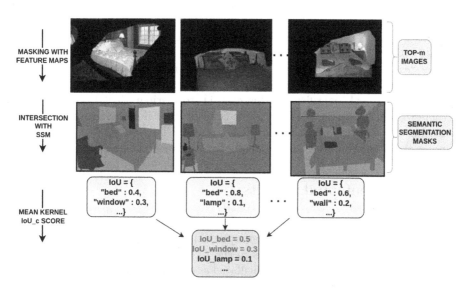

Fig. 2. The calculation of mean IoU_c scores for a kernel.

For a given image $i_j \in I'_m$, the resized feature map generated by every kernel in the kernel group is used to mask the image to obtain $i_j^{\hat{k}_1}, i_j^{\hat{k}_2}, ..., i_j^{\hat{k}_l}$. Figure 2 (top) shows a few images masked with the resized feature maps generated by a kernel. For each of these masked images, the IoU_c score is calculated using Eq. (4) for each concept c, that appears in the corresponding semantic segmentation mask i_j^{Mask} of the image i_j. Figure 2 (middle) shows the semantic segmentation masks of the images at the top. Next, each kernel's IoU_c score for all the *top-m* images, for all concepts c is calculated. Each kernel's mean IoU_c score is calculated by taking the mean score over all images. Finally, the kernel group's IoU_c score is calculated by taking the mean of the mean IoU_c score of each kernel for each concept c.

The algorithm can be summarized as follows:

1. For a given kernel group, find the *top-m* images according to its group kernel norm value.
2. For each kernel in the kernel group find the IoU_c score for each of the *top-m* images.
3. Calculate the mean IoU_c score for each kernel over all images.
4. Calculate the mean of the mean IoU_c score for each kernel to obtain the kernel Group's IoU_c score.

Figure 2 illustrates the IoU_c scores calculation for a single kernel.

The label of the corresponding predicate of a kernel group is chosen as the set of concepts that have their *normalized* IoU_c score in a certain "margin" from the top concept. This is controlled using the user-defined *margin* hyperparameter.

For example, if the IoU_c score for kernel group 12 is {*cabinets* : 0.5, *door* : 0.4, *drawer* : 0.1} then with a *margin* of 0.1 the label for the corresponding predicate will be "*cabinets1_door1*" since the concept *door* is in the 0.1 margin from the top concept *cabinets*. Note that each concept name in the label is appended with a unique numerical identifier (in this case 1), to distinguish it from the other kernel groups that might learn the same concept. Say, if kernel group 25 is also detecting *cabinets* then its predicate's label would be "*cabinets2_...*" where ... denotes the other concepts that the kernel group 25 might be detecting.

6   Experiments and Results

Exp 1 (Setup): We compare the performance of NeSyFOLD-G framework with that of the NeSyFOLD framework on various datasets. We report the accuracy, fidelity, number of unique predicates in the rule-set, number of rules generated and the size of the rule-set. Size is calculated as the total number of predicates in the bodies of the rules that constitute the logic program generated by NeSyFOLD and NeSyFOLD-G.

We used a VGG16 CNN with pre-trained weights on the Imagenet dataset [4]. We trained for 100 epochs with a batch size of 32. We used the Adam [10] optimizer and applied class weights for imbalanced data. We also used $L2$ regularization of 0.005 on all layers and a learning rate of 5×10^{-7}. We used a decay factor of 0.5 and patience of 10 epochs. Also, we resized all images to 224×224. We used $\alpha = 0.6$ and $\gamma = 0.7$ for all the datasets. For this experiment, we used the *German Traffic Sign Recognition Benchmark* (GTSRB) [26], *MNIST* [16] and the Places [39] dataset.

The GTSRB dataset has 43 classes. Each class contains multiple instances of a physical signpost and multiple images of the signpost are provided. We used a 80:20 training-validation split per class and used the provided test set to report the performance metrics of the models.

The MNIST dataset has 10 classes. Each class contains images of a handwritten digit from 0 to 9. We split the standard training set into train and validation set by using the last $10k$ images for the validation set. We used the provided test set to report the results.

The Places dataset has images of various scenes. To see the effect of varying the number of classes $\in \{2, 3, 5, 10\}$ we train on the bathroom and bedroom class (PLACES2) first. Then we add the kitchen class (PLACES3.1), then dining room, living room (PLACES5) and finally home office, office, waiting room, conference room and hotel room (PLACES10). We also selected 2 additional subsets of 3 classes each namely, {desert road, forest road, street} (PLACES3.2) and {desert road, driveway, highway} (PLACES3.3). We obtained the train and the test set by selecting $1k$ images from each class for the test set and the other $4k$ for the training set. We use the given validation set to tune our hyperparameters. All the hyperparameter values used are listed in the supplementary material.

The NeSy-G model was created using the learning procedure described previously using the NeSyFOLD-G framework and the NeSy model was created using the NeSyFOLD framework as described in [18]. The comparison between NeSyFOLD-G and NeSyFOLD is drawn in Table 1. The accuracy (Acc.), fidelity (Fid.), number of predicates (Pred.), are reported on the test set. The results are reported after 5 runs on each dataset. Note, fidelity determines how closely a model follows the predictions of another model. Since the NeSy-G and NeSy models are created from the trained model they should show high fidelity w.r.t. the CNN. The fidelity is calculated as the number of times the NeSy or the NeSy-G model predicts the same class as the CNN, divided by the number of test images.

Exp 1 (Result): Table 1 clearly shows that the NeSy-G model outperforms NeSy model w.r.t. accuracy and fidelity in most cases and is comparable otherwise. More importantly, the advantage of using the NeSyFOLD-G framework is apparent from the reduction in the number of predicates, number of rules and the overall size of the rule-set that is generated.

The reduction in size of the rule-set is a direct indication of the improved interpretability as pointed out by Lage et al. [13]. The main difference between the NeSyFOLD and the NeSyFOLD-G framework is the grouping of similar kernels in the latter. The grouped kernels form better features in the binarization table that is generated after binarizing the group norms. The grouping helps in creating more informative features for the FOLD-SE-M algorithm to generate the rules from. Hence, in a fewer number of predicates and rules, (as compared to NeSyFOLD) the same information can be captured.

Note that as the number of classes increases as in the case of *PLACES2, PLACES3.1, PLACES3.2, PLACES3.3, PLACES5* and *PLACES10* both the models show a decrease in the accuracy and fidelity. This is because as the number of classes increases, more number of kernels are needed to represent the knowledge and consequently more kernels have to be binarized. Thus the loss incurred due to binarization of the kernels increases as the number of classes increases. Notice that for PLACES10 the size of the rule-set generated by NeSyFOLD-G is larger than that generated by NeSyFOLD. This is because for 2 out of the 5 runs, NeSyFOLD could not generate any rule-set as the FOLD-SE-

Table 1. Comparison NeSyFOLD (NF) vs NeSyFOLD-G (NF-G).

Data	Algo	Fid.	Acc.	Pred.	Rules	Size
PLACES2	NF	**0.93 ± 0.01**	0.92 ± 0.01	16 ± 2	12 ± 2	28 ± 5
	NF-G	**0.93 ± 0.0**	**0.93 ± 0.0**	8 ± 1	**7 ± 1**	**11 ± 2**
PLACES3.1	NF	0.85 ± 0.03	0.84 ± 0.03	28 ± 6	21 ± 4	49 ± 9
	NF-G	**0.87 ± 0.01**	**0.86 ± 0.01**	**20 ± 7**	**15 ± 3**	**31 ± 9**
PLACES3.2	NF	**0.94 ± 0.0**	**0.92 ± 0.0**	16 ± 4	13 ± 3	26 ± 7
	NF-G	**0.94 ± 0.01**	**0.92 ± 0.01**	**12 ± 3**	**10 ± 1**	**18 ± 3**
PLACES3.3	NF	**0.83 ± 0.01**	0.79 ± 0.01	32 ± 5	23 ± 3	60 ± 11
	NF-G	**0.83 ± 0.01**	**0.80 ± 0.01**	**30 ± 2**	**21 ± 3**	**53 ± 6**
PLACES5	NF	0.67 ± 0.03	0.64 ± 0.03	56 ± 3	52 ± 4	131 ± 10
	NF-G	**0.68 ± 0.02**	**0.65 ± 0.02**	**41 ± 4**	**34 ± 6**	**83 ± 13**
PLACES10	NF	0.23 ± 0.19	0.20 ± 0.17	**33 ± 28**	**32 ± 27**	**78 ± 66**
	NF-G	**0.33 ± 0.17**	**0.30 ± 0.15**	74 ± 39	73 ± 39	184 ± 97
GTSRB	NF	0.75 ± 0.04	0.75 ± 0.04	206 ± 28	134 ± 26	418 ± 79
	NF-G	**0.76 ± 0.02**	**0.76 ± 0.02**	**176 ± 13**	**98 ± 11**	**320 ± 30**
MNIST	NF	**0.91 ± 0.01**	**0.91 ± 0.01**	132 ± 9	90 ± 7	271 ± 25
	NF-G	0.90 ± 0.01	0.90 ± 0.01	**103 ± 12**	**79 ± 10**	**216 ± 28**

M algorithm could not find good enough features in the binarization table. Due to the size of the training set being relatively large (40k examples) and the large number of classes (10 classes), the loss due to binarization rapidly increases. This is also the reason why the accuracy and fidelity is very low. However, since NeSyFOLD-G uses kernel grouping, the FOLD-SE-M algorithm gets to work with better features in the binarization table and thus the accuracy and fidelity is much higher compared to NeSyFOLD and thus the rule-set size is also high on average. Although in 1 run NeSyFOLD-G also manages to find no rule-set that explains the predictions of the CNN.

Exp 2 (setup): We use the procedure described previously, for semantic labelling of the predicates in the rule-set generated. We use the *ADE20k* dataset [40] in our experiments. It provides manually annotated semantic segmentation masks for a few images of all the classes of the Places dataset. The GTSRB and MNIST datasets do not have any semantic segmentation masks available. Hence, for all the subsets of classes of the Places dataset reported in Table 1, we show the effect of using the semantic labelling algorithm described in Sect. 5. In Fig. 3 we have shown labelled rule-sets for the PLACES2, PLACES3.1 and PLACES3.2, PLACES3.3 and PLACES5 datasets. We used a *ratio* of 0.8 for all datasets, *tail* : $5e^{-3}$ for PLACES2, PLACES3.1 and PLACES3.2, *tail* : $1e^{-2}$ for PLACES3.3 and PLACES5 dataset. A similarity threshold θ_s of 0.8 was used for generating the rule-sets. We used a margin of 0.05 to label the raw rule-sets.

```
RULE-SET 1:
1. target(X,'bedroom') :-
       not sink1_wall2_countertop1(X), not ab2(X).
2. target(X,'bathroom') :- wall1(X).
3. target(X,'bathroom') :- wall3(X).
4. target(X,'bathroom') :- not wall3(X),
       not bed2(X).
5. target(X,'bedroom') :- not bed2(X).
6. target(X,'bedroom') :- not wall3(X).
7. ab1(X) :- not wall4(X), bed4(X).
8. ab2(X) :- not bed3(X), not bed1(X), not bed5(X),
       not ab1(X).
```

```
RULE-SET 2:
1. target(X,'street') :- building5(X).
2. target(X,'forest_road') :- tree1(X),
       not ab1(X), not ab2(X).
3. target(X,'desert_road') :- sky1(X).
4. target(X,'desert_road') :- building7(X),
       not sky1(X), not building6(X).
5. target(X,'forest_road') :- not building3(X),
       not ab3(X).
6. target(X,'street') :- building1(X).
7. ab1(X) :- not tree3_building4(X), sky2(X).
8. ab2(X) :- building2(X), building8(X).
9. ab3(X) :- not tree2(X), not building7(X).
```

```
RULE-SET 3:
1.  target(X,'highway') :- not ground1(X),
        not ab3(X), not ab4(X).
2.  target(X,'driveway') :- house3_building1(X).
3.  target(X,'desert_road') :- not trees2_road5(X),
        not ab6(X).
4.  target(X,'highway') :- house3_building1(X).
5.  target(X,'highway') :- road9(X).
6.  target(X,'driveway') :- house1(X).
7.  target(X,'highway') :- not road9(X), not ab7(X).
8.  ab1(X) :- not road6(X), house3_building1(X).
9.  ab2(X) :- not house2(X), trees3(X), not ab1(X).
10. ab3(X) :- not road7(X), not ab2(X).
11. ab4(X) :- not road2(X), road1(X), not trees4(X).
12. ab5(X) :- not road8_car1(X), not trees1(X).
13. ab6(X) :- not sky2(X), not sky1(X), not ab5(X).
14. ab7(X) :- not road4(X), not road3(X).
```

```
RULE-SET 4:
1. target(X,'living_room') :- sofa2(X), not bed1(X),
       sofa3(X), not sink2(X).
2. target(X,'dining_room') :- cabinet1(X),
       wall4_cabinet3(X), cabinet2(X).
3. target(X,'kitchen') :- floor1_chair1(X),
       not bed3(X).
4. target(X,'bedroom') :- bed3(X),
       not wall2_kitchen_island1(X).
5. target(X,'bathroom') :- wall3(X), not bed2(X).
6. target(X,'living_room') :-
       armchair1_sofa1_wall1(X), not sink1(X),
       not ab1(X).
7. ab1(X) :- wall2_kitchen_island1(X), sofa3(X).
```

Fig. 3. The labelled rule-sets generated by NeSyFOLD-G for PLACES2 (RULE-SET 1), PLACES3.2 (RULE-SET 2), PLACES3.3 (RULE-SET 3) and PLACES5 (RULE-SET 4)

```
RULE-SET 5:
1.  target(X,'kitchen') :- cabinet4_wall5(X),
        not ab1(X), not ab2(X).
2.  target(X,'bedroom') :- bed2(X), not ab3(X).
3.  target(X,'bathroom') :- toilet1(X).
4.  target(X,'bathroom') :- not cabinet1(X),
        wall2_floor1(X), not kitchen_island1(X).
5.  target(X,'bedroom') :- bed3(X), not bed2(X).
6.  target(X,'kitchen') :- cabinet3_door1(X).
7.  target(X,'bathroom') :- wall1(X).
8.  target(X,'bedroom') :- bed1(X).
9.  ab1(X) :- not cabinet3_door1(X), bed4(X).
10. ab2(X) :- not cabinet2(X), wall3(X),
        not range1(X).
11. ab3(X) :- wall4_sink2(X), sink1(X).
```

```
JUSTIFICATION (RULE-SET 5):
'target' holds (for img, and kitchen),
because 'cabinet4_wall5' holds (for img), and
there is no evidence that
'ab1' holds (for img),
    because there is no evidence that
    'cabinet3_door1' holds (for img) and
    'bed4' holds (for img), and
there is no evidence that
'ab2' holds (for img),
    because there is no evidence that
    'cabinet2' holds (for img) and
    'wall3' holds (for img), and
    there is no evidence that
    'range1' holds (for img).
MODEL:
{target(img,kitchen), cabinet4_wall5(img),
not ab1(img), not cabinet3_door1(img), bed4(img),
not ab2(img), not cabinet2(img), wall3(img), not range1(img)}
```

Fig. 4. The justification (right) obtained from s(CASP) for an image "img" when running the query ?- target(img, X). against RULE-SET 5 (left).

We do not show the labelled rule-set for PLACES10 since the accuracy of the NeSy-G model is very low on the dataset.

Exp 2 (result): The labelled rule-sets make intuitive sense to humans. This representation of knowledge in default theory in our opinion makes the rule-set easy to understand. The rule-set captures the knowledge of the trained CNN. For example in RULE-SET 2, the first rule states that "an image X is a 'street' if there is evidence of the concept 'building' in the image". Similarly the second rule states that "an image X is a 'forest road' if there is evidence of the concept 'tree' in the image and there is no evidence of some abnormal conditions 'ab1' and 'ab2'.

Notice how in rules 2,3 of RULE-SET 1 in Fig. 3 the group of kernels, now labelled as 'wall1' and 'wall3' are (most probably) detecting a certain type of patterns on the walls that are indicative of bathrooms, possibly tiles. The kernels are labelled as wall only because the semantic segmentation masks available to us have the label 'wall' for the pixels that denote wall in the image. Hence we are restricted to the expressiveness of the annotations available to us. This can be alleviated by labelling the predicates via manual observation or custom semantic segmentation masks can be generated using tools such as SegGPT [31].

Note that in the first rule of RULE-SET 5 (Fig. 4) there is a predicate `cabinet4_wall5/1`. This predicate corresponds to the kernel group in the CNN that is detecting either both cabinets and walls separately or a specific region in the images that contains a portion of cabinets and wall. It is hard to distinguish between the two cases.

Figure 4 shows a sample justification obtained from s(CASP) for some image "img". The binarized vector associated with "img" is used to write the facts and the query `target(img, X)` is executed against RULE-SET 5. The first rule (shown in red) was satisfied. The first model found by s(CASP) that satisfies the rule-set binds the value of X to 'kitchen'. Hence, the predicted class of the image "img" is kitchen.

7   Related Work

A similar approach of generating rules from the CNN was adopted by Townsend et al. [28,29], where they used a decision tree algorithm to generate the rule-set. However, Padalkar et al. [18] showed that using FOLD-SE-M generates a much smaller rule-set and higher accuracy and fidelity.

There is a lot of past work which focuses on visualizing the outputs of the layers of the CNN. These methods try to map the relationship between the input pixels and the output of the neurons. Zeiler et al. [35] and Zhou et al. [38] use the output activation while others [5,22,25] use gradients to find the mapping. Unlike NeSyFOLD-G, these visualization methods do not generate any rule-set. Zeiler et al. [35] use similar ideas to analyze what specific kernels in the CNN are invoked. There are fewer existing publications on methods for modeling relations between the various important features and generating explanations from them. Ferreira et al. [7] use multiple mapping networks that are trained to map the activation values of the main network's output to the human-defined concepts represented in an induced logic-based theory. Their method needs multiple neural networks besides the main network that the user has to provide.

Qi et al. [19] propose an Explanation Neural Network (XNN) which learns an embedding in high-dimension space and maps it to a low-dimension explanation space to explain the predictions of the network. A sentence-like explanation including the features is then generated manually. No rules are generated and manual effort is needed. Chen et al. [3] introduce a prototype layer in the network that learns to classify images in terms of various parts of the image. They assume that there is a one to one mapping between the concepts and the kernels. We do not make such an assumption. Zhang et al. [36,37] learn disentangled concepts from the CNN and represent them in a hierarchical graph so that there is no assumption of a one to one kernel-concept mapping. However, no logical explanation is generated. Bologna et al. [2] extract propositional rules from CNNs. Their system operates at the neuron level, while NeSyFold-G works with groups of neurons.

Our NeSyFOLD-G framework uses FOLD-SE-M to extract a logic program from the binarization table. There are other works that focus on inductive logic programming [17] such as the ILASP system [14] by Law et al. and the XHAIL [20] system by Ray et al. which induce an answer set program from the data however these systems are more suitable for complex tasks unlike the task of generating rules from simple tabular data, for which FOLD-SE-M is more efficient. Some other works [6,23,24] use a neurosymbolic system to induce logic rules from data. These systems belong to the Neuro:Symbolic → Neuro category whereas ours belongs to the Neuro;Symbolic category.

8   Conclusion and Future Work

In this paper we have shown how the NeSyFOLD-G framework can be used to make a CNN more interpretable. We used the framework with a trained CNN to derive a NeSy-G model that constitutes the CNN with all layers after the last convolutional layer replaced by the rule-set generated by FOLD-SE-M algorithm. We compared the performance of the NeSyFOLD-G framework with that of the NeSyFOLD framework on various datasets. The major difference between the NeSyFOLD-G and the NeSyFOLD framework is that in the former, groups of similar kernels are found and the output of these groups kernels is then binarized to produce the binarization table, that is used as input to the FOLD-SE-M algorithm which generates a rule-set. The kernel grouping algorithm is a novel contribution of this work. In the NeSyFOLD framework each individual kernel's output is binarized and the rules are generated based on the binarization table thus constructed.

We show in the experiments that grouping similar kernels leads to the creation of better features in the binarization table which consequently leads to a more succinct rule-set. The NeSyFOLD-G framework always generates a smaller rule-set than that generated by the NeSyFOLD framework while either outperforming or showing comparable accuracy and fidelity.

We also introduced a novel semantic labelling algorithm that can be used for labelling each predicate that appears in the rule-set with the concepts(s) that its corresponding kernel group represents. We showed two labelled rule-sets and an example justification of a prediction that can be obtained using the s(CASP) ASP system.

Note that both NeSyFOLD-G and NeSyFOLD are aimed at representing the connectionist knowledge of the CNN in terms of a symbolic rule-set. The symbolic rule-set can then be scrutinized by experts to figure out the biases that the CNN might have learnt from the data and these help in avoiding spurious predictions in sensitive domains such as medical imaging. The advantage that NeSyFOLD-G provides is that the interpretability of the rule-set increases as the size of the generated rule-set is significantly smaller.

We acknowledge that the semantic segmentation masks of images may not be readily available depending on the domain, in which case the semantic labelling of the predicates has to be done manually or the semantic segmentation masks can be obtained using transformer-based models such as SegGPT [31] and SAM [11]. Our NeSyFOLD-G framework helps in this regard as well, as it decreases the number of predicates that need to be labelled.

As the number of classes increases, the loss in accuracy also increases due to the binarization of more kernels. We plan to explore end-to-end training of the CNN with the rules generated so that this loss in binarization can be reduced during training itself.

In future, we plan to use NeSyFOLD-G for real-world tasks such as interpretable breast cancer prediction. We also intend to explore combining the knowledge of two or more CNNs by producing a single rule-set that contains the kernels of the corresponding CNNs as predicates. We also plan to investigate how the knowledge from the generated rules can be backpropagated to improve the performance of a CNN [34].

References

1. Arias, J., Carro, M., Salazar, E., Marple, K., Gupta, G.: Constraint answer set programming without grounding. Theory Pract. Logic Program. **18**(3–4), 337–354 (2018)
2. Bologna, G., Fossati, S.: A two-step rule-extraction technique for a CNN. Electronics **9**(6), 990 (2020)
3. Chen, C., Li, O., Tao, D., Barnett, A., Rudin, C., Su, J.K.: This looks like that: deep learning for interpretable image recognition. In: Advances in Neural Information Processing Systems 32 (2019)
4. Deng, J., Dong, W., Socher, R., Li, L.J., Li, K., Fei-Fei, L.: ImageNet: a large-scale hierarchical image database. In: 2009 IEEE Conference on Computer Vision and Pattern Recognition, pp. 248–255. IEEE (2009)
5. Denil, M., Demiraj, A., de Freitas, N.: Extraction of salient sentences from labelled documents (2014). https://doi.org/10.48550/ARXIV.1412.6815. https://arxiv.org/abs/1412.6815
6. Evans, R., Grefenstette, E.: Learning explanatory rules from noisy data. J. Artif. Intell. Res. **61**, 1–64 (2018)
7. Ferreira, J., de Sousa Ribeiro, M., Gonçalves, R., Leite, J.: Looking inside the black-box: logic-based explanations for neural networks. In: Proceedings of the 19th

International Conference on Principles of Knowledge Representation and Reasoning, pp. 432–442, August 2022. https://doi.org/10.24963/kr.2022/45

8. Gelfond, M., Kahl, Y.: Knowledge Representation, Reasoning, and the Design of Intelligent Agents: The Answer-Set Programming Approach. Cambridge University Press, Cambridge (2014)

9. Kanagaraj, N., Hicks, D., Goyal, A., Mishra Tiwari, S., Singh, G.: Deep learning using computer vision in self driving cars for lane and traffic sign detection. Int. J. Syst. Assur. Eng. Manag. **12**, May 2021. https://doi.org/10.1007/s13198-021-01127-6

10. Kingma, D.P., Ba, J.: Adam: a method for stochastic optimization (2014). https://doi.org/10.48550/ARXIV.1412.6980. https://arxiv.org/abs/1412.6980

11. Kirillov, A., et al.: Segment anything (2023)

12. Ko, B., Kwak, S.: Survey of computer vision-based natural disaster warning systems. Opt. Eng. **51**, 0901 (2012). https://doi.org/10.1117/1.OE.51.7.070901

13. Lage, I., et al.: Human evaluation of models built for interpretability. In: Proceedings of the AAAI Conference on Human Computation and Crowdsourcing, vol. 7, pp. 59–67 (2019)

14. Law, M., Russo, A., Broda, K.: The ILASP system for inductive learning of answer set programs. arXiv:2005.00904 (2020)

15. LeCun, Y., et al.: Backpropagation applied to handwritten zip code recognition. Neural Comput. **1**(4), 541–551 (1989). https://doi.org/10.1162/neco.1989.1.4.541

16. LeCun, Y., Bottou, L., Bengio, Y., Haffner, P.: Gradient-based learning applied to document recognition. Proc. IEEE **86**(11), 2278–2324 (1998)

17. Muggleton, S.: Inductive logic programming. New Gen. Comput. **8**(4), 295–318 (1991)

18. Padalkar, P., Wang, H., Gupta, G.: NeSyFOLD: neurosymbolic framework for interpretable image classification (2023). https://arxiv.org/abs/2301.12667

19. Qi, Z., Khorram, S., Fuxin, L.: Embedding deep networks into visual explanations. Artif. Intell. **292**, 103435 (2021). https://doi.org/10.1016/j.artint.2020.103435

20. Ray, O.: Nonmonotonic abductive inductive learning. J. Appl. Logic **7**(3), 329–340 (2009). https://doi.org/10.1016/j.jal.2008.10.007. https://www.sciencedirect.com/science/article/pii/S1570868308000682. Special Issue: Abduction and Induction in Artificial Intelligence

21. Reiter, R.: A logic for default reasoning. Artif. Intell. **13**(1), 81–132 (1980). https://doi.org/10.1016/0004-3702(80)90014-4. https://www.sciencedirect.com/science/article/pii/0004370280900144. Special Issue on Non-Monotonic Logic

22. Selvaraju, R.R., Cogswell, M., Das, A., Vedantam, R., Parikh, D., Batra, D.: Grad-CAM: Visual explanations from deep networks via gradient-based localization. In: Proceedings of the IEEE International Conference on Computer Vision, pp. 618–626 (2017)

23. Sen, P., de Carvalho, B.W., Riegel, R., Gray, A.: Neuro-symbolic inductive logic programming with logical neural networks. In: Proceedings of the AAAI Conference on Artificial Intelligence, vol. 36, pp. 8212–8219 (2022)

24. Shindo, H., Nishino, M., Yamamoto, A.: Differentiable inductive logic programming for structured examples. In: Proceedings of the AAAI Conference on Artificial Intelligence, vol. 35, pp. 5034–5041 (2021)

25. Simonyan, K., Vedaldi, A., Zisserman, A.: Deep inside convolutional networks: visualising image classification models and saliency maps (2013). https://doi.org/10.48550/ARXIV.1312.6034. https://arxiv.org/abs/1312.6034

26. Stallkamp, J., Schlipsing, M., Salmen, J., Igel, C.: Man vs. computer: benchmarking machine learning algorithms for traffic sign recognition. Neural Netw. **32**, 323–332 (2012). https://doi.org/10.1016/j.neunet.2012.02.016. https://www.sciencedirect. com/science/article/pii/S0893608012000457. Selected Papers from IJCNN 2011
27. Sun, W., Zheng, B., Qian, W.: Computer aided lung cancer diagnosis with deep learning algorithms. In: SPIE Medical Imaging (2016)
28. Townsend, J., Kasioumis, T., Inakoshi, H.: ERIC: extracting relations inferred from convolutions. In: Ishikawa, H., Liu, C.L., Pajdla, T., Shi, J. (eds.) ACCV 2020. LNIP, vol. 12624, pp. 206–222. Springer, Cham (2021). https://doi.org/10. 1007/978-3-030-69535-4_13
29. Townsend, J., Kudla, M., Raszkowska, A., Kasiousmis, T.: On the explainability of convolutional layers for multi-class problems. In: Combining Learning and Reasoning: Programming Languages, Formalisms, and Representations (2022). https:// openreview.net/forum?id=jgVpiERy8Q8
30. Wang, H., Gupta, G.: FOLD-SE: an efficient rule-based machine learning algorithm with scalable explainability (2022). https://doi.org/10.48550/ARXIV.2208.07912
31. Wang, X., Zhang, X., Cao, Y., Wang, W., Shen, C., Huang, T.: SegGPT: towards segmenting everything in context. In: Proceedings of the IEEE/CVF International Conference on Computer Vision, pp. 1130–1140 (2023)
32. Xie, N., Sarker, M.K., Doran, D., Hitzler, P., Raymer, M.: Relating input concepts to convolutional neural network decisions (2017). https://doi.org/10.48550/ ARXIV.1711.08006
33. Yang, Y., Kim, S., Joo, J.: Explaining deep convolutional neural networks via latent visual-semantic filter attention. In: Proceedings of the IEEE/CVF Conference on Computer Vision and Pattern Recognition, pp. 8333–8343 (2022)
34. Yang, Z., Ishay, A., Lee, J.: NeurASP: embracing neural networks into answer set programming. In: Proceedings of the Twenty-Ninth International Joint Conference on Artificial Intelligence, IJCAI 2020 (2021)
35. Zeiler, M.D., Fergus, R.: Visualizing and understanding convolutional networks. In: Fleet, D., Pajdla, T., Schiele, B., Tuytelaars, T. (eds.) ECCV 2014. LNCS, vol. 8689, pp. 818–833. Springer, Cham (2014). https://doi.org/10.1007/978-3-319-10590-1_53
36. Zhang, Q., Cao, R., Shi, F., Wu, Y.N., Zhu, S.C.: Interpreting CNN knowledge via an explanatory graph. In: Proceedings of the AAAI Conference on Artificial Intelligence, vol. 32 (2018)
37. Zhang, Q., Cao, R., Wu, Y.N., Zhu, S.C.: Growing interpretable part graphs on convnets via multi-shot learning. In: Proceedings of the AAAI Conference on Artificial Intelligence, vol. 31 (2017)
38. Zhou, B., Khosla, A., Lapedriza, A., Oliva, A., Torralba, A.: Learning deep features for discriminative localization. In: Proceedings of the IEEE Conference on Computer Vision and Pattern Recognition, pp. 2921–2929 (2016)
39. Zhou, B., Lapedriza, A., Khosla, A., Oliva, A., Torralba, A.: Places: a 10 million image database for scene recognition. IEEE Trans. Pattern Anal. Mach. Intell. **40**(6), 1452–1464 (2017)
40. Zhou, B., Zhao, H., Puig, X., Fidler, S., Barriuso, A., Torralba, A.: Scene parsing through ADE20K dataset. In: 2017 IEEE Conference on Computer Vision and Pattern Recognition (CVPR), pp. 5122–5130 (2017). https://doi.org/10.1109/CVPR. 2017.544

Hardware Implementation of OCaml Using a Synchronous Functional Language

Loïc Sylvestre[1]([✉]) [iD], Jocelyn Sérot[2] [iD], and Emmanuel Chailloux[1] [iD]

[1] Sorbonne Université, CNRS, LIP6, 75005 Paris, France
{loic.sylvestre,emmanuel.chailloux}@lip6.fr
[2] Université Clermont Auvergne, CNRS, Clermont Auvergne INP, Institut Pascal,
63000 Clermont-Ferrand, France
jocelyn.serot@uca.fr

Abstract. We present a hardware implementation of the high-level multi-paradigm language OCaml using a declarative language called Eclat. Eclat is tailored for programming reactive hardware applications mixing interaction with physical devices and long-running computations. It is compiled to synthesizable hardware descriptions for configuring Field Programmable Gate Arrays (FPGAs).

We have implemented the OCaml Virtual Machine as an Eclat function to execute complex computations (programmed in OCaml) in reactive applications (programmed in Eclat). This implementation comprises a bytecode interpreter and a runtime system with automatic memory management. The OCaml programmers can customize this runtime by defining external Eclat functions, *i.e.*, hardware accelerators.

Keywords: synchronous programming · functional programming · language design and implementation · FPGA · virtual machine · OCaml

1 Introduction

When programming hardware applications on FPGAs, a classical issue is to reconcile *reactivity* and *expressiveness*.

Reactivity is the ability of an application to respond "quickly enough" to any stimulus occurring from its environment. By contrast, expressiveness refers to the use of abstraction barriers (e.g., high-level programming features with automatic memory management) to hide many low-level implementation details. In particular, the timing behavior of the applications is often left unspecified.

Ensuring reactivity is a founding principle of the so-called synchronous languages [21] (e.g., Lustre [7], Esterel [4] and Signal [13]), which are based on a logical notion of time known as the *Synchronous hypothesis*. In these languages, program execution is divided into a discrete sequence of computation steps separated by clock ticks. Each computation step is logically instantaneous: it processes current inputs and produces outputs before acquiring new inputs at the next clock tick. This offers a proven methodology for designing reactive embedded applications [9].

M. Gebser and I. Sergey (Eds.): PADL 2024, LNCS 14512, pp. 151–168, 2023.
https://doi.org/10.1007/978-3-031-52038-9_10

Synchronous programs can be translated into synchronous hardware, implemented on FPGAs, by associating the *clock tick* of the synchronous model to the *global clock* of the FPGA circuit [3,22]. However, any computation having a long response time must be reformulated (by the programmer) as a sequence of instantaneous computation steps: this is cumbersome and error-prone.

The goal of this paper is to help declarative programmers write reactive applications on FPGAs. We base our work on a new approach [25] for mixing synchronous interaction (modeled as instantaneous functions) and long-running computations (as non-instantaneous functions, *e.g.*, tail-recursive functions); the whole being compiled to VHDL hardware descriptions.

We add to this language more programming features; and implement, on top of it, an OCAML virtual machine (VM) with automatic memory management. This really allows the programmer to mix synchronous interaction on the one hand and complex computations on the other hand; these computations being expressed in OCAML to be compiled by the OCAML bytecode compiler, stored in on-chip memory and executed by the VM circuit.

The contributions of the paper are:

1. the design and implementation of the ECLAT language, which extends the work described in [25] with: coarse-grained parallelism, global arrays, sized integers, and a full support for FPGA synthesis; ECLAT includes a dedicated construct **exec** that bridges interaction and long-running computation;
2. implementing the OCAML VM as an ECLAT function (*i.e.*, a hardware accelerator) using the **exec** construct; automatic memory management is realized by a garbage collector algorithm programmed in ECLAT; the OCAML stack and heap are implemented in on-chip memory as an ECLAT global array;
3. implementing communication and acceleration, both enabling:
   (a) the programmer to extend the OCAML runtime with ECLAT external functions using the OCAML Foreign Function Interface (FFI);
   (b) reactive applications, written in ECLAT, to call the bytecode interpreter.

The resulting framework paves the way for future developments of reactive applications on FPGA using the well-established language OCAML.

The source code of this work is available online:

https://github.com/lsylvestre/PADL24

The paper gives a general view of all the programming possibilities of the proposed approach: from the traditional hardware description, to the execution of OCAML bytecode by a VM circuitry involving custom hardware accelerators, within a reactive FPGA application.

We first present the ECLAT language (Sect. 2); then we describe our implementation of the OCAML VM in ECLAT (Sect. 3) and evaluate it in terms of efficiency and expressiveness (Sect. 4). We show the interoperability possibilities of this VM implementation (Sect. 5). We discuss related work (Sect. 6) and we finally highlight future research perspectives (Sect. 7).

2   Hardware Design Using ECLAT

ECLAT is a synchronous functional language for programming FPGAs. It can be seen both as a hardware description language (with a fine-grained control on timing and parallelism in the applications) and a general-purpose programming language for designing hardware accelerators.

2.1   Circuits as Functions

ECLAT is based on a call-by-value λ-calculus with let-bindings, booleans, conditional, integers and tuples. It is statically typed with let-polymorphism. ECLAT functions are unary. They can be applied to tuples of values and can have functional parameters.

The execution of ECLAT programs is driven by the global clock of the FPGA target. Each ECLAT program is a sequence of top-level definitions (functions and global data) including a function main. This function main is implicitly mapped to physical devices (sensors or actuators) and called at each clock tick. It is said *instantaneous* because, each time it is called with input values from its environment, it returns output values before the next clock tick.

Combinational circuits can easily be described as ECLAT instantaneous functions. For instance, Fig. 1b defines a classical combinational circuit full_add composing two instances of a sub-circuit half_add (Fig. 1a).

Circuit full_add (Fig. 1b) sums two 1-bit integers given a carry input ci; it returns a result s and a carry output co. The two instances of half_add are duplicated at compile time (by function inlining) to form the resulting hardware description. Function main can be mapped to platform-specific I/Os blocks, *e.g.*, three buttons and two LEDs to visualize the behavior of circuit full_add.

Types signatures are inferred by the ECLAT compiler. For example, function half_add (Fig. 1a) has type (bool * bool) $\Rightarrow$ (bool * bool). Type constructor $\tau \Rightarrow \tau'$ denotes an instantaneous function.

```
val half_add : (bool * bool) ⇒ (bool * bool)
val full_add : (bool * bool * bool) ⇒ (bool * bool)
val main : (bool * bool * bool) ⇒ (bool * bool)
```

```
let full_add(a,b,ci) =
  let (s1,c1) = half_add(a,b) in
  let (s,c2) = half_add(ci,s1) in
  let co = c1 or c2 in
  (s, co)

let main(buttons) = full_add(buttons)
```

```
let half_add(a,b) =
  let s = a xor b in
  let co = a & b in
  (s,co)
```

(a)   (b)

Fig. 1. A combinational circuit in ECLAT

2.2   Sequential Circuits

In order to design sequential circuits, ECLAT is enriched with a programming construct **reg**. This construct enables values to be memorized between successive calls to the function main of a given ECLAT program: (**reg** f **last** e_0) represents a register (*i.e.*, a local state) initialized with the instantaneous expression e_0 and updated with instantaneous function f; (**reg** f **last** e_0) is an expression which returns a value: the value of the associated register after updating it with f.

Each function call behaves like circuit instantiation, duplicating (at compile time) the registers that are defined in the body of the callee function. This means that the registers are *not shared* among instances of a same function; they are local and initialized only once.

Figure 2a defines for example a function sum computing a cumulative sum of the values on its input i. A function main is also defined to illustrate the behavior of function calls. The chronogram on Fig. 2b traces a sequence of executions of function main. Each call to function sum produces an output that depends on the current input value and a local state (the register) manipulated by construct **reg** in the body of each instance of function sum. All these registers are initialized to 0 and updated according to the control flow of function main which is re-executed at each clock tick.

```
let sum(i) =
  let update(s) = s + i in
  reg update last 0

let main(i) =
  let x = sum(i) in
  let y = sum(x) in
  let z = if i > 0 then 42
              else sum(-10)
  in (x,y,z)
```

```
val sum  : int ⇒ int
val main : int ⇒ (int * int * int)
```

clock ticks	t_0	t_1	t_2	t_3	t_4	t_5	t_6	$\cdots$
i	2	1	-3	2	-1	-2	3	$\cdots$
x	2	3	0	2	1	-1	2	$\cdots$
y	2	5	5	7	8	7	9	$\cdots$
z	42	42	-10	42	-20	-30	42	$\cdots$

(a)   (b)

Fig. 2. A stateful function in ECLAT

In the body of function main, the expression sum(i) updates its internal register by adding the value of its argument i; the value of the register is then returned and bound to name x. Then, the expression sum(x) behaves similarly: it returns a value which is bound to name y. Notice that each instance of sum refers to a different register. Conditional in ECLAT activates only one branch a time (the *then* part or the *else* part) according to the condition. Therefore, the expression (**if** i > 0 **then** 42 **else** sum(-10)) executes sum(-10) only when i is less or equal than 0. This is similar to the *when* operator of LUSTRE [7]; however, ECLAT has call-by-value semantics; ECLAT values are not streams.

2.3   Expressing Computations

ECLAT provides the ML construct **let rec** for defining tail-recursive functions. Tail-recursion in ECLAT can be unbounded: a pause of one clock cycle is performed at each tail-call, delaying the result of the computation.

ECLAT offers also coarse-grained parallelism using a generalized form of let-bindings (**let** $x = e_1$ **and** $x_2 = e_2$ **in** e) for running the expressions e_1 and e_2 in parallel with a synchronization point (the keyword "**in**") and a continuation e.

Figure 3a defines for instance a tail-recursive function gcd computing the greatest common divisor of two integer values. The figure defines also a function example illustrating both sequential and parallel compositions in ECLAT; the chronogram on Fig. 3b traces the execution of this function.

```
let rec gcd(a,b) =
  if a < b then gcd(a,b-a)
  else if a > b then gcd(a-b,b)
  else a

let example() =
  let x = gcd(2,2) in
  let y = x + 1 in
  let z = gcd(5,10) in
  let x1 = gcd(18,12) and
      x2 = gcd(5,10) in
  let s = x1 + x2 in (x,y,z,s)
```

```
val gcd : (int * int) → int
val example : unit →
                   (int * int * int * int)
```

clock ticks	t_0	t_1	t_2	t_3	t_4	t_5	t_6
x	ε	2	2	2	2	2	2
y		3	3	3	3	3	3
z		ε	ε	5	5	5	5
x1				ε	ε	ε	6
x2				ε	ε	5	5
s							11

(a)   (b)

Fig. 3. A long-running computation in ECLAT

Symbol ε on Fig. 3b represents the value of an expression that is still running. Each empty cell ▪ represents a computation that has not yet started. First, gcd(2,2) is computed. It responds in one clock cycle because gcd is a recursive function: the direct call takes one clock cycle; the two arguments are equal and thus the body of gcd instantaneously returns the value 2. Once x is bound to value the 2, y is instantaneously bound to the value of x + 1 and the computation gcd(5,10) starts. It takes two clock ticks (one for the direct call plus one for the recursive call). Then, two calls to gcd are performed in parallel[1]: gcd(18,12) takes three clock ticks; gcd(5,10) takes two clock ticks and waits at the synchronization point. Then s is bound to x1 + x2 and a tuple is returned.

ECLAT assigns a type $\tau \to \tau'$ to non-instantaneous functions (such as gcd). The static type system distinguishes instantaneous functions (of type $\tau \Rightarrow \tau'$) and non-instantaneous functions (of type $\tau \to \tau'$) as explained in Sect. 2.5.

---

[1] At the circuit level, there are two parallel instances of gcd.

2.4 Mixing Interaction and Computation

Any expression calling a recursive function (such as gcd on Fig. 3a) is non-instantaneous: it cannot directly be used for real-time interaction since the inputs may be ignored and the outputs delayed while the computation is running.

This motivates the introduction of a new programming construct **exec** for executing a long-running computation step by step: (**exec** e **default** e_0) computes the expression e by performing one computation step per clock tick, with respect to the control flow, and always returns a value: either the result of the computation of the expression e if available or the value of the instantaneous expression e_0 (which provides a default value). This value is paired with a boolean rdy indicating when the computation of e is complete. Every time the computation of e terminates, it restarts at the next clock tick and acquires new inputs.

Figure 4a defines, for instance, a function main (*i.e.*, the entry point of the ECLAT program) calling both function sum (Fig. 2a) and function gcd (Fig. 3a). A chronogram is given Fig. 4b for a sequence of input values. Symbol "-" denotes the input values that are ignored by the program.

val main : (int * int * int) ⇒ (bool * int)

```
let main (i,a,b) =
    let s = sum(i) in
    let (x,rdy) = exec
                    gcd(a,b)
                  default 0
in
    let r = if rdy then x else s in
    (rdy,r)
```

clock ticks	t_0	t_1	t_2	t_3	t_4	t_5	t_6	$\cdots$
i	2	1	-3	2	-1	-2	3	$\cdots$
a	18	-	-	-	2	-	5	$\cdots$
b	12	-	-	-	2	-	10	$\cdots$
s	2	3	0	2	1	-1	2	$\cdots$
x	0	0	0	6	0	15	0	$\cdots$
rdy	⊥	⊥	⊥	⊤	⊥	⊤	⊥	$\cdots$
r	2	3	0	6	1	15	2	$\cdots$

(a)   (b)

Fig. 4. Reactive program mixing interaction and computation

As specified in the type signature, function main is instantaneous: it is called at each clock tick, acquiring inputs and returning outputs in a synchronous way. At each clock tick, the register associated with the instance of function sum is updated with input i and the updated value is bound to name s. The long-running computation gcd(a,b) is guarded by **exec**: it progresses step by step, *i.e.*, one step per clock tick. At time t_3 and t_5, the computation gcd(a,b) returns a value, which is bound to name x, and rdy is set to value ⊤ for one clock cycle. The output r of function main is defined as the value of x if rdy is ⊤, otherwise s.

2.5 A Type System for Ensuring Reactivity

The static type system infers the response time of each ECLAT expression using a one bit abstraction: *instantaneous* (**0**) vs. *non-instantaneous* (**1**). The typing judgement for expression $\Gamma \vdash e : \tau|\delta$ means that, in a typing environment Γ, expression e has type τ and response time δ. Here are for instance two typing rules belonging to this type system:

$$\frac{\Gamma \vdash e_1 : \texttt{bool}|\delta_1 \qquad \Gamma \vdash e_i : \tau|\delta_i \qquad i \in \{2,3\}}{\Gamma \vdash \textbf{if } e_1 \textbf{ then } e_2 \textbf{ else } e_3 : \tau|\delta_1 + \max(\delta_2, \delta_3)} \qquad \frac{\Gamma \vdash e : \tau|\mathbf{0} \qquad \Gamma(f) : \tau \Rightarrow \tau}{\Gamma \vdash \textbf{reg } f \textbf{ last } e : \tau|\mathbf{0}}$$

The left one indicates that the response time of a conditional is the response of the condition plus the maximum response time between the *then* and *else* parts. The right one assigns an instantaneous response time to the **reg** construct but also enforces both the update function f and the initialization expression e to be instantaneous. The typing judgment for programs $\vdash \pi : \tau|\mathbf{0}$ means that program π is well-typed if it has type τ and response time $\mathbf{0}$. In other words, *well-typed programs are reactive!* Other programs are rejected at compile time.

2.6 Compilation to Synthesizable Hardware Descriptions

ECLAT is compiled to synchronous circuits by inlining all non-recursive functions and translating ECLAT immediate values into statically allocated bit vectors. Tuples are also immediate values, implemented as concatenations of bit vectors.

The ECLAT compiler is built as a pipeline of semantic-preserving transformations. Each input program is put in ANF-form (Administrative Normal Form) [15] (to make all the evaluation contexts explicit using let bindings), then specialized (to obtain an equivalent first-order program), and λ-lifted [14] (to make all lexical environments explicit using additional parameters, and globalize all functions). Then, non-recursive functions are inlined, and the program is translated into a Finite State Machine (FSM), each tail-recursive function definition becoming a state in this FSM.

Figure 5 for instance gives the FSM obtained by compiling ECLAT expression (gcd(10,11) * 2). This FSM is depicted as a state-transition diagram. The arrows of the diagram are transitions labelled with guarded actions of the form ck · *condition*/*action*, meaning that *action* is executed at the end of the current clock tick if *condition* is true.

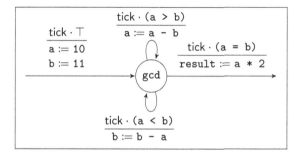

Fig. 5. FSM generated from an ECLAT expression

On Fig. 5, both direct and tail-recursive calls to `gcd` are implemented as transitions (pausing for one clock cycle) with variable assignments for argument passing. The subexpression `gcd(10,11)` is first computed, then the result is instantaneously multiplied by two and assigned to variable `result`, which encodes the return value of the computation.

2.7   Expressing Complex Computations in ECLAT

ECLAT features global mutable arrays, that are implemented using on-chip memory (*i.e.*, RAM blocks available on the FPGA target). This will allow the definition of large heap and stack for the OCAML VM in Sect. 3. Arrays are defined using top-level declarations of the form **let static** $x = c\verb|^|n$, where n denotes the size of the array x to be defined and c is an initial value for all its elements. Each array read $x[v]$ takes two clock ticks (a clock tick for setting the read pointer of the RAM block and another for waiting the result provided by the interface of the RAM block). Each array modification $x[v] \leftarrow v'$ takes one clock tick (for setting both the write pointer of the RAM block and the value to be written). Parallel accesses to a given array x are forbidden and rejected at compile time[2].

We also provide assertions and print primitives for simulation purpose[3]. This is an important aspect for developing large hardware applications.

Finally, ECLAT has sized integers for limiting the area of the generated circuits and implementing specific computations on large integers. ECLAT integers are signed. The type constructor for integers is `int<`θ`>` where θ is a size variable that can be quantified by *let*. A primitive `resize_int<`n`>` is provided for resizing integers; it has the type scheme $\forall \theta \cdot$ `int<`θ`>` $\Rightarrow$ `int<`n`>`. Type `int` is a shortcut for `int<32>`. Typing for arithmetic operations enforced both the arguments and the result to have the same size, the result being implicitly resized. For instance:

$$\textbf{val } (+) \; : \; \forall \theta \cdot \; (\texttt{int<}\theta\texttt{> * int<}\theta\texttt{>}) \; \Rightarrow \; \texttt{int<}\theta\texttt{>}$$

ECLAT does not directly support high-level features, such as general recursion and dynamic data structures with automatic memory management – features that are important in practice to implement algorithms. However, as we will see in the next sections, ECLAT is sufficiently efficient for implementing a high-level language and thus enabling the programmer to express complex algorithms in it.

3   Hardware Implementation of the OCAML VM in ECLAT

This section presents our compilation flow for OCAML on FPGA, which consists of implementing, in ECLAT, both the OCAML virtual machine and a runtime system for OCAML. We present our implementation choices for representing OCAML values and managing dynamic memory with garbage collection.

---

[2] This includes parallel reads due to an implementation limitation.

[3] These constructs are not synthesizable; they are all removed by the ECLAT compiler, using two specific flags, when targeting FPGA synthesis tools.

3.1   The OCAML Virtual Machine

The OCAML VM [17] is a stack machine adapted from the Krivine machine [16] with strict application rather than call-by-name. It enables closure allocation, with an optimized execution model for ML-style unary functions to prevent the allocation of intermediate closures. The VM instruction set comprises 148 instructions manipulating a stack, a heap, a global data segment, and specialized registers such as the stack pointer.

The hardware implementation we propose closely follows the OCAML VM specification. As a limitation, it currently does not support floating point operations and object-oriented features.

3.2   Our Compilation Flow for OCAML on FPGA

Figure 6 schematizes our compilation flow for OCAML on FPGA.

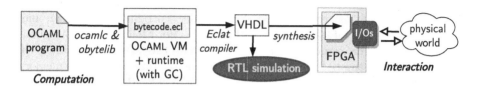

Fig. 6. Implementing OCAML on FPGA using ECLAT

The bytecode produced by the OCAML bytecode compiler `ocamlc`, is first processed using the `obytelib`[4] library to obtain a more compact representation that we encode as an ECLAT file named `bytecode.ecl`. This file contains:

1. an initialization function `init_data` for loading into the VM memory the global data from the OCaml program;
2. a function `external_call` for dispatching external function calls from the OCAML interpreter;
3. a global array `code` encoding each bytecode instruction of the OCAML program as a sequence of integers (*e.g.*, the sequence "19; 2" stands for instruction `POP(2)`, where 19 is the opcode of the bytecode instruction `POP`, which has one parameter: here the integer literal 2).

This generated file is added to the source code of the OCAML VM and runtime (written in ECLAT). The whole application is compiled into a hardware description language (VHDL in our case) by the ECLAT compiler. The resulting hardware description can be used for simulating the bytecode execution at the Register Transfer Level (RTL), *i.e.*, the computational model on which hardware description languages rely. Finally, it can be synthesized using a synthesis tool (in the work described here, we have used the Intel Quartus FPGA tool chain).

---

[4] https://github.com/bvaugon/obytelib.

3.3   A Parametrizable Runtime System

The OCAML compiler adopts a uniform representation of values. Any OCAML value is either an integer (*i.e.*, an immediate value) or a pointer to a memory block. A *mark bit* is used to differentiate integers from pointers. On CPU architectures, addresses are aligned to the size of the word (e.g., 32 or 64 bits). Therefore, their least significant bit is always equal to zero. The standard implementation of the OCAML VM (called `ocamlrun`) uses this bit as the mark bit **0**. Conversely, integers have the mark bit **1**. Therefore OCAML native integers are 31-bit integers (or 63-bit integers depending on the word size) shifted to the left.

Our ECLAT implementation uses a different encoding, defined Fig. 7a. Each OCAML value, represented with type `value` in ECLAT, is a pair formed of one integer (of type `long`) and one mark bit (of type `bool`). The type `long` is an integer having a customizable size.

All the memory needed by the VM is statically allocated in a global array `ram` of customizable size, in which are placed global data, stack and heap (Fig. 7b). Accesses and modifications of this ECLAT array are sequentialized. Each memory block allocated in this array is made of one header (encoding a size, a tag, and, possibly, additional information for garbage collection) followed by contiguous OCAML values. For example, we represent OCAML lists as either the integer 0 (representing the empty list) or a pointer to a block of three contiguous memory cells: one for the header, one for the list head and one for the list tail.

```
type long = int<31> ;;
type value = long * bool ;;

let is_int(_,b) = b ;;
let long_val(n,_) = n ;;
let val_int(n) = (n,true) ;;
```

```
let static ram = (0,true)^16384 ;;

let data_start = 0 ;;
let stack_start = 1000 ;;
let heap_start = 4000 ;;
let heap_size = 6000 ;;
```

(a)   (b)

Fig. 7. Parametrizable word size and memory partitioning for OCAML in ECLAT

We have implemented a Stop&Copy garbage collector (GC) [8] for managing dynamic memory in the array `ram`. This GC requires doubling the size of the heap to organize it in two *semi spaces*: the bytecode interpreter allocates memory blocks in one semi-space. Once the semi-space is full, the program execution is stopped in order to copy, from the current semi-space to the other, all blocks being reachable from the roots of the garbage collector (*i.e.*, the values contained in the stack, the global data segment and the registers); addresses are then updated within the remaining values; and the two semi-spaces are swapped.

4   Experimental Evaluation

In this section, we evaluate the performances of our VM implementation, written in ECLAT, compiled to VHDL and synthesized on an Intel Max10 FPGA. This evaluation is carried out by comparing these performances with that obtained with O2B (*OCaml on Board*) [24], an implementation of the OCAML VM written in C and running on a softcore processor also synthetized on a Max10 FPGA.

The Max10 FPGA has 50K logic cells, 200 Kbytes of on-chip memory, and a clock frequency of 50 MHz. It is embedded on a Terasic DE10-Lite FPGA board. We program it using the Intel Quartus II tool chain (version 22.1). The C code of the OCAML VM in O2B targets the Intel Nios II softcore processor and is compiled with `gcc -Os`.

Both VM implementations are configured to have 32-bit words, a stack of 3,000 words and a Stop&Copy garbage collector (GC) manipulating two semi-spaces of 6,000 words each. They use `obytelib` for preparing the OCAML byte-code generated by the OCAML compiler (version 4.14.1).

The proposed benchmarks[5] involve the following OCAML features: tail-recursive function (Gcd), general recursive function Takeuchi (Tak), intensive composition of higher-order functions (Apply), problem solving (Queens), dynamic creation and worst-case search in a binary search tree (BST), dynamic list creation and filtering preserving sharing for a maximal sublist, using an exception (Share). Programs Tak and Queens make intensive use of the GC.

For each of these programs, we measure the speedups and resource usage (number of used logic cells) for our VM implementation (hereafter, VM_{ECLAT}) versus that obtained with O2B.

4.1   Results

Figure 8 reports speedups for VM_{ECLAT} vs. O2B. The average speedup for the proposed benchmark is 50. This clearly shows the benefits of implementing the OCAML runtime and bytecode interpreter as a custom hardware accelerator instead of running them on a softcore processor.

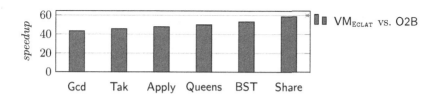

Fig. 8. Speedups achieved by our VM implementation (on the FPGA)

Our OCAML implementation (that does not embed any softcore) uses 44% of the logic cells and 33% of the on-chip memory blocks available on the Max10

---

[5] https://github.com/lsylvestre/PADL24/tree/main/benchs.

FPGA. The softcore-based O2B implementation uses 8% of the logic cells and 66% of the on-chip memory. It is likely that the speedups related above are due, at least in part, to a better usage of the resource in logic cells by the ECLAT VM.

4.2 Comparison with a PC

Being based upon OMicroB (*OCaml on Microcontroller Boards*) [27], which is a generic OCAML VM implementation for programming micro-controllers, O2B can also target a personal computer (PC). We have therefore compared the performances of our VM implementation (VM_{ECLAT}) to that obtained by OMicroB running on PC ($OMicroB_{pc}$), with the same VM configuration (*e.g.*, heap size of 6,000 words). The PC used for this experiment has an Intel Core i7 with a frequency of 2.2 GHz and 16 GB of RAM.

Figure 9 reports speedups for $OMicroB_{pc}$ vs. VM_{ECLAT}. Our VM implementation VM_{ECLAT} is around 38 times slower than $OMicroB_{pc}$. This can be explained by the huge difference in frequency between the low-end FPGA used and the PC: 2.2 GHz/50 MHz = 44. Furthermore, with these settings, OMicroB on PC is approximately 3 times slower than `ocamlrun` (the standard implementation of the OCAML VM), notably because OMicroB is space-optimized to fit on micro-controllers with few resources.

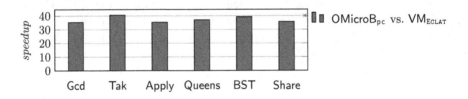

Fig. 9. Comparison between PC and FPGA execution

This section has shown the efficiency of our VM implementation targeting a small FPGA, versus another VM implementation configured in the same way and targeting a softcore processor synthesized on a same FPGA. The benchmarks presented are limited to sequential bytecode execution: in this practical case, the use of a dedicated VM circuitry cannot compensate the frequency gap between a such FPGA and a PC. The next section will show how to achieve better performances by calling external ECLAT functions from OCAML bytecode.

5 Interoperability Between ECLAT and OCAML

For accelerating certain computations or extending the OCAML runtime with new primitives that are not definable in OCAML, we have implemented the OCAML Foreign Function Interface (FFI). This allows OCAML programs, executed by the VM, to call external functions defined in ECLAT. Furthermore, the VM itself is an ECLAT function, that can be embedded in ECLAT applications.

5.1   Calling ECLAT Functions from OCAML Programs

Let's suppose that, in order to improve performances, we want to use the ECLAT version of the gcd function defined Fig. 3 in an OCAML program instead of its direct OCAML version[6]. Function gcd cannot be directly applied to OCAML values since OCAML and ECLAT do not have the same value representation (see the type "value" and primitives long_val/val_long defined Fig. 7a). Therefore, we use an ECLAT wrapper function gcd_glue converting two OCAML values v1 and v2 (and up to five values in nested pairs) and passing them to gcd:

```
let gcd_glue ((v1,(v2,_)),st) =
   (val_long(gcd(long_val(v1),long_val(v2))),st)
```

By convention, such functions to be called from OCAML take also an additional parameter st (the state of the machine) which is also returned. Function gcd_glue can then be called in OCAML programs using the OCAML FFI[7], *e.g.*:

```
external gcd_ext : int -> int -> int = "gcd_glue"

let _ = List.filter (fun x -> x != 1) @@
        List.map2 gcd_ext [18;2;5;1; ··· ] [12;2;10;8; ··· ]
```

This enables significant performance gains by calling, in OCAML, hardware accelerators written in ECLAT.

For instance, function gcd_ext is experimentally <u>65 times faster</u> than an OCAML equivalent function of type (int -> int -> int) compiled to byte-code and executed by our OCAML VM interpreter on the same FPGA.

Moreover, the ECLAT external functions can have parallel implementations (using the ECLAT **let/and/in** construct presented in Sect. 2.3) to increase speedups even further, depending on the degree of available parallelism. For instance, calling 16 times gcd in parallel with the same arguments is <u>1,000 times faster</u> than a pure OCAML execution using our VM implementation.

5.2   Accessing OCAML Data Structures from ECLAT Functions

ECLAT external functions can operate on OCAML data structures using primitives defined in our OCAML runtime library, which also is written in ECLAT.

Figure 10 for instance defines an ECLAT function length computing the length of an OCAML list (*i.e.*, a pointer of the type **value** defined Fig. 7a). It uses two primitives: is_empty (of type value ⇒ bool) to check if a list is empty, and list_tail (of type value → value) accessing to the tail of a list.

Experimentally, this ECLAT function length is <u>17 times faster</u> than an equivalent OCAML version compiled to bytecode and executed by our VM implementation. This speedup is reasonable, since function length performs little computation (only one increment, acc + 1): computation time is dominated by sequential memory accesses, which take equal time in ECLAT and OCAML.

---

[6] Which, incidentally, is perfectly similar to the ECLAT version.

[7] This general mechanism for making OCAML interoperable with its implementation language is very similar to that used in C implementations of OCAML on CPUs, with C external functions.

val length : value → int

```
let length(lst) =
  let rec aux(lst,acc) =
    if is_empty(lst) then acc
    else aux(list_tail(lst),acc + 1)
  in aux(lst,0)
```

Fig. 10. ECLAT function computing the length of an OCAML list

5.3   Embedding OCAML Code in Reactive Applications

Our OCAML VM is written in ECLAT as an instantaneous function `ocaml_vm` (using the **exec** and **reg** constructs). Processing one instruction always takes several clock ticks. For this reason, the function `ocaml_vm` has a special output *busy* corresponding to the *rdy* output of the **exec** construct used internally. It also has an output *stop* indicating when the execution of the OCAML program is complete. Other inputs and outputs can be added to `ocaml_vm` depending on the application to be implemented.

Figure 11 is a simple example of reactive application, written in ECLAT. This application takes two buttons (`button1` and `button2`) as inputs and controls three LEDs as outputs. The entry point (function `main`) is called at each clock tick: it executes the OCAML VM (specialized for a given OCAML program) by calling function `ocaml_vm` with `button2` as an argument.

val ocaml_vm : bool ⇒ (bool * bool * value)
val main : (bool * bool) ⇒ (bool * bool * bool)

```
let main(button1,button2) =
  if button1 then (false,false,false)
  else (let (stop,busy,result) = ocaml_vm (button2) in
        let (red,green) = (busy,stop) in
        let blue = stop && (long_val(result) == 42) in
        (red,green,blue))
```

Fig. 11. A reactive ECLAT application calling the OCAML VM

When `button1` is pressed, the VM execution is suspended, and the three LEDs are switched off. Otherwise, the red LED indicates if the VM is busy; the green LED indicates if the execution of the OCAML bytecode is finished; the blue LED indicates if the OCAML bytecode has produced, in a dedicated register `result`, a value equal to 42.

6   Related Work

Numerous languages for hardware design have been embedded as libraries in programming environments [12]. We can cite CλASH [1] in Haskell; Hardcaml[8] in OCaml; HML in Standard ML [18]; Koika [6] or Π-ware [20] on top of the proof assistants Coq and Agda for building correct hardware. These languages exploit the expressiveness of the host programming environment, *e.g.* Coq, focussing on the effective design of hardware components, whereas our work aims at implementing high-level programming features into hardware accelerators.

Closer to our work is SAFL (*Statically Allocated Functional Language*), which is an ML-like language compiled into hardware [19]. SAFL limits the expressiveness (*e.g.*, avoiding general recursion) to offer good performances.

Shard (*Scheme on Hardware*) [23] is a hardware compiler for a functional subset of Scheme. It features parallel let-bindings and global arrays, like in our approach. It also supports closure allocation: each closure can be called only once and is immediately freed.

FHW (*Functional hardware*) [26] is a compilation flow for the intermediate representation of the Haskell Compiler GHC. It applies semantic-preserving transformations (e.g., elimination of general recursion by introducing explicit stacks [28]) to produce dataflow circuits. The associated runtime comprises a garbage collector for immutable Haskell values [2] allocated in on-chip memory.

O2B (*OCaml on Board*) [24] is an implementation of the OCaml VM on a softcore processor. It allocates the OCaml heap in the memory of the softcore processor, either in on-chip memory or in external (SDRAM) memory. O2B can be used in combination with the hardware compiler Macle (*ML accelerator*) for accelerating certain OCaml functions (by compiling them into VHDL). Like our approach, the accelerated code can operate on OCaml data structures. However, the timing behavior of Macle functions is unspecified (the compiler can choose), and synchronizations are not instantaneous, notably for let-bindings. Macle therefore cannot be used for designing synchronous circuits. Macle provides built-in algorithmic skeletons, such as a parallel *map* for OCaml arrays. In the context of our OCaml VM implementation, these skeletons could be directly expressed by the programmer, in Eclat.

Hardware implementations of the Warren Abstract Machine (WAM) [11] have also been proposed. The Archlog system [10] for instance, similarly to our two-level approach, enables the implementer to generate custom VM architectures using a Prolog-like language, to run realistic Prolog applications on them.

The design of Eclat has been influenced by the programming construct *exec* of Esterel for calling asynchronous tasks from synchronous code. This programming style has lead to the synchronous reactive language HipHop.js [5], which adds synchronous concurrency and preemption to Javascript. A major difference between our work and these approaches is that execution of Eclat long-running computations is deterministic and fair by construction, since Eclat is compiled to synchronous circuits, including its computational part.

---

[8] https://github.com/janestreet/hardcaml.

7   Conclusion

This paper presents ECLAT, a synchronous functional language for programming reactive hardware applications on FPGA. ECLAT unifies interaction and computation in the applications, by expressing both as ML-like functions. These functions are either instantaneous (*e.g.*, a sequential circuit) or non-instantaneous (e.g., a tail-recursion producing a result after several clock cycles). The language features a construct to execute, within an instantaneous function, a computation whose response time is not necessarily known statically: the computation progresses step by step, *i.e.*, makes one step each time the caller is re-executed. The language also has global arrays (implemented in on-chip memory) and parallel let-bindings to exploit coarse-grained parallelism at the circuit level.

The ECLAT synchronous semantics unify the logical clock tick and the global clock of the FPGA; the synthesis tool ensuring that the applications meet the timing constraints of the target. Therefore, the programmer does not need to compute a Worst Case Execution Time (WCET) on the generated code.

To demonstrate the effectiveness of the ECLAT language, we have implemented in it an entire VM and runtime system for the OCAML language. This VM implementation achieves a ×45 speedup vs. another implementation of the OCAML VM, written in C and targeting a softcore processor. It allows the programmer to define ECLAT external functions using the OCAML FFI. This is intended for hardware acceleration purpose, with important speedup possibilities. Moreover, this VM can be embedded in reactive ECLAT applications.

This paper focuses on the practical aspect of our approach (*i.e.*, the programming possibilities) without detailing the technical aspects. Compiling a synchronous language like ECLAT to hardware is challenging: especially for mixing interaction and computation. Furthermore, deep circuitry can be involved in computation-oriented reactive applications, forcing the implementer to consider carefully the space-time trade-off. For this purpose, ECLAT lets the programmer (1) define instantaneous functions (inlined at compile time) to have a better throughput, or (2) annotate certain functions with keyword **rec** (to be shared among all its call sites and introduce a pause), breaking the critical path and reducing the area of the resulting hardware. Certainly, implementing low-level primitives, such as floating-point operations, requires knowledges in hardware design. However, once these primitives are efficiently implemented, they can be called transparently by the declarative programmer using our VM approach, to express complex computations, while interacting with the physical world.

As future work, we plan to support external memory (SDRAM) to allow larger memory footprints. Loading OCAML bytecode from the environment would be useful for dynamically reconfiguring the code of the OCAML VM without having to re-synthesize it on the FPGA. We also plan to use this work for teaching hardware design and the implementation of declarative languages.

References

1. Baaij, C., Kooijman, M., Kuper, J., Boeijink, A., Gerards, M.: CλaSH: structural descriptions of synchronous hardware using haskell. In: 2010 13th Euromicro Conference on Digital System Design: Architectures, Methods and Tools (DSD 2010), pp. 714–721. IEEE (2010). https://doi.org/10.1109/DSD.2010.21
2. Barker, M., Edwards, S.A., Kim, M.A.: Synthesized in-BramGarbage collection for accelerators with immutable memory. In: 2022 32nd International Conference on Field-Programmable Logic and Applications (FPL 2022), pp. 47–53. IEEE (2022). https://doi.org/10.1109/FPL57034.2022.00019
3. Berry, G.: A hardware implementation of pure ESTEREL. Sadhana **17**, 95–130 (1992). https://doi.org/10.1007/BF02811340
4. Berry, G., Gonthier, G.: The ESTEREL synchronous programming language: design, semantics, implementation. Sci. Comput. Program. (SCP) **19**(2), 87–152 (1992). https://doi.org/10.1016/0167-6423(92)90005-V
5. Berry, G., Serrano, M.: HipHop.js: (a)synchronous reactive web programming. In: Proceedings of the 41st ACM SIGPLAN Conference on Programming Language Design and Implementation (PLDI 2020), pp. 533–545 (2020). https://doi.org/10.1145/3385412.3385984
6. Bourgeat, T., Pit-Claudel, C., Chlipala, A., Arvind: The essence of Bluespec: a core language for rule-based hardware design. In: 41st ACM SIGPLAN Conference on Programming Language Design and Implementation (PLDI 2020), pp. 243–257 (2020). https://doi.org/10.1145/3385412.3385965
7. Caspi, P., Pilaud, D., Halbwachs, N., Plaice, J.A.: LUSTRE: a declarative language for programming synchronous systems. In: 14th Annual ACM Symposium on Principles of Programming Languages (POPL 1987), vol. 178, pp. 178–188. ACM (1987). https://doi.org/10.1145/41625.41641
8. Cheney, C.J.: A nonrecursive list compacting algorithm. Commun. ACM **13**(11), 677–678 (1970). https://doi.org/10.1145/362790.362798
9. Colaço, J.L., Pagano, B., Pouzet, M.: SCADE 6: a formal language for embedded critical software development. In: 2017 International Symposium on Theoretical Aspects of Software Engineering (TASE), pp. 1–11. IEEE (2017). https://doi.org/10.1109/TASE.2017.8285623
10. Fidjeland, A., Luk, W.: Archlog: high-level synthesis of reconfigurable multiprocessors for logic programming. In: 2006 International Conference on Field Programmable Logic and Applications, pp. 1–6. IEEE (2006). https://doi.org/10.1109/FPL.2006.311234
11. Fidjeland, A., Luk, W., Muggleton, S.: Scalable acceleration of inductive logic programs. In: 2002 IEEE International Conference on Field-Programmable Technology 2002 (FPT). Proceedings, pp. 252–259. IEEE (2002). https://doi.org/10.1109/FPT.2002.1188689
12. Gammie, P.: Synchronous digital circuits as functional programs. ACM Comput. Surv. (CSUR) **46**(2), 1–27 (2013). https://doi.org/10.1145/2543581.2543588
13. Gautier, T., Le Guernic, P., Besnard, L.: SIGNAL: a declarative language for synchronous programming of real-time systems. In: Kahn, G. (ed.) FPCA 1987. LNCS, vol. 274, pp. 257–277. Springer, Heidelberg (1987). https://doi.org/10.1007/3-540-18317-5_15
14. Johnsson, T.: Lambda lifting: transforming programs to recursive equations. In: Jouannaud, J.-P. (ed.) FPCA 1985. LNCS, vol. 201, pp. 190–203. Springer, Heidelberg (1985). https://doi.org/10.1007/3-540-15975-4_37

15. Kennedy, A.: Compiling with continuations, continued. In: 12th ACM SIGPLAN International Conference on Functional programming (ICFP 2007), pp. 177–190 (2007). https://doi.org/10.1145/1291151.1291179
16. Krivine, J.L.: A call-by-name lambda-calculus machine. High.-Order Symb. Comput. **20**, 199–207 (2007). https://doi.org/10.1007/s10990-007-9018-9
17. Leroy, X.: The ZINC experiment: an economical implementation of the ML language. Technical report, INRIA (1990)
18. Li, Y., Leeser, M.: HML, a novel hardware description language and its translation to VHDL. IEEE Trans. Very Large Scale Integr. (VLSI) Syst. **8**(1), 1–8 (2000). https://doi.org/10.1109/92.820756
19. Mycroft, A., Sharp, R.: A statically allocated parallel functional language. In: Montanari, U., Rolim, J.D.P., Welzl, E. (eds.) ICALP 2000. LNCS, vol. 1853, pp. 37–48. Springer, Heidelberg (2000). https://doi.org/10.1007/3-540-45022-X_5
20. Pizani Flor, J.P., Swierstra, W., Sijsling, Y.: Π-Ware: hardware description and verification in Agda. In: 21st International Conference on Types for Proofs and Programs (TYPES 2015). Schloss Dagstuhl-Leibniz-Zentrum fuer Informatik (2018). https://doi.org/10.4230/LIPIcs.TYPES.2015.9
21. Potop-Butucaru, D., De Simone, R., Talpin, J.P.: The synchronous hypothesis and synchronous languages. In: The Embedded Systems Handbook, pp. 1–21 (2005)
22. Rocheteau, F., Halbwachs, N.: Implementing reactive programs on circuits a hardware implementation of LUSTRE. In: de Bakker, J.W., Huizing, C., de Roever, W.P., Rozenberg, G. (eds.) REX 1991. LNCS, vol. 600, pp. 195–208. Springer, Heidelberg (1992). https://doi.org/10.1007/BFb0031993
23. Saint-Mleux, X., Feeley, M., David, J.P.: SHard: a Scheme to hardware compiler. In: Workshop on Scheme and Functional Programming (2006)
24. Sylvestre, L., Chailloux, E., Sérot, J.: Accelerating OCaml programs on FPGA. Int. J. Parallel Program. (IJPP) **51**(2–3), 186–207 (2023). https://doi.org/10.1007/s10766-022-00748-z
25. Sylvestre, L., Chailloux, E., Sérot, J.: Work-in-Progress: mixing computation and interaction on FPGA. In: 2023 International Conference on Embedded Software (EMSOFT 2023), pp. 5–6. IEEE (2023). https://doi.org/10.1145/3607890.3608454
26. Townsend, R., Kim, M.A., Edwards, S.A.: From functional programs to pipelined dataflow circuits. In: 26th International Conference on Compiler Construction (CC 2017), pp. 76–86 (2017). https://doi.org/10.1145/3033019.3033027
27. Varoumas, S., Pesin, B., Vaugon, B., Chailloux, E.: Programming microcontrollers through high-level abstractions: the OMicroB project. J. Comput. Lang. (COLA) **77**, 101228 (2023). https://doi.org/10.1016/j.cola.2023.101228
28. Zhai, K., Townsend, R., Lairmore, L., Kim, M.A., Edwards, S.A.: Hardware synthesis from a recursive functional language. In: 2015 International Conference on Hardware/Software Codesign and System Synthesis (CODES+ISSS 2015), pp. 83–93. IEEE (2015). https://doi.org/10.1109/CODESISSS.2015.7331371

Ontological Reasoning over Shy and Warded Datalog+/− for Streaming-Based Architectures

Teodoro Baldazzi[1]([✉]), Luigi Bellomarini[2], Marco Favorito[2], and Emanuel Sallinger[3,4]

[1] Università Roma Tre, Rome, Italy
teodoro.baldazzi@uniroma3.it
[2] Banca d'Italia, Rome, Italy
{luigi.bellomarini,marco.favorito}@bancaditalia.it
[3] TU Wien, Vienna, Austria
sallinger@dbai.tuwien.ac.at
[4] University of Oxford, Oxford, UK

Abstract. Recent years witnessed a rising interest towards Datalog-based ontological reasoning systems, both in academia and industry. These systems adopt languages, often shared under the collective name of Datalog$^\pm$, that extend Datalog with the essential feature of existential quantification, while introducing syntactic limitations to sustain reasoning decidability and achieve a good trade-off between expressive power and computational complexity. From an implementation perspective, modern reasoners borrow the vast experience of the database community in developing streaming-based data processing systems, such as volcano-iterator architectures, that sustain a limited memory footprint and good scalability. In this paper, we focus on two extremely promising, expressive, and tractable languages, namely, Shy and Warded Datalog$^\pm$. We leverage their theoretical underpinnings to introduce novel reasoning techniques, technically, "chase variants", that are particularly fit for efficient reasoning in streaming-based architectures. We then implement them in Vadalog, our reference streaming-based engine, to efficiently solve ontological reasoning tasks over real-world settings.

Keywords: Ontological reasoning · Datalog · Chase · Vadalog

1 Introduction

In the last decade there has been a growing interest, both academic and industrial, towards novel solutions to perform complex reasoning tasks in an efficient and scalable fashion. This fostered the development of modern *intelligent systems* enriched with *reasoning capabilities* that employ powerful languages for *knowledge representation* [21,24]. To enable the full potential of ontological reasoning and effectively address relevant tasks of *ontology-based query answering* (QA) and *knowledge graph* navigation, the languages implemented by such reasoners

M. Gebser and I. Sergey (Eds.): PADL 2024, LNCS 14512, pp. 169–185, 2023.
https://doi.org/10.1007/978-3-031-52038-9_11

should provide high expressive power, jointly supporting, for instance, recursion and existential quantification. At the same time, they should fulfil decidability and tractability requirements for QA, so as to fit large-scale applications [9].

Among the languages for *Knowledge Representation and Reasoning* (KRR), the *Datalog*$^\pm$ [15] family became the subject of flourishing research and applications in recent years. Its members (technically, *fragments*) extend Datalog [1] with existential quantification in rule heads, relying on syntactical restrictions such as *guardedness* [13], *weak-acyclicity* [19], and *stickiness* [16], etc., to prevent the QA undecidability caused by a naive integration of existentials [13]. Their semantics can be specified via the *chase* [28] procedure, an algorithmic tool that takes as input a database D and a set Σ of rules, and modifies D by adding new facts until Σ is satisfied. In this paper, we consider two particularly promising fragments, namely, *Shy* [26] and *Warded* [16,21]. They both cover the requirements for KRR, offering a very good trade-off between expressive power, being able to express all SPARQL queries under OWL 2 QL entailment regime and set semantics, and computational complexity, featuring PTIME in data complexity for Boolean conjunctive QA. Reasoning over Shy and Warded is based on powerful chase variants that limit the generation of unavailing facts and ensure termination, namely, the *parsimonious* chase, which does not allow creating new facts for which a homomorphism exists to a fact already in D, and the *isomorphic* chase, preventing the generation of isomorphic facts instead.

Shy and Warded, together with such chase methodologies, are both implemented in state-of-the-art reasoners, namely $DLV^\exists$ [25] and the *Vadalog* [8,10] system. While the data complexity of Shy and Warded is the same, their representative reasoners work quite differently in practice. In fact, $DLV^\exists$, which extends DLV [27] to reason over Shy, employs a *materialization* approach, producing and storing all the facts via *semi-naïve* evaluation [1], in which the rules in Σ are activated over D according to a bottom-up *push-based* strategy. It requires reading the whole D first and then keeping both the original and the newly generated facts in memory throughout the entire reasoning, which is impractical with large and complex datasets [32]. Conversely, to enable scalable QA with a limited memory footprint, recent reasoners like Vadalog leverage the vast experience of the database community and adopt *streaming-based* data processing architectures based, for example, on the *volcano-iterator model* [22]. They operate in a *pull-based query-driven* fashion in which, ideally, facts are materialized only at the end of the evaluation and if they contribute to the QA [8].

The chase is naturally fit for bottom-up evaluations and materialization, yet the need for repeated homomorphism checks to avoid generating duplicates and the consequential requirement to keep in memory an updated version of D, or at least stratum-based intermediate results, highly affects scalability. At the same time, the streaming architectures, inherently memory-bound, are naturally incompatible with these computational tactics. Enabling powerful chase variants such as isomorphic and parsimonious, which tend to be significantly smaller than semi-naïve chase due to the more restrictive homomorphism condition [3], would allow to better exploit the scalability of the streaming architecture for QA.

Contribution. This paper strives to leverage the theoretical underpinnings of Shy and Warded and propose for the first time, to the best of our knowledge, novel reasoning methodologies that are highly suited for streaming-based architectures. Bridging the gap between the theory and practice of these two fragments, we develop an effective *streaming-friendly* chase variant for streaming-based reasoning engines, implementing and evaluating it in the Vadalog system. More in detail, in this paper we provide the following contributions.

- We **systematize the semantic relationship** between Shy and Warded w.r.t. the applicability of parsimonious and isomorphic chase for QA.
- We **develop novel variants of isomorphic and parsimonious chase**, suitable in a streaming-based environment for ontological reasoning.
- We **discuss the integration of the chase procedure in Vadalog streaming architecture**, presenting novel foundations and features of the system.
- We **provide an experimental comparison of Vadalog** with modern materialization-based systems, showing its efficiency over complex QA tasks.

Related Work. Modern reasoners that encapsulate Datalog$^\pm$ expressive power and make use of chase-based methodologies recently emerged in the literature. Relevant examples include, but are not limited to, the already mentioned $DLV^\exists$ [26] with its parsimonious chase, and DLV [27], *Llunatic* [20], and $RDFox$ [31] based on the *Skolem* chase instead [29]. While featuring different reasoning capabilities and performance, they share the common trait of a materialization-based architecture that employs variants of the semi-naïve evaluation. Vadalog is, to our knowledge, the first fully-fledged Datalog$^\pm$ reasoner that effectively synergizes powerful chase methodologies with a streaming-based architecture, with very good results in performance and scalability over real-world tasks.

Overview. In Sect. 2 we discuss chase-based reasoning over Shy and Warded. In Sect. 3 we present the streaming-friendly versions of the chase. In Sect. 4 we illustrate the chase integration in the Vadalog architecture. Section 5 features the experimental evaluation and we draw our conclusions in Sect. 6. An extended technical report is made available online [4].

2   Chase-Based Reasoning over Shy and Warded

To guide our discussion, we provide relevant results on ontological reasoning over Shy and Warded with the chase, also taking into account their recently introduced intersection Protected [3].

2.1   Preliminaries

Let Δ_C, Δ_N, and Δ_V be disjoint countably infinite sets of *constants*, *nulls* and *variables*, respectively. A (*relational*) *schema* P is a finite set of relation symbols (or *predicates*) with associated arity. A *term* is either a constant or a variable. An *atom* over P is an expression of the form $R(\bar{v})$, where $R \in P$ is of arity $n > 0$

and $\bar{v}$ is an n-tuple of terms. A *database* (*instance*) over P associates to each symbol in P a relation of the respective arity over the domain of constants and nulls. The members of the relations are called *tuples* or *facts*. Given a fact $\mathbf{a}$, const($\mathbf{a}$) is the set of constants and nulls($\mathbf{a}$) is the set of nulls in $\mathbf{a}$. Given two conjunctions of atoms ς_1 and ς_2, a *homomorphism* from ς_1 to ς_2 is a mapping $h :$ $\Delta_C \cup \Delta_N \cup \Delta_V \rightarrow \Delta_C \cup \Delta_N \cup \Delta_V$ s.t. $h(t) = t$ if $t \in \Delta_C$, $h(t) \in \Delta_C \cup \Delta_N$ if $t \in \Delta_N$ and for each atom $a(t_1, \ldots, t_n) \in \varsigma_1$, then $h(a(t_1, \ldots, t_n)) = a(h(t_1), \ldots, h(t_n)) \in$ ς_2. An *isomorphism* between ς_1 and ς_2 is a homomorphism h from ς_1 to ς_2 s.t. h^{-1} is a homomorphism from ς_2 to ς_1.

Syntax and Dependencies. A Datalog$^\pm$ program Π consists of a set of tuples and *tuple-generating dependencies* (TGDs), i.e., function-free Horn clauses of the form $\forall \bar{x} \forall \bar{y} (\varphi(\bar{x}, \bar{y}) \rightarrow \exists \bar{z} \, \psi(\bar{x}, \bar{z}))$, where $\varphi(\bar{x}, \bar{y})$ (the *body*) and $\psi(\bar{x}, \bar{z})$ (the *head*) are conjunctions of atoms, $\bar{x}, \bar{y}$ are vectors of universally quantified variables ($\forall$-*variables*) and constants, and $\bar{z}$ is a vector of existentially quantified variables ($\exists$-*variables*). Quantifiers can be omitted and conjunction is denoted by comma. Given a set Σ of Datalog$^\pm$ rules and a position $R[i]$ (i.e., the i-th term of a predicate R with arity k, where $i = 1, \ldots, k$), $R[i]$ is *affected* if (i) R appears in a rule in Σ with an $\exists$-*variable* in i-th term or, (ii) there is a rule in Σ such that a $\forall$-*variable* is only in affected body positions and in $R[i]$ in the head.

Shy, Warded and Protected. Let Σ be a set of Datalog$^\pm$ rules. A position $R[i]$ is *invaded* by an $\exists$-*variable* y if there is a rule $\sigma \in \Sigma$ such that $head(\sigma) = R(t_1, \ldots, t_k)$ and either (i) $t_i = y$ or, (ii) t_i is a $\forall$-variable that occurs in $body(\sigma)$ only in positions invaded by y. Thus, if $R[i]$ is invaded, then it is affected, but not vice versa. Let $x \in \mathbf{X}$ be a variable in a conjunction of atoms $\varsigma_{[\mathbf{X}]}$. Then x is *attacked* in $\varsigma_{[\mathbf{X}]}$ by y if x occurs in $\varsigma_{[\mathbf{X}]}$ only in positions invaded by y. If x is not attacked, it is *protected* in $\varsigma_{[\mathbf{X}]}$. Thus, Σ is *Shy* if, for each rule $\sigma \in \Sigma$: (i) if a variable x occurs in more than one body atom, then x is protected in $body(\sigma)$; and, (ii) if two distinct $\forall$-variables are not protected in $body(\sigma)$ but occur both in $head(\sigma)$ and in two different body atoms, then they are not attacked by the same variable [26]. A $\forall$-variable x is *harmful*, wrt a rule σ in Σ, if x appears only in affected positions in σ, otherwise it is *harmless*. A (join) rule that contains a harmful (join) variable is a *harmful* (*join*) *rule*. If the harmful variable is in $head(\sigma)$, it is *dangerous*. Thus, Σ is *Warded* if, for each rule $\sigma \in \Sigma$: (i) all the dangerous variables appear in a single body atom, called *ward*; and, (ii) the ward only shares harmless variables with other atoms in the body [21]. Without loss of generality (as more complex joins can be broken into steps [8]), an *attacked harmful join* rule $\tau : A(x_1, y_1, h), B(x_2, y_2, h) \rightarrow \exists z \, C(\bar{x}, z)$ is a rule in Σ where $A[3]$ and $B[3]$ are positions invaded by (at least) one common $\exists$-variable, $x_1, x_2 \subseteq \bar{x}$, $y_1, y_2 \subseteq \bar{y}$ are disjoint tuples of harmless variables or constants and h is an attacked harmful variable. If h is otherwise protected, τ is a *protected harmful join* rule. Thus, Σ is *Protected* if, for each rule $\sigma \in \Sigma$: (i) σ does not contain attacked harmful joins; and, (ii) σ is Warded. Protected corresponds to the *intersection* between Shy and Warded [3]. The rewriting of a Warded set Σ of rules with attacked harmful joins into an equivalent Protected set is achieved via the *Attacked Harmful Join Elimination* (AHJE). It replaces each attacked harmful join rule τ with a set of protected rules that cover the generation of all the facts derived from activating τ, thus preserving correctness [5].

Reasoning and Query Answering. An ontological reasoning task consists in answering a *conjunctive query* (CQ) Q over a database D, augmented with a set Σ of rules. More formally, given a database D over P and a set of TGDs Σ, we denote the *models* of D and Σ as the set $\mathbf{B}$ of all databases (and we write $\mathbf{B} \models D \cup \Sigma$) such that $\mathbf{B} \supseteq D$, and $\mathbf{B} \models \Sigma$. A conjunctive query Q is an implication $q(\bar{x}) \leftarrow \psi(\bar{x}, \bar{z})$, where $\psi(\bar{x}, \bar{z})$ is a conjunction of atoms over P, $q(\bar{x})$ is an n-ary predicate $\notin P$, and $\bar{x}, \bar{z}$ are vectors of variables and constants. A *Boolean* CQ (BCQ) $Q \leftarrow \psi(\bar{x}, \bar{z})$ over D under Σ is a type of CQ whose answer is *true* (denoted by $D \models q$) iff there exists a homomorphism $h: \Delta_C \cup \Delta_V \rightarrow \Delta_C \cup \Delta_N$ s.t. $h(\psi(\bar{x}, \bar{z})) \subseteq D$. It is known that the query output tuple problem (i.e., the decision version of CQ evaluation) and BCQ evaluation are AC_0-reducible to each other [14]. Thus, for simplicity of exposition and without loss of generality, we will state our results in terms of BCQ Answering (BCQA).

Semantics and Chase. The semantics of a Datalog$^\pm$ program can be defined in an operational way with the *chase procedure* [23,28]. It enforces the satisfaction of a set Σ of rules over a database D, incrementally expanding D with facts entailed via the application of the rules over D, until all of them are *satisfied*. Such facts possibly contain fresh new symbols ν (*labelled nulls*) to satisfy existential quantification. A TGD $\sigma : \varphi(\bar{x}, \bar{y}) \rightarrow \psi(\bar{x}, \bar{z})$ is satisfied by D if, whenever a homomorphism θ occurs (is *fired*) such that $\theta(\varphi(\bar{x}, \bar{y})) \subseteq D$, there exists an *extension* θ' of θ (i.e., $\theta \subseteq \theta'$) such that $\theta'(\psi(\bar{x}, \bar{z})) \subseteq D$. In the naïve chase (namely, *oblivious* or *ochase*), an applicable homomorphism θ from σ over D occurs if $\theta(\varphi(\bar{x}, \bar{y})) \subseteq D$. When applied, it generates a new fact $\theta'(\psi(\bar{x}, \bar{z}))$ that enriches D, if not already present, where θ' extends θ by mapping the variables of $\bar{z}$ (if not empty) to new nulls named in a lexicographical order [14]. Without loss of generality, we assume nulls introduced at each fire functionally depend on the pair $\langle \sigma, \theta \rangle$ that is involved in the fire. Regardless of the order in which applicable homomorphisms are fired, $ochase(D, \Sigma)$ is unique.

2.2   Boolean QA over Shy and Warded with the Chase

In the joint presence of recursion and existentials, an infinite number of nulls could be generated in *ochase*, inhibiting termination and QA decidability [14].

Example 1. Consider the following Datalog$^\pm$ set Σ of rules

$$Employee(x) \rightarrow \exists s\ WorksFor(x, s) \qquad (\alpha)$$

$$HasBoss(x, y), WorksFor(x, s) \rightarrow WorksFor(y, s) \qquad (\beta)$$

$$WorksFor(x, s), WorksFor(y, s) \rightarrow Knows(x, y) \qquad (\gamma)$$

$$Knows(x, y) \rightarrow \exists s\ WorksFor(x, s), WorksFor(y, s) \qquad (\delta)$$

For each employee x there exists an entity s that x works for (rule α). If x has y as boss, then y also works for s (rule β). If x and y work for the same s, then they know each other (rule γ) and vice-versa (rule δ). Consider the database D = {Employee(Alice), Employee(Bob), HasBoss(Alice, Bob)}.

Due to the existential quantification in rule δ and its interplay with the recursion in rules β and γ, the result of computing $ochase(D, \Sigma)$ contains an infinite set $\bigcup_{i=1,...} \{ WorksFor(Alice, \nu_i), WorksFor(Bob, \nu_i) \}$. To cope with this, Datalog$^\pm$ fragments make use of distinct versions of the $ochase$ based on *firing conditions* to limit the applicability of the homomorphisms and preserve termination and decidability. Among them, we focus on the *parsimonious* (or *pchase*) and the *isomorphic* (or *ichase*) chase. Consider a database I'. In the former, an applicable homomorphism θ of a rule σ is fired if, additionally, there is no homomorphism from $\theta(\text{head}(\sigma))$ to I' (HOMOMORPHISMCHECK) [26]. In the latter, θ is fired if, additionally, there is no isomorphic embedding of $\theta(\text{head}(\sigma))$ to I' (ISOMORPHISMCHECK) [8]. Observe that for any database D, Datalog$^\pm$ set Σ of rules and query q, $pchase(D, \Sigma) \subseteq ichase(D, \Sigma)$, since the homomorphism check is a stricter firing condition than the isomorphism one, and that they are finite ([26, Prop. 3.5] and [7, Theorem 3.14]). We now investigate their applicability over Shy and Warded. Note that QA over them is EXPTIME-complete in combined complexity, and PTIME-complete in data complexity.

Atomic BQA over Shy and Warded. Observe that both *pchase* and *ichase* proved to work only to answer atomic queries, whereas they do not ensure correctness for generic BCQA [8,26]. Now, given a Shy set Σ of rules, a database D, and a BAQ q, we recall that $ochase(D, \Sigma) \models q$ iff $pchase(D, \Sigma) \models q$ [26, Theorem 3.6]. Similarly, since $pchase(D, \Sigma) \subseteq ichase(D, \Sigma)$, we have that $ochase(D, \Sigma) \models q$ iff $ichase(D, \Sigma) \models q$. Both claims also hold for Protected, since it is the intersection of Shy and Warded. On the other hand, neither *pchase* nor *ichase* are complete for Boolean Atomic Query Answering (BAQA) over Warded. We can disprove completeness by counterexample via the Warded Σ in Example 1 and by considering $q = Knows(Alice, Bob)$. Indeed, there exists a rule activation order in which the result of computing $ichase(D, \Sigma)$ is $D \cup \{WorksFor(Alice, \nu_1), WorksFor (Bob, \nu_2), Knows(Alice, Alice), Knows(Bob, Bob\}$. Now, $WorksFor(Bob, \nu_1)$ is not added to $ichase(D, \Sigma)$, as it is isomorphic with $WorksFor(Bob, \nu_2)$. The attacked harmful join rule γ does not generate $Knows(Alice, Bob)$ and $ichase(D, \Sigma) \not\models q$. The same claim holds for *pchase* by definition.

Conjunctive BQA over Shy and Warded. To cover BCQA decidability and preserve the correctness of the evaluation, the chase can be extended with the *resumption* technique [26]. Originally developed for *pchase*, it consists in iteratively "resuming" the procedure in the same state it was after termination (i.e., when the answer to the BCQ is *true* or all the applicable homomorphisms have been examined), performing a promotion of the labelled nulls to constants by the firing condition. More formally, we call *freezing* the act of promoting a null from Δ_N to a novel constant in Δ_C, and given a database instance I, we denote by $\lceil I \rfloor$ the set obtained from I after freezing all of its nulls. We denote $pchase_r(D, \Sigma, i)$ the i-th iteration of resumption for *chase*, where $pchase(D, \Sigma, 0) = D$ and $pchase(D, \Sigma, i) = pchase(\lceil pchase(D, \Sigma, i - 1) \rfloor, \Sigma)$ for $i \geq 1$. Furthermore, we can extend the definition of *ichase*, to perform BCQA, by introducing the *isomorphic chase with resumption* (*ichase_r*), analogous to the *pchase_r*. Formally,

$ichase_r(D, \Sigma, 0) = D$, and $ichase_r(D, \Sigma, i) = ichase(\lceil ichase_r(D, \Sigma, i - 1)\rfloor, \Sigma)$ for $i \geq 1$. Finiteness follows from the definition of *pchase*, *ichase*, and resumption. Indeed, the maximum number of iterations for the resumption that can be performed to answer a certain BCQ q depends on the query itself, and it corresponds to the number of variables in the BCQ $|\mathsf{vars}(q)| + 1$. We interchangeably adopt the notation $chase_r(D, \Sigma, |\mathsf{vars}(q)| + 1)$ and $chase_r(D, \Sigma)$. Now, given a Shy set Σ of rules, a database D, and a BCQ q, we recall that $ochase(D, \Sigma) \models q$ iff $pchase_r(D, \Sigma, |\mathsf{vars}(q)| + 1) \models q$ [26, Theorem 4.11]. Similarly, since $pchase(D, \Sigma) \subseteq ichase(D, \Sigma)$ and by definition of resumption, we have that $ochase(D, \Sigma) \models q$ iff $ichase_r(D, \Sigma) \models q$. Both claims also hold for Protected, since it is the intersection of Shy and Warded. On the other hand, leveraging the above results for BAQA by counterexample via Example 1, we conclude that neither $pchase_r$ or $ichase_r$ are complete for BCQA over Warded.

3   Streaming-Friendly Firing Conditions in the Chase

Leveraging the theoretical underpinnings provided in Sect. 2, we now lay a foundation towards the integration of the chase in streaming-based reasoning environments by proposing novel variants of homomorphism- and isomorphism-based firing conditions (HOMOMORPHISMCHECK$_S$ and ISOMORPHISMCHECK$_S$, resp.) for Shy and Protected Datalog$^\pm$ that avoid fact materialization and strive to achieve low time and memory consumption. Indeed, streaming architectures involve data processing with low memory footprint, without accessing the whole database or fully materializing intermediate results, thus are naturally incompatible with standard *pchase* and *ichase*.

3.1   Aggregate-Based Homomorphism Check

We recall that a fact **a** is homomorphic to a fact **b** if they belong to the same predicate, **b** features the same constants as **a** in the same positions, and there exists a mapping of the labelled nulls in **a** to the constants and nulls in **b**. To present a streaming-friendly homomorphism-based (i.e., parsimonious) firing condition (HOMOMORPHISMCHECK$_S$), we first introduce the notion of *aggregate fact tree* in the chase.

Definition 1. *Given a predicate p and a set I of facts, an* aggregate fact tree *(af-tree) T_p is a tree s.t.: (i) the root T of T_p is labelled by $[\ ]$; (ii) a fact $\mathbf{a} = p(\bar{a}) = p(a_0, \dots, a_k) \in I$ iff there exists a path of k nodes $n_{\bar{a}_0}, \dots, n_{\bar{a}_k}$, where $n_{\bar{a}_i}$ $(0 \leq i \leq k)$ is labelled by $[a_0, \dots, a_i]$, in T_p; and, (iii) two nodes $n_{\bar{a}_j}$ and $n_{\bar{a}_{j+1}} \in T_p$, labelled by $[a_0, \dots, a_j]$ and $[a_0, \dots, a_{j+1}]$ $(0 \leq j < k)$, respectively, iff there exists an edge from $n_{\bar{a}_j}$ to $n_{\bar{a}_{j+1}}$ labelled by a_{j+1}.*

Indeed, the path from the root node T to a leaf $n_{\bar{a}}$ denotes that the fact $p(\bar{a}) \in I$. By construction, facts of a predicate p that share the same arguments up to a position i will share the same root-to-node path up to length i in the aggregate fact tree T_p. Thus, the following statement holds.

Proposition 1. *Let* $\mathbf{a} = p(a_1, \ldots, a_k)$ *be a fact,* I *a set of facts s.t.* $\mathbf{a} \notin I$, *and* T_p *the af-tree for* $\mathsf{pred}(\mathbf{a}) = p$ *in* I. *Then there exists a homomorphism* θ *from* $\mathbf{a}$ *to* $\mathbf{b} \in I$ *iff there exists a root-to-leaf path* t *in* T_p *s.t.* $\theta(\mathbf{a}[i]) = t[i], 1 \le i \le k$.

Algorithm Overview. Leveraging Definition 1 and Proposition 1, we devise a procedure, shown in Algorithm 1, to perform a novel firing condition for the parsimonious chase with low memory footprint. Intuitively, it verifies whether a new fact **a** resulting from an applicable homomorphism in the chase is homomorphic to previously generated ones by performing a form of *path matching* in the corresponding aggregate fact tree. Indeed, if there exists a root-to-leaf path such that a

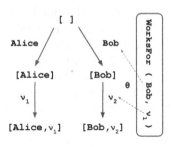

Fig. 1. $\mathrm{T}_{WorksFor}$.

homomorphism occurs from **a**'s arguments to the ones in the path, then the firing condition prevents the applicable homomorphism from being fired and **a** from being generated. More specifically, given $\mathbf{a} = p(a_1, \ldots, a_k)$ and its corresponding aggregate fact tree T_p, the algorithm recursively visits the tree in a depth-first fashion via the function VISITNODE (line 23) and checks whether a homomorphism holds from **a** to the arguments labelling the edges of a root-to-leaf path. It makes use of a *nullMap* structure to keep track of the mappings from the labelled nulls in **a** to constants and nulls in the path.

Algorithm 1. HOMOMORPHISMCHECK$_S$.

```
 1: function VISITNODE(currNode, nullMap, aᵢ)
 2:    if currNode is a leaf node then
 3:        return true
 4:    if aᵢ is a constant then
 5:        if ∄ edge e = (currNode, v) s.t. label(e) = aᵢ then
 6:            return false
 7:        return VISITNODE(v, nullMap, tᵢ₊₁)
 8:    else
 9:        if ∃(aᵢ, b) ∈ nullMap then
10:            if ∄ edge e = (currNode, v) s.t. label(e) = b
    then
11:                return false
12:            return VISITNODE(v, nullMap, aᵢ₊₁)
13:        for edge e = (currNode, v) do
14:            nullMap ← nullMap ∪ (aᵢ, label(e))
15:            if VISITNODE(v, nullMap, aᵢ₊₁) then
16:                return true
17:            nullMap ← nullMap \ {(aᵢ, label(e))}
18:        return false
19:
20: function AGGRHOM_FIRINGCONDITION(a)
21:    T_pred(a) ← getAggregateFactTree(pred(a))
22:    currNode ← T; nullMap ← ∅
23:    if VISITNODE(currNode, nullMap, a[0]) then
24:        return false
25:    T_pred(a).addFact(a)
26:    return true
```

Given the current argument a_i and the reached node *currNode*, if the latter is a leaf of the tree, then the homomorphism has been found (line 3). Otherwise, the homomorphism check over a_i occurs. If a_i is a constant, then the algorithm checks whether such a term also labels one of the outgoing edges of *currNode* (line 5), in which case the target node v is visited. Otherwise, a homomorphism could not be found and the function returns false. If a_i is a null instead, distinct behaviours occur depending on whether *nullMap* features a mapping from a_i to an argument b in a previous edge of the path. If it does, then by definition of mapping function only a node in the tree whose incoming edge is labelled by b can be visited next (line 10). Otherwise, the algorithm carries on the depth-first visit of the tree from *currNode*, attempting to map a_i to the label of each outgoing edge (lines 13–17). Finally, if the homomorphism is not found, $T_{\mathsf{pred(a)}}$ is updated with a new path corresponding to **a**'s arguments and the firing condition returns *true*, thus enabling the generation of **a** in the chase.

The inherent nature of a homomorphism-based approach causes the parsimonious firing condition to be unsuitable for streaming-based architectures. Nevertheless, employing the aggregate tree data structure and performing the homomorphism checks as a path matching task achieves very good time performance, as shown in Sect. 5, while limiting memory consumption in the general case. Figure 1 shows the aggregate fact tree corresponding to predicate *WorksFor* in Example 1. Let us consider a new fact *WorksFor(Bob, ν_1)*. Its generation is prevented by Algorithm 1 due to the existence of path t, corresponding to fact *WorksFor(Bob, ν_2)* in the chase.

3.2 Hash-Based Isomorphism Check

We recall that a fact **a** is isomorphic with a fact **b** if they belong to the same predicate, feature the same constants in the same positions, and there exists a bijection of their labelled nulls. To present a streaming-friendly isomorphism-based firing condition (ISOMORPHISMCHECK$_S$), we first introduce the notion of *null canonicalization*.

Definition 2. *Let Δ_N^c be a set of numbered labelled nulls $\{\varphi_1^c, \varphi_2^c, \ldots, \varphi_n^c\}$ not appearing in Δ_N or in the set I of facts generated in the chase. The* canonicalization *of a fact **a**, denoted* canonical(**a**), *is a new fact $\mathbf{a}^c$ s.t.: (i)* $\mathsf{pred}(\mathbf{a}^c) = \mathsf{pred}(\mathbf{a})$; *(ii) if $\mathbf{a}[i] \in \mathsf{const}(\mathbf{a})$, then $\mathbf{a}^c[i] = \mathbf{a}[i]$; and, (iii) if $\mathbf{a}[i] \in \mathsf{nulls}(\mathbf{a})$, then $\mathbf{a}^c[i] = \varphi_j^c$, where $j = \arg\min_k \mathbf{a}[k] = \mathbf{a}[i]$. A fact **a** is* canonical *if $\mathsf{nulls}(\mathbf{a}) \subseteq \Delta_N^c$.*

Intuitively, given a fact **a**, its canonicalization $\mathbf{a}^c = \mathsf{canonical}(\mathbf{a})$ differs from it only if **a** includes labelled nulls, which are replaced by numbered fresh nulls φ_j^c, where j is the index of the first position in $\mathbf{a}^c$ featuring $\mathbf{a}[i]$. For instance, given a fact $\mathbf{a} = p(\varphi_x, \varphi_y, \varphi_x, const_1)$, $\mathsf{canonical}(\mathbf{a})$ corresponds to the fact $\mathbf{a}^c = p(\varphi_1^c, \varphi_2^c, \varphi_1^c, const_1)$. Thus, the following results hold.

Lemma 1. *Let **a** be a fact and $\mathbf{a}^c$ its* canonical(**a**). *Then there exists an isomorphism between **a** and $\mathbf{a}^c$.*

Proposition 2. *Let **a**, **b** be two facts and $\mathbf{a}^c$, $\mathbf{b}^c$ their canonical form, respectively. Then **a** is isomorphic to **b** iff $\mathbf{a}^c = \mathbf{b}^c$.*

Algorithm Overview. Definition 2 and Proposition 2 provide a powerful foundation to reduce the isomorphism-based firing condition to an equivalence check between hashes of facts by means of canonicalization. A simple and yet effective *hash-based* firing condition ISOMORPHISMCHECK$_S$ is provided in Algorithm 2.

Algorithm 2. ISOMORPHISMCHECK$_S$.

```
1: function HASHISO_FIRINGCONDITION(a)
2:    aᶜ ← canonical(a)
3:    hashSet ← getGeneratedFactsHashSet()
4:    hashₐᶜ ← createStrongHash(aᶜ)
5:    if hashSet.contains(hashₐᶜ) then return false
6:    hashSet.add(hashₐᶜ)
7:    return true
```

The procedure employs a *hashSet*, i.e., a set data structure storing hash values, to check for membership. Note that there might be false positives, i.e. facts that should have been generated, but they are not generated because the check mistakenly detects them as isomorphic to already generated ones. However, using a *hash function with strong collision resistance* should make this event improbable, as witnessed in practice. Whenever an applicable homomorphism for a fact **a** is considered, it first computes canonical(**a**) = $\mathbf{a}^c$, and then checks whether the *hashSet* contains such a newly generated fact (line 5). If that is the case, then $\mathbf{a}^c$ has already been added in a previous iteration by another fired homomorphism over a fact **b**, s.t. canonical(**a**) = $\mathbf{a}^c$ = canonical(**b**). By Proposition 2, this entails that **a** and **b** are isomorphic, thus the isomorphism check returns *false* (as the firing condition is not satisfied). Instead, if $\mathbf{a}^c$ is not contained in *hashSet*, then it updates *hashSet* with the new hash and returns *true*.

Note that the amortized running time complexity of the hash-based isomorphism check is $\mathcal{O}(1)$ if the set is implemented using hash tables [17], which makes such a firing condition particularly suitable for big data and streaming settings. If the occurrence of collisions (i.e. two facts with the same hash value) could not be completely avoided, a collision resolution must be performed. Nevertheless, if a strong hash function is employed, this occurs very rarely in practice. With reference to Example 1, the canonicalization of *WorksFor*(*Bob*, ν_1) is *WorksFor*(*Bob*, ϕ_1), which is the same as *WorksFor*(*Bob*, ν_2) already in the chase, and the generation of the former is prevented by Algorithm 2.

4   The Chase in Streaming-Based Architectures

We now discuss the integration of the chase in streaming-based architectures. We recall that in such systems facts can only be materialized at the end of the reasoning evaluation and, ideally, only the chase steps that are required to answer the query will be activated, without generating the full output of the procedure. While we consider Vadalog as reference, the approach is generic for reasoners based on similar architectural principles.

Vadalog Streaming Architecture. First, we briefly illustrate how Vadalog streaming architecture operates. The logic core of the system adheres to the *pipes and filters* [12] data processing pattern and consists in an active pipeline that reads data from the input sources, performs the needed transformations, and produces the desired output as a result [10]. Given a database D, a set Σ of Datalog$^\pm$ rules, and a query q, the system compiles a processing pipeline by adding a *data scan* (a *filter*) for each rule in Σ and an edge (a *pipe*) connecting a scan β to a scan α if the head of rule β unifies with a body atom of rule α. The reasoning is then performed in a pull-based query-driven fashion that generalizes the *volcano iterator model* [22], where each scan (hence, each rule) reads facts from the respective parents, from the output scan corresponding to q down to the data sources that inject ground facts from D into the pipeline. Interactions between scans occur via primitives such as next(), which asks the parent scans whether there exists a fact to read, and employ specific *routing strategies* to determine which interaction occurs first [8].

Streaming Chase with Resumption. With the goal of enabling generic BCQA in a streaming-based architecture, we recall from Sect. 2 that resumption is required. In fact, an alternative approach would consist in splitting the conjunctive query into an atomic one and a rule, which is then included in the input set Σ of rules. However, it is often unfeasible in practice, as will be demonstrated in Sect. 5, due to the restrictions that would be required to limit the new rule to the syntax of Σ's fragment. For instance, if the query were to feature an attacked harmful join, the AHJE rewriting would be required, which however causes the generation of a number of Protected rules that is in the worst case exponential to the number of attacked harmful joins.

Algorithm 3. The $chase_s$ for streaming BCQA.

```
1: function CHASEₛ(D, Σ, q)
2:     maxRes ← |vars(q)| + 1
3:     p ← compile-pipeline(D, Σ, q)
4:     while next(p) do
5:         ⟨s, f⟩ ← get(p)
6:         if isApplicableHomomorphism(⟨s, f⟩) then
7:             θ ← applicableHomomorphism(⟨s, f⟩)
8:             a ← fire(s, θ)
9:             if FIRINGCONDITION(a) then
10:                 s.addFact(a)
11:                 if answer(q) then return true
12:                 if not frozen(a) and a.resIt < maxRes then
13:                     a ← freeze(a)
14:                     a.resIt ← a.resIt + 1
15:                     go to Line 9
16:     return false
```

Standard resumption consists in performing full iterations of the chase and materializing the intermediate results, both prohibitive operations in a streaming environment. Thus, we enable the Vadalog system to perform generic BCQA by developing a novel resumption-based chase procedure ($chase_s$) for streaming environments, provided in Algorithm 3. Leveraging the pull-based processing pipeline approach, resumption is here treated as a *fact-level property*, that is, each generated fact in the chase belongs to a specific iteration of resumption corresponding to the maximum between the iterations of its parent facts. Thus, it can experience *labelled null freezing*, up to the maximum number of resumptions $|vars(q)| + 1$ allowed by the query q, without performing a global chase iteration. Note that this approach is only applicable if Σ does not feature attacked harmful joins, that is, in the context of Vadalog it belongs to Protected Datalog$^\pm$. More specifically, given a database D, a set Σ of Protected rules and a BCQ q which enables $maxRes$ iterations of resumption, first the procedure compiles the corresponding processing pipeline p as discussed above, and stores it in a map of scans and parent scans (line 3). Then, at each iteration, it propagates via next the request to read facts from the query scan to its parents, down to the scans that read ground data from D, following a fixed routing strategy. If the primitive returns *true*, then it entails that there exists a scan s in p such that it can read a fact f from its parents. Thus, f is read via **get** primitive and the algorithm checks whether an

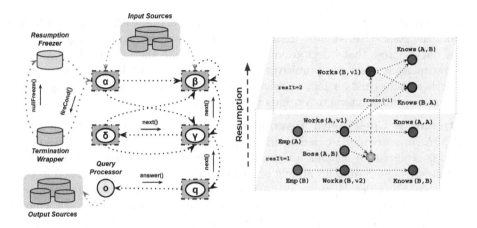

Fig. 2. Vadalog processing pipeline and streaming chase for Example 1.

applicable homomorphism θ may occur from the rule corresponding to s to f (lines 5–7). If that is the case, **a** is the fact derived from firing θ over s. To determine whether **a** is generated in the chase, the procedure will make use of ad-hoc firing conditions (such as the streaming-friendly HOMOMORPHISMCHECK$_S$ and ISOMORPHISMCHECK$_S$ discussed in Sect. 3). If the firing condition is satisfied, **a** is added to the set of facts that can be read from s. Moreover, it checks whether the facts in q are now able to provide a positive answer for the corresponding query, in which case the procedure terminates (line 11). If the firing condition prevents the generation of **a** instead, then the fact-level resumption occurs. Let *resIt* be **a**'s initial resumption iterations, derived from its parent facts. If there exists at least a null in **a** that has not already been subjected to freezing and *resIt* < *maxRes*, then **a** is frozen, the frozen nulls are tagged as constants, and *resIt* is increased (lines 12–14). Finally, the firing condition check is performed again for the frozen **a**. If the facts from all the scans in p have been read but a positive answer for q was not achieved, then the procedure returns *false*.

From an architectural perspective, this novel streaming-based chase with resumption is encapsulated in a *termination wrapper* connected to each scan s. It is responsible for enforcing the firing condition for each fact **a** resulting from an applicable homomorphism on s, as well as for performing null freezing via a *resumption freezer* component. Additionally, a *query processor* is connected to the query scan and checks after each chase step whether q has a positive answer.

Streaming Chase over Example 1. To support the explanation of Algorithm 3, we illustrate its application over Example 1, guided by a visual representation of Vadalog processing pipeline and the streaming chase resulting from a specific rule activation order in Fig. 2. Note that, for space reasons, we do not explicitly address the rewriting of the attacked harmful join in rule γ via AHJE to make Σ Protected and enable the *chase$_s$* procedure. Let us consider the BCQ $q : Q \leftarrow Knows(Alice, x), Knows(Bob, x)$, which asks whether there exists an x

who knows both *Alice* and *Bob* and enables up to 2 iterations of resumption. First, the processing pipeline is compiled, featuring a scan for q and each rule in Σ, connected by the logical dependencies between them. Then, the actual chase procedure begins with next calls from the scan q to its parents, down to scan α, which reads the facts *Employee(Alice)* and *Employee(Bob)* from the input sources and fires applicable homomorphisms to generate *WorksFor(Alice, ν_1)* and *WorksFor(Bob, ν_2)*, respectively. The new facts are in turn read by scan β, together with *HasBoss(Alice, Bob)* from the data sources. The same scan attempts the generation of *WorksFor(Bob, ν_1)*, which is however prevented by the termination wrapper as it is isomorphic with *WorksFor(Bob, ν_2)*. Thus, the freezing of *WorksFor(Bob, ν_1)* is performed by the dedicated component and ν_1 is tagged as a constant. Then, scan γ reads the above facts and it generates *Knows(Alice, Alice)*, *Knows(Bob, Bob)*, *Knows(Alice, Bob)*, and *Knows(Bob, Alice)*. Finally, q reads the resulting facts and it returns a positive answer to the query processor, thus terminating the procedure.

Correctness and Firing Conditions. As firing conditions for Algorithm 3 we employ the HOMOMORPHISMCHECK$_S$ and ISOMORPHISMCHECK$_S$ presented in Sect. 3. Furthermore, this novel approach allowed us to integrate Shy into the Vadalog engine, thus supporting for the first time, to the best of our knowledge, both these powerful and expressive fragments in a streaming-based reasoning system. We will delve into it in a future work. We now argue the correctness of Algorithm 3.

Theorem 1. *For any database D, a Shy set Σ of rules, a BCQ $q = \psi(\bar{z})$, we have that $pchase_r(D, \Sigma) \models q$ iff $chase_s(D, \Sigma) \models q$ with firing condition* HOMOMORPHISMCHECK$_S$.

Theorem 2. *For any database D, a Shy set Σ of rules, a BCQ $q = \psi(\bar{z})$, we have that $ichase_r(D, \Sigma) \models q$ iff $chase_s(D, \Sigma) \models q$ with firing condition* ISOMORPHISMCHECK$_S$.

5   Experimental Evaluation

We experimentally compared the chase variants presented above over well-known scenarios with existential quantification in the context of benchmarking $Datalog^{\pm}$ reasoners. The experiments were run on a cloud-based virtual machine equipped with a CPU Intel Xeon Platinum 8171M @ 2.60 GHz (4 cores) and with 16 GB of RAM. The results of the experiments, as well as the steps to reproduce them, were made available as supplementary material [2], whereas the Vadalog system will be made available upon request. Note that VADALOG-I is the Vadalog configuration based on ISOMORPHISMCHECK$_S$, VADALOG-P is the one based on HOMOMORPHISMCHECK$_S$, VADALOG-IR and VADALOG-PR are the ones in streaming resumption mode for generic conjunctive query answering based on ISOMORPHISMCHECK$_S$ and HOMOMORPHISMCHECK$_S$, respectively. Thus, in the presence of a CQ, both VADALOG-I and VADALOG-P require splitting it into an atomic one and a rule, which is then integrated in the set Σ, possibly performing rewriting steps such as AHJE to restrict its syntax to the one of Σ.

(a) Strong Link. The scenario is a variant of a financial recursive use case about relationships between companies [10, Example 3] over real data extracted from DBPedia [18]. It consists in finding strong links between "significantly controlled companies", that is, companies for which there exist common significant shareholders (persons who hold more than 20% of the stocks). Together with Fig. 3(b), the goal of this experiment is to compare the performance of the four Vadalog configurations. In this scenario, the query contains a simple attacked harmful join between two variables, which was included as a rule in the program via AHJE in the VADALOG-I and VADALOG-P configurations. We used source instances of $1K$, $10K$, $25K$, $50K$ and $67K$ companies and we ran the experiment for 10 iterations, averaging the elapsed times. As shown in Fig. 3(a), the configurations achieve comparable performances. The overhead introduced by the aggregate-fact tree in VADALOG-P and VADALOG-PR does not significantly influence this setting, being balanced out by the higher number of intermediate facts generated in VADALOG-I and VADALOG-IR, and neither does the AHJE in VADALOG-I and VADALOG-P, due to the simplicity of the attacked harmful join.

(b) Has-Parent. The scenario is the simple set of rules: $r_1 : Person(x) \rightarrow \exists y \, HasParent(x, y)$ and $r_2 : HasParent(x, y) \rightarrow person(y)$. It consists in running the following query $q : Q_n(x) \leftarrow person(x_0), hasParent(x_0, x_1), hasParent(x_1, x_2), \ldots, hasParent(x_{n-2}, x_{n-1})$, where n is the scaling parameters, over a database with a single fact: $D = \{person(Alice)\}$. Note that, similarly to Fig. 3(a), the query is conjunctive and it features an attacked harmful join, therefore both VADALOG-I and VADALOG-P require to perform the AHJE rewriting. However, as shown in Fig. 3(b), VADALOG-I and VADALOG-P do not scale, timing out from $n = 4$ onwards due to the AHJE step, which could not handle the increasing number of attacked harmful join to rewrite [5,6]. On the other hand, both VADALOG-IR and VADALOG-PR achieve very low running times, almost constant for all values of the scaling parameter. This experiment highlights the importance of integrating the resumption in Vadalog to keep the query unaffected by the limits of the fragment, as well as the general effectiveness of the implemented resumption approaches when the query rewriting becomes unfeasible.

(c) Doctors. The scenario is a data integration task from the schema mapping literature [30]. While non-recursive, it is rather important as a plausible real-world case. In this experiment, we compare the performance of VADALOG-I, VADALOG-P and the materialization-based $DLV^{\exists}$ [25]. Note that the resumption-based configurations are not included since the maximum number of resumption iterations for the queries is 1. We used source instances of $10K$, $100K$, $500K$, $1M$ facts and we ran 9 queries for 10 iterations, averaging the elapsed times. As shown in Fig. 3(c), $DLV^{\exists}$ performs slightly better than the two configurations of Vadalog over smaller instances. On the other hand, the gap considerably shrinks with the increase in the dataset size. This

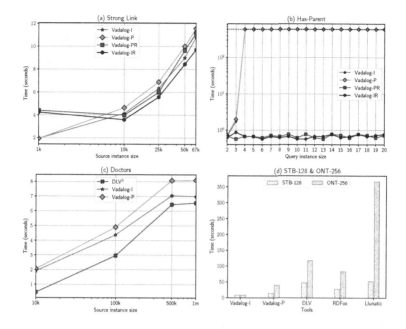

Fig. 3. Reasoning times for the experimental evaluation.

can be explained by the time spent by Vadalog to perform program optimizations before the actual execution of the reasoning. Regarding VADALOG-I and VADALOG-P, we observe that once again there is no heavy performance degradation due to the adoption of HOMOMORPHISMCHECK$_S$.

(d) STB-128 & ONT-256. The scenarios are featured in the *ChaseBench* [11] benchmarks. Specifically, *STB-128* is a set of about 250 Warded rules, 25% of which contain existentials. The expected target instance contains 800K facts, with 20 of labelled nulls. We ran 16 different queries for 10 iterations, averaging the elapsed times. Queries are rather complex, as they involve on average 5 joins, and 8 of them are attacked harmful. On the other hand, *ONT-256* is a set of 789 Warded rules, 35% of which contain existentials. Rules are even more complex than STB-128, and contain multiple joins as well as pervasive recursion. The expected target instance contains 2 million facts, with an incidence of 50% of labelled nulls. We ran 10 different queries, averaging the elapsed times. Queries involve an average of 5 joins, and 5 of them are attacked harmful. In this experiment, we compare the performance of VADALOG-I, VADALOG-P, DLV [27], RDFox [31], and LLUNATIC [20]. Note that VADALOG-IR and VADALOG-PR were not tested as the queries did not require resumption, and that AHJE is performed, on the queries with attacked harmful joins, without significantly affecting the performance. As shown in Fig. 3(d), Vadalog, both in VADALOG-I and VADALOG-P, outperforms all the other systems in both scenarios: VADALOG-I and VADALOG-P ran in 8.88 and

14.34 s for *STB-128* and in 8.86 and 40.24 s for *ONT-256*. Indeed, VADALOG-I is on average 3 times faster than RDFOX, and 7 times faster than LLUNATIC.

6   Conclusion

To perform QA tasks over large and complex datasets, modern $Datalog^{\pm}$ reasoners such as Vadalog shift from a materialization approach to a streaming-based one, which enables scalable query-driven evaluations. In this paper, we focus on the expressive Shy and Warded fragments of $Datalog^{\pm}$. Leveraging their theoretical underpinnings, we develop variants of the chase procedure that are highly suited for streaming-based architectures, and we integrate them in Vadalog to efficiently answer generic conjunctive queries in complex settings.

Acknowledgments. This work was partially supported by the Vienna Science and Technology Fund (WWTF) [10.47379/ICT2201, 10.47379/VRG18013, 10.47379/NXT22018]; and the Christian Doppler Research Association (CDG) JRC LIVE.

Disclosure of Interests. The authors have no competing interests to declare that are relevant to the content of this article.

References

1. Abiteboul, S., Hull, R., Vianu, V.: Foundations of Databases (1995)
2. Baldazzi, T., Bellomarini, L., Favorito, M., Sallinger, E.: Supplementary material. https://bit.ly/47DHCTS. Accessed 20 Nov 2023
3. Baldazzi, T., Bellomarini, L., Favorito, M., Sallinger, E.: On the relationship between shy and warded datalog+/−. In: KR (2022)
4. Baldazzi, T., Bellomarini, L., Favorito, M., Sallinger, E.: Ontological reasoning over shy and warded datalog+/− for streaming-based architectures (Technical report) (2023)
5. Baldazzi, T., Bellomarini, L., Sallinger, E., Atzeni, P.: Eliminating harmful joins in warded datalog+/−. In: Moschoyiannis, S., Peñaloza, R., Vanthienen, J., Soylu, A., Roman, D. (eds.) RuleML+RR 2021. LNCS, vol. 12851, pp. 267–275. Springer, Cham (2021). https://doi.org/10.1007/978-3-030-91167-6_18
6. Baldazzi, T., Bellomarini, L., Sallinger, E., Atzeni, P.: Reasoning in warded datalog+/− with harmful joins. In: SEBD. CEUR Workshop Proceedings, vol. 3194, pp. 292–299. CEUR-WS.org (2022)
7. Bellomarini, L., Benedetto, D., Brandetti, M., Sallinger, E.: Exploiting the power of equality-generating dependencies in ontological reasoning. Proc. VLDB Endow. **15**(13), 3976–3988 (2022)
8. Bellomarini, L., Benedetto, D., Gottlob, G., Sallinger, E.: Vadalog: a modern architecture for automated reasoning with large knowledge graphs. IS **105**, 101528 (2022)
9. Bellomarini, L., Gottlob, G., Pieris, A., Sallinger, E.: Swift logic for big data and knowledge graphs. In: IJCAI, pp. 2–10 (2017). https://www.ijcai.org/

10. Bellomarini, L., Sallinger, E., Gottlob, G.: The vadalog system: datalog-based reasoning for knowledge graphs. Proc. VLDB Endow. **11**(9), 975–987 (2018)
11. Benedikt, M., et al.: Benchmarking the chase. In: PODS, pp. 37–52. ACM (2017)
12. Buschmann, F., Henney, K., Schmidt, D.C.: Pattern-oriented software architecture, a pattern language for distributed computing, vol. 4 (2007)
13. Calì, A., Gottlob, G., Kifer, M.: Taming the infinite chase: query answering under expressive relational constraints. J. Artif. Intell. Res. **48**, 115–174 (2013)
14. Calì, A., Gottlob, G., Lukasiewicz, T.: A general datalog-based framework for tractable query answering over ontologies. J. Web Semant. **14**, 57–83 (2012)
15. Calì, A., Gottlob, G., Lukasiewicz, T., Marnette, B., Pieris, A.: Datalog+/−: a family of logical knowledge representation and query languages for new applications. In: LICS, pp. 228–242. IEEE Computer Society (2010)
16. Calì, A., Gottlob, G., Pieris, A.: Advanced processing for ontological queries. Proc. VLDB Endow. **3**(1), 554–565 (2010)
17. Cormen, T.H., Leiserson, C.E., Rivest, R.L., Stein, C.: Introduction to Algorithms, 3rd edn. MIT Press, Cambridge (2009)
18. DBpedia: Web site (2018). https://www.dbpedia.org. Accessed 20 Nov 2023
19. Fagin, R., Kolaitis, P.G., Miller, R.J., Popa, L.: Data exchange: semantics and query answering. Theor. Comput. Sci. **336**(1), 89–124 (2005)
20. Geerts, F., Mecca, G., Papotti, P., Santoro, D.: That's all folks! LLUNATIC goes open source. Proc. VLDB Endow. **7**(13), 1565–1568 (2014)
21. Gottlob, G., Pieris, A.: Beyond SPARQL under OWL 2 QL entailment regime: rules to the rescue. In: IJCAI, pp. 2999–3007. AAAI Press (2015)
22. Graefe, G., McKenna, W.J.: The volcano optimizer generator: extensibility and efficient search. In: ICDE, pp. 209–218. IEEE Computer Society (1993)
23. Johnson, D.S., Klug, A.C.: Testing containment of conjunctive queries under functional and inclusion dependencies. J. Comput. Syst. Sci. **28**(1), 167–189 (1984)
24. Krötzsch, M., Thost, V.: Ontologies for knowledge graphs: breaking the rules. In: Groth, P., et al. (eds.) ISWC 2016. LNCS, vol. 9981, pp. 376–392. Springer, Cham (2016). https://doi.org/10.1007/978-3-319-46523-4_23
25. Leone, N., Manna, M., Terracina, G., Veltri, P.: DLV^E system (2017). https://www.mat.unical.it/dlve/. Accessed 20 Nov 2023
26. Leone, N., Manna, M., Terracina, G., Veltri, P.: Fast query answering over existential rules. ACM TOCL **20**(2), 12:1–12:48 (2019)
27. Leone, N., Pfeifer, G., Faber, W., Eiter, T., Gottlob, G., et al.: The DLV system for knowledge representation and reasoning. ACM TOCL **7**(3), 499–562 (2006)
28. Maier, D., Mendelzon, A.O., Sagiv, Y.: Testing implications of data dependencies. ACM TODS **4**(4), 455–469 (1979). https://doi.org/10.1145/320107.320115
29. Mecca, G., Papotti, P., Raunich, S.: Core schema mappings: scalable core computations in data exchange. Inf. Syst. **37**(7), 677–711 (2012)
30. Mecca, G., Papotti, P., Santoro, D.: IQ-METER - an evaluation tool for data-transformation systems. In: ICDE, pp. 1218–1221. IEEE Computer Society (2014)
31. Nenov, Y., Piro, R., Motik, B., Horrocks, I., Wu, Z., Banerjee, J.: RDFox: a highly-scalable RDF store. In: Arenas, M., et al. (eds.) ISWC 2015. LNCS, vol. 9367, pp. 3–20. Springer, Cham (2015). https://doi.org/10.1007/978-3-319-25010-6_1
32. Pitoura, E.: Pipelining. In: Liu, L., Özsu, M.T. (eds.) Encyclopedia of Database Systems, pp. 2768–2768. Springer, New York (2018). https://doi.org/10.1007/978-1-4614-8265-9_872

Explanation and Knowledge Acquisition in Ad Hoc Teamwork

Hasra Dodampegama[✉][iD] and Mohan Sridharan[iD]

Intelligent Robotics Lab, School of Computer Science, University of Birmingham,
Birmingham, UK
hhd968@student.bham.ac.uk, m.sridharan@bham.ac.uk

Abstract. State of the art frameworks for ad hoc teamwork i.e., for enabling an agent to collaborate with others "on the fly", pursue a data-driven approach, using a large labeled dataset of prior observations to model the behavior of other agents and to determine the ad hoc agent's behavior. It is often difficult to pursue such an approach in complex domains due to the lack of sufficient training examples and computational resources. In addition, the learned models lack transparency and it is difficult to revise the existing knowledge in response to previously unseen changes. Our prior architecture enabled an ad hoc agent to perform non-monotonic logical reasoning with commonsense domain knowledge and predictive models of other agents' behavior that are learned from limited examples. In this paper, we enable the ad hoc agent to acquire previously unknown domain knowledge governing actions and change, and to provide relational descriptions as on-demand explanations of its decisions in response to different types of questions. We evaluate the architecture's knowledge acquisition and explanation generation abilities in two simulated benchmark domains: Fort Attack and Half Field Offense.

Keywords: Non-monotonic logical reasoning · Ecological rationality · Knowledge acquisition · Explanation generation · Ad hoc teamwork

1 Introduction

Ad hoc teamwork (AHT) refers to the problem of enabling an agent to collaborate with others without any prior coordination [27]. For example, consider the simulated multiagent domain *Fort Attack* (FA, Fig. 1a), with a team of guards trying to defend a fort from a team of attackers [8], or *Half Field Offense* (HFO, Fig. 1b), with a team of offense agents trying to score a goal against a team of defenders [16]. Agents in these domains have limited knowledge of each other, no prior experience of working as a team, and have to operate under partial observability and limited communication; these conditions also exist in many practical applications such as disaster rescue and surveillance.

The state of the art in AHT has moved from using predetermined policies for selecting actions in specific states to methods based on a key "data-driven"

© The Author(s), under exclusive license to Springer Nature Switzerland AG 2023
M. Gebser and I. Sergey (Eds.): PADL 2024, LNCS 14512, pp. 186–203, 2023.
https://doi.org/10.1007/978-3-031-52038-9_12

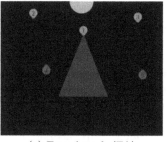

(a) Fort Attack (FA)   (b) Half Field Offense (HFO)

Fig. 1. Screenshots from FA and HFO environments.

component [20]. This component uses a long history of prior experiences to build probabilistic or deep network methods that model the behavior of other agents (or agent types) and optimize the behavior of the ad hoc agent. However, in practical domains, it is difficult to gather such large training datasets of different situations and to adapt to unforeseen changes. Also, these methods lack transparency, and make it difficult to leverage commonsense domain knowledge to revise existing knowledge over time. Unlike existing work, we follow a *cognitive systems* approach, formulating AHT as a joint reasoning and learning problem. Our prior work developed a knowledge-guided architecture for AHT (**KAT**), which combined the principles of *refinement* and *ecological rationality*, enabling an ad hoc agent to determine its actions based on non-monotonic logical reasoning with prior domain knowledge and rapidly-learned predictive models of other agents' behaviors. In this paper, we significantly extend the architecture, enabling the ad hoc agent to:

1. Incrementally learn and revise previously unknown axioms and models that govern the dynamics of the domain; and
2. Provide on-demand relational descriptions of its decisions, and those of other agents, as *explanations* in response to different types of questions.

We demonstrate and evaluate these capabilities in the two simulated benchmark domains (FA, HFO). In particular, we illustrate how the interplay between representation, reasoning, and learning leads to incremental, reliable, and efficient knowledge acquisition and explanation generation.

2   Related Work

AHT has been researched under different names, as described in a recent survey [20]. Early work encoded specific protocols (or plays) for different scenarios, with an agent choosing specific protocols in specific states [6]. Subsequent work used sampling-based methods such as Upper Confidence bounds for Trees (UCT) to determine the ad hoc agent's action selection policy [5].

Many recent studies include a data-driven component that uses probabilistic, deep-network, and reinforcement learning (RL)-based methods to learn action choice policies for the ad hoc agent based on a lengthy history or prior observations of different *types* of teammates or situations [4,22]. For example, a RL method has been used to learn different policies for different teammate types, computing and using the best policy among the learned policies for a new teammate [4]. Also, attention-based deep neural networks have been used to jointly learn policies for different agent types [7], and to account for different team compositions [22]. Sequential and hierarchical variational auto-encoders have been used to model beliefs over other agents, and approximate belief inference has been achieved through meta-learning for a given prior [29]. Other work has combined learned policy methods with adversarial teammate prediction to account for changes in the agents' behavior [24], and used Convolutional Neural Networks to detect and adapt to changing teammate types [23]. Sampling strategies have also been combined with such learning methods to optimize performance [28]. Such methods based on a data-driven learning component require considerable computation, memory, and training examples, build opaque models, and make it difficult to adapt to unexpected changes. Our architecture addresses these limitations by leveraging the complementary strengths of knowledge-based reasoning and data-driven learning methods.

Given the increasing use of AI methods in different applications, many architectures have utilized knowledge-based and data-derived methods to provide transparency in the operation of such methods [1,19]. For example, prior work proposed a theory for explanation generation in human-robot interaction, using the declarative programming paradigm of Answer Set Prolog (ASP) to represent and reason with domain knowledge [25]. Other work has adapted this theory to support transparency in the decisions made by agents in scene understanding tasks [21]. In addition to transparency, agents operating in complex domains often need to revise their existing knowledge, and many different methods have been developed to support this ability. For example, a system based on inductive learning has been developed to learn new knowledge in the form of an ASP program [18]. Other approaches have used non-monotonic logical reasoning together with inductive learning and relational reinforcement learning to identify new rules for answer set programs [26].

The architecture developed in this work draws inspiration from the existing work to support reliable, efficient, and transparent reasoning and learning in ad hoc teamwork, enabling the ad hoc agent to adapt to different teammates and opponents, acquire and revise domain knowledge, and provide on-demand explanations in response to different types of questions.

3   Architecture

Figure 2 provides an overview of KAT, our architecture for ad hoc teamwork. Our ad hoc agent performs non-monotonic logical reasoning with prior commonsense domain knowledge and models of other agents' behaviors learned and revised

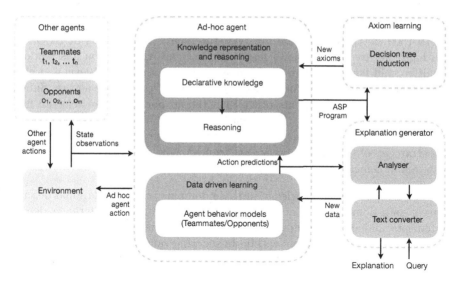

Fig. 2. Architecture combines complementary strengths of knowledge-based and data-driven reasoning and learning.

incrementally from limited examples, using heuristic methods to guide reasoning and learning. At each step, all agents receive observations of the domain state, and they independently determine and execute their individual actions in the environment. The *axiom learning* component enables the ad hoc agent to acquire and revise its knowledge governing changes in the domain, and the *explanation generator* component enables it to provide relational descriptions as explanations of its decisions in response to questions. Please note that the basic reasoning components of our architecture were introduced in our conference papers [9, 10]. This paper primarily contributes the components for axiom learning and explanation generation; for completeness, we describe all components of our architecture in the following two example domains.

Example Domain 1 *[Fort Attack (FA) Domain]*
Consider three guards defending a fort from three attackers in the FA domain—Fig. 1a [8]. An episode of the game ends if: (a) guards protect the fort for a given period of time; (b) all members of a team are terminated; or (c) an attacker reaches the fort. Each agent can move in one of the four cardinal directions with a specific velocity, rotate clockwise or anticlockwise, do nothing, or shoot an opponent within a range. The environment has four kinds of built-in policies for guards and attackers as described in Sect. 4.1. In our work, one of the guards is the ad hoc agent that can adapt to changes in the team and domain.

Example Domain 2 *[Half Field Offense (HFO) Domain]*
Consider a simulated 2D soccer domain where a team of offense agents are trying to score a goal against a team of defense agents (including a goalkeeper)—Fig. 1b [16]. An episode of the game ends if: (a) offense team scores a goal; (b)

ball leaves the field; (c) defense team captures the ball; or (d) maximum episode
length (500) is reached. There are two state space abstractions in HFO: low
and high; we use the high-level features. There are three action abstractions:
primitive, mid-level, and high-level; we use a combination of mid-level and high-
level actions. In our work, our ad hoc agent is one of the offense agents. Similar
to prior AHT methods, agents other than the ad hoc agent are selected from
teams in the 2013 Robocup 2D simulation league competitions; offense agents
are from *helios, gliders, cyrus, axiom, aut* and defense agents are from *agent2D*.
The strategies of these agent types were trained using data-driven (probabilistic,
deep, reinforcement) learning methods.

Prior commonsense knowledge in these domains includes relational descriptions of some domain/agent attributes, *e.g.*, location and shooting range, default
statements, and axioms governing change, *e.g.*, an agent can only move to a location nearby, only shoot others within its shooting range (FA), and only score a
goal from a certain angle (HFO). This knowledge may need to be revised over
time.

3.1 Knowledge Representation and Reasoning

In KAT, the transition diagram of any domain is described using an extension of the action language $\mathcal{AL}_d$ [13]. KAT's domain representation comprises a system description $\mathcal{D}$, a collection of statements of $\mathcal{AL}_d$, and a history $\mathcal{H}$. $\mathcal{D}$ has a sorted signature Σ with basic sorts, e.g., *x_value, y_value,
ad_hoc_agent, external_agent, step* (for temporal reasoning); actions, e.g.,
pass(ad_hoc_agent, external_agent), dribble(ad_hoc_agent, x_value, y_value);
statics, i.e., domain attributes whose values cannot be changed by actions, e.g.,
next_to(x_value, y_value, x_value, y_value) which describe the relative arrange-
ment of places; and fluents, i.e., attributes whose values can be changed by
actions. Fluents can be *inertial*, i.e., obey laws of inertia and changed by actions,
e.g. *ball_loc(x_value, y_value)* encodes the ball's location in the field; and *defined*,
i.e., not obey inertia laws and not directly changed by ad hoc agent's actions,
e.g., an external agent's location: *agent_loc(external_agent, x_value, y_value)*.

The domain dynamics are described in $\mathcal{D}$ using three types of axioms: *causal
law*, *state constraint*, and *executability condition*. Examples in HFO include:

$$dribble(R, X, Y) \textbf{ causes } loc(R, X, Y) \tag{1a}$$

$$\neg has\_ball(A1) \textbf{ if } has\_ball(A2), \ A1 \neq A2 \tag{1b}$$

$$\textbf{impossible } pass(R, T) \textbf{ if } \neg has\_ball(R) \tag{1c}$$

Statement 5(a) is a causal law that states that dribbling to a place changes
the location of the agent to that place. Statement 5(b) is a state constraint
that implies only one agent can control the ball at any time. Statement 5(c)
is an executability condition that prevents the ad hoc agent from considering
the action of passing the ball when it does not control the ball. History $\mathcal{H}$
is a record of observations and action executions, *i.e.*, relations of the form

$obs(fluent, boolean, step)$ and $hpd(action, step)$ respectively, at specific time steps. It also includes initial state defaults, *i.e.,* statements initially believed to be true in most circumstances.

To reason with knowledge, the domain description is automatically translated to a program $\Pi(\mathcal{D}, \mathcal{H})$ in CR-Prolog [3], an extension to Answer Set Programming (ASP) that supports consistency restoring (CR) rules. ASP encodes *default negation* and *epistemic disjunction*, and supports non-monotonic reasoning; the ability to revise previously held conclusions. This ability is essential in practical multiagent collaboration domains in which agents often have to reason with incomplete knowledge and noisy observations. The CR rules allow the agent to recover from situations when the program $\Pi(\mathcal{D}, \mathcal{H})$ is inconsistent. For example, consider the situation in which an encoded default states that *attackers usually spread and attack* but the ad hoc agent observes an attacker displaying different behavior, e.g., mounting a frontal attack or staying back away from the shooting range of the guards. To address such exceptions to defaults, a CR rule is added to $\Pi(\mathcal{D}, \mathcal{H})$ for every default, allowing the ad hoc agent to assume that the default's conclusion is false under exceptional circumstances, as a means of restoring consistency. For example:

$$\neg spread\_attack(X) \xleftarrow{+} attacker(X)$$

allows the ad hoc agent to consider the rare situation of attackers mounting a frontal attack or display any behavior that does not agree with the default behavior.

$\Pi(\mathcal{D}, \mathcal{H})$ includes statements from $\mathcal{D}$ and $\mathcal{H}$, inertia axioms, reality check axioms, closed world assumptions for defined fluents and actions, helper relations, e.g., $holds(fluent, step)$ and $occurs(action, step)$ to imply that a fluent is true and an action is part of a plan at a time step, and helper axioms that define goals and drive planning and diagnosis. Once the program Π is constructed, all reasoning tasks (e.g., planning, diagnostics, and inference) are reduced to computing *answer sets* of Π. We use the SPARC system [2] to write and solve CR-Prolog programs. Example programs for FA and HFO domains are in our open source repository [11].

3.2   Agent Behavior Models

The ad hoc agent's decisions must take into account the state of the domain which is also governed by the actions of other agents. KAT thus also reasons with models that predict the behavior of the other agents. Our prior work introduced the use of the *Ecological Rationality* (ER) principle, which is based on Herb Simon's definition of *Bounded Rationality* [14], and the algorithmic theory of heuristics [14, 15] to rapidly learn and revise these predictive models. The ER-based approach enables the ad hoc agent to choose relevant attributes and learn models of the behavior of other agents from limited training data (*e.g.,* 10000) while supporting rapid, incremental updates. Specifically, KAT enables the ad hoc agent to learn an ensemble of "fast and frugal" (FF) decision trees

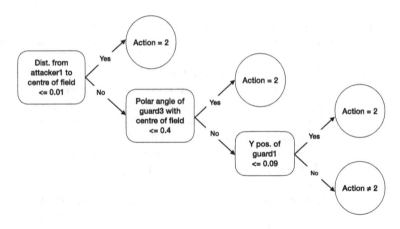

Fig. 3. FF tree in the ensemble for an attacker in the FA domain.

that predict the behavior of each type of other agents; each FF tree provides a binary class label and the number of leaves in the tree is limited by number of attributes [17]. An individual FF tree learned for an attacker agent in the FA domain is shown in Fig. 3.

Note that unlike state of the art AHT methods, KAT enables the predictive models of the other agents' behavior to be learned and revised rapidly. Also, consistent agreement (disagreement) with predictions of an existing model triggers model choice (revision); the ad hoc agent is thus able to quickly adapt to changes in the domain or in the team composition.

3.3   Axiom Induction

Incrementally learning previously unknown domain knowledge is essential in complex domains such as ad hoc teamwork. One contribution of this paper is an approach to learn previously unknown causal laws and executability conditions governing the domain's dynamics. Acquiring this knowledge will reduce ambiguity and enable the ad hoc agent to make more informed (also more reliable and efficient) decisions. We do so by adapting work that combined *decision tree induction* with knowledge-based reasoning [21], as described below.

For each candidate action, we collect possible state transitions involving this action and incrementally build a decision tree model by splitting nodes at each time step based on unused attributes. Every split must meet a minimum requirement of samples at each child. Then we build the candidate axioms by exploring different paths from the root to the leaves of the tree. These axioms are then validated for identifying further inconsistencies in the system. Specifically we:

1. Select an action and simulate the execution in different initial states to collect state transition information (e.g., start and end states, executed action, and presence or absence of inconsistency). If the expected outcome is not observed after an action execution, that indicates the potential absence of

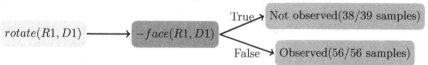

(a) Part of a tree created for a missing executability condition in the HFO domain.

(b) Part of a tree created for a missing causal condition in the FA domain.

Fig. 4. Examples of part of trees created for missing axioms.

an executability condition. If additional effects are observed (than what is expected), that indicates a missing causal law.

2. All fluent literals that exist in the answer set or initial state, and have an object constant that occurs in the executed action, are then stored as training data. The ground terms in the literals are further replaced by variables.

3. After data from a few execution traces are available, the decision tree models are created with relevant fluent literals as leaf nodes and the executed action as the root node. For executability conditions, the output or class label for each example is the presence or absence of an inconsistency. For causal laws, the output or class label for each example is the presence of unexpected fluent literals observed in the resultant state.

4. The candidate axioms are then generated along the path from the root node to the leaves in the decision trees. Examples of such path (*i.e.,* part of the decision tree) are illustrated in Fig. 4 for the executability condition and the causal law below.

$$\neg occurs(shoot(R), I) \leftarrow \neg holds(has\_ball(R), I). \tag{2}$$

$$occurs(rotate(R, D), I + 1) \leftarrow holds(face(R, D), I). \tag{3}$$

The candidate axioms then go through a series of validation checks. In particular, we only retain axioms that have sufficient support from the samples collected during the construction of the decision tree model of prior state transition experiences. In addition, we test the candidate axioms in some simulated situations similar to those used to collect the training examples and only retain axioms that do not cause any new inconsistencies. Furthermore, candidate axioms that pass the validation checks are merged with existing axioms to ensure that the more general version of the axioms (e.g., replace individual ground arguments of literals with their sorts) are included in the ad hoc agent's knowledge base.

3.4   Transparency

Unlike methods in the existing literature that seek to make an entire learned model interpretable, or to explain (or justify) all the choices made by a reasoning system, KAT focuses on quickly identifying the relevant information to construct relational descriptions as *explanations* in response to causal, contrastive, or counterfactual questions about its decisions and beliefs. An automated decision-making system's ability to reliably answer such questions about its decisions and beliefs promotes acceptability [1,12]; this ability has been shown to play an important role in human reasoning and learning as well. KAT's use of knowledge-based reasoning and simple predictive models provides the foundation of the approach introduced in this paper to support the desired transparency in the ad hoc agent's operation. In addition, KAT's approach for generating these descriptions on-demand promotes computational efficiency. We build on prior work that demonstrated the ability to provide on-demand answers by iteratively and selectively identifying the axioms and literals that influence the desired action and belief, and have their antecedents satisfied in the relevant answer sets [21]. Specifically, KAT's *"Explanation Generator"* in Fig. 2 generates relational descriptions in response to four types of questions identified as being important in work on explainable planning [12]:

1. (**Action justification questions**) *Why did you do action A at step I?* When asked to justify an executed action, the ad hoc agent will:
    - extract actions A_{af} that occurred after A.
    - identify the axioms with a ($\in A_{af}$) in its head.
    - extract literals that would have prevented such an action from happening, e.g., from the body of its executability conditions.
    - identify that any such literal that exists in answer set at step I but not in I + 1 was caused by the execution of A and thus enabled subsequent steps.
2. (**Contrastive questions**) *Why did you not do action A at step I?* When asked why an action was not included in the plan, the ad hoc agent will:
    - find executability conditions with A as its head to identify preconditions.
    - extract corresponding literals and check if they are satisfied by the answer set; each such literal prevented consideration of A.
    - if no preconditions of A are identified, compute cost of adding A to the computed plan. This will identify reasons for not selecting A.
3. (**Justify beliefs**) *Why did you believe L at step I?* To justify a belief at a specific step, ad hoc agent will:
    - find axioms that have given belief in its head.
    - extract related literals and check whether they are satisfied by the answer set. These will be the supporting statements for the belief.
    - if there are multiple supporting statements explaining a target belief, select one to provide the explanation. We leave the ranking of explanations and multi-step tracing of beliefs to future work that can build on ideas from [21].

4. **(Counterfactual Questions)** *What action do you think agent R will take at step I and why? What would be the outcome if you/agent R did action A instead?* When answering questions about the action choices of agents or the potential future state of the world, the agent will:

   - make sure that it starts with the current best estimate of the state of the world, e.g., answer set at step I.
   - perform mental simulation of future steps from the current state using existing knowledge, including the action choices of other agents based on their behavior prediction models, and any specific ad hoc agent actions to be explored. Specifically, create potential next states of the world and explore the effects of specific actions or observations of interest.
   - use the newly acquired information to generate the explanation tailored to the question posed.

The newly acquired information/experience may also be used to further train the KAT system, specifically the behaviour prediction models of the other agents, for specific situations of interest. For all types of questions, the identified literals are processed with existing software tools and templates to generate textual descriptions provided as responses (i.e., explanations). We provide an execution trace in Sect. 4.3 of this approach, which can be used to answer questions during both planning and execution.

4   Experimental Setup and Results

Since KAT's ability to reason with domain knowledge and learn behavior prediction models was already evaluated in our prior work, the work described in this paper evaluated three hypotheses:

- **H1:** KAT enables an ad hoc agent to accurately learn previously unknown causal laws and executability conditions;
- **H2:** Reasoning with incrementally learned axioms improves the performance of the ad hoc agent and the team; and
- **H3:** KAT supports the generation of relational descriptions as explanations of the ad hoc agent's decisions and beliefs.

H1 was evaluated in both FA domain and HFO domain, with accuracy determined by the fraction of literals identified correctly in the learned axioms. As performance measures for H2, we used the team of guards' win percentage in the FA domain, and the fraction of the goals scored by offense team in the HFO domain. H3 was evaluated in the FA domain, including qualitative evaluation. Further details of experiments and baselines are provided below.

4.1   Experimental Setup

FA domain provides four types of built-in policies for the attacker and guard agents as described below.

- **Policy220:** guards place themselves in front of the fort and shoot continuously; attackers try to approach the fort.
- **Policy650:** guards try to block the fort; attackers sneak in from all sides.
- **Policy1240:** guards spread and shoot the attackers; attackers spread and sneak in from all sides.
- **Policy1600:** guards are willing to move from the fort; some attackers approach the fort and shoot to distract guards while others try to sneak in.

For experiments in FA domain our ad hoc agent replaced one of the guard team members and each other agent in the team(guard/attacker) was assigned a policy from these built-in policies.

For the experiments in the **HFO domain**, we used six external agent teams from 2013 RoboCup simulation competition. The ad hoc agent represented one of the offense team members and the teammates were selected from *helios, gliders, cyrus, axiom and aut*, and the defense agents were based on *agent2d* team.

To evaluate **H1**, we used KAT in two sets of experiments; **Exp1**, in which we removed three axioms (two causal laws and one executability condition) from the agent's knowledge base in the FA domain; **Exp2**, in which we removed four axioms (one causal law and three executability condition) from the agent's knowledge base in the HFO domain.

FA domain:

$$holds(face(R, D), I + 1) \leftarrow occurs(rotate(R, D), I). \tag{4a}$$

$$holds(in(R, X, Y), I + 1) \leftarrow occurs(move(R, X, Y), I). \tag{4b}$$

$$\neg occurs(shoot(R, A), I) \leftarrow \neg holds(in\_range(R, A), I). \tag{4c}$$

HFO domain:

$$holds(in(R, X, Y), I + 1) \leftarrow occurs(dribble(R, X, Y), I). \tag{5a}$$

$$\neg occurs(dribble(R, X, Y), I) \leftarrow \neg holds(has\_ball(R), I). \tag{5b}$$

$$\neg occurs(shoot(R), I) \leftarrow \neg holds(has\_ball(R), I). \tag{5c}$$

$$\neg occurs(pass(R, T1), I) \leftarrow \neg holds(has\_ball(R), I). \tag{5d}$$

We ran the axiom learning algorithm 40 times; 20 times for each domain. Each time the ad hoc agent selected a different action and simulated its effects in each domain to incrementally learn all the missing axioms (see Sect. 3.3). As the performance measure we recorded the precision and recall of learning the missing axioms in terms of accurately identifying the literals in the axioms.

Next, in **Exp3** and **Exp4**, we allowed the agent to use the axioms it learned in **Exp1** and **Exp2** in the FA domain and HFO domain respectively. We conducted 100 game episodes in each domain with each built-in policy. As the baselines for these experiments (**Base1**) we used an ad hoc agent that does not use the learned axioms in its planning. These experiments were used to evaluate **H2**.

Finally to evaluate **H3**, in **Exp5** we randomly selected 10 sets of state observation and agent available domain knowledge from different game episodes in the FA domain. Then we posed 27 different questions (belonging to the four types

Table 1. Precision and recall of the learned axioms in FA (Exp1) and HFO (Exp2) domains.

Domain	Precision	Recall
FA	1.00	0.43
HFO	0.89	0.47

of questions described in Sect. 3.4) to the agent from each plan and recorded the precision and recall of retrieving relevant literals for constructing answers to these questions as explanations. Next, in **Exp6** we removed the axioms the agent learned in **Exp1** from its knowledge base and repeated the experiment. Additionally, we also provide execution traces as qualitative examples of the architecture's performance in the FA domain to support **H3**.

4.2 Experiment Results

We first discuss the results of evaluating **H1**. As stated earlier, in **Exp1**, three axioms (two causal laws and one executability condition) were removed from the ad hoc agent's knowledge in the FA domain, and the axiom learning algorithm was executed 20 times. In **Exp2**, four axioms (one causal law and three executability conditions) were removed from the ad hoc agent's knowledge in the HFO domain, and the axiom learning algorithm was executed 20 times. We then measured the precision and recall of the agent learning these missing axioms in each run and summarized the results in Table 1. We observe high precision and average recall values in Table 1. The lower recall can be explained by the fact that only axioms with a high degree of support from the observed transitions were added to the ad hoc agent's knowledge, i.e., a correct candidate axiom could be filtered and not added to the ad hoc agent's knowledge if its addition is not justified by sufficient experiences of the ad hoc agent. We observed that the recall values improved with additional experiences. These results support **H1**.

Tables 2 and 3 summarize the results of **Exp3** and **Exp4** respectively. Compared with **Base1**, which corresponds to not using the learned axioms from **Exp1** and **Exp2**, i.e., reasoning without some key axioms, there was a significant improvement in the number of games/episodes in which the guards won in the FA domain, particularly with policies 220, 650 and 1240. Similar performance was observed in the HFO domain, with a substantial improvement in the fraction of goals scored by the offense team when the ad hoc agent included the learned axioms during reasoning and the other agents used the policies *helios, gliders, cyrus* and *axiom*. With both the built-in policy 1600 in the FA domain and the *aut* policy in the HFO domain the results are comparable with and without the learned axioms; note that the learned axioms are not necessarily used in each episode. This is a good outcome and supports **H2**.

Next, we discuss the results of evaluating **H3**. Specifically, Table 4 summarizes the precision and recall values corresponding to **Exp5** that evaluated the ability to generate relational descriptions as explanations of the agents decisions

Table 2. Win(%) of the team of guards in the FA domain with and without the learned axioms (Exp3).

Policy	Without(%)	With(%)
220	81	86
650	38	46
1240	47	56
1600	21	21

Table 3. Fraction of goals scored by the offense team in HFO with and without the learned axioms (Exp4).

Policy	Without(%)	With(%)
Helios	30	35
Gliders	25	29
Cyrus	32	38
Axiom	14	24
Aut	19	19

Table 4. Precision and recall of retrieving relevant literals for constructing explanations in the FA domain with the learned axioms (Exp5).

Question type	Precision	Recall
Action justification	1.00	1.00
Contrastive	0.96	0.94
Belief justification	0.95	0.85
Counterfactual	1.00	1.00

Table 5. Precision and recall of retrieving relevant literals for constructing explanations in the FA domain without the learned axioms (Exp6).

Question type	Precision	Recall
Action justification	1.00	0.34
Contrastive	0.90	0.90
Belief justification	0.88	0.63
Counterfactual	1.00	1.00

and beliefs. In these experiments, the learned axioms were included in the knowledge used by the ad hoc agent for reasoning. Table 5 summarizes the precision and recall values from **Exp6**, where the ad hoc agent generated the explanations for different queries while the learned axioms were removed from the knowledge base. The observed higher values of precision and recall in Table 4 compared with the values in Table 5, i.e., the observed improvement in retrieving the relevant literals needed to construct the (correct) responses to the questions, provides strong support for hypothesis **H3**.

4.3   Execution Trace

This section provides some execution traces illustrating some of the capabilities of our architecture. Consider, for example, the scenario in Fig. 5, in which an ad hoc agent in grid (3, 13) at time step 0, has the goal of shooting an attacker in grid (9, 8). The plan generated by the ad hoc agent was:

$$occurs(move(learner, 4, 13), 1),$$
$$occurs(move(learner, 5, 13), 2),$$
$$occurs(move(learner, 6, 13), 3),$$
$$occurs(move(learner, 7, 13), 4),$$
$$occurs(shoot(learner, attacker1), 5)$$

As an example of providing relational descriptions of decisions and beliefs, consider an exchange with the ad hoc agent after it executed this plan successfully;

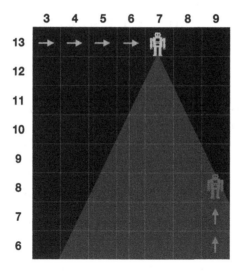

Fig. 5. Part of the domain showing the ad hoc guard agent (green) moving to track and shoot an attacker (red). (Color figure online)

- **Human:** "Why did you move to (7, 13) in step 4 ?"
- **Ad hoc Agent:** "Because attacker1 was not in range for shooting and my goal was to shoot the attacker1 in step 5".

This response was generated using the approach in Sect. 3.4. For example, since the *shoot* action occurred immediately after *move*, the relevant axiom identified included:

$$\neg occurs(shoot(R, A), I) \leftarrow \neg holds(in\_range(R, A), I) \qquad (6)$$

Next, the ad hoc agent explored the related answer sets and identified that ground literal *in_range(learner, attacker1)* was present in step 5 but not in step 4. This literal was then selected to construct the answer (above) justifying the action execution.

- **Human:** "Why did you not shoot attacker1 in step 2?"
- **Ad hoc Agent:** "Because attacker1 was not in the shooting range at step 2 since it had moved towards fort in step 0 and step 1."

The agent first tried to identify axioms with action *shoot* in the head, e.g., Statement 6 in this scenario. Next the agent ground the body of the axiom and verified whether it was included in the answer set. Since the $\neg in\_range(learner, attacker1)$ was valid in step 2, the agent identified it as a literal that prevented it from considering the shooting action at step 2. Since the location of *attacker1* is also a key factor here, the agent also included the immediate actions of the attacker1 when generating its response (above).

In a scenario where the agent does not find any preconditions that prevents it from executing an action mentioned in a contrastive question, recall that it will still compare the cost of its plans including and excluding that particular action. An example for such a scenario is shown below.

- **Human:** "Why did you not move to (3,13) in step 2?"
- **Ad hoc Agent:** "Because that action increases the cost of the plan; new plan cost = 8, old plan cost = 7."
  In this scenario, the ad hoc agent tried to create a plan with the suggested action. Then it computed the cost for the new plan and compared it with the cost of its original plan. Since the new plan's cost was higher than that of the original plan, this information was used to justify its action choice and to generate the answer (above) to the question posed.
- **Human:** "Why did you believe attacker1 was in shooting range at step 5?"
- **Ad hoc Agent:** "Because I observed that the attacker1 was located in 9,9 in step 5 and I was in 7, 13 facing south."
  When probed to expand on this answer, the ad hoc agent also mentioned that "This further satisfied the conditions $Y2-Y1 <= 5, Y2-Y1 >= 4, X2-2 <= X1, X1 <= X2 + 2$."
  When posed with a question about its beliefs, the ad hoc agent first identified the valid axioms (e.g., state constraints) that could influence the belief:

$$holds(in\_range(L, A), I) \leftarrow$$
$$holds(in(L, X2, Y2), I),$$
$$holds(agent\_in(A, X1, Y1), I),$$
$$holds(face(L, south), I),$$
$$Y2 - Y1 <= 5, Y2 - Y1 >= 4,$$
$$X2 - 2 <= X1, X1 <= X2 + 2.$$

By grounding and verifying that the relevant literals are available in the answer set, the ad hoc agent generated the explanation described above. This answer demonstrates the agent's ability to answer questions regarding its beliefs. A similar process can be used to trace the evolution of beliefs over multiple time steps. The ad hoc agent can also be asked about hypothetical situations, including those involving other agents, through counterfactual questions.

- **Human:** "What do you think the attacker will do in step 2?"
- **Ad hoc Agent:** "Attacker will move up in step 2."
- **Human:** "Why do you think the attacker will move up in step 2?"
- **Ad hoc Agent:** "Attacker will decide to move up since all the attackers are alive and attacker is in front of the fort."

In this scenario the agent retrieved the current state estimate stored and initialized a new FA environment. Then it simulated the environment for the desired future time steps while using the agent behaviour models to predict the actions of the other agents. Next, it went through the FF tree model predicting the attacker's behavior, and identified rules that caused it to believe the attacker agent will 'move up' in step 2. This information was used to generate the responses (above) to the questions posed. A similar approach was followed to generate the explanations to queries such as:

- **Human:** "What will happened if guard1 shoots in step 2?"
- **Ad hoc Agent:** "If guard1 shoots in step 2, the number of alive attackers will be reduced to 1 in step 3. There will be 3 guards alive, and the nearest attacker to the fort will be attacker3."

These results support hypothesis **H3**.

5 Conclusions

This paper described KAT, a knowledge-driven AHT architecture that supports non-monotonic logical reasoning with prior commonsense domain knowledge and predictive models of other agents' behaviors that are learned and revised rapidly using heuristic methods. In this paper, we focused on describing KAT's ability to incrementally learn and revise previously unknown axioms that govern action and change in the domain, enabling an ad hoc agent to better adapt to the environment. Moreover, we described KAT's ability to provide transparency by generating on-demand relational descriptions of the ad hoc agent's (and other agents) decisions in response to different types of questions. In the future, we will explore scenarios with multiple ad hoc agents, investigate scalability of our architecture to more complex domains, and use our architecture on physical robots in AHT settings.

References

1. Anjomshoae, S., Najjar, A., Calvaresi, D., Framling, K.: Explainable agents and robots: results from a systematic literature review. In: International Conference on Autonomous Agents and Multiagent Systems (AAMAS), Montreal, Canada (2019)
2. Balai, E., Gelfond, M., Zhang, Y.: Towards answer set programming with sorts. In: Cabalar, P., Son, T.C. (eds.) LPNMR 2013. LNCS (LNAI), vol. 8148, pp. 135–147. Springer, Heidelberg (2013). https://doi.org/10.1007/978-3-642-40564-8_14
3. Balduccini, M., Gelfond, M.: Logic programs with consistency-restoring rules. In: AAAI Spring Symposium on Logical Formalization of Commonsense Reasoning (2003)
4. Barrett, S., Rosenfeld, A., Kraus, S., Stone, P.: Making friends on the fly: cooperating with new teammates. Artif. Intell. **242**, 132–171 (2017)
5. Barrett, S., Stone, P., Kraus, S., Rosenfeld, A.: Teamwork with limited knowledge of teammates. In: AAAI Conference on Artificial Intelligence, vol. 27, pp. 102–108 (2013)
6. Bowling, M., McCracken, P.: Coordination and adaptation in impromptu teams. In: National Conference on Artificial Intelligence, pp. 53–58 (2005)

7. Chen, S., Andrejczuk, E., Cao, Z., Zhang, J.: AATEAM: achieving the ad hoc teamwork by employing the attention mechanism. In: AAAI Conference on Artificial Intelligence, pp. 7095–7102 (2020)
8. Deka, A., Sycara, K.: Natural emergence of heterogeneous strategies in artificially intelligent competitive teams. In: Tan, Y., Shi, Y. (eds.) ICSI 2021. LNCS, vol. 12689, pp. 13–25. Springer, Cham (2021). https://doi.org/10.1007/978-3-030-78743-1_2
9. Dodampegama, H., Sridharan, M.: Back to the future: toward a hybrid architecture for ad hoc teamwork. In: AAAI Conference on Artificial Intelligence (2023)
10. Dodampegama, H., Sridharan, M.: Knowledge-based reasoning and learning under partial observability in ad hoc teamwork. Theory Pract. Log. Program. **23**(4), 696–714 (2023). https://doi.org/10.1017/S1471068423000091
11. Dodampegama, H., Sridharan, M.: Code (2023). https://github.com/hharithaki/KAT
12. Fox, M., Long, D., Magazzeni, D.: Explainable planning. In: IJCAI Workshop on Explainable AI (2017)
13. Gelfond, M., Inclezan, D.: Some properties of system descriptions of AL_d. Appl. Non-Class. Log. Spec. Issue Equilibr. Log. ASP **23**(1–2), 105–120 (2013)
14. Gigerenzer, G.: What is bounded rationality? In: Routledge Handbook of Bounded Rationality. Routledge (2020)
15. Gigerenzer, G., Gaissmaier, W.: Heuristic decision making. Ann. Rev. Psychol. **62**, 451–482 (2011)
16. Hausknecht, M., Mupparaju, P., Subramanian, S., Kalyanakrishnan, S., Stone, P.: Half field offense: an environment for multiagent learning and ad hoc teamwork. In: AAMAS Adaptive Learning Agents Workshop (2016)
17. Katsikopoulos, K., Simsek, O., Buckmann, M., Gigerenzer, G.: Classification in the Wild: The Science and Art of Transparent Decision Making. MIT Press, Cambridge (2021)
18. Law, M., Russo, A., Broda, K.: The ILASP system for inductive learning of answer set programs. CoRR abs/2005.00904 (2020). https://arxiv.org/abs/2005.00904
19. Miller, T.: Explanations in artificial intelligence: insights from the social sciences. Artif. Intell. **267**, 1–38 (2019)
20. Mirsky, R., et al.: A survey of ad hoc teamwork: definitions, methods, and open problems. In: European Conference on Multiagent Systems (2022)
21. Mota, T., Sridharan, M., Leonardis, A.: Integrated commonsense reasoning and deep learning for transparent decision making in robotics. Springer Nat. CS **2**, 242 (2021). https://doi.org/10.1007/s42979-021-00573-0
22. Rahman, M.A., Hopner, N., Christianos, F., Albrecht, S.V.: Towards open ad hoc teamwork using graph-based policy learning. In: International Conference on Machine Learning, pp. 8776–8786 (2021)
23. Ravula, M., Alkoby, S., Stone, P.: Ad hoc teamwork with behavior switching agents. In: International Joint Conference on Artificial Intelligence (2019)
24. Santos, P.M., Ribeiro, J.G., Sardinha, A., Melo, F.S.: Ad hoc teamwork in the presence of non-stationary teammates. In: Marreiros, G., Melo, F.S., Lau, N., Lopes Cardoso, H., Reis, L.P. (eds.) EPIA 2021. LNCS (LNAI), vol. 12981, pp. 648–660. Springer, Cham (2021). https://doi.org/10.1007/978-3-030-86230-5_51
25. Sridharan, M., Meadows, B.: Towards a theory of explanations for human-robot collaboration. KI - Künstliche Intelligenz **33**, 1–12 (2019). https://doi.org/10.1007/s13218-019-00616-y

26. Sridharan, M., Meadows, B., Gomez, R.: What can i not do? Towards an architecture for reasoning about and learning affordances. In: Proceedings of the International Conference on Automated Planning and Scheduling, vol. 27, no. 1, pp. 461–469 (2017). https://doi.org/10.1609/icaps.v27i1.13852. https://ojs.aaai.org/index.php/ICAPS/article/view/13852
27. Stone, P., Kaminka, G., Kraus, S., Rosenschein, J.: Ad hoc autonomous agent teams: collaboration without pre-coordination. In: AAAI Conference on Artificial Intelligence, pp. 1504–1509 (2010)
28. Zand, J., Parker-Holder, J., Roberts, S.J.: On-the-fly strategy adaptation for ad-hoc agent coordination. In: International Conference on Autonomous Agents and Multiagent Systems, pp. 1771–1773 (2022)
29. Zintgraf, L., Devlin, S., Ciosek, K., Whiteson, S., Hofmann, K.: Deep interactive Bayesian reinforcement learning via meta-learning. In: International Conference on Autonomous Agents and Multiagent Systems (2021)

Automated Interactive Domain-Specific Conversational Agents that Understand Human Dialogs

Yankai Zeng[1]($\boxtimes$), Abhiramon Rajasekharan[1], Parth Padalkar[1], Kinjal Basu[2],
Joaquín Arias[3], and Gopal Gupta[1]

[1] The University of Texas at Dallas, Richardson, TX, USA
{Yankai.Zeng,Abhiramon.Rajasekharan,Parth.Padalkar,
Gupta}@utdallas.edu
[2] IBM T. J. Watson Research Center, Yorktown Heights, NY, USA
Kinjal.Basu@ibm.com
[3] CETINIA, Universidad Rey Juan Carlos, Madrid, Spain
Joaquin.Arias@urjc.es

Abstract. We present the AutoConcierge system that can "understand" human dialogs in a specific domain, namely, restaurant recommendation. AutoConcierge will interactively "understand" a user's utterances, and request the user to provide required information via a natural language reply. AutoConcierge uses GPT-3 to convert human dialogs into predicates that represent knowledge implicit in the dialogs. These predicates are then input into the goal-directed s(CASP) answer set programming (ASP) system for performing commonsense reasoning to compute responses in the form of predicates. GPT-3 is used again to convert these computed predicates into natural language sentences that are communicated to the user. To the best of our knowledge, AutoConcierge is the first automated conversational agent that can realistically converse like a human based on *truly understanding* user utterances. The framework used for AutoConcierge provides a recipe for developing other task-specific chatbots leveraging large language models and answer set programming.

Keywords: Chatbot · LLMs · Answer Set Programming

1 Introduction

Conversational agents are designed to understand dialogs and generate meaningful responses to communicate with humans. The recently popular ChatGPT, with its surprising performance and powerful conversational ability, brought *Large Language Models* (LLMs) such as GPT-3 [7], PaLM [11], and LLaMa [35] as the solution to the vexing problem of developing conversational AI systems. These LLMs work quite well in content generation tasks, but their deficiency in fact-and-knowledge-oriented tasks is well-established by now [5]. The reason for this flaw is that LLMs generate text that is purely based on a pattern-matching mechanism, and consequently have absolutely no understanding of the meaning of sentences and thus lack *awareness* [5]. In contrast, humans understand the meaning of sentences, then use their reasoning capabilities to

© The Author(s), under exclusive license to Springer Nature Switzerland AG 2023
M. Gebser and I. Sergey (Eds.): PADL 2024, LNCS 14512, pp. 204–222, 2023.
https://doi.org/10.1007/978-3-031-52038-9_13

draw further conclusions, check for consistency, or determine missing information from this meaning. Thus, to make the machine-generated response reliable and consistent, we believe that we need to follow a similar approach.

Following the above insights, in this paper we report on developing an elaborate conversational agent that can "understand" human dialog and respond properly according to human expectation. We narrow the domain of our conversational agent to give advice about finding restaurants in the user's vicinity. Our agent, called AutoConcierge, is able to provide precise information based on user preferences. User preference is elicited by AutoConcierge via a natural language dialog with the human user. Auto-Concierge will first ask the user a few questions to which the user responds in natural language. These are questions that a human concierge will also ask. Once enough information is collected, AutoConcierge will find a restaurant in its knowledge base that satisfies (most of) the user's requirements, and that does not violate any restriction imposed by the user. Users can also ask AutoConcierge for other possible recommendations, or even modify their requirements mid-conversation.

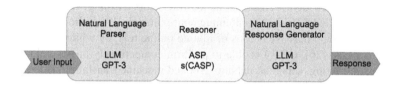

Fig. 1. The AutoConcierge Architecture

Figure 1 shows the high-level architecture of our AutoConcierge system. We use GPT-3 to "translate" the dialog from English to predicates, and then feed these predicates to an Answer Set Programming [6] system. The predicates are fixed in advance and can be thought of as a pre-defined ontology that the reasoner understands. We can think of this ontology as the common vocabulary between the LLM and the ASP reasoner. We use the s(CASP) ASP system [3] to represent the commonsense knowledge for making restaurant recommendations and to compute a response. The response is computed as one or more logical predicate(s). The predicate(s) are then converted into human-understandable natural language expression, by using GPT-3 as a reverse translator, to generate the bot's dialogs. Detailed implementation of the AutoConcierge system is discussed in the rest of this paper.

To the best of our knowledge, AutoConcierge is the first conversational agent to communicate with humans based on *truly understanding* human dialogs. It leverages both the LLM as well as ASP technology. Crucially, it relies on the s(CASP) goal-directed ASP system [3] for commonsense reasoning [18]. The AutoConcierge system has several advantages over an approach that is purely based on LLMs: (1) Auto-Concierge can check if the knowledge extracted from the user utterance is consistent, correct, and complete. This is because it possesses commonsense knowledge about the domain represented as ASP rules [18]. (2) It gives reasonable advice based on the knowledge of the user's likes and dislikes, which LLM-only agents are not able to explicitly consider. (3) It is capable of precisely justifying its recommendations. The methodology used by AutoConcierge can be easily adapted for developing other task-specific chatbots, such as for automatically making airline reservation, automated order-taking system at a McDonald's drive-through, automated bank teller, etc.

We performed significant quantitative testing of the AutoConcierge Chatbot. Our experiments to measure efficiency show that AutoConcierge generates replies in an acceptable time, and the human evaluation experiment indicates that it outperforms state-of-the-art systems, especially in *Truthfulness* and *Fluency*.

2   Background

2.1   Large Language Models (LLMs)

Until recently, transformer-based deep learning models have been applied to NLP tasks by training and fine-tuning them on task-specific datasets [8]. With the advent of Large Language Models, the paradigm changed to teaching a language model any arbitrary task using just a few demonstrations, called *in-context learning*. Brown et al. introduced an LLM called GPT-3 [7] containing approximately 175 billion parameters that has been trained on a massive corpus of filtered online text, on which the well-known ChatGPT is based [26]. GPT-3 is able to perform competitively on several tasks such as question-answering, semantic parsing [31] and machine translation. However, such LLMs tend to make simple mistakes in tasks such as semantic (commonsense) and mathematical reasoning [5,15,38].

2.2   Answer Set Programming and s(CASP)

Answer Set Programming (ASP) is a logic programming paradigm suited for knowledge representation and reasoning [6] that facilitates commonsense reasoning [18]. The s(CASP) system [3], is an answer set programming system that supports predicates, constraints over non-ground variables, uninterpreted functions, and, most importantly, a top-down, query-driven execution strategy. These features make it possible to return answers with non-ground variables (possibly including constraints among them) and compute partial models by returning only the fragment of a stable model that is necessary to support the answer.

Complex commonsense knowledge can be represented in ASP and the s(CASP) query-driven predicate ASP system can be used for querying it [10,42]. Commonsense knowledge can be emulated using (i) default rules, (ii) integrity constraints, and (iii) multiple possible worlds [16,18]. Default rules are used for jumping to a conclusion in the absence of exceptions, e.g., a bird normally flies, unless it's a penguin.

```
1  flies(X) :- bird(X), not abnormal_bird(X).
2  abnormal_bird(X) :- penguin(X).
```

Integrity constraints allow us to express impossible situations and invariants. For example, a person cannot sit and stand at the same time.

```
1  false :- person(X), sit(X), stand(X).
```

Finally, multiple possible worlds allow us to construct alternative universes that may have some parts common but other parts inconsistent. For example, the cartoon world of children's books has a lot in common with the real world (e.g., birds can fly in both worlds), yet in the former birds can talk like humans but in the latter they cannot. Default rules are used to model a bulk of our commonsense knowledge. Integrity constraints help in checking the consistency of the information extracted. Multiple possible worlds allow us to perform assumption-based (or abductive) reasoning.

A large number of commonsense reasoning applications have already been developed using ASP and the s(CASP) system [10,23,29,42]. The query-driven s(CASP) ASP system is crucial for the AutoConcierge system. It is used to perform commonsense reasoning resembling a human concierge: to draw conclusions, to check for inconsistencies in the knowledge derived from user's dialogs, etc. Justification for each response can also be given as the s(CASP) system can generate justifications for successful queries as proof trees [2].

3   Design Philosophy

The main philosophy we follow in realizing a conversation agent is to emulate how humans process dialogs: (i) converting a sentence to knowledge, (ii) processing the knowledge to check the consistency, correctness, and completeness of the extracted knowledge, and then drawing conclusions from it, and (iii) converting the conclusions into a response sentence. These three phases (Fig. 1) are realized as three separate modules—a module for predicate extraction, a module for reasoning, and a module for response generation. Our idea is to make the three parts self-contained while having them communicate with each other through clear, well-defined interfaces. Therefore, an intermediate filter is designed to parse and filter out irrelevant information from the output of the LLM before being passed to the reasoner. Following this structure, predicate generation is completely done by the Large Language Model GPT-3, all the reasoning is performed by the goal-directed s(CASP) system, while the natural language response generation is done by yet another invocation of GPT-3.

3.1   Translating Sentences to Predicates

In our method, GPT-3 works as a "translator" that translates sentences spoken by a human to predicates that can be understood by the machine. Essentially, we use GPT-3 purely as a semantic parser that generates predicates capturing the meaning ("deep structure") of the sentences. For simplicity, this set of predicates is designed by us and restricted to a specific domain. This parsing step is realized by prompting the GPT-3 model with a few examples—referred to as in-context learning. An instance is shown below:

> There is a restaurant in the city center, Alimentum, which is not family-friendly.
> ### restaurant-name(alimentum), establishment(restaurant), family-friendly(no)

The example contains a sentence and the corresponding (essential) predicates we want to extract from its meaning, separated by '###'. These examples are carefully selected so that they cover most of the cases and all types of predicates with their possible values. Some extra natural language instructions are also added at the beginning of the prompt to make GPT-3 better understand the task.

What is remarkable is that a small number of such examples are enough for GPT-3 for in-context learning. This is due to GPT-3 being pre-trained on a vast amount of human-generated text [7]. We tested GPT-3 specialized to our in-context learning on the E2E dataset [25], and obtained an accuracy of **89.33%**. The high accuracy of predicate generation supports the feasibility of using the specialized GPT-3 as a semantic parser for AutoConcierge.

3.2 Commonsense Reasoning

Once a sentence has been translated into predicates, the generated predicates are input into the reasoning module to compute the missing information. To find this missing information, the reasoning module may have to seek more information from the human user which it does through additional dialogs. If it determines that all the information has been acquired, it finds the restaurant to be recommended and communicates to the user.

Knowledge Base: The AutoConcierge system aims to recommend a user's local restaurants that satisfy his/her preferences. To achieve this, information about local restaurants is necessary. For each restaurant, nine properties have been collected: the name of the restaurant, its cuisine type, its establishment type (bar, restaurant, coffee shop, etc.), its distance from the location of the concierge, its location address, its contact numbers, its price range, the average rating from the reviewers, and whether it is suitable for a family. This information is stored in the s(CASP) knowledge base. Note that the predicate representation of these nine properties, plus additional predicates (i) indicating user preferences, (ii) that the user is interested in another answer, and (iii) the user is interested in a past answer, respectively, were used for GPT-3's in-context learning. The in-context learning we provided to GPT-3 also helps it identify if a statement relates to the user being thankful or saying pleasantries. If no predicate of interest is identified in a sentence, it is labeled as irrelevant.

Conversational Knowledge Template: In a conversation where we are trying to help someone with a specific task, we have a plan in our mind on how to provide that help. The plan generally entails systematically asking for information from the other person, and then reaching a decision. For each domain-specific task, the corresponding conversation plan has to be represented. We represent the plan as a *conversational knowledge template* (CKT) that has been designed for implementing socialbots [4]. A CKT can be thought of as a state machine that allows AutoConcierge to systematically ask for information from a human user. It can be represented as a set of ASP rules coded in the s(CASP) system. In our AutoConcierge system, the CKT is used to explore users' preferences by directly asking them about their preferred type of food, their budget, etc. We define a set of properties that should be asked to get this user-preference information. These properties correspond 1-to-1 to the predicates representing meaning discussed earlier. For each response, the agent picks one of the properties from the set that has not been discussed before and generates a question for it. After collecting all the preference information in the set, the agent will generate an appropriate restaurant recommendation.

Preference-Based CKT Navigation: While using CKT for achieving the task at hand, AutoConcierge may need additional commonsense knowledge that has to be explicitly represented as well. This knowledge is for related concepts apart from the properties defined in the knowledge base. For instance, when people say "I prefer curry", our commonsense knowledge tells us that they are referring to the cuisines that provide food with curry. As a result, we may automatically select Indian or Thai as the food type due to the preference for curry. Similarly, if someone is planning to drink alcohol, a pub or a bar is a good place to go. As much of this commonsense knowledge as possible—that we expect a human concierge to know—must be explicitly represented in the reasoning module.

The predicates that are needed for decision-making are considered in order in the next-topic selection step that is part of the CKT, implemented as an ASP program in the s(CASP) system. We keep a pre-defined priority order in the reasoning module via a list, and the CKT always picks the property with a higher rank to generate the next question. However, if the users consider some properties more important than others, they can always ask for these requirements to be satisfied at the beginning of the dialog. Likewise, a user can change their mind at any time, and the order coded in the CKT is overridden. We refer to the reasoning module that contains the CKT implemented in s(CASP) as the *reasoner*.

3.3   AutoConcierge Response Generation

AutoConcierge has to generate a response in two cases (i) to communicate the final restaurant recommendation, and (ii) to seek information from the user about their preferences (intermediate question generation).

Once a target restaurant is identified by the reasoner, its detailed information is computed by the reasoner in the form of logical predicates, containing the information that the user is seeking and the corresponding restaurant details. These predicates are translated into natural language sentences using GPT-3 in a reverse example format. For instance, the in-context learning example for this module is structured as follows:

place(0, name, The Waterman), place(0, food type, Japanese), place(0, phone number, 414-247-2758) ### Perhaps you are interested in The Waterman, which offers Japanese cuisine. To make a reservation, you can call 414-247-2758.

In the case of intermediate question generation, the reasoner outputs the property for the next question. A template is then applied to this property to generate a question, for example: *Do you have any preference for the [property] of the place?* Similarly, if the agent fails to find a satisfying restaurant, or the user is saying something irrelevant, the reply is generated based on the corresponding template.

To make the response more polite, natural, and varied, we further rephrase the generated reply using another GPT-3-based wording module, enhancing the agent's human-like quality with respect to producing a natural language response.

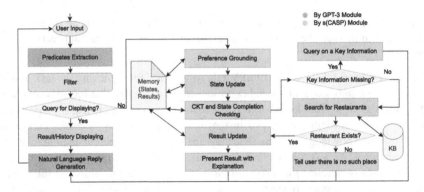

Fig. 2. AutoConcierge Architecture; Green-colored boxes are handled by GPT-3, orange-colored by the s(CASP) system. (Color figure online)

4   AutoConcierge Implementation

We provide specific details of the AutoConcierge system in this section. Figure 2 shows high-level details of how the system works.

4.1   Knowledge Representation

The knowledge base collects nine properties for each restaurant: *name, food type, establishment type, price range, customer rating, address, phone number, family-friendliness,* and *distance*. Each property for a specific restaurant is expressed as a predicate in the following example format:

$$\textbf{place}(restaurant\_ID, property\_name, property\_value)$$

For simplicity, the *price range* predicate is defined for only three values: expensive, moderate, and cheap. Likewise, the *customer rating* predicate is defined for three values: high, average, and low. The *food type* of a restaurant is usually its cuisine. When a restaurant's cuisine is not obvious, we record the food type it mainly serves. For example, the *food type* of a fried chicken restaurant is chicken. The *food type* of food shops and drink shops is marked as the food or drink they are serving. The *food type* of different bars is set as "bar", while the bar type can be further distinguished through the *establishment* predicate that is defined for a regular restaurant, a shop, or a fast-food restaurant. In the longer run, these concepts and associated commonsense knowledge have to be formally represented via a well-defined ontology and constitute future work.

4.2   Interaction of Modules

When the specialized GPT-3 model generates predicates from the natural language sentences, the input is usually the user's reply, but when AutoConcierge asks for the user's (positive or negative) preference, the question posed by AutoConcierge is also made as part of the input to GPT-3 augmented with in-context learning. The predicate domains are restricted to the nine properties in the knowledge base, as well as extra "prefer" and "not_prefer" that are used to capture user's additional preferences. The information the user is querying for (e.g., name of a restaurant, or its address) is indicated as "query". The format of the predicates generated by the predicate generation module is shown in the following example:

```
1   restaurant-name(query),
2   price range(moderate),
3   establishment(restaurant),
4   establishment(bar),
5   prefer(spicy),
6   prefer(noodle),
7   not_require(food type, Indian),
8   not_require(food type, Thai),
9   address(query)
```

The predicates in the example indicate that we need to find a restaurant's name and its address. The establishment could be a restaurant or bar, with moderately priced food that serves spicy food and noodles.

The in-context learning aid we provide to GPT-3 allows for predicates to contain multiple arguments. In predicates other than "prefer" or "not_prefer", this denotes the disjunction of these values, whereas in these two predicates indicating the preference, it denotes a conjunction. This is designed for simplicity of the parsing phase, based on the characteristic of the properties. For properties such as *food type*, *customer rating*, etc., a restaurant can only have one value for these properties. However, a user may ask for "Indian or Thai" food, for example, and both options chosen must be recorded. For the "prefer" or "not_prefer" predicate, however, it is possible that one may seek a restaurant, for example, with both spicy food and noodles, and preference for both should be recorded.

There are also two special predicates generated by the GPT-3 based parser, "another_option" and "view_history", which are used, respectively, to seek the next possible recommendation according to the current preference list and to keep track of the restaurants that the agent has recommended previously in the dialog. In addition to the above predicates, our specialized GPT-3 model also classifies the input sentences into different labels, such as **"irrelevant"** and **"thank"**. If a sentence is classified as **"irrelevant"** by the parser, a filter that sits between the parser and the reasoner will generate (some variation of) a courteous response like "Sorry, I am only a concierge. Can I assist you with recommending a restaurant?" This ensures that AutoConcierge stays focused on the task (LLM-based bots, notoriously, will enter into irrelevant conversations, if the user so desires). The **"thank"** label represents a sentence from the user that is expressing gratitude, and an appropriate response is generated (e.g., "You are welcome"). The filter also works as a format modifier that adapts the parser output to the format the reasoner accepts, as illustrated in Fig. 2.

The format of the information provided as input to the reasoner is slightly different from the parser output. The extracted predicates in the above example are rewritten as terms to fit the format of the reasoner as shown below.

```
require('name', ['query']),
require('price range', ['moderate']),
require('establishment', ['restaurant','bar']),
require('prefer', ['spicy', 'noodle']),
not_require('food type', ['Indian','Thai']),
require('address', ['query'])
```

The filter represents all the properties using just two predicates: "require/2" and "not_require/2". This makes our implementation more flexible.

4.3 Recommendation Generation

CKT Implementation: In AutoConcierge, at the top level, the CKT keeps asking questions of the user until all the information is collected. The properties *food type*, *price range*, and *customer rating* are the key pieces of information that are acquired from the user. Users may state their preference positively (e.g., "I want a cheap price range") or negatively (e.g., "Don't want it too expensive"). Note that users can provide multiple pieces of information in a single sentence (e.g., "Can you recommend an inexpensive Chinese restaurant for my family?"). After each piece of information is acquired, the state is updated. Once all the information is available, the reasoner searches the query property present in the state (e.g., restaurant-name(query)). The reasoner then finds all possible restaurants that satisfy the property preferences. The high-level code for the CKT is shown below. Note that neg_member relies on *negation as failure*. The reasoner runs on the s(CASP) goal-directed ASP system [3].

```
1   next_action('ask',Question) :- state(State),
2       next_info(Question, State).
3   next_action('recommend', Result) :-
4       state(State), recommend(State, Result).
5
6   next_info(X,State) :- key_info(L), member(X,L),
7       member(require(X, ['query']), State).
8   next_info(X,State) :- key_info(L), member(X,L),
9       forall(A,neg_member(require(X, A), State)),
10      forall(B,neg_member(not_require(X,B),State)).
11
12  recommend(State, Result) :-
13      merge([require('name',['query'])],State,Next),
14      recommend_(Next, Result).
15  recommend_(State, Recommendation) :-
16      get_query_list(State, Queries),
17      get_satisfied_places(State, X),
18      fill_query(X, Queries, Recommendation).
```

The rule for get_query_list/2 predicate extracts properties that are queried, while the rules for get_satisfied_places/2 and fill_query/3 predicates generate the response, that is passed on to the next module that will generate a natural language response for the user.

Updating State: In Sect. 4.2, we discussed the predicate "prefer" and "not_prefer" that captures the user's preference for food type. To update the state, we first extract these two predicates from the dialog and find the corresponding *food type* property. The newly acquired requirements are merged into the agent's state following the priority order discussed in Sect. 3.2. The `update_state/3` predicate below shows the high-level code.

```
1   update_state(L1, L2, L3) :-
2       set_prefer(L1, L4, Recm_List),
3       set_not_prefer(L4, Not_Recm_List, L5),
4       add_state(L5, L2, L6),
5       add_state(Recm_List, L6, L7),
6       add_state(Not_Recm_List, L7, L3).
```

Once a negated property is recorded in the state, no matter whether the non-negated property exists, the reasoner would not ask for this property again. Meanwhile, when a state is updated with requirements, any negative requirements wrt this property will be removed from the state. In the recommendation step, these negative requirements act as constraints that any of the results cannot violate.

Computing Responses: At each step, the reasoner examines the state, finds the information that it is still missing, crafts a term, and passes it to the response module that uses GPT-3 to translate it into a natural language response or question. Once all the user querying is done, the reasoner finds the restaurants that fit the criteria. An appropriate term is crafted again, and communicated to the response module. If there are no answers (because the criteria are too strict, for example), the representation of "no answer found" is communicated to the response module. The response module generates the natural language response. It either gives the answer or asks the user to relax the criteria. If there are multiple restaurants that satisfy the criteria, they are stored in an output list. The first one in the output list is returned, and is subsequently removed from the output list to another list that maintains the history of recommendations. If the user rejects the current recommendation and asks for another one (e.g., "Can you recommend another one?"), GPT-3 model extracts the predicate "another_option" as an input to the reasoner, and the top one remaining in the output list is returned, and so on. Similarly, the "view_history/1" predicate prompts the reasoner to recall previous recommendations. For instance, when the user asks "Can you show me the restaurant you recommended at first?", GPT-3 will convey the semantics to the reasoner through the "view_history(first)" predicate. The "view_history" predicate can take numbers as values indicating the ith previous recommendation, or "first" or "last" that refers to the first or the last recommendation. The specialized GPT-3 model has also been trained to generate the "view_history" predicate for the appropriate sentence.

4.4 Explanation

One feature of AutoConcierge is that it is able to explain the reason for the generated recommendation. This is primarily because it has a complete understanding of user preferences and it uses commonsense reasoning to compute its response. Whenever a recommendation is made, the reasoner explicitly explains how the restaurant meets the user's criteria. If the agent is not able to make any recommendation based on the preference provided, it also explains and suggests a possible change in the preference that helps find a solution. Failure to recommend happens if the search query fails. The reasoner can then run a negated query on s(CASP), that is guaranteed to succeed, and then analyze its proof trace to find the property to relax. The property relaxed is the one that contributes to the success of the negated query, and thus the cause of the original failed query (details omitted due to space). Note that s(CASP) system's goal-driven nature and its justification facility [2] is crucial.

5   Experiments and Results

We have extensively tested the AutoConcierge system. Below, we show one example conversation between the AutoConcierge and the user. We show the state that the reasoner maintains after each user utterance for the conversations. Note that because we use GPT-3, user dialogs don't have to be syntactically perfect, they can be slightly ungrammatical or colloquial.

Bot: Hi there, how can I assist you?
User: Can you recommend me a restaurant?

```
1  require('name', ['query']),
2  require('establishment', ['restaurant'])
```

Bot: Is there a particular type of food you would like to eat?
User: I can try any food except curry.

```
1  require('name', ['query']),
2  require('establishment', ['restaurant']),
3  not_require('food type', ['Indian','Thai'])
```

Bot: Are you looking for a certain price range of restaurants?
User: Less than fifteen dollars.

```
1  require('name', ['query']),
2  require('establishment', ['restaurant']),
3  not_require('food type', ['Indian','Thai']),
4  require('price range', ['cheap'])
```

Bot: Are you looking for a place with a particular customer rating?
User: No, I'm not looking for a specific rating score.

```
1  require('name', ['query']),
2  require('establishment', ['restaurant']),
3  not_require('food type', ['Indian','Thai']),
4  require('price range', ['cheap']),
5  require('customer rating', ['low','average','high'])
```

Bot: Southern Recipes Grill has an average customer rating and serves budget-friendly American cuisine.
User: Sounds nice. Can you give me its address?

```
1  require('name', ['query']),
2  require('establishment', ['restaurant']),
3  not_require('food type', ['Indian','Thai']),
4  require('price range', ['cheap']),
5  require('customer rating', ['low','average','high']),
6  require('address', ['query'])
```

Bot: Located at 621 W Plano Pkwy #229, Plano, TX 75075, Southern Recipes Grill offers delicious food at an affordable price. Customers have given it an average rating.
User: Thank you for your help.
Bot: It's my pleasure to help. No need to thank me.

Table 1. Run-Time (seconds) comparison in different modes. We experimented with the question generation mode with one and three requirement(s) in the current state, and with the recommendation mode with five requirements.

	Next Question (1 Req.)	Next Question (3 Req.)	Recommendation (5 Req.)
Find First	0.624	0.626	0.637
Find All	0.633	0.638	1.384
End-to-End	1.571	1.672	4.602

5.1 Efficiency Evaluation

The AutoConcierge system is reasonably efficient. We conducted experiments to evaluate the execution efficiency of our AutoConcierge system, with a focus on time taken for *next question generation* and *computing final recommendation* in the reasoning phase (Table 1). We varied the number of requirements for the next question generation. We set the number of requirements to five for the recommendation mode. We also measured the time taken by the reasoner in finding the first (partial) answer set as well as in finding all the (partial) answer sets. The time taken by the reasoner was measured via the s(CASP) system's command-line interface. The End-to-End row in Table 1 includes the time for predicate generation, reasoning, and natural language response generation combined. We conducted 10 runs of each experiment and calculated the average results. Our findings, presented in Table 1, reveal that the number of requirements in the question generation stage does not significantly affect performance. Our results also show that GPT-3 components (parsing and response generation) take more time than the reasoner. Note that these response times are quite fast even compared with a human.

Table 2. Human Evaluation Results comparing our AutoConcierge with the sota PPTOD model. We tested on ten conversations with ten human evaluators.

	AutoConcierge (ours)	PPTOD
Understanding	**7.24**	6.88
Truthfulness	**7.47**	6.19
Coherency	**7.19**	6.58
Fluency	**7.55**	6.82
Task Ease	**6.97**	6.44
Expected Behavior	**6.77**	6.06
Total Satisfaction	**6.74**	5.86

5.2 Human Evaluation

We designed a manual evaluation experiment to test the performance of ten conversations generated by AutoConcierge. To compare, we also generate the conversations for the same goal through the SOTA task-oriented model, PPTOD [33]. PPTOD is an end-to-end system trained for multi-task situations, initialized with the T5 model [28]. It reads the entire dialog as the input, and outputs 1) the current state, 2) the next action, and 3) the reply generated. When the next action requires the database involved, it will send the entire state to the database and the database will return a list of results. Below is one example of the PPTOD conversation with the user.

Bot: Hello what can I do for you today?
User: Hey today is my son's birthday. We want to hold
 a party for him
State: <sos_b> <eos_b>
Action: <sos_a> [restaurant] [request] city <eos_a>
Bot: What kind of party?
User: Birthday party
State: <sos_b> [restaurant] greeting Hello date today party
 type birthday party <eos_b>
Action: <sos_a> [restaurant] [request] city <eos_a>
Bot: What city?
User: Dallas
State: <sos_b> [restaurant] greeting Hello date today occasion
 birthday party city Dallas <eos_b>
Action: <sos_a> [restaurant] [request] date <eos_a>
Bot: What time?
User: 3 pm
State: <sos_b> [restaurant_reservation] restaurant location
 Dallas reservation time 3 pm <eos_b>
Action: <sos_a> [restaurant] [request] number of people
 <eos_a>
Bot: What kind of food?
User: He loves tiramisu. So maybe somewhere with tiramisu
State: <sos_b> [restaurant_reservation] restaurant location
 Dallas reservation time 3 pm <eos_b>
Action: <sos_a> [restaurant] [request] number of people
 <eos_a>
Bot: I have a few options. How about a restaurant called
 amaro?
User: Sounds good! Where is it?
State: <sos_b> [restaurant_reservation] restaurant location
 Dallas reservation time 3 pm <eos_b>
Action: <sos_a> [restaurant] [inform] address <eos_a>
Database Input: (No Result)
Bot: It is at 333 North Congress Avenue
User: Cool! Have a nice day
State: <sos_b> [restaurant_reservation] restaurant location
 Dallas reservation time 3 pm <eos_b>
Action: <sos_a> [restaurants] [goodbye] <eos_a>
Bot: You too!

The conversations were anonymously demonstrated to ten different graders who graded on a scale of 1 to 10 and the final score was calculated by averaging. The volunteers are well-educated, and recruited from people we approached with a variety of backgrounds. We used the four metrics from the PPTOD system's human evaluation [33]: **Understanding**, **Truthfulness**, **Coherency**, and **Fluency**. We also added **Task Ease** and **Expected Behavior** [36]. We also asked the testers for the **Total Satisfaction** score. Note that PPTOD is purely based on machine learning technology where a corpus of dialogs is used for fine-tuning the system based on a pre-trained LLM.

Table 2 reflects the final result of the quantitative test, showing that AutoConcierge performs better in all the metrics. Moreover, it has a remarkably higher score in *Truthfulness* and *Fluency*, suggesting that our AutoConcierge, using s(CASP) goal-directed ASP system, is more reliable than the deep-learning-based models. The use of GPT-3 allows AutoConcierge to generate more natural replies.

5.3 Comparison with Bing AI

We also conducted an experiment to test restaurant recommendations using Microsoft's Bing AI [22], a recently released GPT-based chatbot with a search engine. To ensure fairness, we limited the scope of the search for a restaurant to two miles around our location. A sample Bing AI conversation and detailed analysis are presented below (location is removed to preserve author anonymity).

Similar to PPTOD, Bing AI is based on pattern matching and therefore lacks an understanding of the user's purpose and generates responses with hallucinations. Even worse, the data is from popular websites and consequently, many local restaurants cannot be retrieved.

Bing: What can I assist you with now?
User: Hi I'm now at (university name), could you recommend me a nearby restaurant within 2 mile ride?
Bing: Sure! There are several restaurants near (university name) within 2 miles. (gives two top-result recommendations) Is there a specific type of cuisine you're interested in?
User: I'm looking for Italian food.
Bing: There are several Italian restaurants near (university name) within 2 miles. (gives another two examples for Italian restaurants) Would you like more information on these restaurants?
User: I don't have a high budget, are these restaurants expensive?
Bing: One affordable Italian restaurant near (university name) within 2 miles is Jimmy's Food Store, a specialty food market that offers exquisite Italian food. Another option is Botolino Gelato Artigianale, which serves Italian gelato. Would you like more information on these restaurants?
User: Can you tell me where is Jimmy's Food Store?
Bing: Jimmy's Food Store is located at 4901 Bryan Street, Dallas. Is there anything else you would like to know?
User: But it seems very far away from (university name). Any other options?
Bing: Yes, another option for affordable Italian food near (university name) within 2 miles is Botolino Gelato Artigianale, which serves Italian gelato. Would you like more information on this restaurant?
User: Tell me more about Botolino Gelato Artigianale.
Bing: (gives details for Botolino Gelato Artigianale) Would you like more information on this restaurant?
User: No thanks. It is also very far away from (university name). Please recommend the restaurant nearby within 2 miles drive.
Bing: I'm sorry but I couldn't find any affordable Italian restaurants within 2 miles of (university name). Would you like me to look for other options?
User: ...

As evident from the example Bing AI conversation, the GPT-based search engine, despite generating natural language responses similar to a human concierge, exhibits several deficiencies. These include:

- Bing AI does not ask for detailed user preferences like a human concierge would. It arbitrarily recommends restaurants. Any request for preference by Bing AI, e.g., asking for a specific type of cuisine, is driven by what the user said. In contrast, AutoConcierge actively seeks information to achieve the task goal.
- Bing AI only recommends popular restaurants on the web. It cannot recommend restaurants that are not listed on any website. On the other hand, our AutoConcierge possesses knowledge of all restaurants stored in the knowledge base and can make precise recommendations. It can even recommend a nearby grocery store to buy a sandwich if all restaurants nearby are closed. This is an obvious advantage that task-oriented bots have over generic search-engine-based systems such as Bing AI.
- Bing AI is limited to generating only ten responses, which requires the user to provide accurate and detailed information in a few questions. It may sometimes ignore specific requirements, necessitating their repeated mention. The limitation to 10 responses is there because of Microsoft's worry that Bing AI will go haywire or can become offensive, etc. AutoConcierge, on the other hand, allows users to reply as many times as they like, and the agent remembers the requirements once it is mentioned.
- Bing AI can accurately convey information available through search, but it may hallucinate information if it cannot be found on the current page. For instance, in the example above, several of the restaurants recommended were more than 10 miles away, while the bot asserted that they were within 2 miles. AutoConcierge ensures that all information provided by the agent is reliable.

6   Related Work

Conversational agents (chatbots) have been an active area of research for a long time. Many chatbots have been deployed by businesses, especially e-commerce websites, but they are really deficient, and quickly handover to a human operator after one or two rounds of dialogs. Other commercial chatbots such as Amazon Alexa, Siri, and Google Assistant are more of information retrieval devices rather than actual effective chatbots that can have a stateful conversation. The task-oriented chatbots are designed with a closed set of instructions (ontology) and a mapping method matching user commands to the ontology. The CKT [4] enables the system to control the dialog flow and shift topics among the ontology. Rule-based or finite-state-based systems, like Eliza [39,40], Chat-80 [37], PARRY [12], IRIS [13], and DAISY [20], encode the mapping by rules or states. The main challenge in these chatbots, some such as Chat-80 developed by logic programmers decades ago, is parsing the dialogs and correctly extracting the knowledge conveyed in the dialogs. Our experience indicates that extracting knowledge via parsing is still a major challenge and conventional NLP parsing technology is not highly effective despite existence of sophisticated parsers such as Stanford Core NLP parser [21]. AutoConcierge overcomes this problem by using an LLM as a semantic parser. With the popularity of deep learning in NLP tasks, neural models are employed for the Dialogue State Tracing (DST) task [9,17,24,27,33]. A recent line of related research uses different sizes of transformer-based models to build chatbots [1,32,34,41,43]. These models are similar to GPT-3 [7], and are based purely on pattern matching, and thus are similar to Bing AI and therefore suffer from similar disadvantages discussed earlier.

To evaluate the quality of a conversation, different metrics [30,36] are proposed in different aspects like understanding, engagingness, humanness, etc. Other works use different ways of collecting human feedback. Blenderbot 3 [32] allows users to give a thumbs down for a conversation and select if the bot behaves unproperly. The XiaoIce system [44] evaluates its model using conversation-turns per session arguing that an engaging chatbot will motivate users to interact longer with it. PPTOD [33] deploy human graders to score four aspects: understanding, truthfulness, coherency, and fluency.

7   Conclusion and Future Work

In this paper, we developed a domain-specific conversational agent that called Auto-Concierge, that "understands" human dialogs, for restaurant recommendations. Auto-Concierge uses GPT-3 with in-context learning as a semantic parser and a response generator. The reasoning is achieved by the s(CASP) goal-directed ASP system that performs commonsense reasoning. AutoConcierge emulates humans in how it holds conversations: It extracts the knowledge from a sentence spoken by the user; next, it reasons over this knowledge to draw a conclusion; and, then uses the conclusion to generate a natural language response. AutoConcierge outperforms the state-of-the-art task-oriented conversation bots, especially in reliability, and is even better than the LLM-based Bing AI on the restaurant recommendation task.

Our future work includes building a more general chatbot by making the knowledge representation more general through the use of existing ontologies such as WordNet [14]. AutoConcierge guarantees the responses generated to be correct and reliable, but the price paid is its scalability. It cannot operate beyond the commonsense knowledge that it possesses. However, with clear application functions and well-defined rules, other domain-specific task-oriented conversation bots similar to AutoConcierge can be readily developed. We are confident that such chatbots based on our method can outperform state-of-the-art commercial bots based largely on machine learning technology.

We also plan to develop a framework based on LLMs (GPT-3) and ASP (s(CASP)) for making the development of chatbots such as AutoConcierge significantly easier and faster. We also plan to develop a socialbot similar to AutoConcierge that can hold a conversation with humans about movies, books, sports, video games, etc., similar to Amazon Alexa socialbots [4,19].

References

1. Adiwardana, D., et al.: Towards a human-like open-domain chatbot (2020). https://doi.org/10.48550/ARXIV.2001.09977, https://arxiv.org/abs/2001.09977
2. Arias, J., Carro, M., Chen, Z., Gupta, G.: Justifications for goal-directed constraint answer set programming. In: Proceedings 36th ICLP (Tech. Comm.). EPTCS, vol. 325, pp. 59–72 (2020). https://doi.org/10.4204/EPTCS.325.12
3. Arias, J., Carro, M., Salazar, E., Marple, K., Gupta, G.: Constraint answer set programming without grounding (2018). https://doi.org/10.48550/ARXIV.1804.11162
4. Basu, K., et al.: CASPR: a commonsense reasoning-based conversational Socialbot (2021)
5. Borji, A.: A categorical archive of chatgpt failures (2023). https://arxiv.org/abs/2302.03494
6. Brewka, G., Eiter, T., Truszczynski, M.: Answer set programming at a glance, December 2011. https://doi.org/10.1145/2043174.2043195
7. Brown, T., et al.: Language models are few-shot learners. In: NeurIPS, vol. 33, pp. 1877–1901. Curran Associates, Inc. (2020). https://proceedings.neurips.cc/paper/2020/file/1457c0d6bfcb4967418bfb8ac142f64a-Paper.pdf
8. Casola, S., Lauriola, I., Lavelli, A.: Pre-trained transformers: an empirical comparison (2022). https://doi.org/10.1016/j.mlwa.2022.100334, https://www.sciencedirect.com/science/article/pii/S2666827022000445
9. Chen, L., Lv, B., Wang, C., Zhu, S., Tan, B., Yu, K.: Schema-guided multi-domain dialogue state tracking with graph attention neural networks. In: Proceedings of the AAAI Conference on Artificial Intelligence, vol. 34, pp. 7521–7528 (2020)
10. Chen, Z., Marple, K., Salazar, E., Gupta, G., Tamil, L.: A physician advisory system for chronic heart failure management based on knowledge patterns (2016)
11. Chowdhery, A., et al.: Palm: scaling language modeling with pathways. arXiv preprint arXiv:2204.02311 (2022)
12. Colby, K.M.: Human-computer conversation in a cognitive therapy program. In: Machine Conversations, pp. 9–19 (1999)
13. Fast, E., Chen, B., Mendelsohn, J., Bassen, J., Bernstein, M.S.: Iris: a conversational agent for complex tasks. In: Proceedings of the 2018 CHI Conference on Human Factors in Computing Systems, pp. 1–12 (2018)
14. Fellbaum, C. (ed.): WordNet: An Electronic Lexical Database. MIT Press, Cambridge, MA (1998)
15. Floridi, L., Chiriatti, M.: GPT-3: its nature, scope, limits, and consequences, December 2020. https://doi.org/10.1007/s11023-020-09548-1
16. Gelfond, M., Kahl, Y.: Knowledge Representation, Reasoning, and the Design of Intelligent Agents: Answer Set Programming Approach. Cambridge Univ. Press, Cambridge (2014)
17. Gordon-Hall, G., Gorinski, P.J., Lampouras, G., Iacobacci, I.: Show us the way: learning to manage dialog from demonstrations. arXiv preprint arXiv:2004.08114 (2020)
18. Gupta, G.: Automating common sense reasoning with ASP and s(CASP), Technical report (2022). https://utdallas.edu/gupta/csr-scasp.pdf
19. Hu, S., et al.: Further advances in open domain dialog systems in the fourth Alexa prize socialbot grand challenge. In: Alexa Prize SocialBot Grand Challenge 4 Proceedings (2021). https://www.amazon.science/publications/further-advances-in-open-domain-dialog-systems-in-the-fourth-alexa-prize-socialbot-grand-challenge

20. Leo John, R.J., Patel, J.M., Alexander, A.L., Singh, V., Adluru, N.: A natural language interface for dissemination of reproducible biomedical data science. In: Frangi, A.F., Schnabel, J.A., Davatzikos, C., Alberola-López, C., Fichtinger, G. (eds.) MICCAI 2018. LNCS, vol. 11073, pp. 197–205. Springer, Cham (2018). https://doi.org/10.1007/978-3-030-00937-3_23

21. Manning, C.D., Surdeanu, M., Bauer, J., Finkel, J., Bethard, S.J., McClosky, D.: The Stanford CoreNLP NLP toolkit. In: ACL System Demonstrations, pp. 55–60 (2014)

22. Microsoft: Bing AI: The search engine that knows what you need (2023). https://www.bing.com/new/

23. Morris, J.: Blawx: user-friendly goal-directed answer set programming for rules as code. In: Proceedings of the Programming Language and the Law (ProLaLa) (2023)

24. Mrkšić, N., Séaghdha, D.O., Wen, T.H., Thomson, B., Young, S.: Neural belief tracker: data-driven dialogue state tracking. arXiv preprint arXiv:1606.03777 (2016)

25. Novikova, J., Dušek, O., Rieser, V.: The E2E dataset: new challenges for end-to-end generation (2017)

26. OpenAI: Optimizing language models for dialog (2022). https://openai.com/blog/chatgpt/

27. Peng, B., Li, C., Li, J., Shayandeh, S., Liden, L., Gao, J.: Soloist: building task bots at scale with transfer learning and machine teaching. Trans. Assoc. Comput. Linguist. **9**, 807–824 (2021)

28. Roberts, A., et al.: Exploring the limits of transfer learning with a unified text-to-text transformer (2019)

29. Sartor, G., Davila, J., Billi, M., Pisano, G., Contissa, G., Kowalski, R.: Integration of logical English and s(CASP). In: Proceedings of the ICLP Workshops: GDE'22. CEUR Workshop Proceedings, vol. 2970. CEUR-WS.org (2022)

30. See, A., Roller, S., Kiela, D., Weston, J.: What makes a good conversation? How controllable attributes affect human judgments. arXiv preprint arXiv:1902.08654 (2019)

31. Shin, R., Van Durme, B.: Few-shot semantic parsing with language models trained on code. In: Proceedings of the ACL-HLT, pp. 5417–5425 (2022)

32. Shuster, K., et al.: BlenderBot 3: a deployed conversational agent that continually learns to responsibly engage. ArXiv abs/2208.03188 (2022)

33. Su, Y., et al.: Multi-task pre-training for plug-and-play task-oriented dialogue system. arXiv preprint arXiv:2109.14739 (2021)

34. Thoppilan, R., et al.: Lamda: language models for dialog applications (2022). https://doi.org/10.48550/ARXIV.2201.08239, https://arxiv.org/abs/2201.08239

35. Touvron, H., et al.: Llama: open and efficient foundation language models. arXiv preprint arXiv:2302.13971 (2023)

36. Walker, M., Kamm, C., Litman, D.: Towards developing general models of usability with paradise. Nat. Lang. Eng. **6**(3–4), 363–377 (2000)

37. Warren, D.H., Pereira, F.C.: An efficient easily adaptable system for interpreting natural language queries. Am. J. Comput. Linguist. **8**(3–4), 110–122 (1982)

38. Wei, J., et al.: Chain of thought prompting elicits reasoning in large language models. In: NeurIPS (2022)

39. Weizenbaum, J.: Eliza-a computer program for the study of natural language communication between man and machine. Commun. ACM **9**(1), 36–45 (1966)

40. Weizenbaum, J.: Eliza-a computer program for the study of natural language communication between man and machine. Commun. ACM **26**(1), 23–28 (1983)

41. Wolf, T., Sanh, V., Chaumond, J., Delangue, C.: Transfertransfo: a transfer learning approach for neural network based conversational agents (2019). https://doi.org/10.48550/ARXIV.1901.08149, https://arxiv.org/abs/1901.08149

42. Xu, Z., et al.: Jury-trial story construction and analysis using goal-directed answer set programming. In: Hanus, M., Inclezan, D. (eds.) Practical Aspects of Declarative Languages. PADL 2023. LNCS, vol. 13880, pp. 261–278. Springer, Cham (2023). https://doi.org/10.1007/978-3-031-24841-2_17

43. Zhang, Y., et al.: DIALOGPT: large-scale generative pre-training for conversational response generation. In: Proceedings of the 58th Annual Meeting of the Association for Computational Linguistics: System Demonstrations, pp. 270–278. Association for Computational Linguistics, Online, July 2020. https://doi.org/10.18653/v1/2020.acl-demos.30, https://aclanthology.org/2020.acl-demos.30

44. Zhou, L., Gao, J., Li, D., Shum, H.Y.: The design and implementation of XiaoIce, an empathetic social chatbot. Comput. Linguist. 46(1), 53–93 (2020). https://doi.org/10.1162/coli_a_00368, https://aclanthology.org/2020.cl-1.2

Author Index

M. Gebser and I. Sergey (Eds.): PADL 2024, LNCS 14512, p. 223, 2023.
https://doi.org/10.1007/978-3-031-52038-9

Printed in the United States
by Baker & Taylor Publisher Services